Research Review *for* School Leaders

Volume III

EDITORIAL BOARD

Charlene E. Carper, Assistant Principal, McKelvie Middle School, Bedford, New Hampshire

Raymond Cooper, Principal, Tenino High School, Tenino, Washington

Linda Fox, Principal, Elizabeth High School, Elizabeth, Colorado

Geneva Gay, Professor of Education, University of Washington

James J. Hayden, Principal, Freehold Township High School, Freehold, New Jersey

LeRoy Hoehner, Principal, McCook Junior–Senior High School, McCook, Nebraska

Ann Lieberman, Codirector, National Center for Restructuring Education, Schools, and Teaching, Columbia University

Laurel N. Tanner, Senior Professor of Education, Temple University

Research Review *for* School Leaders

Volume III

Co-sponsored by the National Association of Secondary School Principals and the National Association of Elementary School Principals

Edited by

William G. Wraga
University of Georgia

Peter S. Hlebowitsh
University of Iowa

Founding Editor

Daniel Tanner
Rutgers University

LEA

LAWRENCE ERLBAUM ASSOCIATES, PUBLISHERS
2000   Mahwah, New Jersey   London

Copyright © 2000 by Lawrence Erlbaum Associates, Inc.
All rights reserved. No part of this book may be reproduced in any form,
by photostat, microfilm, retrieval system, or any other means, without prior
written permission of the publisher.

Lawrence Erlbaum Associates, Inc., Publishers
10 Industrial Avenue
Mahwah, NJ 07430

Cover design by Kathryn Houghtaling Lacey

ISBN 0-8058-3508-3 (cloth : alk. paper)
ISSN 1528-8498

Books published by Lawrence Erlbaum Associates are printed on acid-free
paper, and their bindings are chosen for strength and durability.

Printed in the United States of America
10 9 8 7 6 5 4 3 2 1

To Lloyd Campbell Chilton

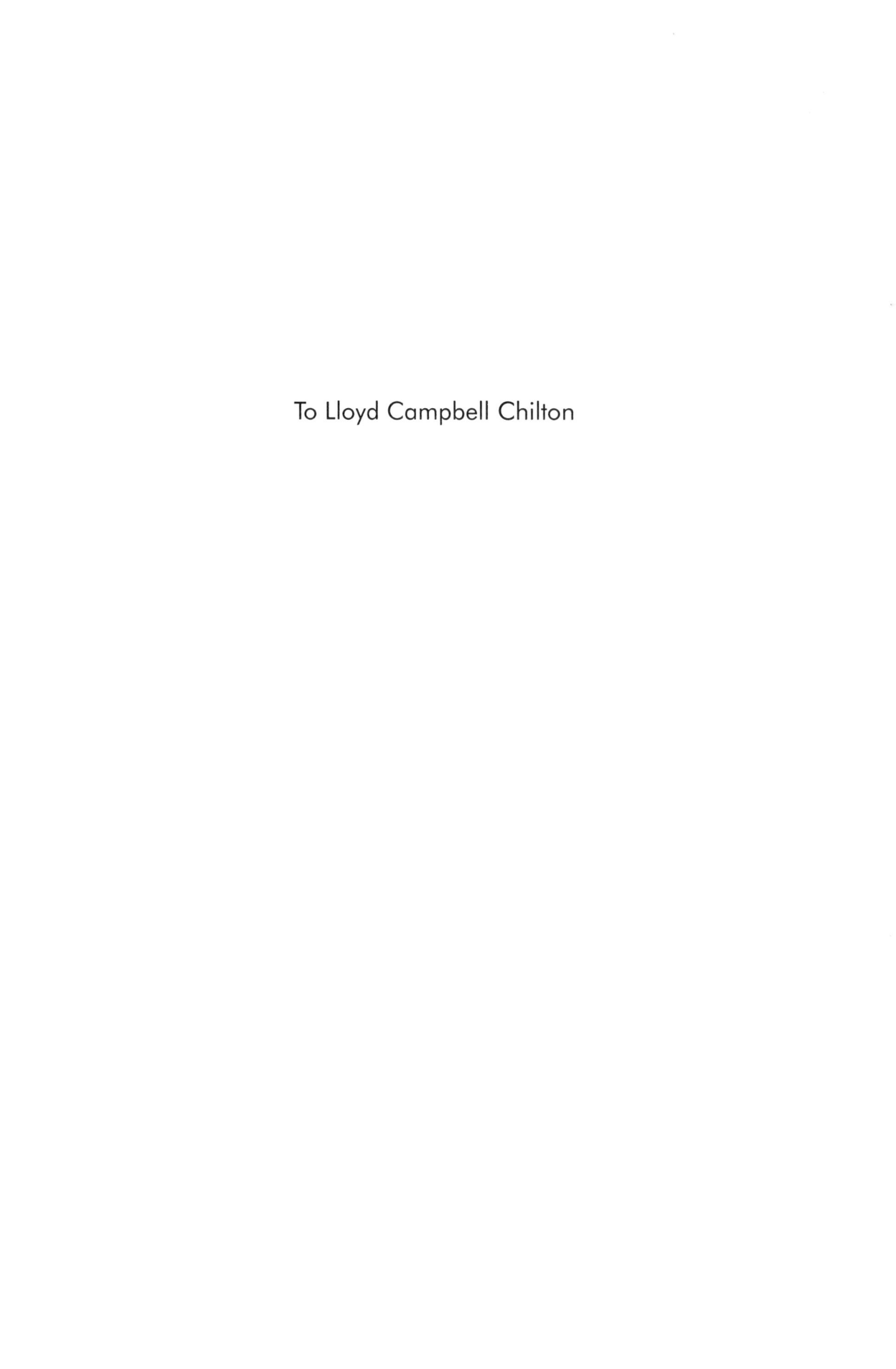

Contents

Foreword *Daniel Tanner*	ix
Preface	xiii

Part I — 1
Citizenship Education—The Democratic Prospect

1. Improving the Outcomes of Civic Education — 5
   Phillip J. VanFossen

2. Citizenship Education in the Elementary School — 33
   James M. Shiveley

3. Citizenship Education in the Secondary School — 61
   Gregory E. Hamot

Part II — 101
Multicultural Education

4. Multicultural Education and the Civic Mission of Schools — 103
   John J. Patrick

5. Best Practices in Multicultural Education: Recommendations to School Leaders — 135
   Carl A. Grant and Kim Wieczorek

Part III — 179
Gifted and Talented Education

6. Policy Implications of Continuing Controversies in Gifted Education — 183
   Nancy Ewald Jackson and Heidi L. Doellinger

Part IV — 197
Classroom Assessment

7. The Principal's Assessment Responsibilities — 201
   Richard J. Stiggins

8. The Construction of Standardized Tests and Their Uses — 237
   Michelle A. Mengeling

9. External Portfolio Assessment: Where Has the Reflection Gone?   261
   Julie Cheville

10. Computer Software Products for Classroom Assessment Purposes   277
    Michelle A. Mengeling

11. High Stakes, Low Stakes Testing: Do Stakes Really Matter?   301
    Lucy L. Payne

Part V   **329**
Scheduling

12. Secondary School Scheduling   331
    Henry Traverso

13. Block Scheduling: What We Have Learned   347
    Robert Lynn Canady and Michael D. Rettig

Author Index   375

Subject Index   385

Foreword

Daniel Tanner, Founding Editor
Rutgers University

There is a story behind every new idea or venture. The idea for this project grew out of an expressed need. Through the course of my 10-year tenure as a founding member of the Curriculum Council of the National Association of Secondary School Principals, I had the privilege of meeting on a regular basis with members of the association's Curriculum Committee, composed of school leaders from throughout the nation. Most impressively, the school leaders did not use our forums to vent their frustrations. Instead they addressed common concerns and shared ideas in the most constructive ways. To my mind, this was all the more impressive when considering how school leaders have been subjected to incessantly shifting external pressures from the mass media, political opportunists, special-interest groups, and local factions with regard to education priorities and practices. The slogan of "reform" has been shouted from the rooftops by opposing sides of educational issues as though reform itself is a solution to any education problem. The consequence has been that many reforms have had questionable consequences for children and youth—so that reforms of today have to be undone by the counterreforms of tomorrow.

"One former is worth a thousand reformers," stated Horace Mann. It is a truism that reformers come and go with their bandwagons, leaving school leaders to face the consequences of misguided reforms. Mann and later John Dewey held that education progress comes from constructive action through problem solving—the implementation of action guided by the best available evidence. At the joint meeting of the Curriculum Council and the Curriculum Committee, the education leaders expressed their concern that the members of the education research community all too often neglect to draw on the problems of those who are engaged in the work of the schools and tend to be self-serving in that their publications are largely for internal consumption. Further, the school leaders expressed concern over the tendency for the education research community to follow opportunistic lines in grantsmanship, largely determined by dominant and shifting political priorities. And most significantly, the education leaders expressed their need for a professional publication that would connect current research to the practical problems in the real world of the schools—so as to provide education practitioners with the best available evidence as a guide to practice. In this way, education practitioners and their schools would also gain support against misguided and unfair attacks from external sources. Indeed, the American education experience has revealed that the most promising and fruitful research ideas have been derived from the practical need for problem solutions, and reciprocally that research findings must be evaluated and put to the test of widening practical conditions—marking the vital connections between research and practice.

With these concerns in mind, I met with Lloyd C. Chilton, my long-term editor at Macmillan Publishing Company, who, after his retirement from Macmillan, moved to the position of executive director of leadership/policy/research professional publishing at Scholastic, Inc. We proceeded to identify the prospective coeditors for the project, Peter S. Hlebowitsh and William G. Wraga, both of whom share an abiding commitment to bridging research and practice for school improvement and the advancement of professional knowledge. Together we met in Reston, Virginia, at NASSP headquarters. Lloyd Chilton and I discussed the proposed project at a joint meeting of the NASSP Curriculum Council and Curriculum Committee under the chairmanship of James W. Keefe, then NASSP's director of research. The proposal for a research review for school leaders was met enthusiastically by all concerned. Thomas F. Koerner, then deputy executive director of NASSP, immediately lent his support to the project.

The school leaders offered many invaluable suggestions and expressed their preference for a hardbound publication series that would have a working place on their professional bookshelves as an authoritative current source for informed practitioners. Significantly, they agreed that the problems and issues addressed in the *Annual Review of Research for School Leaders* should not be concentrated on secondary schools, in recognition that practical problems almost invariably have ramifications throughout all levels of the education system—elementary, middle, and high school.

The first volume was published by Scholastic in 1996. With the retirement of Lloyd C. Chilton, Scholastic discontinued the publication of professional books despite the initial success of the project. Lloyd suggested that Macmillan Reference would be ideally suited for the project. During the proposal stage with Macmillan, I spoke with Tom Koerner about the idea of placing the *Annual Review of Research for School Leaders* under the joint sponsorship of the National Association of Secondary School Principals and the National Association of Elementary School Principals. Tom Koerner agreed that the project should indeed span all phases of schooling. We proceeded to discuss this with Samuel G. Sava, executive director of the National Association of Elementary School Principals, and he readily supported the idea for joint sponsorship. The second volume was published by Macmillan in 1998. However, Macmillan, which had been subjected to successive takeovers by corporate conglomerates, was undergoing repeated restructuring, so we decided to move the project to Lawrence Erlbaum Associates under the able editorship of Naomi Silverman. We were very fortunate also in having the continuing guidance and assistance of Lloyd C. Chilton.

Research Review for School Leaders is a unique and pioneering project that should prove invaluable as a resource for informed school leaders, teachers, and other school professionals, and also for professors and students of education. As with the earlier volumes, this volume of *Research Review for School Leaders* focuses on nationalizing influences on the school from the vantage points of education policy and practice. The implications for school and society are clear and profound. The problems and issues addressed are pervasive, not passing. *Research Review for School Leaders* should help bridge the gap between research and practice—a long-expressed need for those working in the real world of the schools.

PREFACE

School leaders increasingly face pressures to improve the efficacy of local educational programs. Calls for improvement, however, often include advocacy of a favored "reform" measure. Too often, the proposed reform is justified more by current popularity and compelling anecdotes than by sound principles of professional practice or a favorable record of rigorous research. Confronted with relatively short time frames within which to respond to pressures for such reforms, school leaders have few places to turn for reliable reviews of research and professional practice.

The *Research Review for School Leaders* is designed to serve as a practical resource for school leaders whose schedules preclude opportunities to locate and review related research on every issue they must address. Professionals can make sound decisions when they have available reviews of the research pertaining to the problems with which they grapple. The *Research Review for School Leaders* aims to place comprehensive, current, and accessible reviews of educational research at the fingertips of the practicing educational leader.

This is the third volume of the *Review*. Although the name of this volume has changed, its purpose and substance are continuous with the work of the earlier volumes. The first *Annual Review of Research for School Leaders* (Scholastic, 1996) summarized research on the topics of the status of public schooling, interdisciplinary curriculum, and educational applications of computers. The second *Annual Review of Research for School Leaders* presented research reviews on the topics of middle-level education, the extracurriculum, mathematics education reform, and dropouts. The present volume, newly named *Research Review for School Leaders*, offers the educational leader reviews of research on five timely educational issues: citizenship education, multicultural education, gifted and talented education, classroom assessment, and scheduling.

Citizenship education is arguably the very reason public schools exist. The original intent of the Founders of the United States was that education would create the enlightened citizenry essential to the success of a system of government based on popular sovereignty. Yet civic education typically receives short shrift in both educational policy and practice. The chapters in this important part review both the research about and practice of citizenship education in K–12 schooling. Closely related to the civic mission of public schooling is the task of fostering a sense of social cohesion among the diverse individuals and groups that comprise this multicultural society. Issues of research and practice of multicultural education are reviewed in Part II of this volume. The education of another recognized subgroup in the student population, gifted and talented youth, is examined in Part III.

Among the pressures placed on the public schools during the past 20 years, perhaps none has been greater than the demand to raise standardized test scores. In the minds of many politicians, policymakers, and parents, standardized tests have become virtually synonymous with assessment. Human behavior, however, is too complex to reduce to any single indicator. Reliance on standardized tests as the principal, if not the sole, source of information about student learning greatly oversimplifies the assessment process. Part IV presents in-depth reviews of research about various dimensions of classroom assessment. Finally, as assessment generally affects nearly all aspects of a local educational program, so does scheduling. With the sudden emergence of renewed interest in block scheduling, a review of research on block scheduling and of other scheduling options is in order. Part V is devoted to the issue of scheduling.

We hope that school leaders find the research and practices summarized in this volume useful in their professional endeavors. It is worth bearing in mind, however, that research is best not simply imposed on a local setting. The nature of the particular problem to be solved will invariably bear on the relevance of research to a local setting. This said, we envision school leaders engaged in important discussions of this research with teachers, school board members, parents, and other interested parties as they collaboratively seek effective resolutions to local educational problems.

—*William G. Wraga*
—*Peter S. Hlebowitsh*

PART I

Citizenship Education—
The Democratic Prospect

PUBLIC SCHOOLS HAVE LONG BEEN viewed as fundamental agencies in the sociocivic development of children. Although most educators tend to see their work largely in academic terms, few would deny the role they play in the process of educating youth for enlightened participation in a democratic society. Citizenship education, to give it a name, does not simply belong to the social studies teacher. It is the work of all educators who understand the school's mission to shape informed and socially conscious individuals. If educators take any interest at all in student performance as it relates to critical thinking, character education, moral development, current events, government knowledge, or community involvement, they are likely to find themselves working in the interests of citizenship education. The chapters in this section are dedicated to showing the pedagogical face of the sociocivic mandate of schooling.

It is fair to say that civic purposes have been undervalued in the practice of the school. According to data taken by the National Center for Education Statistics (Anderson, 1990), 23% of fourth-graders reported never being exposed to topics dealing with the rights and responsibilities of citizenship in their social studies classes; 34% were never exposed to topics dealing with elections and voting. Among eighth-graders, 27% reported never being exposed to topics dealing with the principles of government. Few schools take much of an interest in assessing citizenship-related skills. In short, the place of citizenship education in the school curriculum is not always easy to find.

School leaders interested in promoting a more visible and deliberately designed citizenship education program might find it difficult to know exactly how to proceed. The chapters in the section speak to such possibilities, not only in terms of directly to forms of pedagogy, but also in terms that relate to potential objectives and outcomes in the domain of citizenship education. At the elementary school level, for instance, the issues are largely microcurricular, meaning they reside in the instructional judgments of teachers whose duties range across the various content areas of the curriculum. Removed from pressures to offer highly specialized education, elementary school teachers could find any number of reasonable ways to inject citizenship education into the common learning experience. At the high school level, however, the issue is largely macrocurricular, meaning it is mostly a matter of deciding how to privilege the place of citizenship education in the coursework and in the larger school experience in a way that goes beyond what might be happening in the social studies class.

REFERENCE

Anderson, L. (1990). *The civics report card.* Washington, DC: U.S. Department of Education.

CHAPTER 1

IMPROVING THE OUTCOMES OF CIVIC EDUCATION

Phillip J. VanFossen
Purdue University

Democracy is not, I repeat, a natural or universal habit of the human mind; it is a cultivated spirit. And if we wish to maintain a democracy we cannot neglect its constant cultivation.

—*Joseph Tussman (1997, p. 143)*

*T**HE GOAL OF THIS CHAPTER IS TO SUMMARIZE EMPIRICAL findings on the effectiveness of various forms and strategies of civic (or citizenship) education for increasing the necessary and desired characteristics of democratic citizens. This summary is presented within the context of education for democratic citizenship, with a brief discussion of the characteristics of democracy and the role of democratic citizenship education in perpetuating these characteristics, and an outline of desired characteristics for democratic citizens. The final section provides an overview of recent data on how well the nation's students and young adults are acquiring these desired characteristics and a summary of recent research on effective strategies for fostering the characteristics of democratic citizens. The chapter concludes with a summary of the results and a discussion of the implications of these findings.*

OUR DEMOCRATIC CIVIC SOCIETY AND EDUCATION

The citizens of this unique experiment in constitutional democracy have a demanding set of obligations. Included among these obligations are a knowledge of the rights and responsibilities of the democratic citizen and an understanding of the civic values—democracy among them—that undergird this civic society. Moreover, these obligations include a "commitment to and participation in a community's civic life" with such participation being seen as the "engine of a constitutional democracy and a free society" (National Assessment of Educational Progress [NAEP] Civics Consensus Project, 1996, p. 1). Indeed, without the informed participation of a responsible citizenry, a democratic republic—by its very definition—cannot exist for long.

As the Center for Civic Education (1995) reported, "Democracy is not a 'machine that will go of itself,' but must be consciously reproduced, one generation instructing the next in the knowledge and skills, as well as the civic character and commitment needed for its sustenance" (p. 3). This implies that democratic societies must provide the means for socializing citizens in the necessary requirements for democratic citizenship. Barber (1992) stressed that "education and democracy are inextricably linked and that in a free society the link is severed at our own peril" (p. 9).

The American public school system was developed, at least in part, to ensure the socialization—through education—of young citizens into this democratic society. As Patrick and Hoge (1990) noted, "From Washington's time to our own, schools have had the mission of inducting 'future guardians of the liberties of the Country' into the civic culture" (p. 427).

Certainly then, as the chapter opening from Tussman implies, a democratic society should be concerned with the education of its citizens in order to meet their democratic obligations. Put more simply, Barber (1992) pointed out that "democracy is less the enabler of education, than education is the enabler of democracy" (p. 14). This then is the role given to civic (or citizenship) education in a democracy: the preparation of once and future democratic citizens.

Democratic Citizenship Education

One view of civic (citizenship) education is that it should "prepare students to participate intelligently in public affairs by giving them the understandings they need to make sense of civic issues" and to help students "appreciate the principles ... that are central to American democracy" (Anderson et al., 1990, p. 6). Patrick (1997) extended this view by noting that "if the polity would survive and thrive, citizens must have knowledge of its principles and institutions, skills in applying this knowledge and dispositions that incline them to protect individual rights and promote the common good" (p. 2).

A second view implies that citizenship education must go beyond the transfer of knowledge of civic issues and institutions to help students acquire the skills needed to be effective participants in a democratic society. Engle and Ochoa (1988) argue that "decision-making skills and all of the knowledge and attitudes that go into the making of intelligent decisions are at the heart of democratic citizenship" (p. 18) and citizenship education must seek to foster these skills in future citizens.

Although perspectives on civic (citizenship) education do vary, a robust consensus on the desired outcomes of such education seems to exist. Illustrative of this consensus is *The Civics Framework for the 1998 National Assessment of Educational Progress* (NAEP Civics Consensus Project, 1996), which divided student progress in civic education into three components: basic civic knowledge, intellectual and participatory skills, and civic dispositions. The National Council for the Social Studies' *Position Statement: The Essentials of Social Studies* (1980) outlined four broad categories of desired outcomes of citizenship education: the acquisition of basic knowledge, the development of democratic beliefs, the development of thinking and political skills, and the facilitation of civic participation. Engle and Ochoa (1988) divided the education needed by democratic citizens into four similar headings: Basic Knowledge, Commitment to the Democratic

Ideal, Intellectual Skills, and Political Skills. Parker and Jarilomek (1997) described the concept of "civic efficacy"—those things needed by citizens for full participation in a democracy—as consisting of three broad areas: knowledge drawn from history and the social sciences, development of values and attitudes that support democracy, and the acquisition of intellectual and participation skills. Similarly, in an extensive review of research on civic education, Patrick and Hoge (1990) chose to divide civic learning into the categories of: knowledge about government, civics, and law; civic attitudes and values; and skills in cognitive processes and participation.

Obviously, there is broad general agreement on the nature of the characteristics that are desired outcomes of citizenship education and are needed by democratic citizens. Given this broad level of agreement then, and for the purposes of this chapter, these outcomes are subsumed into four categories: basic civic knowledge, development of democratic values/attitudes, democratic participation skills, and citizen participation. Table 1.1 demonstrates how the desired outcomes outlined by various authors fit under these four categories.

TABLE 1.1
Summary of Desired Outcomes of Civic (Citizenship) Education

Author(s)	Basic Civic Knowledge	Development of Democratic Values/Attitudes	Democratic Participation Skills	Citizen Participation
NAEP (1996)	Basic civic knowledge	Civic dispositions	Intellectual and participatory skills	
NCSS (1980)	Basic knowledge	Development of democratic beliefs	Thinking and political skills	Facilitation of civic participation
Patrick & Hoge (1990)	Knowledge about government, civics, and law	Civic attitudes and values	Skills in cognitive processes	Participation
Engle & Ochoa (1988)	Basic knowledge	Commitment to the democratic ideal	Intellectual skills and political skills	
Parker & Jarilomek (1997)	Knowledge drawn from history and the social sciences	Values and attitudes that support democracy	Intellectual and participation skills	

CATEGORIES OF DESIRED OUTCOMES OF CIVIC (CITIZENSHIP) EDUCATION

This section examines the four categories of desired outcomes in greater detail, beginning with an overview of each category. It then moves on to review data on how well American students and young adults have acquired the desired characteristics under each category. Finally, recent empirical evidence for improving civic (citizenship) education in each category is summarized.

BASIC CIVIC KNOWLEDGE

What knowledge—facts, concepts, and ideas—must citizens possess in order to participate effectively in a democratic society?[1] Patrick and Hoge (1990) noted that "citizens of a constitutional democracy are expected to know principles and facts necessary for meaningful participation in government and political affairs" (p. 431). The NAEP Civics Consensus Project (1996) divided basic civic knowledge into five categories: knowledge of civic life, politics, and government; knowledge of the foundations of American political life; knowledge of the purposes, values, and principles of American democracy; knowledge of the relation of the United States to other nations and to world affairs; and knowledge of the roles of citizens in American democracy (p. 18).

Engle and Ochoa (1988) took a slightly broader interpretation of basic "civic" knowledge, but echoed the NAEP Civics Consensus Project when they stressed the importance of knowing what institutions—governmental among them—exist in society and how such institutions work. Engle and Ochoa also stressed the importance of knowing not only the current manifestations of these democratic institutions, but also their evolution. "Present day democracy ... should not be seen as an end product but as a stage of development ... and one that is still in the process of development" (Engle & Ochoa, 1988, p. 19).

How much of such basic civic knowledge do students in the nation's schools possess? In order to answer this question, this section draws from Patrick and Hoge's (1990) summary of research on teaching government, civics, and law, the NAEP *Civics Report Card* (Anderson et al., 1990), and several other large studies of the civic knowledge of young adults.

The results reported by Patrick and Hoge (1990) are uneven at best. Although "most 17-year-olds (more than 60%) have general and superficial knowledge of governmental institutions and officials" and can describe the "purposes and functions of constitutional rights and liberties" (p. 431), most high school students' (and many adults') grasp of civic knowledge ends here. Indeed, Patrick and Hoge noted that most high school students have very little knowledge of the processes of government, law, and politics in the United States, with barely half of a national

---

[1] This section draws heavily from the National Assessment of Education Progress (NAEP) conducted in 1988 on civics and government and on the report describing the 1998 NAEP on civics. NAEP is a survey (mandated by the U.S. Congress) of a large, nationally representative sample designed to collect data on student achievement in a variety of core subjects, civics and government among them. The first such collection took place in 1969–1970 and included data on science, writing, and citizenship or civics. Subsequent surveys on civic education have been conducted in 1975–1976, 1981–1982 and 1987–1988. Another NAEP for civics was conducted in 1998.

TABLE 1.2
Trends in Average Civics Proficiency at Ages 13 and 17, 1976–1988

	Assessment Year		
	1976	1982	1988
Age 13	49.1 (.2)	49.1 (.4)	50.0 (.4)
Age 17	61.7 (.3)*	61.3 (.5)*	59.6 (.5)

Note. Data from Anderson et al. (1990).
*Indicates statistically significant difference from 1988 at the .05 level. Standard errors are presented in parentheses. 95% confidence interval is equal to the average proficiency ± 2 standard errors of the estimated proficiency.

sample of 17-year-olds able to correctly answer basic questions concerning the U.S. Constitution (NAEP, 1983).

The NAEP *Civics Report Card* (Anderson et al., 1990) summarized findings from two surveys of U.S. civics achievement: a trend assessment of American students at ages 13 and 17 carried out from 1975 through 1988 and an assessment of 4th-, 8th-, and 12th-graders' civics achievement conducted in 1988. The NAEP *Civics Report Card* suggested that a lack of civic knowledge among high school students and young adults may be a worsening trend: "The seventeen year olds participating in the most recent assessment tended to perform significantly less well then their counterparts in the earlier assessments" (p. 7). However, the 1987–1988 NAEP data did suggest that for 13-year-olds, the level of civic

TABLE 1.3
Levels of Civics Proficiency by Grade, 1988

	Percentage of Students at or Above Level	
Proficiency Level	Grade 8	Grade 12
Level 200		
Recognizes existence of civic life	94.4 (0.4)	98.8 (0.2)
Level 250		
Understand the nature of political institutions and the relationship between citizen and government	61.4 (1.0)	89.2 (0.7)
Level 300		
Understands specific government structures and functions	12.7 (0.7)	49.0 (1.1)
Level 350		
Understands a variety of political institutions and processes	0.3 (0.1)	6.0 (0.5)

Note. Data from Anderson et al. (1990). Standard errors are presented in parentheses. 95% confidence interval is equal to the average proficiency ± 2 standard errors of the estimated proficiency.

knowledge may actually have increased slightly over previous assessments. Table 1.2 presents the results of these analyses.

Other findings from the NAEP *Civics Report Card* (Anderson et al., 1990) indicated that students lacked in-depth knowledge of political institutions and processes. Only half the 12th- grade students assessed displayed a detailed knowledge of governmental structures and only 6% of students sampled demonstrated an understanding of a wide range of political or governmental institutions. Table 1.3 provides data on the level of civic proficiency attained by students in the 1988 NAEP study.

It would seem, based on the evidence presented, that the level of basic civic knowledge among students in the nation's schools is less than ideal. As Patrick and Hoge (1990) concluded, "A major objective in teaching government, civics and law has been to transmit [civic] knowledge [and] ... assessments of the knowledge of older adolescents and adults suggest only modest success in this important dimension" (p. 431).

Given these results, what, if anything, can citizenship educators do to increase the acquisition of basic civic knowledge among the nation's students? Stated another way, what variables, if any, impact the level of basic civic knowledge of public school students and young adults? This section summarizes relevant empirical evidence in an effort to answer these questions and to provide insight into strategies for teaching civics and/or models of citizenship education that may increase the level of basic civic knowledge among students and young adults.

Patrick and Hoge (1990) provided a summary of research on the acquisition of basic civic knowledge by American students. They concluded that the "civic knowledge of ... secondary students is increased through direct instruction" and that "civic knowledge is related to the number of courses taken ... and the amount of time spent on civics lessons in the classroom and on homework" (p. 432).

Indeed, as self-evident as this conclusion may seem, it is clear that simply taking a course entitled "civics" or "government" during high school can increase students' civic knowledge. Whereas it might be assumed that most American students would be required to take such a course in civics or government before graduation, Niemi and Junn (1999) reported that 8% of the students in the 1987–1988 NAEP study had never taken a civics course, more than one quarter of the students had taken only one-half year of civics or less, and that more than 40% of students had less than one full year of civics (p. 66).

Niemi and Junn (1999) sent a questionnaire to each of the social studies directors of the 50 states and the District of Columbia asking about civics/government course requirements. Forty-two (82%) directors indicated that their state had such a requirement. However, Niemi and Junn also indicated that in "only twenty of those states does the requirement demand that there be a separate course (in civics or government); most states simply require that the material be covered in some way during the high school years" (p. 64). In other words, most states have adopted an "infusion" model in which key civics knowledge is integrated into other social studies courses.

This finding is especially troubling as Niemi and Junn (1993), using data collected during the 1987–1988 NAEP, found that participation in courses explicitly entitled "civics" or "government" had a significant, positive effect on the level of basic civics knowledge demonstrated by students. Niemi and Junn reported a "relatively large difference in civics knowledge between those who had no civics course and those who had one or more—even if that course was in 9th or 10th grade" (p. 16).

This last statement refers to a second finding concerning recency of coursework. Not surprisingly, Niemi and Junn (1999) reported that students who had reported taking civics or government courses most recently demonstrated significantly greater levels of civics knowledge, all other things equal. These results, however, make the impact of taking a course entitled civics or government all the more noteworthy.

Similarly, Niemi and Junn (1993) reported that the frequent discussion of current events during a high school civics or government course and the treatment of a "broad range of subjects" within the course resulted in significant positive effects on students' civics knowledge (p. 18). In a book-length analysis of the 1988 NAEP data, Niemi and Junn (1999) concluded that frequent discussion of current events "improves student test scores by as much as 4 % if one contrasts having no discussion at all with having daily discussion" (p. 122). The authors concluded that "the impact of classroom attention to current events is all the more impressive because the NAEP assessment did not specifically call for knowledge of contemporary politics" (p. 122).

Niemi and Junn (1993) also described the significant positive effect of participation in student government on civics knowledge. They concluded that although student government is not "part of the civics curriculum, per se," such participation does "genuinely enhance student knowledge" (p. 23).

Sinatra, Beck, and McKeon (1992) attempted to determine the effects of participation in a stand-alone unit on the American Revolution and the formation of the U.S. government on fifth- through eighth-graders' knowledge of basic structures of government. Using a longitudinal, qualitative design, including interview techniques, the authors gathered data on student responses to questions such as: "How is our country run? What kind of government do we have? and What does it mean to be a 'free country'?" (p. 638).

The results indicated that an isolated instructional unit had very little impact on increasing student knowledge of basic governmental structures. The student responses were generally very superficial and often "not well-grounded in the structure of government" (p. 659). Sinatra et al. (1992) concluded that "the most striking finding evident in the longitudinal data was the consistency of students' responses over the 3-year period" (p. 659). The authors explanation of this consistency—a continued lack of anything more than superficial knowledge of governmental structures—lay in the "need for greater attention to students' understanding of major ideas and underlying issues in social studies" (p. 659). In other words, students understanding suffered from a lack of in-depth treatment of key issues.

Although this study was very limited in its scope, these conclusions do call into question the efficacy of the use of single stand-alone units on the "government" in order to increase adolescents' basic civic knowledge. In this, Sinatra et al. (1992) supported the Niemi and Junn (1993) thesis that entire courses on civics or government (or at least long-term study) are more effective in increasing basic civic knowledge.

Results from the 1988 NAEP indicated that participation in certain forms of classroom instruction may contribute to students' civic knowledge. Students were asked to report how often they had participated in, for example, classroom simulations, including mock trials and mock elections. Whereas relatively few students reported they had participated in these types of activities, "those who had tended to perform better in the assessment than their peers who had occasionally or never participated in these activities" (Anderson et al., 1990, p. 85). Niemi and Junn (1999) found that participation in a mock election or government contributed significantly to individual student achievement (p. 120).

Law-related education (LRE) is a broad curricular movement within citizenship education. Defined as a curriculum that provides students with "opportunities to develop the knowledge ... skills, attitudes and appreciations necessary to respond effectively to the law and legal issues," LRE has long been touted as a successful vehicle for improving citizenship education in general (Study Group on Law-Related Education, 1978, p. 50). Patrick and Hoge (1990) reported that "students in systematic and extensive law-related education (LRE) programs have increased their knowledge of the purposes and types of law, state and federal judicial institutions and rights and responsibilities of citizens" (p. 433).

Hardin (1991) conducted a survey of more than 1,200 teachers in order to determine the impact of LRE on students' attitudes toward and knowledge about legal and political issues. The questionnaire employed in this study asked teachers to provide fixed-item responses on the impact of LRE on students' interest in the course, interest in current events, and class participation. Teachers were also asked to provide additional written comments about the impact of LRE on their students. Teachers clearly attributed increases in student interest in civics class and in current events to LRE. Similarly, teachers indicated that students in LRE programs demonstrated more "critical thinking skills" than students who were not in such programs (Hardin, 1991, p. 23).

The results concerning increased civic knowledge, however, were mixed. Some teachers suggested that students' civics knowledge often increased dramatically with the implementation of a systematic LRE program: "Before LRE was included, the mid-term Civics failure rate was 50%. After LRE was added, the mid-term failure rate dropped to 20%" (Hardin, 1991, p. 25). Curiously, such knowledge gains seemed to extend to special education students in particular. Teacher responses indicated that the only special education students who "knew their rights and responsibilities" were students "in the only school district [in that state] to offer LRE to special education students" (Hardin, 1991, p. 25).

Results here were mixed, however, as a number of teacher responses indicated little or no impact of LRE on students' civic knowledge. Teachers indicated that students often "show interest in LRE, but no marked improvement otherwise" (Hardin, 1991, p. 26).

DEMOCRATIC AND POLITICAL VALUES AND ATTITUDES

What values and/or attitudes should the democratic citizen hold or aspire to? What dispositions or character traits are essential to democratic citizens? The NCSS *Position Statement: Essentials of Social Studies* (1980) stated that "fundamental beliefs drawn from the Declaration of Independence and the U.S. Constitution ... form the basic principles of our democratic constitutional order" (p. 2). Among the list of democratic beliefs that civic (citizenship) education should seek to foster are justice, equality, responsibility, freedom, diversity, and privacy (NCSS, 1980, p. 2). Patrick and Hoge (1990) agreed that civic education is "heavily weighted with attitudes and values associated with constitutional democracy in the United States" (p. 431).

Parker and Jarilomek (1997) noted that "without certain dispositions, self governance and civic life would be impossible" (p. 11). Their list of such dispositions was more sophisticated in scope than those already noted and included such character traits as "a reasoned commitment to the public values of this society ... knowing the basic rights guaranteed all citizens (and) ... treating oneself and others with respect" (p. 12).

The NAEP Civics Consensus Project (1996) described several important civic dispositions that "contribute to the ... nation's well-being (p. 32). Among these were "public-spiritedness, civility, respect for law, critical mindedness and a willingness to listen, negotiate and compromise" (NAEP Civics Consensus Project, 1996, p. 32).

Engle and Ochoa (1988) expressed similar goals. They noted that students "should come to have a more reasoned understanding of democracy, including such ideas as freedom of choice, openness to new ideas ... the protection of minority rights and opinions; freedom of the press, freedom of religion, freedom to speak one's mind and academic freedom" (p. 23).

What civic values/attitudes do students in the nation's schools possess? To what degree do students leaving school hold the vital democratic dispositions noted previously? What attitudes toward government and governmental institutions do students hold? In order to answer these questions, this section draws primarily from Patrick and Hoge's (1990) summary of research on teaching government, civics, and law and from several other large studies of the civic and political attitudes of American youth and young adults.

Unfortunately, research conducted in this area has tended to focus nearly exclusively on student attitudes toward government and governmental institutions and has thus failed to address other attitudes or dispositions that may be needed for successful democratic citizenship (e.g., the "reasoned commitment to public values," "civility," or "critical mindedness" mentioned earlier). This dearth of research may be due to several factors, including the difficulty inherent in measuring the presence of such dispositions in large, representative samples.

The summary of research on civic attitudes and values developed by Patrick and Hoge (1990) is illustrative of this focus in that it was guided by two questions: "To what extent have students formed commitments to standards (values) associated with the Constitution and system of government in the United States? And, to what extent have they developed positive orientations (attitudes) ... toward constitutional democracy in the United States?" As Patrick and Hoge concluded, civic (citizenship) education "is heavily weighted with attitudes and values associated with Constitutional democracy in the United States" (p. 431).

Despite this somewhat narrow approach to describing the civic and political values and attitudes students hold, Patrick and Hoge (1990) nonetheless provided important insight into the nature of political beliefs and attitudes among the nation's students. Based on their review of relevant research, Patrick and Hoge presented seven general findings related to adolescent/young adult political beliefs, attitudes, and values:

1. Adolescents and young adults tend to have favorable attitudes toward the Constitution, democracy, and the nation.
2. Most children have developed these positive attitudes without solid civic knowledge.
3. Students generally express support for majority rule and minority rights, but support for certain rights tends to decline when applied to unpopular groups or individuals.
4. Studies in the 1950s (Purdue Youth Opinion Polls) have shown that a large proportion of students were authoritarian in their attitudes toward the Bill of Rights, opposing rights for certain groups (e.g., African Americans). Adolescents in the 1980s were given the same type of questions and the results were mixed: On a few responses, students were more democratic than their 1950s counterparts, but a larger percentage of the 1980s high school stu-

dents were willing to allow police searches without warrants, deny legal counsel to criminals, and accept restrictions on religious freedom.
5. Students have a persistent lack of commitment to the values inherent in the central paradox of a constitutional democracy: majority rule, minority rights.
6. Students hold favorable views of political participation, especially voting and participating in political campaigns.
7. However, students also express low levels of political interest and efficacy and socioeconomic status remains the best predictor of student interest and activity.

Are these characteristics manifest across all segments of the student population? Nearly all of the research on student's political attitudes and values that Patrick and Hoge summarized focused on heterogeneously grouped individuals. Sidelnick (1989) claimed that "only a few studies ... examined the political attitudes of low-ability adolescents" (p. 92).

Sidelnick attempted to describe the political attitudes of low, average and above average ability students and to determine if across-group differences existed. Using a random sample of 9th- and 12th-grade students stratified across ability level, Sidelnick used standardized scales to gather data on three main topics: students' respect for law, students' dogmatism or lack of receptiveness, and students' beliefs in the fundamental freedoms of the Bill of Rights.

The results indicated significant differences in the dogmatism and fundamental freedoms scale ratings across ability level. In other words, lower ability students were more dogmatic in their attitudes than average ability students who, in turn, were more dogmatic than the higher ability students. The same relationship held for the fundamental freedoms scale. No significant differences across ability levels were reported for the respect for law scale. Sidelnick concluded that "low-ability subjects are more dogmatic and consequently less likely to support fundamental freedoms embodied in ... the Bill of Rights" (p. 95). Sidelnick proposed that "educators should seek ways to ... decrease the dogmatism or close-minded attitudes evident in many low- and average-ability level students" (p. 95).

In an attempt to summarize the political attitudes and beliefs of the American electorate, Branson (1994) examined two national surveys: the annual "American Freshman" report on attitudes and behaviors of first-year students at American colleges and universities (Astin, Korn, & Riggs, 1993) and the *Times Mirror* Center for the People and the Press (1994) survey on underlying political beliefs.

The "American Freshman" report (Astin et al., 1993) gathered data on a number of topics from 220,000 incoming freshmen at 427 colleges and universities. Several of the questionnaire topics dealt directly with students' political attitudes and beliefs. Results from these items indicated that students held a somewhat negative perception of government, governmental institutions, and politics. Indeed, a large majority of respondents agreed with negative statements such as "the government is not protecting the consumer," "the government is not controlling pollution," and "the government needs to do more to control handguns."

When asked to identify activities in which they had engaged in their senior year of high school, only 18% of respondents indicated they discussed politics on a regular basis. Curiously, however, 40% of respondents indicated they had participated in some form of demonstration, which begs the question of whether students discussed these protests beforehand. Students also put personal goals above public or civic goals: "Keeping up with politics," "promoting racial understanding," and "influencing the political structure" were goals identified by less than 40% of respondents.

The *Times Mirror* Center for the People and the Press (1994) conducted a national survey of 3,300 randomly selected adults, age 18 or older. Branson (1994) concluded that the results of the *Times Mirror* survey highlighted three important results with respect to political attitudes and beliefs: Americans' have become either polarized or indifferent toward social and public issues, Americans' attitudes toward both major parties have undergone a marked change, and Americans are increasingly distrustful of both politicians and governmental institutions. As Branson (1994) concluded, these results seem to indicate a "who cares" attitude on the part of the American polity that makes the avoidance of political participation all the more likely (p. 9).

As with the basic knowledge component of civic education, the results concerning the civic attitudes and values that secondary students and young adults hold seemed mixed. Although students generally believe in the efficacy of democratic institutions, these beliefs are superficial in that they are not based on a fundamental knowledge of civil society. This superficiality is reflected in the lack of understanding of the central paradox of democracy (majority rule, minority rights) that allows students to hold much more authoritarian views where unpopular groups or individuals are concerned (Patrick & Hoge, 1990). Lower and average ability students are even more likely to hold such authoritarian and dogmatic views than their higher ability counterparts. The superficiality of student belief is also manifest in increasingly distrustful attitudes toward government and governmental institutions held by young adults and the continued downward spiral in rates of political participation (Branson, 1994).

Given these results concerning students' political attitudes and beliefs, what, if anything, can citizenship educators do to improve these attitudes and beliefs among the nation's students? What variables, if any, impact the political attitudes and beliefs of public school students and young adults? This section summarizes relevant empirical evidence in an effort to answer these questions and to provide insight into strategies for teaching civics and models of citizenship education that may improve the democratic and political attitudes and beliefs of secondary students and young adults.

It is clear from previous research in this area that the direct teaching of civic values and attitudes—as well as the direct teaching of civic knowledge—has no discernable impact on the development of such values and attitudes (Patrick & Hoge, 1990). Moreover, Torney, Oppenheim, and Farnen (1975) found that an overemphasis on the direct teaching of such values as patriotism among Western European students actually led to *diminished support* for civic values and lower levels of civic knowledge.

If direct teaching does not positively influence student attitudes, then what other variables might do so? Classroom climate has long been a variable of interest in this area. Patrick and Hoge (1990) concluded that "the classroom climate established by the teacher is one key to the development of (positive) civic attitudes" (p. 433). Further, they concluded that "teachers who emphasize analysis and appraisal of controversial public issues in an 'open' classroom environment, where students feel free and secure ... , are likely to enhance the learning of democratic attitudes" (p. 433).

Research has indicated that participatory civic learning experiences can have a positive impact on students' political attitudes. Harwood (1990) conducted an investigation of the impact of the Close-Up Foundation's experiential citizenship education program on students' attitudes. The Close-Up Foundation is a private, nonprofit organization that sponsors a week-long series of simulations, field trips, discussion groups, and programs held annually in Washington, DC, which is attended by some 30,000 students and teachers from all ability and socioeconomic levels and from all 50 states and Puerto Rico.

Using a pre- and posttest design, Harwood administered a political attitudes questionnaire to two civics classes who participated in the Close-Up Foundation experience and to four comparison classes. The results of the study indicated that students who attended the Close-Up program scored significantly higher on measures of political confidence, political interest, and political trust than the comparison group. In addition, students who participated in the program stated they were more likely to become politically active than students who had not attended. Harwood concluded that the Close-Up experience had "a strong impact" on the students who had participated in the program (p. 18).

Patrick and Hoge (1990) concluded that whereas direct instruction in democratic or politic values may have limited impact, the use of activities and strategies that require students to use critical thought may lead to improved student attitudes. "Teachers increase their students' potential for development of democratic attitudes and values when they provide systematic instruction in thinking about public issues ... " (p. 433).

Brody (1994) studied the impact of a commercial curriculum (the *We the People ...* curriculum,[2] developed by the Center for Civic Education) that described the impact of systematic discussion of current public issues on students' level of political tolerance. Brody defined political tolerance as a citizen's respect for the political and civil rights of all people in the society, no matter how unpopular a group or an individual.

Brody collected data from a sample of 1,351 high school students from across the United States. Analysis of the results indicated that students who were involved in a civics or government class displayed higher levels of political tolerance than the typical American citizen did and that students who were participating in the *We the People ...* program had the highest level of political tolerance of all. Brody concluded that the *We the People ...* program fostered increased tolerance because it promoted higher levels of self-confidence and the perception of fewer limits on students' political freedom.

In a study of the relation between classroom climate and political attitudes, Harwood (1991) used four characteristics to define classroom climate in the civics classroom: classroom activities, teacher characteristics, student involvement, and social atmosphere. Harwood defined political attitudes as the feeling students had toward political institutions, public officials, and political processes. Using both qualitative and quantitative methods, Hardwood studied three senior-level civics classrooms for the entire 11-week period during which the classes met. Harwood used data collected during classroom observations to construct a teacher characteristic profile based on the perceived openness of the classroom. Attitudinal data were collected using four normed, standardized scales that measured political efficacy, political interest, political trust and political confidence.

Harwood found a strong, significant relation between two elements of the classroom climate variable and two of the four attitude scales. Students of teachers who were rated as being more open tended to score higher on the political efficacy and political trust scales. Similarly, students in classes where the level of student involvement was high tended to score higher on the political efficacy, political trust, and political interest scales. Harwood also found that students of teachers who had higher openness ratings and who allowed higher levels of student involvement were more likely to be engaged in political discussion outside of the classroom.

Overall school climate has also been shown to impact students' political attitudes and values positively. "Nonclassroom attributes of schools, such as style of

---

[2] *We the People ... The Citizen and the Constitution* is designed to promote civic competence and responsibility among the nation's elementary and secondary students. The instructional program enhances students' understanding of the institutions of American constitutional democracy. At the same time, students discover the contemporary relevance of the Constitution and Bill of Rights. The culminating activity is a simulated congressional hearing in which students "testify" before a panel of judges. Students demonstrate their knowledge and understanding of constitutional principles and have opportunities to evaluate, take, and defend positions on relevant historical and contemporary issues (Center for Civic Education, 1997).

administration, executive organizations, school governance, peer interactions and extracurricular programs, are likely to affect profoundly the civic learning of students" (Patrick & Hoge, 1990, p. 433).

Research on school climate variables has indicated that school governance and organization are related to the political attitudes of students. For example, Ehman (1980), in a study that examined the role of the school in the political socialization process, concluded that "more participation and less authoritarian climates (in the schools generally) are linked to positive political attitudes" (p. 113). However, Patrick and Hoge (1990) cautioned that research on school climate in the field of character education suggested that schools where adults "authoritatively and unambiguously support core values of the community as standards of responsible behavior" (p. 434) may be more effective in preparing students for democratic citizenship after leaving school. The results concerning overall school climate remain mixed.

It has long been accepted that students who participate in extracurricular activities (e.g., student government, athletics, and interest group clubs) are more likely to hold positive attitudes and to engage in political participation outside of school. Patrick and Hoge (1990) concluded that student participation in such extracurricular events is "positively related to the development of political efficacy and to the propensity for participation in civil life outside the school" (p. 433). Some research (Ehman, 1980) has suggested that these student activities may be more influential than the formal curriculum in developing positive attitudes toward political participation and public affairs.

DEMOCRATIC PARTICIPATION SKILLS

> If citizens are to exercise their rights and discharge their responsibilities as members of self-governing communities, they not only need to acquire a body of knowledge about civic life, politics and government, they also need to acquire relevant intellectual and participatory skills (NAEP Civics Consensus Project, 1996, p. 24)

Remy (1976) argued persuasively that—in addition to knowledge about politics and government—education for democratic citizenship must include the development of students' abilities to make and judge civic decisions, to act on such decisions and to influence them. The Center for Civic Education (1995) concluded that students need to develop "the intellectual and participatory skills necessary for competent and responsible participation" (p. 5) in this democratic society.

What intellectual and participatory skills are needed by democratic citizens in order to participate fully in a democratic, civic society? The NAEP Civics Consensus Project (1996) divided the necessary intellectual skills into three categories: identifying and describing (e.g., defining key terms, describing functions of government); explaining and analyzing (e.g., explaining causes and effects, distinguishing between fact and opinion); and evaluating, taking, and defending positions (e.g., identifying, evaluating, and defending the validity of arguments).

The Center for Civic Education (1995) offered a similar categorical distinction, but went on to define intellectual skills as inseparable from civic content: "To be able to think critically about a political issue, for example, one must have an understanding of the issue, its history, its relevance, as well as command of a set of intellectual tools or considerations useful in dealing with such an issue. Thus equipped, a citizen is better able to evaluate, take and defend positions on issues" (p. 5).

Engle and Ochoa (1988) stressed that the skills needed by citizens went beyond the simple ability to retrieve and remember information. They concluded that "the skills needed by citizens of a democracy are more complex in nature and focused on the utilization of knowledge in making decisions" (p. 25). Among these skills were the ability to make reasoned judgments in light of conflicting evidence, being able to see a problem in its broadest possible context, and being able to select and apply the most relevant information for a particular problem.

NAEP Civics Consensus Project (1996) stressed that "education for citizenship must not only address the acquisition of knowledge and of intellectual skills; it must also focus on the development of skills required for informed, competent and responsible participation in the political process and civil society" (p. 28). These skills might be categorized as follows:

Interacting—skills citizens need to cooperate and work with other citizens, to be responsive, to question, to be civil, to build coalitions.

Monitoring—skills needed to monitor actions of government, gathering and analyzing information, attending public meetings.

Influencing—skills required to affect the processes of politics and government: voting, writing, petitioning (NAEP, 1996).

Keeping this array of intellectual and participatory skills in mind, how well prepared to exercise these skills are the nation's students and young adults? Unlike the domains of civic knowledge and political values and attitudes, research into the realm of civic skill acquisition is almost nonexistent. As Patrick and Hoge (1990) wrote, "There is a paucity of data about cognitive- and participation-skill learning associated with civic education" (p. 432).

Moreover, the limited data on cognitive and participation skill acquisition that has been reported has often relied on standardized instrumentation as a proxy for certain cognitive or participation skills: at best, a questionable methodology. For example, the 1983 NAEP report concluded that more than 60% of 17-year-olds have certain "middle range cognitive skills" (Patrick & Hoge, 1990, p. 432) Niemi and Junn (1999) reported that several items (3 out of 150 on the questionnaire) on the 1988 NAEP asked students to use inferential skills in order to answer the question correctly. Results on those three items indicated that approximately 70% of students were able to draw the correct inference based on the data provided. Niemi and Junn (1999) concluded that "it was disconcerting to see that many students were unable to answer what we considered to be easy questions" (p. 43) and went on to express concern over these results. However, these claims should be interpreted cautiously as these conclusions were based entirely on responses to just a few standardized questions.

Civic education scholars have posited that most of the nation's adolescents are not prepared to use the skills needed to identify relevant public issues and make rational decisions about them. For example, Ravitch and Finn (1987) provided a syllogistic argument to support this hypothesis. They argued that (a) data have indicated that students have very superficial civic knowledge about the U.S. Constitution (Anderson et al., 1990), (b) thus students cannot recognize and comprehend their rights as articulated in the Constitution, and therefore (c) they will not be able to reflect on public issues associated with those rights. Although this argument holds a certain intuitive attractiveness, it is one that must be cautiously interpreted as little empirical data has been reported to support this conclusion.

Patrick and Hoge (1990) summarized two other arguments concerning the development of intellectual and participation skills. First, the low levels of civic participation among adolescents and young adults may be due to a lack of knowledge about how to participate in civic affairs. Niemi and Junn (1999) noted that very little attention is given to such skill development at the high school level. Miller (1985) concluded that a lack of overall civic knowledge may also be a factor contributing to lack of participation skills.

Finally, Patrick and Hoge (1990) summarized Goodlad's argument, first developed in *A Place Called School* (1984), that the low levels of participations skills among adolescents were due to the lack of emphasis on this aspect of civic learning in the classroom. Goodlad's national study of schools found little evidence of intellectual skill development in classrooms across the nation and concluded that social studies, in particular, had a preoccupation with low level intellectual processes.

Given the lack of data regarding student acquisition of intellectual and participation skills integral to democratic citizens, it is not at all surprising to find that very few studies have reported on effective strategies for increasing student levels of these skills. In light of this fact, Patrick and Hoge (1990) resorted to summarizing broad, general studies of critical thinking and decision making in social studies classrooms. For example, Cornbleth (1985) found that, in the social studies classroom, students' decision-making capabilities are likely to be enhanced if they practice these skills within the context of specific subject matter such as government. Cornbleth concluded that the successful decision maker in any domain must have discipline-based knowledge related to the issue at hand. Stated differently, Cornbleth encouraged civics educators to deal more explicitly with issues of civic decision making and participation in the formal curriculum.

CIVIC PARTICIPATION

If the goal of civic education is the informed participation of a responsible citizenry, then it follows that the success or failure of such education can be judged "by the extent to which the citizenry takes a reflective and active part in the political and social community" (Ferguson, 1990, p. 385). Distinct from participation skills, civic participation has been defined as voluntary acts engaged in by private citizens who seek to influence or bring about change in either a political or social context. Political participation can take one of two forms (electoral or nonelectoral), but either way its ultimate outcome is influencing the selection of government personnel and/or the actions they take. Social participation may take the form of work with service organizations, volunteerism, presentations to youth groups and church-related activities (Ferguson, 1990).

What are the current levels of citizen participation among students in the nation's schools and among young adults? Much of the news—at least with respect to political participation—is not good. For example, the level of voter participation among citizens under age 30 is approximately 30%, down from a decade ago, and 20% to 30% below voter participation rates among citizens over age 30 (Bennett, 1997).

Unfortunately, these results point to a trend in declining voter participation rates. As Ferguson (1990) reported, voter participation rates for the 18–24 age group have been falling steadily since the 1970s. "In 1984, only one-half the 18–24 year olds were registered to vote, and only 16.6% of the eligible voters in (this) group voted in the 1986 elections" (Ferguson, 1990, p. 387).

As noted earlier, the American Freshman report indicated that only 18% of incoming college and university freshmen reported regularly engaging in political discussions (Astin et al., 1993). This percentage was exactly one half the percentage of three decades ago (Bennett, 1997). Less than 20% of first-year college students claimed to follow what goes on in government and political affairs most of the time, as compared with 32% of citizens over age 30 (Bennett, 1997).

One should be cautious, however, to avoid simple generalizations about the level of civic (or even political) participation of adolescents and young adults based solely on voting patterns or a lack of political discourse. Indeed, whereas participation in the electoral process may be waning for this age group, some evidence indicates that overall levels of civic participation may be rising. Ferguson noted that "declines in voting percentages may not necessarily indicate a diminution in civic interest but may be attributed in part to changes in the nature of participation" (p. 388). One cross-national study (Dalton, 1988) concluded that although U.S. voting rates are the lowest among Western democracies, when all forms of civic participation are factored in, U.S. citizens may be the most civically active of all.

A recent study conducted by the University of Michigan's Political Studies Center found that whereas citizens are indeed less inclined to vote than in previous generations, they are no less inclined to belong to community organizations, to participate in civic groups, or to be otherwise engaged in their communities (Raasch, 1998). The PEW Charitable Trust conducted a survey of Philadelphia residents that reached similar conclusions. The results indicated that 9 out of 10 Philadelphians had taken part in some form of civic engagement over the past year (Raasch, 1998). Some of the types of civic activity reported were town meetings, writing elected officials, contributing money or time to a campaign, and working on neighborhood issues.

The evidence concerning nonvoting civic participation is encouraging, but the degree of civic involvement of adolescents and young adults remains troubling. What can be done to increase the levels of civic participation among these citizens? What strategies or models in civic education increase the likelihood of citizen participation? In order to answer these questions, this section relies on Ferguson's (1990) summary of research on social and political participation and several recent studies on civic participation.

Although general levels of education and educational attainment correlate highly with civic participation, classroom-level factors in general, and the civics curriculum in particular, have little discernable impact on levels of participation. Ferguson (1990) reported that "there is limited empirical support for the assumption that social studies courses [which include civics] exert a positive influence on participation" (p. 390). Miller (1985) is an illustrative case. After analyzing 35,000 responses from the High School and Beyond and National Longitudinal Study data, Miller found that formal civics course exposure is weakly correlated with future civic participation. Ferguson (1990) concluded that "the civics curriculum appears to be more instrumental in the acquisition of political knowledge than in shaping the dispositions and skills related to participation" (p. 389).

Ferguson (1990) reported a number of studies that found significant correlation between school activities—extracurricular activities in particular—and rates of participation among young adults. "Studies of participation in school governance and extracurricular activities have supported [the] hypothesis that active participation in one setting is likely to be transferred to new political situations" (Ferguson, 1990, p. 389). Although participation in extracurricular activities was found to be the strongest predictor of future participation, "years of schooling ... was the second strongest predictor" (p. 389). In other words, those who attend school the longest (in the case of high school, those who graduate) are those who are most likely to engage in future civic participation.

Ferguson (1990) summarized the empirical findings related to civic participation as follows:

1. Students who take part in extracurricular activities are more likely to become civically active as adults.
2. The formal school curriculum has little impact on civic behavior.
3. Social studies instruction promotes knowledge acquisition more effectively than it promotes participation.
4. The socialization that does occur in civics classroom is primarily an academic experience; few opportunities are provided to learn through hands-on community service.
5. There is no evidence to support or to challenge the hypothesis that community- and school-related participation experiences are more effective than traditional classroom-bound methods of instruction.

Recent investigations into the efficacy of a service learning model have, to some degree, refuted Ferguson's last point. Indeed, advocates of service learning programs point to increased civic participation as one of the realized benefits to such a program. As Garman (1995) claimed, students who participate in service learning "are endowed with a sense of civic efficacy, the attitude that they should, can and will have an impact on civic affairs" (p. 1). Can a service learning program increase students' civic participation as adults?

Community service learning has been defined as the integration of meaningful service to one's community with academic learning and structured reflection on the service experience (Kraft & Kielsmeier, 1995). Wade (1995) described examples of service learning activities as "those in which students gather oral histories from senior citizens for their social studies curriculum or create a bird sanctuary as a means for helping the environment while they learn science and math skills" (p. 122).

Eyler, Giles, and Braxton (1997) gathered data from 1,100 students at 30 colleges and universities who had completed a one semester service learning program and from 400 students who had not. Eyler et al. used a pre- and posttest design to determine changes in, among other things, "students' assessments of their citizenship skills (and) their confidence that they can and should make a difference in their communities" (p. 2). The results indicated that student participation in a service learning program "was a significant predictor of growth in students' confidence they can be effective in their community, that they are connected to it and that the community can be effective in solving its problems" (p. 5). These results should be cautiously interpreted as student self-report of plans to engage in future community service are not the actual service itself. However, it was clear from this study that attitudes toward community service among students who participated in the service learning project were more positive than those who had not participated.

Wade (1995) reported on a semester-long study of a pre-service teacher education class. Within this class, students were required to complete a personal service learning project that included reflective journals and a two-page summary of the project at the end of the semester. Wade used semantic differentials to determine changes in student attitudes toward service learning and community service. The results suggested that "on the whole, students came to see being active in the community as easier, more important and more interesting and many expressed a stronger commitment to engage in community service following their experiences" (p. 126).

Nolin, Chaney, Chapman, and Chandler (1997) conducted a national survey of student participation in community service activities. Among the findings reported were the rates of service learning participation in the nation's schools. Results indicated that nearly one half of all public school students had participated in some form of community service. Among private schools (both secular and church-related) more than two thirds of students reported participating in some form of community service. Other results indicated that 93% of students who were asked to participate (but were not required to participate) in community service projects eventually did so, as compared with only 24% of students who participated without being asked (Nolin et al., 1997).

Most interestingly, Nolin et al. (1997) found that the likelihood of future (voluntary) participation in community service was related to whether or not the initial community service was required and arranged by the students' school. Students who participated in a program required and arranged by their school were twice as likely to plan to participate (voluntarily) the following year when compared to students whose service participation was not required. Nolin et al. concluded that school policies regarding service projects may have tremendous influence on future student participation.

Conclusions

This chapter began with a definition of civic (citizenship) education and of the desired outcomes of successful civic education programs. A brief overview of the degree to which the nation's adolescents and young adults possess these desired outcomes was then presented. Finally, this chapter provided a summary of relevant research on effective strategies for fostering these characteristics. Having reviewed this research, what conclusions can be drawn about various strategies and what are the implications of these conclusions for civic (citizenship) educators in the nation's schools?

BASIC CIVIC KNOWLEDGE

Several recent national surveys have indicated that the nation's adolescents and young adults have limited civic knowledge. As many as half of the students studied were unable to identify basic governmental structures or demonstrate more than a superficial understanding of the workings of the government or of the rights and responsibilities of democratic citizens. What approaches to civic (citizenship) education have been linked to improving students' basic civic knowledge?

It is clear that taking a course entitled "civics" or "government" during high school (preferably in 12th grade) has a positive impact on students' knowledge. Isolated or "infused" units of study on the government have little impact on student knowledge. Several classroom variables have been shown to have positive impact on student knowledge. Among these are the treatment of a wide variety of topics, the use of mock elections and other classroom simulations, and the frequent discussion of current events. Finally, the implementation of a systematic law-related education program may increase students' knowledge of governmental structures and of the nation's legal system.

DEMOCRATIC AND POLITICAL VALUES AND ATTITUDES

Students generally hold favorable views of the Constitution, democracy, and the nation, but these views are based on very weak background knowledge. Students tend to express support for the fundamental value of majority rule/minority rights but often balk at extending rights to unfavorable groups or individuals. Students hold favorable views of voting and other forms of political participation. Low ability students tend to be more dogmatic and less supportive of freedoms found in the Bill of Rights than are average or high level students. Few students view political discourse as important in their daily lives. Incoming college students tend to be apathetic toward politics in general and are often distrustful of government and politicians. Given this somewhat mixed picture, what factors might help develop more positive attitudes among the nation's adolescents and young adults?

Research has indicated that whereas the direct teaching of political or democratic values is ineffective and perhaps even detrimental, certain curricular activities have demonstrated a positive impact on students' attitudes. For example, systematic instruction in public issues increases student potential for developing democratic attitudes. Student participation in ongoing civic/political simulations and curriculum (e.g., Close-Up, *We the People* ...) leads to greater degrees of political trust and tolerance and results in a desire to be more politically active.

Classroom and school climate may impact student attitudes. Open classrooms (i.e., those where students feel free to discuss and debate issues) appear to lead to more positive political attitudes. A high degree of student involvement in civics classes leads to more positive political attitudes and greater political participation. However, the results concerning school climate variables remain mixed.

Finally, students who participate in extracurricular activities (including, but not limited to, student government) demonstrated more positive attitudes toward political participation than students who do not participate in such activities.

DEMOCRATIC PARTICIPATION SKILLS

Civic education scholars have hypothesized that students have low levels of civic participation skills, but little empirical support exists for such a hypothesis. Very limited evidence from the 1988 NAEP study indicated that students lack inferential reasoning skills. Research on critical thinking indicates that civics students may be like other social studies students and possess low levels of participation skills. These reportedly low levels of participation skills may be due to a lack of treatment of such skills in the civics curriculum. Civic and social studies educators have recommended a greater emphasis on these skills in the curriculum.

CITIZEN PARTICIPATION

Studies show the level of political participation among the nation's adolescents and young adults is, and has been, particularly low. Voting rates among the 18- to 24-year-old population are only half the rates of older adults. Young adults do not participate in, nor do they value, political discussions. However, young adults do participate in community service and other, nonelectoral, forms of civic participation.

Research on citizen participation has indicated that the formal civics curriculum has little impact on students' level of political or social participation. This may be due to the fact that there are few instances within the formal curriculum where participation is emphasized beyond an academic treatment. Research indicates a high degree of correlation between years of schooling and rates of participation, highlighting the importance of focusing efforts on dropout prevention programs.

Service learning appears to increase the likelihood of political and social participation. Students who have participated in such programs regularly report increases in their desire to engage in community service in the future.

FINAL THOUGHTS

In conclusion, the research reviewed in this chapter has the potential to inform civic educators. Although some of the research suffers from methodological flaws or is overly limited in scope, some important, albeit tentative, findings have emerged.

As with all social science inquiry, further research and study on civic education should be conducted. Future studies will serve to replicate or refute initial findings reported here or to indicate new variables that may influence students' civic learning.

In particular, further study should focus on three areas. First, a continued examination of the formal civics curriculum—what is taught as civics and/or government at the high school level and how it is taught—and its impact on civic learning is warranted. Second, more formal study of the development of students' civic skills—intellectual and participatory—and how best to facilitate that development must be conducted. As noted earlier, research in this area is almost nonexistent. Finally, research on citizen participation should seek to confirm the initial findings regarding the impact of a service learning model on civic attitudes and participation.

REFERENCES

Anderson, L., Jenkins, L., Leming, J., MacDonald, W., Mullis, I., Turner, M., & Wooster, J. (1990). *The civics report card.* Princeton, NJ: National Assessment of Education Progress, Educational Testing Service.

Astin, A., Korn, W., & Riggs, E. (1993, December). *The American freshman: National norms for fall, 1993.* Cooperative Institutional Research Program, American Council on Education, UCLA.

Barber, B. (1992). *An aristocracy of everyone: The politics of education and the future of America.* New York: Oxford University Press.

Bennett, S. (1997, March). Why young Americans hate politics and what we should do about it. *Politics and Political Science,* 47–53.

Branson, M. (1994). *What does research on political attitudes and behavior tell us about the need for improving education for democracy?* Paper presented at the International Conference on Education for Democracy, Malibu, CA. (ERIC Document Reproduction Services No. 387 433)

Brody, R. (1994). *Secondary education and political attitudes: Examining the effects on political tolerance of the We the People ... curriculum.* Final Report. Palo Alto, CA: Stanford University.

Center for Civic Education. (1995). *The role of civic education: A report of the task force on civic education to the second annual White House conference on character building for a democratic, civic society.* Calabasas, CA: Author.

Center for Civic Education. (1997). *Programs of the center for civic education.* Center for Civic Education WWW HomePage: http://www.civiced.org/programs.html. Calabasas, CA: Author.

Cornbleth, C. (1985). Critical thinking and cognitive processes. In W. Stanley (Ed.), *Review of research in social studies education, 1976–1983* (pp. 51–63). Washington, DC: National Council for Social Studies.

Dalton, R. (1988). *Citizen politics in Western democracies.* Chatham, NJ: Chatham House.

Ehman, L. (1980). The American school in the political socialization process. *Review of Research in Education, 50*(1), 99–119.

Engle, S., & Ochoa, A. (1988). *Education for democratic citizenship: Decision-making in the social studies.* New York: Teacher's College Press.

Eyler, J., Giles, D., & Braxton, J. (1997). *Report of a national study comparing the impacts of service-learning program characteristics on post secondary students.* Paper presented at the annual meeting of the American Educational Research Association. (ERIC Document Reproduction Services No. 408 505)

Ferguson, P. (1990). Impacts on social and political participation. In J. Shaver (Ed.), *Handbook of research on social studies teaching and learning* (pp. 385–399). New York: Macmillan.

Garman, B. (1995). *Civic education through service learning. ERIC/ChESS Digest.* (ERIC Document Reproduction Services No. 390 720)

Goodlad, J. (1984). *A place called school.* New York: McGraw-Hill.

Hardin, J. (Ed.). (1991). *Teachers speak out on law-related education: Summary report on the SPICE IV national teachers' survey.* Winston-Salem, NC: Center for Research and Development in Law-Related Education.

Harwood, A. (1990, April). *The effects of Close-Up participation on high school students political attitudes.* Paper presented at the annual meeting of the American Educational Research Association, Boston. (ERIC Document Reproduction Service No. 320 846)

Harwood, A. (1991, April). *The difference between "democracy sucks" and "I may become a politician": Views from three high school civics classes.* Paper presented at the annual meeting of the American Educational Research Association, Chicago. (ERIC Document Reproduction Services No. 341 604)

Kraft, R., & Kielsmeier, J. (Eds.). (1995). *Experiential learning in schools of higher education.* Dubuque, IA: Kendall/Hunt.

Miller, J. (1985, April). *The influence of high school social studies courses on political participation of young adults.* Paper presented at the annual meeting of the American Educational Research Association (ERIC Document Reproduction Service No. 265 086)

National Assessment of Educational Progress. (1983). *Citizenship and social studies achievement of young Americans: 1981–1982 performance and changes between 1976 and 1982.* Denver: Education Commission of the States.

National Assessment of Educational Progress Civics Consensus Project. (1996). *Civics framework for the 1998 National assessment of educational progress.* Washington, DC: NAEP Governing Board.

National Council for the Social Studies. (1980). *Position statement: The essentials of social studies.* Washington, DC: Author.

Niemi, R., & Junn, J. (1993, September). *Civics courses and the political knowledge of high school seniors.* Paper presented at the annual meeting of the American Political Science Association, Washington, DC (ERIC Document Reproduction Service No. 372 001)

Niemi, R., & Junn, J. (1999). *Civic education: What makes students learn.* New Haven, CT: Yale University Press.

Nolin, M. J., Cnaney, B., Chapman, C., & Chandler, K. (1997). *Student participation in community service activity. The national household education survey.* Washington, DC: U.S. Department of Education, OERI.

Parker, W., & Jarilomek, J. (1997). *Social studies in the elementary education.* Columbus, OH: Merrill–Prentice-Hall.

Patrick, J. (1997). *The framework for the National Assessment of Educational Progress in civics. ERIC/ChESS Digest.* (ERIC Document Reproduction Service No. 410 179)

Patrick, J., & Hoge, J. (1990). Teaching government, civics and law. In J. Shaver (Ed.), *Handbook of research on social studies teaching and learning* (pp. 427–436). New York: Macmillan.

Raasch, C. (1998, January 12). Researchers: Low voter turnout not necessarily bad sign for democracy. *Lafayette Journal and Courier*, p. A5.

Ravitch, D., & Finn, C., Jr. (1987). *What do our 17-year olds know? A report of the first national assessment of history and literature.* New York: Harper & Row.

Remy, R. (1976). Making, judging and influencing political decisions: A focus for citizen education. *Social Education, 40*(6), 360–365.

Sidelnick, D. (1989). Effects of ability, grade and gender on three measures of citizenship with high school students. *The Social Studies, 80*(3), 92–97.

Sinatra, G., Beck, I., & McKeown, M. (1992). A longitudinal characterization of young students' knowledge of their country's government. *American Education Research Journal, 29*(3), 633–661.

Study Group on Law-Related Education. (1978). *Final report of the U.S. Office of Education Study Group on Law-Related Education.* Washington, DC: U.S. Government Printing Office. (ERIC Document Reproduction Service No. 175 737)

Times Mirror Center for the People and the Press. (1994). *The people, the press and politics: The new political landscape.* News Release: Sept. 21, Washington, DC.

Torney, J., Oppenheim, A., & Farnen, R. (1975). *Civic education in ten countries.* Stockholm, Sweden: Almqvist & Wiksell.

Tussman, J. (1977). *Government and the mind.* New York: Oxford University Press.

Wade, R. (1995, May/June). Developing active citizens: Community service learning in social studies teacher education. *The Social Studies,* pp. 122–128.

CHAPTER 2

CITIZENSHIP EDUCATION IN THE ELEMENTARY SCHOOL

James M. Shiveley
Miami University, Oxford, Ohio

CITIZENSHIP EDUCATION HAS ALWAYS BEEN AT THE CENTER of the public school curriculum in this country. The goal of citizenship education, regardless of grade level, has been to create democratic citizens,[1] a concept that seems simple enough on the surface, yet has remained fertile ground for divergent thoughts and recommendations. This chapter discusses citizenship education as it relates to the elementary school setting,[2] describing past and current practice and examining the research base that supports this practice.

Drawing from the relevant literature and research on citizenship outcomes, this chapter has been organized into four sections. The first section describes the background and historical context of citizenship education. The following three sections review the methods most commonly found in the primary grades for teaching democratic citizenship today. These categories are: a *content-based approach* —where instruction on citizenship is direct and explicit, and where content is usually taken from the social science disciplines; a *thematic infusion approach*—where citizenship traits are taught more indirectly through curricular materials and concepts stressed in several prevalent national movements found in the elementary school today; and *classroom and school practice*—where key aspects of citizenship education are taught, often unintentionally, through teacher modeling, classroom strategies, and student activities.

OVERVIEW OF CITIZENSHIP EDUCATION: NOT WHETHER, BUT HOW?

Citizenship education has always been one of the central challenges of public education in the United States. As early as 1796, President George Washington called for "the education of our Youth in the science of Government. In a Republic, what species of Knowledge can be equally important? And what duty more pressing on the Legislature, than to patronize a plan for communicating it to those who are to be the future guardians of the liberties of the Country" (Washington, cited in Patrick & Hoge, 1991, p. 427).

---

[1] This chapter uses the definition of a democratic citizen offered by Parker and Jarolimek (1984): "an informed person, skilled in the processes of a free society, who is committed to democratic values and is able, and feels obligated, to participate in social, political, and economic processes" (p. 6).
[2] This chapter uses civic education and citizenship education interchangeably and elementary school refers to public schools, grades 1–6.

Since then, this charge has been implemented in a variety of ways, depending on how the nation has interpreted the concept of civic education. Patriotic poems, songs, parades, biographies, and histories of the relatively new nation constituted the curriculum of civic education through much of the 19th century. In the elementary school, geography was the primary social science taught in the lower grades, with history becoming more prominent after sixth grade.

The content of civic education merged with two late 19th-century pressures—the desire to assimilate millions of immigrants to the growing nation, and the need to train workers for the industrialization of the United States. The results were an emphasis on the concept of the United States as a "melting pot" and on developing skills helpful to citizens who would fill the jobs available during the industrial revolution. Specific courses in civics were rarely found in the curriculum during this time, but were instead imbedded in the subjects of history, geography, and moral education (Freeland, 1991).

The past century has seen additional shifts in the emphasis of civic education. As the United States became more infatuated with science at the turn of the 20th century, so too did the notion of educational content. For the first time, the term *political science* was used in the curriculum for courses designed specifically for civic purposes. This curricular movement was reinforced by reports issued at that time by the National Education Association and the American Political Science Association calling for courses in civics, government, and constitutional law (Patrick & Hoge, 1991).

The period following World War II saw a shift toward preparing citizens to be able to fight off the effects of propaganda. As a result, the development of critical thinking skills became a primary area of focus. Immediately following the launching of Sputnik in 1957, schools shifted their attention away from directly developing better citizens in favor of emphasizing more technical information in the maths and sciences. The 1960s saw a turn toward building consensus, values clarification, and decision making, much of this being housed under the umbrella of "The New Social Studies." As this movement lost momentum in the early 1970s, law-related education (LRE) moved to fill the void, and has retained a prominent place in the civic education curriculum ever since (Battistoni, 1985; Mathews, 1996).

In recent years, citizenship education has become influenced by three additonal movements. The first has stressed a return to a core set of courses in civics, most often taught in the upper grades. The second has been an emphasis on fighting citizen apathy and in preparing students to become more engaged in the political process. The third trend has been the inclusion of some form of service learning in the school curriculum.

Democracy does not just happen. Despite differences in the weight given to different trends, educators have never assumed that just because students were immersed in a democratic culture, these students automatically would develop the appropriate democratic knowledge, skills, and attitudes needed in a democratic society and the disposition to use them. A conscious, deliberate, and ongoing effort is needed to promote these traits. This responsibility has rested squarely with the institutions of public education and remains a primary reason why schools are maintained at public expense (Franzosa, 1988).

The question of citizenship education, then, has never been whether, but how. In other words, what "counts" as good citizenship (Pratte, 1988)? This debate has remained fervent in recent decades. Barr, Barth, and Shermis (1978) made the case that "good citizenship in a democracy" is interpreted very differently by different people. They suggested that there are three main traditions: social studies taught as citizenship transmission, in which citizenship is best promoted by inculcating "right" values as a framework for making decisions; citizenship taught as social science, where citizenship is best promoted by mastery of already established democratic concepts, processes, and problems; and citizenship taught as reflective inquiry, where democratic principles are best promoted through a process of inquiry in which knowledge is driven from what citizens need to know to make decisions and solve problems. Whereas all three approaches agree that citizenship is the primary purpose, there has always been disagreement about how best to go about achieving this goal.

Shaver (1977) identified eight alternative (but not necessarily exclusive) approaches to civic education. They were:

Academic disciplines—teaching the content of history and the social sciences.

Law-related education—a series of courses on the Constitution and the structure of government.

Social problems—concentrating on the social issues of the day.

Critical thinking—developing in students skills to enable them to be informed, autonomous thinkers, resistant to manipulation.

Values clarification—assisting students in making their own decisions based on central values they support.

Moral development—seeking to advance students from lower to higher levels of moral reasoning.

Community involvement—promoting student involvement in real-world community projects.

Institutional school reform—giving students a meaningful role in school governance.

Shaver claimed that it was possible to identify one or more of these themes in any citizenship education curriculum.

Such groupings serve primarily as an example of how much diversity remains within the field of citizenship education. Additional groupings could be offered, but regardless of how the content is organized, choices would have to be made between differing, and at times competing, conceptions of citizenship (Franzosa, 1988).

A review of the literature highlights three additional points on citizenship education in the elementary schools. First, the primary responsibility for citizenship education has traditionally fallen under the domain of the social studies. The major goal of the social studies has always been to promote citizenship in a democracy. Whelen (1992) pointed out that "since social studies emerged as a school subject early in the twentieth century, consensus about its rationale, purposes and curricular organization has been rare. In fact, the only issue generally agreed upon has been that social studies has a special responsibility for citizenship education" (p. 2). Although social studies is not the only area in the school curriculum held accountable for such an obligation, "this is where, if anywhere, the core knowledge base of citizenship will be debated and developed. Social studies is the only place in the school curriculum where focused inquiry on democratic ideals and practices might be located" (Parker, 1990, p. 17).

Second, citizenship attainment, although agreed on in principle, remains somewhat elusive, regardless of the approach. The Center for Civic Education analyzed more than 40 state curricula, all dealing with citizenship, and sadly concluded that "little was said about the aims of citizenship education." In fact, "the question of what citizenship means was seldom addressed" (Butts, 1993, p. 91).

Parker (1990) also acknowledged this ambiguity, but believed this has really become more an excuse not to move forward in achieving the goal of creating good citizens. In his words:

> Some critics have charged that citizenship education is at once so vague and all-encompassing that it can mean anything to anybody. In other words, it works nicely as a rhetorical device in the written curriculum but malfunctions in the taught curriculum where it is used to justify virtually anything (including nothing at all). This complaint has wrongly been taken as reason enough to abandon the citizenship goal. I read it differently, however, as a legitimate complaint about the difficulty of achieving a goal that is left too vague. (p. 18)

Third, the role of citizenship education has traditionally been minimized at the elementary school level. This has occurred despite research that indicates the elementary years are perhaps the most critical for citizenship development. During these formative years, young students need to develop a context for civic education, learn content associated with civic education in a systematic manner, and begin to develop some sense of efficacy (Davis & Fernlund, 1995).

One finds instead that the elementary school day is more often filled with reading, mathematics, and classroom management. When issues related to citizenship are addressed, they are often relegated to any remaining time at the end of the day, or to whatever time may be left on a Friday afternoon. Reasons cited for this practice include a lack of citizenship content knowledge for elementary teachers and administrators (and therefore lack of a comfort zone when teaching it), and pressures to raise test scores in reading and math, rather than civics (Parker, 1991).

Not surprisingly, elementary students often rate their interest in citizenship education low in relation to other subjects. Three studies revealed that social studies (again, the primary area in which citizenship education falls in the primary grades) did not inspire students' interest. Students rated the subject "very low," never in the students' top five favorite subjects, and this rating further declined as students progressed through the elementary grades (Freeland & Dickinson, 1984; Shaughnessy & Haladyna, 1985; Shaver, 1979). The good news is that despite this lack of interest in the content of citizenship education, upper elementary students somehow still develop positive and supportive attitudes toward their Constitution, system of government, and nation (Dalton, 1988; Hess & Torney, 1967).

How is citizenship education most often taught in the elementary school? A multitude of approaches is used. The teaching of citizenship has been categorized into three broad categories. The first includes those efforts that are part of the explicit external curriculum, which is referred to as the *content-based approach*. A second category, the *infusion approach*, includes movements or themes that are interdisciplinary in nature. Finally, there is a category of strategies and methods used by teachers that reinforce essential democratic concepts called *classroom and school practice*. Each of these areas is not exclusive of the others, but serves only an organization function here. Some areas of citizenship education fall neatly into one of these three categories and others are more difficult to categorize precisely, having characteristics associated with each category.

THE CONTENT-BASED APPROACH

The content-based approach refers to teaching the content traditionally associated with citizenship development. This content is usually found in the social science disciplines and is considered part of the explicit curriculum. Teachers have lesson plans for this content, often have textbooks and other materials, and evaluate student progess. Assessment often takes the form of state proficiency tests, in addition to the teacher's own formal and informal evaluation. This is the area most people think of when considering where citizenship education is mostly being taught.

Rarely are specific courses devoted solely to citizenship education or civics at the elementary level, however. Instead, in the upper elementary grades, there are courses in the school curriculum in which citizenship education is embedded (i.e., American history, state history, and geography). These courses usually last a semester rather than a full year. In the lower elementary grades, these content areas and the citizenship concepts associated with them are more often taught in the form of units or projects that are done within the context of a larger interdisciplinary theme. For example, a brief overview of civics, history, geography, and economics is provided as each is related to citizenship education in the elementary school.

CIVICS, HISTORY, GEOGRAPHY, AND ECONOMICS

Civics fell from favor as a separate course in the upper elementary grades in the years following the 1920s. In recent decades, however, citizenship related curricula has seen a resurgence as a variety of national commissions called for more core civics in the elementary grades. Often this has taken the form of government, civics, and law being infused into history and geography courses (Bennett, 1987). The Education for Democracy Project (1987) of the American Federation of Teachers made a similar recommendation, suggesting that the teaching of civic values of a constitutional democracy be included throughout the elementary grades. In 1988, two curriculum projects were initiated, *CIVITAS* and *Our Democracy: How America Works*, both emphasizing government and civics as a major component of the curriculum at all grade levels (Patrick, 1991).

The teaching of history has long been associated with promoting the core values of citizenship. Thomas Jefferson, in his "Notes on the State of Virginia," claimed that history lessons were essential tools that allowed citizens to be "guardians of their own Liberty." It is believed that history can teach students "the collective genius and action of peoples in the past" and allow them to "compare peoples' ideals and speeches with their actions, a trait essential in preparing for citizenship" (Battistoni, 1985, p. 98).

Traditionally, history in the elementary grades does not begin in earnest until the fifth or sixth grade. This trend is due, in part, to earlier research indicating that children slowly acquired conceptions of physical time (Fraisse, 1963; Hallam, 1972; Lello, 1980; Piaget, 1969). This assumption has been recently called into question. It is now believed that young children understand historical time better and in a variety of ways than previously believed. Young students are able to see patterns and sequences in real events, link history to chronology, and use broad time categories to describe times past (Levstik & Pappa, 1987).

Others suggest that history should become a vital part of the early elementary curriculum as long as student development is considered and activities are used to enhance young learners' "history readiness" (Bradley Commission, 1988; Elkind, 1981; Seefeldt, 1984). Such activities include working on a daily schedule, telling time, developing chronology and sequence in daily and weekly activities and events, using time-oriented vocabulary (e.g., month, hour, calendar, after, today, tomorrow, winter), and using timelines (Freeland, 1991).

Another device used with increasing regularity in the elementary grades to enhance historical understanding is the use of narrative. Research here indicates that historical narrative may help children interpret historical information better because it contextualizes history requiring some interpretation by the reader or listener (White, 1980). History and civic proponents use this data to argue for earlier introduction to historical instruction in the elementary school.

Geography, along with history, has traditionally been one of the major content areas in which civics education and citizenship concepts have been embedded. The rationale for this connection has been that effective citizenship involves participation and decision making and these traits are aided by a geographic perspective that gives insight to political, economic, environmental, and social concerns. Geographic education, then, is thought to complement citizenship education, giving a context to local, national, and international issues (Center for Civic Education, 1991).

Arguments for increasing students' geographic understanding have come since the early 1980s as the media began to report that large numbers of young Americans demonstrated a low level of geographic knowledge. Politicians began to raise questions regarding how ineffective U.S. citizens could be in the world economic and political arena if they were geographically ignorant. Elementary administrators and teachers also saw the connections between geographic literacy and a "child's social education aimed at citizenship in an increasingly interdependent world" (Winston, 1988, p. 35).

In response, the National Geographic Society took the leadership role in the movement to increase the prominence of geography in the elementary curriculum. They worked primarily through teacher workshops, materials development, and media attention (Center for Civic Education, 1991). A network of State Geographic Alliances was established for this purpose. These centers promote geographic literacy in the elementary grades through activities such as Geography Bees, the establishment of a Geography Awareness Week, and a web page on the Internet where students and teachers have geographic resources and activities readily available.

Economics has also been a content area closely associated with the explicit curriculum of citizenship education. The case for economic literacy as it is connected to democratic citizenship is built on the premise that Americans think and talk about economic issues, that these issues affect them as citizens, and that economic issues are primarily concerned with making decisions—a primary attribute of democratic citizenship (Schug & Walstad, 1991). Miller (1987) stated the connection this way:

> Economics is for everyone in part because we live in an economic world. Most of the major decisions that confront us are fundamentally economic. Effective decision making and participation in a democratic republic requires citizens to have at least a minimum of competency in economics. (p. 162)

The elementary school remains fertile ground for the development of economic competency (Ramsett, 1977; Schug & Armento, 1985; Smith, 1997). Key economic principles need to be developed in the early grades, using children's informal learning as a basis for the formal development of critical thinking and economic knowledge (Kourilsky, 1987). Such economic instruction is contingent on developmental theory, allowing childrens' economic ideas to become more flexible and abstract with age (Schug & Birkey, 1985).

The teaching of economics, for its own sake or for the sake of democratic citizenship, has yet to be developed in the elementary grades as much as economic educators would like. Reasons for this include a lack of confidence by teachers in teaching economic concepts, poor teacher preparation in economics, weak curricular materials, and limited time in the curriculum available for economics (Walstad & Watts, 1985). Indications that this trend is starting to change have come recently. Televised economic programs such as *Trade-Offs* and instructional programs such as the mini-society and kinder-economy have shown successful results at the elementary school level. Such programs allow for active student participation in real economic experiences. When elementary age students are encouraged to make economic decisions and learn from the consequences of those decisions, they begin to develop economic concepts in concrete ways (Schug & Walstad, 1991).

That civic education is taught as part of the formal elementary school curriculum, and how it is taught, are two different issues, however. Research into the methods and materials used at the elementary level to teach civics, history, geography, and economics reveal surprisingly similar, and unfavorable, results. Goodlad (1984) found that elementary students liked history and civics less than any other topic in school, in large part due to the materials and methods that were used often to kill the students' interests. Civics and history textbooks tend to be dry, redundant, supportive of the status quo, and designed for passive learning and the transmission of facts rather than active involvement in the pursuit of knowledge (Carroll et al., 1987; Larkins, Hawkins, & Gilmore, 1987).

Whereas today's textbooks are more attractive and more sensitive to ethnic and racial diversity than those of a generation ago, most of the criticisms levied are the same as those reported in a similar study in the 1960s (Price, 1966). This would not be so alarming except that studies also report that, when teaching these topics, from 65% to 90% of classroom time involved the use of textbooks and other commercially prepared curricular materials (Fancett & Hawke, 1982; Ravitch & Finn, 1987; Shaver, Davis, & Helburn, 1980).

Elementary teachers do use small groups and independent work more often than secondary teachers, and also make more efforts to connect civics, history, geography, and economics to citizenship (Stodolsky, 1988). Still, the predominant means of teacher instruction for these courses remains traditional lecture, recitation, homework from the textbook, and an occasional use of an audiovisual aid or field trip. This type of instruction has been remarkably stable over the past 50 years, with any changes in methodology being more incremental than fundamental (Cuban, 1991). Still other studies indicate a lack of treatment by teachers to democratic rights and values, with the focus being mainly on respect for rules, laws, and authorities. Little effort is given to include time for reflective or critical thinking (Harrington, 1980).

The content of citizenship education is most often delivered using direct instruction techniques. This direct content-based instruction on citizenship remains a fundamental part of the elementary curriculum. However, it is not the only means by which the attributes of democratic citizenship are taught. Other areas help to fill in the gaps left by content-based instruction alone. One of these areas includes a number of educational trends and movements the content of which is found infused throughout the school's curriculum and climate. These trends, whether by intent or serendipity, also serve to emphasize democratic principles. Three of these movements are discussed later.

THEMATIC INFUSION APPROACH

The thematic infusion of citizenship education involves the indirect teaching of citizenship attitudes and values to students through predominant school, community, and national movements now found in the schools. These movements include multicultural education and global education, inclusion, and service learning. The content, skills, and attitudes emphasized by this approach are rarely found in the school curriculum guide or on state and national proficiency tests. Yet, what students learn from these approaches goes a long way toward bolstering some of the attributes of democratic citizenship in young students (Ehman, 1980; Leming, 1985; Patrick & Hoge, 1991).

MULTICULTURAL EDUCATION AND GLOBAL EDUCATION

Multicultural education has among its goals the creation of a school environment in which "all students—regardless of their gender and social class, and their ethnic, racial, or cultural characteristics—should have an equal opportunity to learn" (J. Banks, 1989, p. 2). It is a movement that values cultural pluralism, stressing the positive characteristics of a diverse society and nation. If, as McCormick (1984) stated, "multiculturalism is rooted in one of the highest of American ideals, that of educational equity and equality for all of our citizens" (p. 93), then the connections that are made between multicultural education and citizenship education are strong.

Citizenship education should promote the understanding and appreciation of pluralism vital to a democratic society. A pluralistic democratic society can only work when its diverse groups really believe that they and those around them are an important part of the institutions and social structure in which they are immersed (J. A. Banks, 1991; C. Banks & J. Banks, 1993). When a multicultural perspective is infused throughout a school's curriculum, classrooms become more consistent with key democratic principles. Such a curriculum encourages elementary students to view people from a pluralistic perspective—one that is inclusive, nonstereotypical, and unprejudiced and that helps prepare them to "build authentic, democratic communities" (Alter, 1995, p. 355). According to Parker and Jarolimek (1984), a pluralistic perspective

> is a disciplined respect for human differences—differences of all sorts but particularly of opinion and preference, of race and religion, of ethnicity and, in general, of culture. Their perspective is based on the realization that there is diversity among people and the conviction that this diversity is good. From this perspective, one seeks to understand and appreciate the multiplicity of cultural and subcultural differences among peoples. From this perspective, one regards the existence of ethnic and philosophical differences, not as a problem to be solved but as a healthy, inevitable, and desirable quality of democratic group life. From this perspective came the Founders' determination to protect minorities from the majority. (p. 2)

Many of the goals of multicultural education that are consistent with civic ideals are also shared by global education. Students with a global perspective "understand interdependence, value diversity, and identify not only with their own culture group and nation-state but with the world community as well" (Parker & Jarolimek, 1984, p. 2). Global education hopes to "bring about changes in the content, in the methods, and in the social context of education in order to better prepare students for citizenship in a global age" (L. Anderson, 1979, p.15). The National Council for the Social Studies (1982) defined global education as

> efforts to cultivate in young people a perspective of the world which emphasizes the interconnections among cultures, species, and the planet. The purpose of global education is to develop in youth the knowledge, skills, and attitudes needed to live effectively in a world possessing limited natural resources and characterized by ethnic diversity, cultural pluralism, and increasing interdependence. (p. 1)

Children under age 10 seem more receptive than older children to learning about other cultures and peoples, so the elementary years are arguably the optimal time for learning political, economic, and social systems from a global and multicultural perspective (NCSS, 1992). An elementary school that infuses a global perspective into its curriculum would include dimensions such as perspective consciousness, state of the planet awareness, cross-cultural awareness, knowledge of global dynamics, and awareness of human choices (Anderson, 1982; Hanvey, 1979).

Studies on the influence of multicultural and global education on students' attitudes in the elementary curriculum show some positive results. Research examining the effects of reinforcement techniques, curriculum content, and cooperative classroom environments found that elementary students may develop a more positive racial attitude and that minority students often experienced academic gains as well (Aronson & Gonzalez, 1988; Katz & Zalk, 1978; Slavin, 1989, 1990).

Other studies, however, show inconsistent results on this issue (Litcher & Johnson, 1969; Litcher, Johnson, & Ryan, 1973), with some gender studies revealing that the teaching materials used actually reinforced sex role stereotyping (Katz, 1986; Klein, 1985; McGhee & Frueh, 1980). In a more recent analysis of elementary textbooks, Alter (1995) found that most texts "do not reflect diverse perspectives and multicultural or global realities" (p. 355). Added to this is the criticism that most elementary teachers do not come from diverse backgrounds or believe their teacher training programs have adequately prepared them to teach in such settings (Ishler, Edens, & Berry, 1996).

Recently, more and more elementary teachers have begun to use children's literature to combat such obstacles. Such literature-based instruction has become a powerful tool for assisting young readers to grasp key global and multicultural concepts at the elementary school level (Pugh, Garcia, & Margalef-Boada, 1994). Quality children's literature has been shown to help students better understand ideas such as cultural differences and similarities, multiple perspectives, and interdependence; to increase social sensitivity; to gain a greater recognition of shared and unique cultural values and norms (Norton, 1990); to understand the outside world and question stereotypes (Sullivan, 1996); and to develop an enhanced ability to view issues through multiple perspectives (Garcia, Hadaway, & Beal, 1988; Kim & Garcia, 1996; Turnell & Ammon, 1996). By identifying with the characters in the stories, students are able to develop an increased awareness of the options available to these characters (and to themselves) as they work to solve pressing problems.

INCLUSIONARY PRACTICE

Inclusive education, first mandated by PL 94-142 and reauthorized by PL 101-476, is an another educational movement strongly connected to the concept of equity. A fundamental principle of inclusive education is the valuing of diversity and the belief that individuals can contribute to their community and world (Kunc, 1992). Special educators have long recognized that the idea of participatory democracy lies at the heart of inclusionary practice in the schools. As Curtis (1991) stated, "All citizens in a democratic society are expected to share in the decision-making process.... Failure to provide a particular group with instruction in the means of participation violates a basic tenet of our society by serving to exclude individuals from the democratic process" (p. 157).

Stated in the negative, this means maintaining a separate educational system for students with disabilities, which entails a system that sorts and tracks students, devalues diversity, and undercuts equity, harms all students; and sends the wrong message about democratic citizenship. As L. Granger and B. Granger (1988) asserted, "Every time a child is called mentally defective and sent off to the special class for some trivial defect, the children who are left in the regular classroom receive a message: No one is above suspicion; everyone is being watched by the authorities; nonconformity is dangerous" (p. xii).

Studies indicate that elementary students are more likely to attend inclusive classrooms than middle school or high school students. This increased percentage at the elementary level may be a consequence of a smaller gap in achievement between students believed to have disabilities as compared to their peers. Another factor is that school districts are often hesitant to assign a disability label to students until they are enrolled in the second or third grade. Additionally, it seems that when students are in the primary grades, parents and school districts are more open to ways that address differences in learning abilities in a general education setting (Lipsky & Gartner, 1997).

In a summary of the research on inclusive education, Lipsky and Gartner (1997) found that all students, those in special education as well as general education, experienced an improvement in student outcomes as a result of their inclusive classroom environment. These results indicated this trend not only academically, but socially and behaviorally as well. In contrast, studies of self-contained programs for at-risk and special needs students in the elementary classroom indicated that the preparation these students received for active citizenship roles never was a fundamental objective. Such results cause many to question the ethics and efficacy of maintaining dual educational programs (Inclusive Education Recommendation Committee, 1993), particularly if a primary purpose of education is to develop citizens who are open-minded, committed to resolving societal problems, and are willing and able to participate in the democratic process (Curtis, 1978).

SERVICE LEARNING

Service learning, the integration of community service with academic content, is another educational movement that embodies many of the characteristics fundamental to democratic citizenship. The idea behind service learning is that the act of service should become a fundamental premise of the civic curriculum if students are to realize the obligations associated with democracy (Barber, 1992). If students are to be actively engaged in the citizenship process, then they must be helped to "learn the value of engaging in long-term efforts to revitalize our democratic society and at the same time, assist them in developing the skills to respond compassionately to those whose daily needs cannot wait for societal transformation" (Wade & Saxe, 1996, p. 331). In programs that include service learning, a primary goal is to have students learn some of the skills of democratic society by engaging in them. Individual rights and freedoms remain critical in a democratic society, but not at the expense of public engagement. In this regard, the schools, perhaps even more so than the family, are in a unique position to foster such civic qualities as developing a sense of community or working for the common good (Wade, 1997).

Wade (1997) described a number of service learning projects elementary school classrooms might attempt. An essential component of a service-learning activity is the integration of curriculum-based learning objectives with a project that addresses a true community or school need. Such projects are often included as part of an interdisciplinary unit. Examples (Wade, 1997, pp. 14, 142–143) include having students:

- Design and build a bird sanctuary in conjunction with a unit on birds and trees.
- Create an alphabet book, which is then presented to an area Headstart day care center.
- Interview elderly community members and include these chronicles in a book for the town or school library.
- Learn about the measurement, patterns, and teamwork associated with quilts as they sponsor a local quilting bee.
- Grow a vegetable garden, in conjunction with a senior partner, in the backyard of an elderly center.
- Create a conservation area in the community while studying ecosystems and recycling.
- Become involved in area environmental clean-up efforts.
- Conduct projects that attempt to meet the needs of the homeless or hungry.
- Participate in cross-age tutoring.
- Assist special needs students, recording their experiences in a log, which is later used to create a picture book about the partnership.

Studies on the effects of service learning on democratic beliefs and academic learning reveal mixed, but promising, results. Wade and Saxe (1996) concluded that the inclusion of service-learning projects in the curriculum could contribute to students' involvement in the social and political life of the community. They found that school-based service projects sometimes, but not always, led to increased political efficacy, increased self-esteem and social responsibility, and more future civic involvement. These benefits were also achieved while not detracting from students' academic achievement. Wade and Saxe also concluded that the success of a service-learning project relied on these projects being carefully planned around objectives in the curriculum and implemented effectively in the school and community. Such projects require educators to "reflect on the complexities of service and social action, and decide if they want to encourage students to question the status quo, meet a community need, and/or study the contextual factors underlying social issues" (p. 351).

CLASSROOM AND SCHOOL PRACTICE

A third arena in which citizenship education takes place is in the daily teaching strategies used and the classroom atmosphere created by elementary teachers. Here is where the principles of democratic citizenship are modeled and students are given the opportunities to carry aspects of citizenship into practice. This is where teachers can "walk the walk" of citizenship education.

The strategies, organization, and climate of a classroom and school, sometimes referred to as the implicit, hidden, or indirect curriculum (Eisner, 1985; Pritchard, 1988), often provide the greatest opportunity to influence students' attitudes toward democratic practice. This is because of the positive relation that exists between a democratic school climate and the development of democratic attitudes among students (Ehman, 1980; Leming, 1985).

Although classroom practice can hardly be considered "hidden," the messages sent to students are often quite different than what is explicitly taught. For example, the implicit school curriculum often speaks clearly to students that they should be passive, dependent, and submissive—traits obviously at odds with attributes that are needed in a democratic citizen such as self-reliance and the ability to engage in active discovery (Battistoni, 1985; Parker & Jarolimek, 1984).

Citizenship is taught both directly and indirectly and civic attitudes are best influenced through mutually supportive activities of this formal and informal curriculum. The civic learning experience of particular students depends on the combination of direct instruction of civic content and the indirect practical experiences they have had at school (Patrick & Hoge, 1991).

With this in mind, a sampling of classroom and school practices have been categorized that informally instruct and reinforce the principles of democratic citizenship. These practices, although interrelated, remain vital to citizenship education if the hope is to educate students who will think and act on their own. The categories of classroom practice briefly reviewed here are those dealing with participatory learning, decision making, critical thinking, cooperative learning, extracurricular activities, and, classroom climate.

PARTICIPATORY LEARNING

Besides being an effective way to learn content, active participation by students lies at the heart of democratic citizenship. If students are to move beyond the rhetoric of citizenship, and move toward active participation, they must see participation modeled and be given opportunities in the classroom to practice it. Pahl (1990), after reviewing the research on democratic outcomes, concluded that "almost unanimous agreement exists.... Passive learning of content alone is not sufficient preparation for active participation in a democratic society" (p. 276).

Students must be actively engaged in their learning experience. Participatory learning has been shown to be among the most effective in producing active citizens (Kim, Parks, & Beckerman, 1996; Richardson, 1993). Research findings indicate that when a strong participatory component of civics education is present, students "learn important lessons in direct political decision-making" and "are more likely to exhibit democratic traits" (Battistoni, 1985. p. 122). Other studies demonstrated that elementary students improved their participation-related knowledge and attitudes, and had an increased sense of political efficacy after engaging in a series of activities directly related to political involvement (Glenn, 1972; Sherry, 1976).

Participatory learning at the elementary school level may be as simple as setting up class elections, holding regular class meetings to discuss and voice opinions on class issues, involving students in a class or school project, requiring students to attend a local school board meeting, or teaching the content in the form of a simulation. Active participation in strategies such as simulations have been shown to increase student interest in the topic under study, as well as to increase the likelihood that they would take personal action at a later date on issues important to them (Boocock, 1968; Cherryholmes, 1966; Keating, 1995; VanSickle, 1986).

DECISION MAKING

Decision making is also vital for democratic citizenship. Engle (1960) summarized this position almost four decades ago. He wrote:

> A good citizen has many facts at his command, but more, he has arrived at some tenable conclusion about public and social affairs. He has achieved a store of sound and socially responsible beliefs and convictions. In the process of testing his ideas he has greatly increased his fund of factual information and he has become increasingly skillful at intelligent decision making. (p. 302)

Engle claimed that the first step in improving decision making was to abandon the "ground covering technique" prevalent in the schools in favor of spending more time examining "the significance of the material, or to consider its relevance and bearing to any general idea, or to consider its applicability to any problem or issue past or present" (p. 302).

Students need assistance in making decisions. Some of the skills they need to acquire include collecting, analyzing, and organizing information, and then determining how to best use the information when reaching conclusions. One of the best strategies utilized by elementary teachers to help students develop these skills is teaching through inquiry or discovery.

Simply put, inquiry is "the process by which one goes about rationally resolving doubt" (Gilliom, 1977, p. 2). Inquiry usually begins with a problem, or a "point of perplexity," from which the student rigorously goes through a number of steps, including: defining the problem, developing a tentative hypothesis or solution to the problem, gathering relevant data, testing the hypothesis, accepting or rejecting the hypothesis, and after reaching a conclusion, testing this conclusion in new situations (Dewey, 1933).

An inquiry or discovery-oriented approach to instruction, a method increasingly used at the elementary level, promotes reflection, decision making, and participation more so than a didactic expository approach (Ferguson, 1991). Inquiry asks students to "deal with significant problems relating to people's interaction with other people and with their environment" with the goal of developing an "intellectually autonomous individual—the independent person who blends a commitment to rationality with skill, understandings, and attitudes requisite to thoughtful inquiry" (Gilliom, 1977, p. 2).

CRITICAL THINKING

Critical thinking is seen as "essential to citizenship in a democratic society where citizens are confronted by persistent and complex social problems" (Stanley, 1991, p. 255). It has been defined as the rules of logical inquiry or argument analysis (Newmann, 1975) or as "a collection of discrete skills or operations each of which to some degree or other combines analysis and evaluation" (Beyer, 1985, p. 272). Beyer went on to list what he called the "core of these operations" as distinguishing between verifiable facts and value claims; determining the reliability of a source; determining the factual accuracy of a statement; distinguishing relevant from irrelevant information, claims, or reasons; detecting bias; identifying unstated assumptions; identifying ambiguous or equivocal claims or arguments; recognizing logical inconsistencies or fallacies in a line of reasoning; distinguishing between warranted and unwarranted claims; and determining the strength of an argument (p. 272).

Teaching the skills of critical thinking should be a fundamental component of citizenship education at every grade level, no less so in the elementary school. This idea has gained momentum as programs to develop critical thinking have proven successful in the primary grades (Costello, 1995). Several strategies are commonly mentioned for the enhancement of critical thinking. One involves more in-depth teaching about fewer topics. Some research has indicated that content knowledge may be essential to developing critical thinking abilities (Cornbleth, 1985; Perkins, 1986). Other strategies to consider include aiding in information- processing skills, maintaining a classroom atmosphere conducive to questioning and reflection, and the frequent examination of open-ended social problems (Stanley, 1991).

Programs designed to help increase the critical thinking and decision-making skills of elementary students seem to work best when students practice these skills in concert with the learning of specific content (Cornbleth, 1985). This content may be in the form of the perspective of a character in a children's story, the possible bias present in an editorial in the newspaper, or the factors to consider when obtaining information from the Internet.

COOPERATIVE LEARNING

Democracy relies on more than self-reliance and an independent pioneering spirit. Throughout the nation's history, people's ability to cooperate and compromise has been an important characteristic for a democratic society. Elementary teachers must also prepare their students to succeed in a world that "communicates, cooperates, and that views responsibility in the context of social meanings" (Colomb, Chilcoat, & Stahl, 1992, p. 26). Few strategies provide such opportunities as well as cooperative learning and cooperative learning strategies do, while at the same time improving students' academic achievement (Slavin, 1988; 1990; Stahl & VanSickle, 1992).

Cooperative learning helps teach students to be active, effective citizens (VanSickle, 1992). When done correctly, the group rewards and individual accountability found in cooperative learning promote personal and social responsibility, equal opportunity and individual welfare, and personal responsibility. Furthermore, students engaged in cooperative learning activities have an opportunity to "demonstrate competence, make contributions to team success, and be recognized for those contributions," which then supports "individual welfare, meritocracy, and social responsibility" (VanSickle, 1992, p. 19).

Cooperative learning has the additional benefit of promoting acceptance of special needs students and diverse groups into the elementary classroom environment. Cooperative learning shares the goals of improving social skills, improving the communication techniques of students, enhancing problem-solving abilities, and increasing academic achievement (Farlow, 1994; Slavin, 1985).

EXTRACURRICULAR ACTIVITIES

Activities that occur outside of the elementary classroom can also contribute to citizenship education. Many studies show a strong correlation between student involvement in extra school activities and these same students' participation in community activities outside of school. Patrick (1991), in a review of research on teaching government and civics and law, stated that it is "generally accepted that student participation in extracurricular activities of the school is positively related to the development of political efficacy and propensities for participation in civil life outside the school" (p. 433). Holland and Andre (1987) reported high correlations between extracurricular activities and high self-esteem, improved acceptance of diversity, lower delinquency, and improved later involvement in political and social activity. Other researchers have found that students enrolled in smaller schools benefit more socially and developmentally than students in larger schools, in large part because a higher percentage of students from smaller schools are able to take part in a greater variety and number of outside activities (Holland & Andre, 1987; P. Schoggen & M. Schoggen, 1988). These studies all support earlier work hypothesizing that increased participation in extracurricular school activities often transferred to increased political participation in later years (Almond & Verba, 1963; Barker & Gump, 1964; Hanks, 1981; Milbrath & Goel, 1977).

The creation of elementary school student councils is one way to provide opportunities for students to become more involved. In a study of elementary student councils in one state (approximately one third of all elementary schools in their study had student councils), Heath and Vik (1994) found that the most cited benefits listed by principals were the opportunities student councils gave students to develop leadership skills, resolve conflicts, and manage projects. These principals believed that the student councils also helped to promote school spirit and a sense of ownership and community in their schools. In short, student councils were considered an ideal means to allow students to develop citizenship traits.

These studies do not necessarily prove that providing such activities in an elementary school actually increases citizenship development among all students. A correlation between extracurricular activities and increased political awareness does not necessarily denote that one causes the other. Such a direct cause and effect relation has proven difficult to establish. It could be argued that the students involved in such activities would often be the same students who would be politically active whether or not these extracurricular activities were provided (Holland & Andre, 1987).

CLASSROOM CLIMATE

The classroom climate established by the elementary teacher can also play an important role in developing citizenship traits. An environment that is open to discussion and debate about issues provides opportunities for students to practice articulating their beliefs and for these beliefs to be challenged by differing views. A democratic society requires of its citizens the ability to "use language to question, debate, negotiate, and reshape personal belief systems" (Knipping, 1991, p. 14). When students feel secure enough to express ideas and information in an open climate, they are more likely to learn such democratic attitudes as respect for the opinions of others and a sense of political efficacy (Ehman, 1980; Leming, 1985; Torney, Oppenheim, & Farnen, 1975).

The exploration of controversial issues provides one mechanism by which elementary teachers can engage students in such discussions. Hahn (1991) concluded that when students were given the opportunities to investigate controversial issues, they became more supportive of civil liberties, were better able to analyze arguments, became less dogmatic, and increased their self-esteem. Other studies indicate that in classrooms that included discussion of controversial issues students exhibited an increased interest in the topic at hand, as well as an increase in confidence and trust among class members. This was the case as long as such discussions were held in an open, supportive class environment (Hahn, Tocci, & Angel, 1988).

In the primary grades, the social issues most likely to generate such discussion should come from the lives of the students rather than from classroom textbooks (Knipping, 1991). Cognizant of this, the National Council for the Social Studies (1989) recommended that elementary teachers only use the textbook occasionally to teach social issues, but instead attempt to engage students in more realistic discussions of concerns directly related to their lives at home or in the classroom. These discussions have helped develop skills such as critical thinking and an appreciation for multiple perspectives in students as young as kindergarten through second grade (Knipping, 1991; Martin, 1990).

Unfortunately, the elementary school climate described here is often hard to find. According to VanSledright and Grant (1994),

> Most elementary school climates and the goals they promote do not fully embrace democratic tolerance and the authority-sharing characteristics necessary to engage students in an active, critical, and constructive examination of what they are learning and why. Adults seldom share authority very effectively: Administrators and experts decide, teachers implement, and students comply. In environments organized this way, democracy rarely flourishes. (pp. 335–336).

It seems that a gap remains between theory and practice. This gap may be viewed as an opportunity to continue to improve the ways in which citizenship education is taught directly and indirectly.

CONCLUSIONS

Few would argue against the value of citizenship education in the elementary school. Here again, the question is not whether it should be taught, but the way it should be taught. This chapter reviewed the literature and research concerning citizenship education as it has been and is currently being carried out in the elementary school setting. It has been posited that the goals of democratic citizenship, and therefore the question of the way it is taught, have historically been viewed from a variety of perspectives and that although much is being done, and in a wide variety of ways, there remains much room for improvement.

This chapter has discussed how every elementary school curriculum allows time for some form of citizenship education. Time is set aside—if not daily, then at least each week—for citizenship to be taught formally and directly. It is equally true that many concepts of citizenship are taught indirectly and informally. This may be in the form of educational movements infused throughout the curriculum, or in the day-to-day strategies and climate used and created in the classroom. One result is that democratic citizenship may be taught unconsciously as often as it is consciously.

Hopefully, the presentation of this information will allow elementary teachers and principals interested in improving their citizenship education programs to reexamine the ways in which democratic skills, attitudes, and dispositions are taught in their school. Such reexamination may reveal new opportunities to teach civics directly during the school day, as well as to take advantage of opportunities to stress those democratic principles infused throughout the curriculum. Finally, teachers and administrators may take a new look at the ways in which citizenship is taught throughout the day in the implicit curriculum—the strategies, activities, and school atmosphere that contribute to fostering democratic practice—and then take steps to bring the informal more in line with the formal instruction, that is, to make the unconscious more conscious. Such an effort could assist in creating a citizenship education program that is more consistent, cohesive, and ultimately effective.

REFERENCES

Almond, G. A., & Verba, S. (1963). *The civic culture: Political attitudes and democracy in five nations.* Princeton, NJ: Princeton University Press.

Alter, G. (1995). Transforming elementary social studies: The emergence of a curriculum focused on diverse, caring communities. *Theory and Research in Social Studies, 23*(4), 355–374.

Anderson, C. (1982). Global education in the classroom. *Theory into Practice, 21*(3), 97–105.

Anderson, L. (1979). *Schooling and citizenship in a global age: An exploration of the meaning and significance of global education.* Bloomington, IN: Social Studies Development Center of Indiana University.

Aronson, E., & Gonzalez, A. (1988). Desegregation, jigsaw, and the Mexican-American experience. In P. A. Katz & D. A. Taylor (Eds.), *Eliminating racism: Profiles in controversy* (pp. 301–313). New York: Pelham.

Banks, C., & Banks, J. (1993). Social studies teacher education, ethnic diversity, and academic development. *International Journal of Social Education, 7*(3), 24–38.

Banks, J. (1989). *Multicultural education: Issues and perspectives.* Boston: Allyn & Bacon.

Banks, J. A. (1991). Multicultural education: Its effects on students' racial and gender role attitudes. In J. P. Shaver (Ed.), *Handbook of research on social studies teaching and learning* (pp. 459–469). New York: Macmillan.

Barber, B. R. (1992). *An aristocracy of everyone: The politics of education and the future of democracy.* New York: Ballatine.

Barker, R. G., & Gump, P. V. (1964). *Big school, small school: High school size and student behavior.* Stanford, CA: Stanford University Press.

Barr, R., Barth, J., & Shermis, S. (1978). *The nature of social studies.* Palm Springs, CA: ETC Publications.

Battistoni, R. M. (1985). *Public schooling and the education of democratic citizens.* Jackson, MI: University Press of Mississippi.

Bennett, W. J. (1987). *James Madison High School: A curriculum for American studies.* Washington, DC: U.S. Department of Education.

Beyer, B. (1985). Critical thinking: What is it? *Social Education, 49*(3), 270–276.

Boocock, S. S. (1968). An experimental study of the learning effects of two games with simulated environments. In S. S. Boocock & E. O. Schild (Eds.), *Simulation games in learning* (pp. 107–133). Beverly Hills, CA: Sage.

Bradley Commission on History in Schools. (1988). *Resolutions of the commission: Steps toward excellence in the school history curriculum.* Westlake, OH: Bradley Commission on History in Schools.

Butts, R. (1993). *In the first person singular; The foundations of education.* New York: Teacher's College Press.

Carroll, J. D., Broadnax, W. D., Contreras, G., Mann, T. E., Ornstein, N. J., & Stiehm, J. (1987). *We the people: A review of U.S. government and civics textbooks.* Washington, DC: People for the American Way.

Center for Civic Education. (Ed.). (1991). *Civitas.* Calabasas, CA: Center for Civic Education.

Cherryholmes, C. H. (1966). Some current research on the effectiveness of educational simulations: Implications for alternative strategies. *American Behavioral Scientist, 10,* 4–7.

Colomb, R., Chilcoat, G., & Stahl, N. (1992). Elementary students can learn to cooperate and cooperate for learning. In R. Stahl & R. VanSicle (Eds.), *Cooperative learning in the social studies classroom* (pp. 26–31). Washington, DC: National Council for the Social Studies.

Cornbleth, C. (1985). Critical thinking and the cognitive process. In W. B. Stanley (Ed.), *Review of research in social studies education: 1976–1983* (pp. 51–63). Washington, DC: National Council for the Social Studies.

Costello, P. J. M. (1995). Education, citizenship and critical thinking. *Early Child Development and Care, 107,* 105–114.

Cuban, L. (1991). History of teaching in social studies. In J. P. Shaver (Ed.), *Handbook of research on social studies teaching and learning* (pp. 197–209). New York: Macmillan.

Curtis, C. (1991). Social studies for students at-risk and with disabilities. In J. P. Shaver (Ed.), *Handbook of research on social studies teaching and learning* (pp. 157–174). New York: Macmillan.

Curtis, C. K. (1978). *Contemporary community problems in citizenship education for slow-learning secondary students.* Unpublished doctoral dissertation, Utah State University.

Dalton, R. J. (1988). *Citizen politics in western democracies.* Chatham, NJ: Chatham House.

Davis, J. E., & Fernlund, P. M. (1995). Civics: If not, why not? *The Social Studies, 86,* 56–59.

Dewey, J. (1933). *How we think.* Boston: Heath. (Original work published 1909)

Education for Democracy Project. (1987). *Education for democracy: A statement of principles.* Washington, DC: American Federation of Teachers, Educational Excellence Network, and Freedom House.

Ehman, L. H. (1980). The American school in the political socialization process. *Review of Educational Research, 50*(1), 99–119.

Eisner, E. W. (1985). *The educational imagination* (2nd ed.). New York: Macmillan.

Elkind, D. (1981). Child development and the social science curriculum of the elementary school. *Social Education, 45*(6), 435–437.

Engle, S. (1960). Decision making: The heart of social studies instruction. *Social Education, 24*(6), 301–306.

Fancett, V., & Hawke, S. (1982). Instructional practices in social studies. In Project Span Staff and Associates (Ed.), *The current state of social studies: A report of project SPAN* (pp. 207–263). Boulder, CO: Social Science Education Consortium.

Farlow, L. (1994, June 18). *Cooperative learning to facilitate the inclusion of students with moderate to severe mental retardation in secondary subject-area classes.* Paper presented at the annual conference of the American Association on Mental Retardation, Boston.

Ferguson, P. (1991). Impacts on social and political participation. In J. P. Shaver (Ed.), *Handbook of research on social studies teaching and learning* (pp. 385–399). New York: Macmillan.

Fraisse, P. (1963). *The psychology of time.* New York: Academic Press.

Franzosa, S. D. (Ed.). (1988). *Civic education: Its limits and conditions.* Ann Arbor, MI: Prakken.

Freeland, K. (1991). *Managing the social studies curriculum.* Lancaster, PA: Technomic.

Freeland, K., & Dickinson, G. (1984). Elementary students' rankings for favorite subjects and subjects of highest grades. *Educational Review,* (Spring), 1–5.

Garcia, J., Hadaway, N. L., & Beal, G. (1988). Cultural pluralism in recent nonfiction trade books for children. *The Social Studies, 79,* 252–255.

Gilliom, M.E. (1977). *Practical methods for the social studies.* Belmont, CA: Wadsworth.

Glenn, A. D. (1972). Elementary school children's attitudes toward politics. In B. G. Massialas (Ed.), *Political youth, traditional schools: National and international perspectives* (pp. 51–63). Englewood Cliffs, NJ: Prentice-Hall.

Goodlad, J. I. (1984). *A place called school.* New York: McGraw-Hill.

Granger, L., & Granger, B. (1988). *The magic feather: The truth about "special education."* New York: Dutton.

Hahn, C. L. (1991). Controversial issues in social studies. In J. P. Shaver (Ed.), *Handbook of research on social studies teaching and learning* (pp. 470–480). New York: Macmillan.

Hahn, C. L., Tocci, C., & Angell, A. (1988, June). *Civic attitudes and controversial issue discussions in five nations.* Paper presented at the International Meeting of the Social Studies, Vancouver, British Columbia.

Hallam, R. N. (1972). Thinking and learning in history. *Teaching History, 2,* 337–346.

Hanks, M. (1981). Youth, voluntary associations, and political socialization. *Social Forces, 60,* 211–223.

Hanvey, R. G. (1979). *An attainable global perspective.* New York: Global Perspectives (formerly The Center for War/Peace Studies).

Harrington, C. (1980). Textbooks and political socialization. *Teaching Political Science, 7*(2), 481–500.

Heath, J. A., & Vik, P. (1994). Elementary school student councils: A statewide survey. *Principle,* 31–34.

Hess, R. D., & Torney, J. V. (1968). *The development of political attitudes in children.* Garden City, NY: Doubleday.

Holland, A., & Andre, T. (1987). Participation in extracurricular activities in secondary school: What is known, what needs to be known. *Review of Educational Research, 57,* 437–466.

Ishler, R. E., Edens, K. M., & Berry, B. W. (1996). Elementary education. In J. Sikula (Ed.), *Handbook of research on teacher education* (pp. 348–377). New York: Macmillan.

Katz, P. A. (1986). Modification of children's gender-stereotyped behavior: General issues and research considerations. *Sex Roles, 14,* 591–602.

Katz, P. A., & Zalk, S. R. (1978). Modification of children's racial attitudes. *Developmental Psychology, 11,* 447–461.

Keating, T. (1995, September). Let your school board be a lesson. *American School Board Journal,* 41–42.

Kim, C., & Garcia, J. (1996). Diversity and trade books: Promoting conceptional learning in social studies. *Social Education, 60*(4), 208–211.

Kim, S., Parks, S., & Beckerman, M. (1996). Effects of participatory learning programs in middle and high school civic education. *The Social Studies, 87,* 171–176.

Klein, S. S. (Ed.). (1985). *Handbook of achieving sex equity through education.* Baltimore: John Hopkins University Press.

Knipping, N. Y. (1991). Developing civic discourse: A 2nd-grade example. *Childhood Education,* (Fall), 14–17.

Kourilsky, M. L. (1987). Children's learning of economics: The imperative and the hurdles. *Theory into Practice, 26*(3), 198–205.

Kunc, N. (1992). The need to belong: Rediscovering Maslow's hierarchy of needs. In R. A. Villa, J. S. Thousand, W. Stainback, & S. Stainback (Eds.), *Restructuring for caring and effective education: An administrative guide to creating heterogeneous schools* (pp. 25–39). Baltimore: Paul H. Brookes.

Larkins, A. G., Hawkins, M. L., & Gilmore, A. (1987). Trivial and noninformative content of elementary social studies: A review of primary texts in four series. *Theory and Research in Social Education, 15*(4), 299–311.

Lello, J. (1980). The concept of time, the teaching of history, and school organization. *The History Teacher, 13,* 341–350.

Leming, J. S. (1985). Research on social studies curriculum and instruction: Interventions and outcomes in the socio-moral domain. In W. B. Stanley (Ed.), *Review of research in social studies education: 1976–1983* (pp. 65–121). Washington, DC: National Council for the Social Studies.

Levstik, L. S., & Pappas, C. C. (1987). Exploring the development of historical understanding. *Journal of Research and Development in Education, 21,* 114–119.

Lipsky, D. K., & Gartner, A. (1997). *Inclusion and school reform: Transforming America's classroom.* Baltimore: Paul H. Brookes.

Litcher, J. H., & Johnson, D. W. (1969). Changes in attitudes toward Negros of White elementary school students after use of multiethnic readers. *Journal of Educational Psychology, 60,* 148–152.

Litcher, J. H., Johnson, D. W., & Ryan, F. L. (1973). Use of pictures of multiethnic interaction to change attitudes of White elementary school students toward Blacks. *Psychological Reports, 33,* 367–372.

Martin, A. (1990). Social studies in kindergarten: A case study. *Elementary School Journal, 90,* 305–317.

Mathews, D. (1996). Reviewing and previewing civics. In W. Parker (Ed.), *Educating the democratic mind* (pp. 265–286). Albany, NY: SUNY Press.

McCormick, T. (1984). Multiculturalism. *Theory into Practice, 23*(2), 93–97.

McGhee, P. E., & Frueh, T. (1980). Television viewing and the learning of sex role stereotypes. *Sex Roles, 6,* 179–188.

Milbrath, L. W., & Goel, M. L. (1977). *Political participation: How and why people get involved in politics.* Chicago: Rand McNally.

Miller, S. L. (1987). This issue. *Theory into Practice, 26*(3), 162.

National Council for the Social Studies. (1982). Position statement on global education. *Social Education, 46*(1).

Newmann, F. M. (1975). *Education for citizen action: Challenge for secondary curriculum.* Berkeley, CA: McCutchan.

Norton, D. E. (1990). Teaching multicultural literature in the reading classroom. *The Reading Teacher, 44*(4), 28–40.

Pahl, R. (1990). Review of teaching and learning for social studies outcomes. *The Social Studies, 81*(6), 249–254.

Parker, W. (1990). Assessing citizenship. *Educational Leadership, 48*(8), 17–22.

Parker, W., & Jarolimek, J. (1984). *Citizenship and the critical role of the social studies* (Vol. 72). Washington, DC: National Council for the Social Studies.

Parker, W. C. (1991). Achieving thinking and decision-making objectives in social studies. In J. P. Shaver (Ed.), *Handbook of research on social studies teaching and learning* (pp. 345–356). New York: Macmillan.

Parker, W. C. (Ed.). (1996). *Educating the democratic mind.* Albany, NY: SUNY Press.

Patrick, J. J., & Hoge, J. D. (1991). Teaching government, civics, and law. In J. P. Shaver (Ed.), *Handbook of research on social studies teaching and learning* (pp. 427–436). New York: Macmillan.

Perkins, D. N. (1986). *Knowledge as design.* Hillsdale, NJ: Lawrence Erlbaum Associates.

Piaget, J. (1969). *The child's concept of time.* London: Routledge & Kegan Paul.

Pratte, R. (1988). Civic education in a democracy. *Theory into Practice, 27*(4), 303–308.

Price, R. D. (1966). Textbook dilemma in the social studies. *The Social Studies, 57,* 21–27.

Pritchard, I. (1988). *Moral education and character.* Washington, DC: U.S. Department of Education.

Pugh, S., Garcia, J., & Margalef-Bogda, S. (1994). Multicultural trade books in the social studies classroom. *The Social Studies, 5,* 62–65.

Ramsett, D. E. (1977). Toward improving economic education in the elementary grades. *Journal of Economic Education, 4*(1), 30–35.

Ravitch, D., & Finn, C. (1987). *What do our 17-year-olds know?* New York: Harper & Row.

Richardson, S. (1993). Active civic learning for secondary scool students. *The Social Studies, 84,* 196–202.

Schoggen, P., & Schoggen, M. (1988). Student voluntary participation and high school size. *Journal of Educational Research, 81,* 288–293.

Schug, M. C., & Armento, B. J. (1985). Teaching economics to children. In M. C. Schug (Ed.), *Economics in the school curriculum, K–12* (pp. 33–43). Washington, DC: Joint Council on Economic Education and the National Education Association.

Schug, M. C., & Birkey, C. J. (1985). The development of children's economic reasoning. *Theory and Research in Social Education, 13*(1), 31–42.

Schug, M. C., & Walstad, W. B. (1991). Teaching and learning economics. In J. P. Shaver (Ed.), *Handbook of research on social studies teaching and learning* (pp. 411–419). New York: Macmillan.

Seefeldt, C. (1984). *Social studies for the preschool-primary child* (2nd ed.). Columbus, OH: Merrill.

Shaughnessy, J. M., & Haladyna, T. M. (1985). Research on student attitude toward social studies. *Social Education, 49*(8), 692–695.

Shaver, J. P. (Ed.). (1979). *Building rationales for citizenship education* (Vol. 52). Arlington, VA: National Council for the Social Studies.

Shaver, J. P., Davis, O. L., & Helburn, S. W. (1980). An interpretive report on the status of precollege social studies education based on three NSF-funded studies. In *What are the needs in precollege science, mathematics, and social science education?* (p. 7). Washington, DC: National Science Foundation.

Sherry, F. T. (1976). *A study on the effect of lessons in political science on fifth grade children.* Boston University, Boston.

Slavin, R. (1988). Cooperative learning and school achievement. *Educational Leadership, 46*(2), 31–33.

Slavin, R. (1989). *When and why does cooperative learning increase achievement? Theoretical and empirical perspectives* (Vol. OIRI, No. G86-00061986). Baltimore: John Hopkins University, Center for Research on Elementary and Middle Schools.

Slavin, R. E. (1985). Cooperative learning: Applying contact theory in desegregated schools. *Journal of Social Issues, 41,* 45–62.

Slavin, R. E. (1990). *Cooperative learning: Theory, research, and practice.* Englewood Cliffs, NJ: Prentice-Hall.

Smith, R. M. (Ed.). (1997). *Civic ideals.* New Haven, CT: Yale University Press.

Stahl, R., & VanSicle, R. (Eds.). (1992). *Cooperative learning in the social studies classroom.* Washington, DC: National Council for the Social Studies.

Stanley, W. (1991). Teacher competence for social studies. In J. P. Shaver (Ed.), *Handbook of research on social studies teaching and learning* (pp. 249–262). New York: Macmillan.

Stodolsky, S. (1988). *The subject matters: Classroom activity in math and social studies.* Chicago: University of Chicago Press.

Sullivan, J. (1996). Real people, common themes: Using trade books to counter stereotypes. *Social Education, 60*(7), 399–401.

Torney, J. V., Oppenheim, A. N., & Farnen, R. F. (1975). *Civic education in ten countries: An empirical study.* New York: Wiley.

Turnell, M., & Ammon, R. (1996). The story of ourselves: Fostering multiple historical perspectives. *Social Education, 60*(4), 212–215.

VanSickel, R. L. (1986). Toward more adequate quantitative instructional research. *Theory and Research in Social Education, 14*(2), 171–186.

VanSickle, R. (1992). Cooperative learning, properly implemented, works: Evidence from research in classrooms. In R. Stahl & R. VanSickle (Eds.), *Cooperative learning in the social studies classroom* (p. 62). Washington, DC: National Council for the Social Studies.

VanSledright, B. A., & Grant, S. G. (1994). Citizenship education and the persistent nature of classroom teaching dilemmas. *Theory and Research in Social Education, 22*(3), 305–339.

Wade, R. C. (Ed.). (1997). *Community service-learning.* Albany, NY: SUNY Press.

Wade, R., & Saxe, D. (1996). Community service-learning in the social studies: Historical roots, empirical evidence, critical issues. *Theory and Research in Social Education, 24*(4), 331–359.

Walstad, W. B., & Watts, M. (1985). Teaching economics in the schools: A review of survey findings. *Journal of Economic Education, 16*(2), 135–146.

Whelen, M. (1992). History and the social studies: A response to the critics. *Theory and Research in Social Education, 20*(1), 2–16.

White, H. (1980). The value of narrativity in the representation of reality. *Critical Inquiry, 7*(1), 5–27.

Winston, B. J. (1988). Geography's five fundamental themes. *Social Studies and the Young Learner, 1*(2), 3–6.

CHAPTER 3

CITIZENSHIP EDUCATION IN THE SECONDARY SCHOOL

Gregory E. Hamot
The University of Iowa

PUBLIC SCHOOLING IN ALL SOCIETIES AIMS TO TEACH students the knowledge, skills, and dispositions needed to function as citizens. Secondary schools in a democratic society translate these curricular goals into knowledge of the community, nation, and world; skills required to participate effectively in society while promoting and protecting one's interests; and the democratic dispositions that form the bases for decisions to act on one's behalf while keeping the common good in mind. Citizenship education is the fundamental premise on which the whole secondary school experience functions. However, a 1916 report from the National Education Association's Commission on the Reorganization of Secondary Education placed this responsibility squarely on the shoulders of the secondary social studies curriculum (Dunn, 1916).

This chapter is an evaluative description of exemplary practices for democratic citizenship education in secondary schools that encompass the knowledge, skills, and dispositions necessary for adolescents to function effectively as citizens in this society. As such, two distinct, but related, categories form the basis of this chapter. These categories identify exemplary secondary school citizenship education by its sources of subject matter and by its learning activities. This chapter takes its lead mostly, but not exclusively, from the secondary social studies curriculum's inherent responsibility for citizenship education.

SOURCES OF SUBJECT MATTER FOR CITIZENSHIP EDUCATION

Sources of subject matter that best cultivate citizenship in students have long been the focus of discussion in social studies education (Ross, 1997). This discussion does not center on the importance of knowledge in the life of a citizen, but on what knowledge students should apply to life situations in order for them to function effectively in a democratic society. A secondary school curriculum that claims to foster citizenship in students can approach the question of "What subject matter is most worth considering?" through various perspectives. These perspectives include the individual disciplines of history and the social and behavioral sciences; interdisciplinary approaches such as global education, multicultural education, and issues-centered curricula; and the community. An additional source of subject matter for citizenship education exists in the life of the school itself.

These various perspectives form the foundation of exemplary citizenship education subject matter in secondary schools. Each offers a unique insight into what students should both know and consider when working toward their individual interests within the parameters of the common good. Additionally, all of them can work together—and, ideally, should be employed as such—in the development of effective democratic citizens.

HISTORY AND THE SOCIAL AND BEHAVIORAL SCIENCES

Without doubt, the most common subject matter approach to learning about democratic citizenship on the secondary school level is the academic, compartmentalized study of history and the social and behavioral sciences (Dynneson & Gross, 1991). Traditionally, these subject matter sources emerge from the disciplines of world and U.S. history, political science, geography, economics, sociology, anthropology, and psychology. Each of these disciplines plays a different role in the secondary school curriculum concerned with citizenship education, and each offers different ways of looking at the decisions citizens face in a democratic polity.

History. As a core element of the secondary school curriculum, history is the most commonly experienced subject matter in citizenship education. Social utilitarians, such as Gagnon (1988) and Merriam (1934), viewed history in relation to citizenship education as a way for students to view the experiences of the past, especially from democratic societies, as guides to decision making in the present. As such, history works as a body of knowledge that may be used to avoid Santayana's famous caveat that "those who cannot remember the past are condemned to repeat it" (cited in Seldes, 1985, p. 367).

Kennedy (1991) identified three "issues" along the lines of social utilitarianism that validate history as a source of subject matter for citizenship education:

1. A recognition that historical knowledge is a fundamental form of knowledge and therefore must be available to all citizens.
2. An understanding that history is able to create a sense of an inclusive community to which all citizens belong and to which all, both past and present, contribute.
3. A realization that historical situations are demonstrators of civic intelligence in action, showing us how others have taught and acted in seeking to solve societies' problems in the past. (p. 74)

Together, these issues frame the teaching of history as a part of the curriculum that extends beyond the recall of facts to a higher level of cognitive understanding. Students who learn history in this manner can consider the lessons from the past when making decisions about life in a democratic society. The recent *National Standards for History* (National Center for History in the Schools, 1996) highlighted the basic historical skills required to address such issues as "differentiating between (1) relevant historical antecedents that properly inform analyses of current issues and (2) those antecedents that are clearly irrelevant" (p. 41).

Political Science. The traditional focus of political science in citizenship education is the individual's role as an active participant in the governance of a community. In other words, the subject matter of political science focuses on the rights and responsibilities of the citizenry (Lane, 1972) and active participation in politics (Thompson, 1970; Verba, 1969). The *National Standards for Civics and Government* (Center for Civic Education, 1994) underscored the rationale for learning such subject matter with the following claim: "The goal of education in civics and government is informed, responsible participation in political life by competent citizens committed to the fundamental values and principles of American constitutional democracy" (p. 1). In the secondary school curriculum, this sort of subject matter is found most commonly in government classes.

Ostensibly, political science as an element of citizenship education centers on the need for students to comprehend the institutions of a democratic society with the hope that the bureaucratic mechanisms and political elites of such institutions do not create a feeling of "political alienation" in youth (Woyach, 1991). The belief that knowledge of these public institutions will assist students in learning ways to effect progressive change in society and in their public lives constitutes the value of political science as a pragmatic approach to helping students understand and promote the public good.

Geography. The subject matter of geography assists students in understanding their responsibilities when making decisions, and when considering those of public policymakers, that impact the local and the global environment, both physical and human. In his overview of geography as a source of subject matter for citizenship education, Helburn (1991) identified three themes that geographers address as criteria for analyzing issues of public policy: the interaction of local society with the environment, the interdependence of one's own society with others around the world, and the recognition and acceptance of cultural differences (p. 116). These three themes provide students with a geographic perspective when making decisions on public policies that impact on them and their environment.

Recently, a consortium composed of the American Geographical Society, the Association of American Geographers, the National Council for Geographic Education, and the National Geographic Society developed a set of national standards for students to meet if geographic literacy is to contribute to their education as citizens. Known as the Geography Education Standards Project, this consortium explained the role of geographic subject matter in citizenship education as the basis on which people can make informed decisions and can act on these decisions as they relate to their local and global environments. Among the standards' desired outcomes is the development of a geographically informed person who "applies spatial and ecological perspectives to life situations" (Geography Education Standards Project, 1994, p. 34). The geographical concepts that should be applied to the subject matter of "life situations" include spatial context, place and region, physical processes, and the interactions between humans and their environment.

Economics. In 1994, the Goals 2000: Educate America Act recognized the importance of economic understanding in relation to citizenship education by including it as an essential element of the curriculum. In 1997, the National Council on Economic Education, in partnership with the National Association of Economic Educators and the Foundation for Teaching Economics, developed 20 content standards that defined essential economic knowledge. Based primarily on the microeconomic principles of a free market economy, the content standards contained in *The Voluntary National Content Standards in Economics* treat economics as the study of limited resource allocation among unlimited wants (National Council on Economic Education, 1997).

Banaszak (1991) noted that the importance of economic literacy in a democratic society is essential because citizens interact with the economy in at least three ways: through their influence on the overall direction of economic policy; through their daily decisions on the distribution of resources, goods, and services; and through their decisions on issues such as taxes and levies. With these interactions in mind, Miller (1996) viewed the relation of economic literacy to the role of the citizen in a democratic society as "rooted in the idea that economics provides a set of conceptual tools to help citizens think about their government's relationship to the economy and the many economic issues citizens in a democratic society face" (p. 26). The 20 content standards that make up these conceptual tools contribute knowledge to assist students in understanding the economic forces that effect them daily and in considering the consequences of their personal economic decisions and those of public policymakers in relation to the common good.

Sociology. Defined as the study of human interactions within groups, sociology offers citizenship education the subject matter that looks at citizenship as a completely social act. As such, citizenship "takes form only within the context of interaction between and among people in their daily lives" (Wexler, Grosshans, Zhang, & Kim, 1991, p. 142). Sociology supplies citizenship education with subject matter on two distinct levels: the institutional level and the individual level.

Sociologists and anthropologists have traced the need for social institutions to primitive societies. Over time, these institutions formed patterns that could be found in all cultures. Social (e.g., familial and educational), religious, economic, political, and legal institutions make up the five types of institutions found in virtually every society. The role played by such subject matter with regard to citizenship education rests in clarifying the effects of these institutions on the individual's daily existence. On the individual level, sociology brings to citizenship education the subject matter formed from investigations of the individual's role as a member of a group who influences and can be influenced by social institutions.

Key sociological concepts include socialization, role, norm, sanction, values, conflict, and socioeconomic inequality. Through an understanding of these concepts, and the higher order generalizations that develop from these concepts, students can learn "to make decisions related to social problems and to better understand the groups in which they live" (Banks & Clegg, 1990, p. 308). Concerned, in part, with political institutions, sociology overlaps with the subject matter sources for citizenship education found in political science (Martorella, 1996). As a study of individuals within a group context, sociology shares common disciplinary ground with anthropology and psychology.

Anthropology. As a source of subject matter for citizenship education, anthropology offers students the opportunity to learn about and appreciate cultural diversity, thereby reducing the ethnocentric bias antithetical to a pluralistic democracy (Frech, 1974). This assumption stems, in part, from the anthropological view that "all cultural variations are understandable and valid within their own pattern of development" (Owen & Zevin, 1996, p. 205). This concept, known as cultural relativism, sets the subject matter of anthropology in a position to assist students in understanding that cultures different from their own can offer worthwhile solutions to human problems.

As the holistic study of culture, anthropology approaches life's problematic aspects through key concepts such as diffusion, tradition, acculturation, ethnocentrism, cultural relativism, and the rite of passage. Generally speaking, secondary level anthropology approaches these concepts under the broad subdivisions of physical anthropology, cultural anthropology, and archeology (Banks & Clegg, 1990).

Chilcott's (1986, 1991) application of five anthropological theories of culture to citizenship acts as one example of how students might realize the cultural underpinnings of their citizenship and that of others. These theoretical lenses include the following anthropological perspectives: functionalist, structural/functionalist, structuralist, cultural/ecological, and symbolic/interactionist. Such an approach is indicative of the ways in which anthropological perspectives can move students to understand subject matter that includes the roots of their citizenship in a pluralistic democracy and how and why these roots may differ from those of other cultures.

Psychology. Psychology is a behavioral science concerned with "the dispassionate search for regularities and for predictability of human behavior" (Werthheimer, Yeager, & Jones, 1996, p. 74). Psychology is a source of subject matter for citizenship education on two levels: the personal and the social. First, psychology explores human behavior in order to raise individuals' personal awareness so that they can improve their individual welfare. Second, psychology is the attempt to discover principles of behavior that will lead to a realization of human potentials conducive to the development of a more ideal world. This second level encompasses the subdiscipline of social psychology, which links the two disciplines through the study of "patterns of organization in society ... and the study of individual behavior" (Brandhorst, 1991, p. 161).

The belief that human behavior is determined rather than random underscores the outlook held by the discipline of psychology. This outlook maintains that, by manipulating certain aspects of people's personal and social conditions, it is possible to improve their individual and collective lot in society. In a democratic society, this belief translates into the use of the scientific method to predict and control aspects of people's lives that block democratic behavior, thus improving the human condition. As such, psychology contributes to the secondary school's goal of citizenship education through key concepts related to the personal and social foci of the discipline. These concepts include values, self, motivation, learning (including memory and cognition), and the social psychological theories of human development and personality (Martorella, 1996; Werthheimer, Yeager, & Jones, 1996).

INTERDISCIPLINARY APPROACHES TO SOURCES OF CITIZENSHIP EDUCATION SUBJECT MATTER

The recent National Council for the Social Studies (NCSS) standards restated the council's 1992 definition of social studies as "the integrated study of the social sciences and humanities to promote civic competence" (NCSS, 1994, p. 3). In addition to the core disciplines of the traditional secondary social studies curriculum, the NCSS advocated the application of content from the humanities, mathematics, and science to assist students in making "informed and reasoned decisions for the public good as citizens of a culturally diverse, democratic society in an interdependent world" (NCSS, 1994, p. 3).

This interdisciplinary approach to citizenship education reflects research findings on how adolescents deal with social issues, trends, and problems (e.g., Adelson, 1972, 1982, Connell, 1971). Taken together, these findings illustrate that people begin to move from a concrete to an abstract conception of the social world during adolescence. Mackey (1991) summarized these findings by noting that "classification and serialization skills give adolescents a tool with which they eagerly examine their social concerns" (p. 139). Vars' (1996) overview of research on interdisciplinary curricula showed that "almost without exception, students in innovative interdisciplinary programs do as well as, and often better than, students in so-called conventional programs" (p. 148). In a predictive statement on school reform movements in the 1990s, Hurd (1991) saw the interdisciplinary approach as one in which "a unity of knowledge will make it possible for students to take learning from different fields of study and use it to view human problems in their fullness from several perspectives" (p. 35).

Global Education. One interdisciplinary "movement" in education that promotes citizenship development, and that has gained currency in the last two decades, is global education. This movement defines citizenship education through a perspective that views subject matter as the problematic conditions arising from life in a globally interconnected, multicultural democracy.

The fact that more than 40 states now recommend various forms of global education in their K–12 curricula (Czarra & Smith, 1992) illustrates the growing strength of this movement over the past 20 years. Originally intended as a way to approach social studies education, global education now expands across the curriculum as one approach to fostering citizenship as a whole school mission (Anderson, 1994). People can improve their ability to make effective judgments in an increasingly global environment through an interdisciplinary understanding of their status in the community and the world (Hanvey, 1976).

The subject matter of global education centers on the issues and problems that citizens must face in an age of heightened interconnectedness with other cultures—an interconnectedness that takes place on virtually all levels of human endeavor. Issues such as the global environment, world peace, global economics, and human rights act as subject matter in a curriculum with a global perspective. In facing these issues as members of an international social structure, students develop effective citizenship skills through the application of knowledge drawn from any discipline to decisions about life in a global society. As such, global education approaches citizenship education as an interdisciplinary endeavor.

Merryfield (1997), building from the philosophical and empirical research in global education, identified four elements of global education that rely on interdisciplinary approaches to citizenship education: human values, the interconnectedness of global systems, cross-cultural awareness, and human choices. Each of these elements draws from multiple disciplines in an attempt to give students the knowledge base for determining the best strategies when dealing with global issues and problems on an international, rather than nationalistic, basis.

Multicultural Education. The subject matter of multicultural education rests on the concepts of difference and commonality as earmarks of a constantly changing, culturally diverse society that lives by laws enacted through public consent. Based on difference and commonality, multicultural education subject matter builds from the mindful, interdisciplinary study of culture, religion, language, ethnicity, and race in the national life. Students, through the study of difference and commonality, can analyze critically the assumptions of libertarian, constitutional democracy through mutual cultural understanding and with respect for divergent thought. By definition, then, multicultural education acts as a counterweight to the dualism of monoculturalism and ethnocentrism, breaks down the "we–they" consciousness that comes so easily to the unreflective mind, and nurtures racial and ethnic harmony through the development of a democratic disposition (C. E. Bennett, 1990).

As a movement that supports cultural understanding as a whole school goal (Araboglou, 1996), multicultural education requires an interdisciplinary approach founded on subject matter that grows from the overarching concepts of similarity and difference. Multitudes of issues in everyday life offer subject matter for multicultural education. Students grappling with issues of inequality, racism, nationalism, and those found in the global education movement require the use of interdisciplinary approaches and multiple cultural perspectives in their decision-making processes.

The National Council for the Social Studies Task Force on Ethnic Studies Curriculum Guidelines (1992) highlighted the interdisciplinary nature of multicultural citizenship education by noting that "multicultural content is as appropriate and important in teaching such fundamental skills and abilities as reading, thinking, and decision making as it is in teaching about social issues raised by racism, dehumanization, racial conflict, and alternative ethnic and cultural life-styles" (p. 285). When infused across the secondary school curriculum, multicultural education draws from all disciplines in order to address subject matter based on current multicultural issues that persist in a diverse democracy. Such a curriculum meets the school's sociocivic mandate by enabling students to "analyze cultural, political, economic, and historical patterns and structures so that students will not only better understand society, but affect it" (Hursch, 1997, p. 107).

Issues-Centered Curriculum. The treatment of citizenship education through an issues-centered, interdisciplinary curriculum has been a major movement in social studies education throughout this century. The first notion of an interdisciplinary curriculum for citizenship education grew from the 1916 report of the Committee on Social Studies of the Commission on the Reorganization of Secondary Education. *The Social Studies in Secondary Education* (Dunn, 1916), as the report is commonly known, recommended a course titled "Problems of American Democracy." Explicated by Burch and Patterson (1918), this course framed citizenship education subject matter in the crucial issues and problems of the day and their timeless antecedents. This approach to citizenship education views all disciplinary knowledge as evidence for students to employ when testing hypotheses on the resolution of social issues and problems, thereby, activating within students, the civic duty of problem solving in a democratic society.

Similar to global and multicultural education, issues-centered curricula treat the problems and issues faced by democratic societies with an interdisciplinary approach because "inquiry into any real-world matter related to citizenship is naturally holistic" (Evans, 1997, p. 199). Ongoing social impediments and enigmas confronted by citizens form the basis of the subject matter in an issues-based curriculum. Actual events in public life that illustrate these ongoing impediments and enigmas form the type of subject matter that launches student inquiry into the resolution of controversial issues (Rossi, 1996). Given issues on the environment, for instance, students could employ knowledge not only from the humanities and the social and behavioral sciences, but also from the natural sciences and mathematics; thus, making the issues-centered curriculum a core element of all classes taught in the secondary school.

THE COMMUNITY AS A SOURCE OF SUBJECT MATTER FOR CITIZENSHIP EDUCATION

Dewey (1902, 1933) noted the relation of the curriculum to the life of the child as a natural process for developing thoughtful, reflective citizens. Without this relation, Dewey believed that students saw little purpose for the subjects taught in schools. As participants in their communities, students should understand the direct link between their lives outside of school and the curriculum.

Based on this belief, citizenship education draws subject matter from the community at large: "To this end, [students] require assignments and activities that encourage them to view data from their daily life experiences as relevant and legitimate subject matter for analysis in the classroom" (Martorella, 1996, p. 45). The local community affords sources of subject matter for citizenship education that range from the cultural artifacts preserved in museums to public opinion on local issues. These sources of subject matter are uncovered and tied to the school curriculum through activities such as field trips, collecting oral histories, participation in community service, and gathering survey and interview data on issues pertinent to the community and the students.

Community-based sources of subject matter rely on the interaction of students with their broader social environment. D. Conrad (1991) termed these interactions as experiential in nature, and, on that basis, he found that research on students involved with the exploration of the community environment as a source for subject matter had a positive effect on their social, psychological, and intellectual development.

THE SCHOOL AS A SOURCE OF SUBJECT MATTER FOR CITIZENSHIP EDUCATION

The school itself offers a rich context for citizenship education outside the formal curriculum because secondary school students spend approximately 25% of their waking hours in school and countless hours associating with their peers when outside of school. Because they engulf the life of precollegiate students, school policies, activities, and procedures may be the most obvious sources for subject matter dedicated to the development of adolescents into effective citizens. The school as subject matter for citizenship education, however, is not restricted to the leadership programs and student councils that exist in most secondary schools. The nature of the subject matter found in schools, if it is to contribute directly to the citizenship of the entire student population, must go beyond the notion of limited representative government to a more inclusive view of student involvement in a democratic process of school governance.

School governance that involves the entire student body along with teachers and administrators is based on the idea that democracy cannot be learned through subject matter generated by the disciplines alone. Democracy must be practiced in order for it to be learned. In their advocacy of democratic education that involves the entire student body in deciding issues of school governance, Mosher, Kenny, and Garrod (1994) claimed "experience with the democratic process and its values to be a powerful complement to the traditional curricula" (p. 166). They pointed to low voter turnouts of the past as the results of schooling disengaged from the consideration and the practice of the moral and ethical responsibilities that constitute democratic citizenship. Dewey (1933), while noting that active and meaningful democratic practice in child and adolescent development led to a mature democratic mind, also pinpointed the inherent risks in politically alienating students:

> But if the young are to be prepared when they leave school to take an effective part in a democratic society, the danger must be faced and conquered. Many of the failures of democratic government (which are used by critics to condemn the whole undertaking) are due to the fact that adults are unable to share in joint conference and consultation in social questions and issues. They can neither contribute intelligently, nor can they follow and judge the contributions of others. The habits set up in their earlier schooling have not fitted them for this enterprise; the habits even stand in the way. (pp. 270–271)

Examples of schools that have taken seriously the idea of inclusive democratic practice in school governance can be found in the cases of Brookline High School in Massachusetts and Hanover High School in New Hampshire (Mosher et al., 1994) and Harmony School in Indiana (Goodman, 1992). In each of these cases, the life of the school is the core subject matter for student development toward democratic citizenship.

Learning Activities for Citizenship Education

Research on learning activities that promote citizenship development forms the basis for operationalizing sources of citizenship education subject matter. This section is a descriptive evaluation of eight learning activities addressed commonly in secondary social studies methods texts spanning the past quarter century (Banks & Clegg, 1990; Ehman, Mehlinger, & Patrick, 1974; Gillom, 1977; Martorella, 1996; Social Science Education Consortium, 1996). These learning activities include: cooperative learning; concept learning; values clarification, moral reasoning, and character education; thinking skills; role playing, simulations, and games; service learning; structured questioning; and computer technology. These learning activities can be employed in all of the subject matter approaches to citizenship development in secondary schools. Similar to the subject matter approaches, these activities can and do overlap in practice. This review is a discrete treatment of these activities for the purposes of descriptive evaluation. Emphasis on democratic citizenship education delimited the research base for this section.

COOPERATIVE LEARNING

McBrien and Brandt (1997) defined cooperative learning as a "teaching strategy designed to imitate real-life learning and problem solving by combining teamwork with individual accountability" (p. 24). Windrim (1990) emphasized that cooperative learning, as a socializing and democratizing process, must also include mixed ability within the learning groups. D. W. Johnson and R. T. Johnson (1996) stated that the value of cooperative learning to teach traditional American values (equality, life, liberty, and the pursuit of happiness) lies in the basic assumptions of the founding documents. Citing the opening paragraph of the Constitution ("We the people, in order to form a more perfect union ...") as a timeless charge for national cooperation, they noted that cooperative learning teaches students a form of success, both individually and within a group, that stems from collaborative efforts based on mutual responsibility.

Slavin (1989–1990) forwarded the noteworthy fact that "cooperative learning is one of the most thoroughly researched of all instructional strategies" (p. 52). D. W. Johnson and R. T. Johnson's (1986) review of 122 studies comparing cooperative learning to individualized learning activities indicated overwhelmingly that cooperative learning led to higher achievement, more retention, increasingly positive attitudes toward subject matter, greater motivation, and higher order thinking skills.

Margolis, McCabe, and Schwartz (1990) reviewed the research on how cooperative learning effects the facilitation of mainstreaming for both the mainstreamed and regular student. Although they found that the effects were positive for both groups in understanding each other and breaking down stereotypes, they cautioned that cooperative learning, albeit a research-proven success for many educational goals dealing with citizenship education, must be approached slowly and with care. In the course of their review of the research, they developed a useful heuristic for implementing cooperative learning strategies in the classroom:

> Choose academic and social learning objectives that are appropriate for the students' grade level.
>
> Explain assignment objectives and procedures explicitly and completely.
>
> Describe to students the social-cooperative skills on which they will be evaluated.
>
> Start with small groups working on discrete, easy-to-evaluate tasks.
>
> Publicly value group diversity and full participation.

Monitor and reinforce group collaborative processes as well as individual behavior and accomplishment.

Attend to the physical arrangement and sound level of the classroom.

Periodically hold plenary class meetings.

Establish written guidelines and norms for group work that clearly define suitable behavior.

Employ cooperative learning for an appreciable amount of time.

Adapt cooperative learning strategies to your needs and style of teaching. (pp. 113–114)

With these guidelines as a premise, several case studies highlight cooperative learning as an exemplary practice for citizenship education.

Vocke (1992) employed a Jigsaw II cooperative learning strategy developed by Slavin (1983) and Anderson and Palmer (1988). This strategy assigns students to heterogeneous groups that break into "expert" groups comprised of one student from each of the original groups. The expert groups focus on one particular aspect of the overall assignment, work cooperatively to come to a consensus on the most important aspects of their particular area, and return to their original groups to teach what they have learned. Vocke assigned his students to analyze primary sources for the purpose of formulating a perspective on how the American Civil War effected the lives of individuals. In the expert groups, students examined critically the information offered by different entries in the diary of a well-to-do Southern female. When they returned to their original groups, the students taught each other from their expert perspectives with the goal of writing a two-page interpretation of the effects of the war on individuals. Through cooperative learning activities centered on the critical analysis of primary sources, Vocke's students gained a heightened understanding of history as a highly interpretive academic discipline that offers many perspectives on present-day issues and problems such as the effects of war on individual civilians.

In a case study of her classroom, B. D. Conrad (1988) found that cooperative learning promoted democratic citizenship by reducing prejudice in her students. Based on a global food consumption simulation, her students worked cooperatively in teams representing different countries of the world. Students in these teams worked with each other toward a goal of distributing fairly the foreign aid allotted to their country. Through recorded observations, Conrad found that when grouped heterogeneously and focused on a mutual goal, her students abandoned their previously held prejudices toward each other in order to seek equitable solutions to their assigned nation's problems.

Lindblom (1991) studied student development of critical thinking skills in relation to the media by employing cooperative learning techniques in his classroom during the Gulf War. Using a variation of the Jigsaw II method, his students were assigned to watch one of the national news reports from either NBC, CBS, ABC, or CNN. In expert groups formed for each network, the students analyzed each network's level of opinion formation in relation to its presentation of facts in reporting the events of the war. Once per week, the students would reform into groups of four (one from each expert group) to compare and contrast the approaches used by the four networks in transmitting the events of the war to the public. Using the news as "text" and employing cooperative learning activities, Lindblom found that "in the context of civic responsibility, students practicing such diverse roles [tutors, expert consultants, investigators, and presenters] can become open-minded, critically conscious citizens who are sensitive to the people around them" (p. 57).

CONCEPT LEARNING

A *concept* is a definition, criterion, or set of criteria for categorizing objects and events that exhibit some sort of commonality (Ehman et al., 1974). Learning concepts is essential to any aspect of education. The ability to classify objects and events into existing schema and people's ability to expand their schema through experiences with new objects and events is basic to their quality of thinking and learning.

Concept learning as an aspect of citizenship education lies in the value of concepts to act together as conceptual frameworks. Higher level concept learning of this sort heightens students' capability to interpret their environment, to communicate in a logical form, and to think abstractly without the burden of concrete examples. For example, students with the ability to form higher level concepts in a history class can make historical connections across space and time, thus utilizing history as one way of interpreting and applying information to issues and problems of today (Schechter & Weil, 1996).

Concept learning operates under the research-based assumptions found in cognitive psychology. These assumptions support the need for concept learning, and many examples of ways to teach concepts based on these assumptions exist in social studies methods books and instructional materials. However, studies on the effects of concept learning in citizenship development are rare (Martorella, 1991).

In one such study, Reyes and Smith (1983) found that "loading" concepts into textbooks did not insure they would be learned. In particular, they analyzed social studies textbook approaches to concepts related to the social and behavioral sciences and history. By implication, Reyes and Smith found that mere mention of discipline-based concepts in textbooks did not assist students in understanding essential concepts they could use to apply knowledge from the disciplines to the subject matter of citizenship education. Their study led them to conclude that "teachers of social studies at all levels need to return to systematic instruction in the classroom to assure students comprehension and development of key social concepts; concepts which are central to the understanding of these disciplines" (p. 88). Unfortunately, they offered no suggestions on how teachers can go about planning such systematic instruction.

A comparative study of oral and written techniques for concept learning by Crisman and Mackey (1990) investigated Reyes and Smith's recommendation for systematic instruction in concept learning. One of the questions they sought to answer was whether or not technique and mode of instruction have a significant effect on concept attainment. They surveyed high school students so as to identify two social studies concepts with which students were least familiar. The results yielded two concepts related to citizenship education: "sovereignty" (a relational political science concept) and "comparative advantage" (a conjunctive economic concept). Using expository teaching techniques based on lecture or reading, the researchers developed six approaches to teaching these concepts: definition only (oral), definition followed by four examples (oral), four examples followed by definition (oral), definition only (reading), definition followed by four examples (reading), examples followed by definition (reading). These approaches were taught to 24 classes at a metropolitan high school over a 4-day period. In their summary of primary findings, Crisman and Mackey found that concept attainment was greater when examples were provided; giving the definition prior to the examples helped in learning the relational concept, but there was no significant difference in learning the conjunctive concept based on teaching method; and there was no significant difference between the level of student understanding whether the concepts were taught orally or through the written word.

Intuitively, concept learning is essential if students are to apply the various disciplines to the issues and problems that face society. To date, research from cognitive psychology has provided guides to developing instruction for concept learning. Aside from a few studies, however, the effects of concept learning on citizenship development remain mostly hypothetical abstractions from cognitive psychology that lack rigorous empirical research.

VALUES CLARIFICATION, MORAL REASONING, AND CHARACTER EDUCATION

In contrast to concept learning, research and development in values clarification, moral reasoning, and character education have a direct link to democratic citizenship education practices. The very nature of citizenship in a democratic society rests on the dispositions of each individual in the society. Although certain dispositions are seemingly timeless and expected persistently, the evolution of these dispositions and the development of new ones earmark a progressive democracy. Education for democratic citizenship, therefore, is inextricably bound up in the development of dispositions conducive to promoting people's self-interest in balance with those dispositions necessary for advancing the common good. At the heart of values clarification, moral development, and character education lies the notion that citizens will not always balance personal self-interest with the common good, and citizenship education must prepare students for this inevitable disharmony.

Leming (1996) divided research on the effects of these three practices into two categories: moral/values education and character education. Within the realm of moral/values education, student dispositions are viewed as emerging naturally through teaching approaches based on the values clarification work of Simon (Raths, Harmin, & Simon, 1966) and the moral development research of Kohlberg (1966). Both of these approaches center on decision making and moral questions. The character education movement that emerged during the 1980s is a reincarnation of character trait inculcation evident in American schooling throughout the republic's history. Before the 1980s, the most concerted effort to implement character education in schools appears to have been during the 1920s. Character education focuses on the development of specific, predetermined character traits in students.

Values Clarification and Moral Reasoning. The 1970s and 1980s were the high water mark for values clarification as a citizenship education strategy. One handbook of activities alone sold over 600,000 copies (Simon, Howe, & Kirschenbaum, 1972). Values clarification as a teaching activity involves four major steps, the fourth of which contains processes in value development: choosing a value-laden topic or moral issue; introducing a question or activity to promote discussion of the issue; treating each viewpoint with respect; and value processing: choosing a value, prizing it, and acting on it (Kirschenbaum, 1992).

As these steps and processes unfold, the teacher acts as a facilitator without opinion. The emergent student values are to be respected without question. Critics of the values clarification approach questioned the right of teachers to pry into the private values of students and the moral relativism that ensued from a lack of adult direction in thinking about appropriate values (Leming, 1996).

Kohlberg (1975, 1976) framed the cognitive development approach to moral reasoning. Known commonly as the moral dilemma approach, Kohlberg noted that humans can advance through six moral stages at three levels:

1. Preconventional level
   Stage 1: The punishment-and-obedience orientation (avoid breaking rules, be obedient, do no harm persons or property)
   Stage 2: The instrumental-relativist (follow rules that promote your interests, do what is fair)
2. Conventional level
   Stage 3: The interpersonal concordance or "good boy–nice girl" orientation (measure up to expectations of those you respect, follow the Golden Rule)

Stage 4: The "law and order" orientation (observe the law and rules, contribute to society)
3. Postconventional, autonomous, or principled level
Stage 5: The social contract, legalistic orientation (observe social contract, respect core values)
Stage 6: The universal-ethical-principle orientation (uphold universal ethical principles)

Kohlberg's research showed that people confronted with cognitive dissonance of a moral nature–and who are also exposed to examples of the next stage of moral reasoning–will develop morally. This theoretical foundation gave birth to the most commonly used technique in developing moral reasoning in students: the *dilemma-discussion activity*. This activity involves a discussion during which students must defend their reasons for resolving a morally problematic scenario. Ultimately, the goal of this activity is to expose students to the next highest stage of moral reasoning–through discussion–with the intention of moving students to this next stage (Kohlberg, 1980). Critics of Kohlberg's theories concentrated on the ethnic and gender homogeneity of his subjects (e.g., Gilligan, 1982) and the question of whether or not students would act in real-life moral crises as they act in a classroom setting (e.g., Colby & Damon, 1992).

In a comparative review of the research on values clarification and moral reasoning, Leming (1996) found dilemma-discussion activities to far exceed values clarification activities in achieving their respective intended aims. Regarding moral discussion, he found that "when students are engaged in the process of discussing moral dilemmas accompanied by cognitive disequilibrium and exposure to examples of the next highest stage of moral reasoning, and when the treatment condition lasts at least a semester in length, a shift in student reasoning of one-quarter to one-half stage will result in approximately 80 percent of the studies" (pp. 151–152). His meta-analysis of values clarification research found a confusing array of dependent variables. Nonetheless, he found that values clarification teaching practices resulted in an overall success rate from 0% to 20%. Clearly, however, none of the studies reviewed by Leming looked at changes in student behavior that may have resulted from programs in either moral dilemmas or values clarification. This dearth of research leaves the curriculum planner and teacher at a loss when considering values clarification activities and moral reasoning techniques as approaches to developing desired citizenship behavior.

Character Education. With the blessings of the Reagan administration, then Secretary of Education William Bennett launched a program to reinstall the character education movement into public schools. In stark contrast to the neutrality of the values clarification and moral dilemma approaches, the character education movement seeks to inculcate specific civic virtues.

The call for character education led to a continuing discussion on which virtues are most important to teach in schools. Drawn from three current works on character education, the following series indicates the sort of virtues for inculcation in students in order for them to develop the character necessary for effective citizenship: compassion, self-discipline, responsibility, friendship, work, courage, perseverance, honesty, loyalty, faith, justice, prudence, temperance, fortitude, hope, charity, duty, respect, tolerance, helpfulness, cooperation, fairness, and democratic values (W. Bennett, 1993; Lickona, 1991; Wynne & Ryan, 1993).

Problematic for the character education movement at this time is the almost non-existent research base on the best practices for developing virtuous citizens. For instance, Leming (1985) found that traditional, expository teachers did little to change students' political attitudes. Schultz (1989) supported these findings by asking high school students whom they would trust when considering important decisions. Only 5% of the juniors and seniors surveyed admitted they would turn to a teacher or counselor. Friends, parents, and relatives ranked higher. However, Hartshorne and May (1928) conducted the one study that might hold promise for character education practices in the classroom. Seventy years ago, they found a significant difference in the level of "deceit" exhibited by students in individual classrooms. However, variables such as type of school, age level, intelligence level, or home background seemed to make no difference in their findings. Their conclusion, simply put, was that the atmosphere created by the individual teacher as a role model in the classroom had more to do with the character of the students than any other variable they tested.

Ample evidence exists on the value of learning activities that promote moral and ethical thinking. However, if moral and ethical civic behavior is a goal of public schooling, then research on the connection between teaching techniques, role modeling, and school atmosphere and student behavior in natural social settings seems to hold the most promise. To date, little evidence exists on how best to marshal these variables into coherent curricula for democratic citizenship behavior.

THINKING SKILLS

In his review of research on thinking and decision-making skills, Parker (1991) noted the various terms applied to thinking skills that are essential to democratic citizenship. Critical thinking, creative thinking, problem solving, decision making, divergent and convergent thinking, metacognition, schema, domain-specific and general thinking skills, dispositions, everyday reasoning, and higher order thinking make up the "contemporary clatter of terms" (p. 345). Basically, the notion of solving problems lies at the heart of democratic citizenship education because, unlike totalitarian societies where answers to problems stem solely from the ideology of the ruling elite, solving problems in a democracy is a public responsibility based on the reflective thinking process (Beyer, 1985; Engle & Ochoa, 1988; Griffin, 1992; Hunt & Metcalf, 1968; Wilen, 1996).

Dewey (1916, 1933) outlined the democratic disposition for problem solving that he termed the "method of intelligence." Otherwise known as reflective inquiry, the method of intelligence encompasses a process initiated when people confront subject matter that creates cognitive dissonance. Citizenship education requires subject matter to be both social and personal in nature. The process proceeds as the individual or group frames the problem, hypothesizes solutions, evaluates each hypothetical solution through the best available evidence, searches for the consequences of each tentative solution, and tests through action the solution that appears to offer the best theoretical results.

Wilen (1996) found that the three most prominent models of thinking applicable to citizenship education were those developed by Swartz and Perkins (1990), Beyer (1988), and the National Council for the Social Studies (1994). From these three models, five competencies related to problem solving emerged consistently. They were the abilities to: process data to investigate questions; distinguish between relevant and irrelevant information; determine points of view or bias; determine the strength of an argument; and generate and assess solutions to problems based on evidence and democratic principles.

Teaching strategies for developing thinking and problem-solving skills have dotted the citizenship education landscape throughout the 20th century. Parker (1991) reviewed research conducted on four well-known approaches to problem solving developed during this century: 1936–1941 (propaganda resistance studies), 1964–1966 (Taba's cognitive task studies), 1966–1970 (the Harvard Social Studies Project's jurisprudential studies), and the present (Newmann's classroom thoughtfulness study). Problematic in his findings was the huge array of definitions for thinking and problem solving in each of these approaches. Nonetheless, the studies he reviewed indicated that the propaganda resistance materials succeeded when thinking was taught directly, rather than through subject matter. Studies of the Harvard Social Studies Project brought out the importance of focusing on the development of thinking skills through the discussion of subject matter in the form of controversial issues that plague a democratic society. Research on Taba's cognitive task process yielded successful results when centering the development of thinking skills in the subject matter and in the intellectual processes of the traditional social studies disciplines. Newmann's classroom thoughtfulness studies corroborated Taba's findings that depth, rather than breadth, assists students in developing thinking skills as a democratic disposition. Additionally, research into Newmann's work established the importance of organizational variables that set up democratic school contexts in which to learn higher order thinking.

Wilen (1996), building on Parker's findings, reviewed the research on several strategies for teaching thinking. He found mixed results in approaches that advocated higher order teacher questioning to develop higher order student thinking (Beyer, 1987; Dillon, 1982; Gall & Rhody, 1987; Mills, Rice, Berliner, & Rousseau, 1980). Studies of wait time after higher order teacher questions associated longer wait times for student responses with positive results in student thinking (Atwood & Willen, 1991; Rowe, 1986; Tobin, 1987). Gall (1985) found that discussion between students led to higher order thinking, changed student attitudes, and heightened their ability to carry out group problem solving. Overall, Wilen concluded that thinking and problem-solving skills for democratic citizenship develop best when infused across the curriculum and are taught best when students are "encouraged to speak openly; ask thoughtful questions; engage in hands-on, and minds-on, learning activities; and focus on issues and problems" (p. 136).

ROLE PLAYING, SIMULATIONS, AND GAMES

Role playing, simulations, and games comprise an interrelated set of activities that aim to replicate social situations and social phenomena, in addition to altering attitudes. The relation between role playing and simulations is closer than the relation between games and the other two activities. The difference lies in the replication of reality and not in their aims.

Role playing is a learning activity that facilitates the practice of social competencies such as negotiating, decision making, and communicating. It is a method of introducing students to different social and historical roles. This process takes place when students simulate situations involving specific problems of social life, such as those found in the moral dilemma-discussion activities.

Simulations are an operational model of social processes. They include sequences of events determined by the roles of the participants. Simulations can be a miniature representation of social reality or a model of the process of human interaction. In either case, the purpose of simulations in citizenship education is to learn typical social relations associated with the defined aims and assumptions of a democratic society.

Educational *games* do not represent reality in the same sense as simulations. The intention of gaming in citizenship education is to develop and practice useful skills and concepts in the subject matter areas. The human disposition of competition emerges frequently, but not always, as a key element in educational games. Games proceed through a fixed set of rules usually accompanied by a scoring system and time limitations.

In all three activities, the overarching goal is for students to enact a role other than their normal one for the purpose of taking on a perspective dissimilar to their own. In so doing, students can examine abstract issues and view differing perspectives on particular topics and issues that involve a wide variance in beliefs, attitudes, and moral choices. In each case, teachers who employ role playing, simulations, and games need to help students understand the potentially emotional nature of the activity, initiate instructions accordingly, describe the activity thoroughly, assign roles, monitor the actual activity closely, and conduct a debriefing session (Martorella, 1996).

Educational research on the effects of role playing, simulations, and games is sparse. In fact, VanSickle (1986) reviewed over 400 articles and studies on the overall educational value of simulations and games in the social studies classroom, let alone variables specific to citizenship education, and he found only 42 that researched effects based on comparative experimental methodology.

The research that does exist indicates an overall lack of clear consensus on the value of such strategies in the development of civic competencies. Nonetheless, several reviews of research conducted over the past 35 years lead to several pertinent conclusions on the value of role playing, simulations, and games in the development of effective citizenship. Cherryholmes (1966) conducted one of earliest studies of this sort by analyzing six experimental-control group studies of simulations in social studies classrooms. He found that the experimental groups became more interested in the subject matter than did the control groups. However, no significant changes occurred in the learning and retention of facts and principles, critical thinking and problem solving, or attitudinal adjustment of any sort toward the social phenomena under study. Cherryholmes concluded that the students in these studies tended to memorize, rather than discover, the sociocivic structures being taught in the simulations. Boocock and Schild (1968), in a review of nine studies based on experimental and control groups, found essentially the same results. However, the 26 studies reviewed by Livingston and Stoll (1973) revealed some positive trends beyond the enjoyment of simulations over traditional, expository teaching methods. These studies varied in focus. Student factual knowledge increased in 8 of 16 studies. Eight of 11 studies concerned with attitudinal change revealed a movement by students toward greater understanding and approval of the perspectives associated with the person whose role they played. In seven studies, students believed their motivation to participate with others improved.

VanSickle (1986) conducted the most ambitious meta-analysis of role playing, simulations, and games in social studies education. He analyzed 22 comparative experimental studies that provided sufficient data to calculate effect sizes. Two groups of studies emerged from his meta-analysis: 6 studies employed pre- and posttest or no treatment control group methods and 16 studies compared role playing, simulations, and games to alternative experimental teaching methods. Overall, VanSickle found that these methods produced small gains in recall, retention, and application of knowledge. Attitudinal change showed mixed results, ranging from slight attitudinal gains toward content under study, slight negative attitudinal change toward the social phenomenon under consideration, and virtually no attitudinal change toward self. Clegg (1991), in his summary of findings on role playing, simulations, and games, did not dismiss the value of such learning activities. However, the mixed findings based on the few studies that addressed social studies education in general, and citizenship education in particular, led him to conclude that "despite the promising potential … to help students discover how to relate to others and how to develop social interactions, the limited data suggest that there have been only small, inconsistent effects, as compared to alternative treatments" (p. 526).

To date, research on role playing, simulations, and games as valuable learning activities for developing democratic citizenship is marginal. However, hundreds of descriptive cases bound by individual classroom context exist in the practitioner's literature. Also, there is a growing number of role playing activities, simulations, and games available in both hard copy and computer software forms. These realities indicate that teachers consume these materials and trust them as valuable activities for the development of democratic citizenship in their students.

SERVICE LEARNING

Negative public perceptions of the social structure, of the community, and of youth have drawn attention to a need for schools to link students to public service. Today, 47 states maintain commissions on national service, and school-related service by precollegiate students is on the rise (Schine, 1997a, 1997b). Linking the community to citizenship education subject matter lies at the heart of service learning. This link—the ethic of civic responsibility—is a common thread found in social studies educators' definitions of citizenship (e.g., Engle & Ochoa, 1988; National Council for the Social Studies, 1994; Newmann, Bertocci, & Landsness, 1977; Remy, 1980).

The Alliance for Service-Learning (1993) proposed the following criteria for evaluating programs in service learning on the basis of whether or not these programs include participatory activities:

> that meet actual community needs, that are coordinated in collaboration with the school and community, that are integrated into each young person's academic curriculum, that provide structured time for a young person to think, talk, and write about what he/she did and saw during the actual service activity, that provide young people with opportunities to use newly acquired academic skills and knowledge in real life situations in their own communities, that enhance what is taught in the school by extending student learning beyond the classroom, and that help to foster the development of a sense of caring for others. (p. 1)

In essence, service learning blends the curriculum with the needs of the community in a way that involves students in the decision-making processes essential for effective democratic citizenship. These processes include the rights and responsibilities of citizens as they take social action for the betterment of society.

Findings on the merits of service learning vary in significant ways, but three benefits emerge distinctly from the research literature. First, service and the school's academic pursuits become mutually enriching. Service activities that link subject matter to the life of the community are meaningful to students. When students begin to see the community as subject matter no longer detached from their lives in school, it becomes an integral part of their daily existence (Boyer, 1987; Carter, 1997).

Second, service learning enhances civic-mindedness. Lipka, Beane, and O'Connell (1985) found that such educational programs help students develop an understanding of the procedural and political aspects of life in a democracy. Student-driven models for service learning in which the students are responsible for all aspects of the process engender this understanding. This level of student responsibility develops civic-mindedness because students learn to assess, make a choice, become involved, and reflect on their community experience and how it contributes to society. Zeldin and Tarlov (1997) reviewed service learning programs throughout the country and found that programs successful in promoting civic-mindedness involve students in planning the entire service learning activity; carrying out the activity; and analyzing, reflecting, reporting on, and making new applications of the learning gained from the service activity. Aided by the teacher's guidance, the students construct the service learning project in a collaborative, democratic style. Assuming responsibility for others and themselves is clearly evident in the citizenship displayed by students involved in successful service learning projects.

Third, service learning promotes personal growth through the development of mature decision-making skills and an increased sense of responsibility. In a review of research on experience-based learning programs, D. Conrad (1991) noted that "the most consistent finding of studies of participatory programs is that these experiences do tend to increase self-esteem and promote personal development" (p. 543). Personal growth through service learning indicates the potential for personal moral improvement through cooperation between students while developing and carrying out such projects. Through this cooperative process, students build a learning community, and the strategies they develop throughout the project give them the necessary tools to teach each other and to shape their own behavior.

In spite of these benefits, Wade and Saxe (1996) reviewed 22 studies on service learning that investigated political efficacy and future civic participation as overarching variables, and they found mixed results. They concluded that the inconsistency in student growth on the dimension of political efficacy stemmed from variance in the service learning programs studied: "When programs promote an individualistic, charitable conception of service and do not tie their activities to political issues or organizations, participants are unlikely to gain on this dimension" (p. 346). However, their review of research on service learning activities framed by political issues, focused on local government decisions, and dedicated to social action showed a strengthened sense of political efficacy. Cohort studies of service learning programs that promote civic efficacy also predicted increased civic participation as adults. This finding is perhaps the strongest evidence in support of service learning as an exemplary practice in citizenship education.

STRUCTURED QUESTIONING

Learning activities aimed at developing democratic citizenship are bound to include questions. Properly structured questions can motivate learning and can stimulate reflection (Dewey, 1933). Embedded within each of the learning activities explicated in this chapter is the ability of teachers and students to engage each other through the art of questioning.

Ample evidence exists to support the notion that teacher questioning encourages student learning (Costa, 1985; Dantonio, 1990). However, the types of questions teachers ask have a direct bearing on whether or not students are engaged in higher order thinking. Questions best suited to prompting higher order thinking skills (e.g., Bloom's analysis, synthesis, and evaluation, 1956; or Taba's scripted questioning, 1969) lead students to operationalize content and apply it to any citizenship education subject matter.

In their extensive review of research on exemplary questioning strategies, Wilen and Clegg (1986) found 11 questioning practices that correlated with overall student achievement. Two of these practices lead directly to the development of higher order thinking so essential to effective democratic citizenship.

First, effective citizenship development takes place when teachers engage students with high level cognitive questions that promote both convergent and divergent thinking. Working from studies done by Berliner (1984) and Brophy and Good (1986), Wilen and Clegg (1986) concluded that questions aimed at convergent thinking activate the comprehension and application levels of Bloom's cognitive taxonomy. Divergent questions activate critical thinking on citizenship education subject matter, and they move students to the analysis, synthesis, and evaluation levels of the cognitive taxonomy. Wilen (1985) found that higher order questions emerge most commonly during reflective discussions.

Second, as evidenced by the research of Brophy and Good (1986) and Weil and Murphy (1982), effective questioning will probe students to clarify, support, or stimulate thinking on a point of view. These studies found that if student responses to initial questions were incomplete, probing questions assisted them to refine, augment, or justify their initial responses. Again, this finding was most evident in studies of teachers and students engaged in reflective discussions.

The art of questioning is also an activity that should be practiced by students. After formal schooling, higher order thinking will stem only from a person's learned ability to ask higher order questions. Marzano et al. (1988) reasoned that effective questioning by teachers should act as a model of how students should approach the formulation of questions as adult citizens. Learning activities that promote higher order questioning (e.g., the Socratic method; Ogle's, 1986, KWL strategy; and Palincsar and Brown's, 1984, reciprocal questioning technique) helped students develop and apply critical thinking skills when addressing the issues and problems that earmark the subject matter of democratic citizenship education.

COMPUTER TECHNOLOGY

Without doubt, digital technology (e.g., microcomputers, CD-ROMS, and interactive video systems) has changed the world of work and play for millions of citizens, and sales of computers have surpassed those of televisions in society (Levy, 1994). Assuredly, digital technology's impact on education will be a research concern for many years to come. The Clinton administration's call for increased educational use of computers, especially in the form of the Internet's "information highway," is symptomatic of the digital technology explosion. At present, digital technology and citizenship education meet in the various computer programs teachers and students can use in conjunction with any of the learning activities described in this chapter.

Additionally, the integration of computers with citizenship education is imperative. As future citizens, students will require computer proficiency for accessing, evaluating, and communicating information and for solving increasingly complex problems (Peck & Dorricott, 1994). The recent standards in civics and government support computer literacy as a performance standard for citizenship development (Center for Civic Education, 1994). Berson (1996) pointed out the increased use of computers in social studies classrooms as both a method of instruction and topic of discussion. The indispensability of computer literacy in the lives of citizens is also a growing economic concern for public schools because the cost of digital technology could impact greatly on students' chances to become computer literate, thereby creating critical gaps between graduates of the "have" and "have not" schools (Bowers, 1988).

In a theoretically directionless review of the research on digital technology in the social studies classroom, Pahl (1996) concocted 10 questions addressing some of the issues faced by schools in the computer age. Nonetheless, he did manage to point out the recent growth in research that connects an increasing knowledge of how the brain functions to the value of computers in the mental development of the child. This sort of research holds the most promise in viewing the role of computer technology in the development of citizenship because it addresses the use of computers as tools to enhance exemplary learning activities that address higher order thinking skills and problem-solving skills.

Unfortunately, research on computer use in secondary school citizenship education is, overall, inconclusive (Berson, 1996). This may be the case, in part, because the use of computers by secondary social studies teachers ranks among the lowest in all of education (Ehman & Glenn, 1991). However, recent research indicates that computers increase student access to and motivation to learn information. Roedding (1990) found modest gains in examination preparation and level of class participation by secondary social studies students using drill and practice software. Studies reviewed by Ehman and Glenn (1991) indicated limited gains in student knowledge outcomes when teachers used drill and practice computer programs in the social studies. Higgins and Boone (1992) looked at the use of hypermedia study guides with ninth-grade students and concluded that ease of information access through such guides outweighed the use of lectures in both comprehending and retaining basic information. Overall, studies on information access and the use of software to enhance study skills looked primarily at knowledge level skills with no view toward higher taxonomic thinking skills.

Studies of computer programs aimed at developing problem-solving skills indicated positive effects. Benenson, Braun, and Klass (1992) studied 42 eighth-grade students using a computerized simulation on decision making. The treatment group received direct instruction on decision-making skills before the simulation began. This treatment showed a negative effect on student use of higher order thinking skills. Self-directed student use of the simulation facilitated higher order thinking in the control group. Unfortunately, this study did not explore student prior knowledge of computers and the possible effect this variable may have had on the self-directed findings. Ehman, Glenn, Johnson, and White (1992) studied eight social studies classrooms where teachers employed databases to enhance problem-solving skills. Modeling, student practice, debriefing, sharing outcomes, and previous integration of computers in these classrooms indicated the types of computer-based teaching strategies that resulted in high levels of problem solving by their students. Berson's (1996) review of studies in classrooms where databases were employed for enhancement of higher order thinking and problem solving showed that "databases have been especially useful for managing the extensive knowledge base in the social studies; they also foster students' development of inquiry strategies through the manipulation and analysis of information" (p. 492).

Findings that indicate positive facilitation of student access to information, motivation to learn information, and development of higher order thinking and problem-solving skills through the use of computers in the classroom are encouraging. Nonetheless, as more digital technology enters the classroom, research on the effects of such technology to enhance citizenship development is essential. To date, much of the literature on computers and citizenship education is descriptive and only implies the success of specific computer-based activities (e.g., Stevens, 1993; Vockell, 1992; Vockell & Brown, 1992; Yeager & Morris, 1995). Until a concerted research effort comes about, the relation of computer-assisted instruction to citizenship development will remain largely hypothetical.

FINDINGS AND RECOMMENDATIONS

In *A Place Called School*, Goodlad (1984) proposed 10 goals that could assist teachers, administrators, and the community in devising a common direction for American schooling. These goals, drawn from historical school documents and contemporary state government educational policy statements, fell into four categories. One of these categories (social, civic, and cultural goals) indicates clearly the long-standing mandate for the public schools to carry out the mission of citizenship education. However, his findings on the importance of social studies courses, the curricular home of citizenship education throughout much of this century, revealed ambivalence by high school students and negativism by junior high school students.

Given this review of exemplary practices in secondary school citizenship education, Goodlad's findings make sense. Primarily, but not exclusively, this chapter addressed citizenship education in secondary schools as the curricular mantle placed on the shoulders of social studies education. Reviewing hundreds of articles, books, ERIC documents, and dissertations revealed a wide-ranging rhetorical discussion on the subject matter of exemplary citizenship education, but a dearth of research findings related directly to the essential school mandate of citizenship education. Social studies educators philosophize about the value of certain subject matter approaches and expend great amounts of energy on writing about what works for them, but the vast research base in social studies activities focuses primarily on cognitive processing associated with the social and behavioral sciences and history as fields of inquiry. With the exception of research in values clarification and moral reasoning, few researchers' pay attention to specific dispositions necessary for democratic citizenship. The same holds true for research on behaviors necessary for civic competence, with some studies on service learning and cooperative learning being the exceptions.

FINDINGS

Two findings can be inferred from this review. First, although the school mandate for citizenship education is clear, the meaning of citizenship is a vastly different story. For example, Burstyn (1996), Kennedy (1997), and Oldenquist (1996) edited three books on the nature of citizenship. In each case, the chapter authors offered differing interpretations of democratic citizenship that ranged generally from the traditional-philosophical, through the modern-industrial, to the postmodern/postindustrial. This is not a criticism. A healthy democracy should be involved in a continuous debate over the essential nature of citizenship. However, this reality leaves school leaders in a quandary and educational researchers looking elsewhere for less contentious variables.

Second, the research on exemplary citizenship education learning activities suffers from this lack of agreement. For reasons that may include specific disciplinary training, philosophical shyness, or a combination of both, few researchers in social studies education attempt to put their views of citizenship education "on the line," so to speak, as both the premise and the focus of their investigations. Most often, studies leave it to the consumer of research to decide if the findings relate to some form of citizenship education. Researchers appear to work under the assumption that individual teachers, administrators, and other scholars will decide what is or is not valuable based on their idiosyncratic interpretations of democratic citizenship. Again, the intent here is not to criticize, because in a democratic society, the value of research findings should be left to the consumer. However, what remains beyond the subject matter rhetoric and a few research studies are myriad publications explaining successful citizenship education practices based seemingly on logical premises and intuition. Full scale studies, either statistical or interpretive, based on the various explications of democratic citizenship are in dire need if teachers and administrators seek to take from the literature ideas that make practical sense in their individual contexts and align with their community's view of democratic citizenship.

At this point, exploring the nature of individual school contexts and the community's interpretation of democratic citizenship becomes the task of teachers and other school leaders. Framing the research base within these two areas can lead teachers and school leaders to a pragmatic evaluation of the literature based on local needs. In so doing, school leaders should mount investigations into: the meaning and subject matter of citizenship, appropriate activities for learning and examining this meaning, and in-service programs aimed at energizing the school toward internalizing this meaning in day-to-day practice. The scope of this chapter allows a recommendation for both investigating the meaning and subject matter of citizenship and identifying related, appropriate learning activities.

RECOMMENDATIONS

This study indicates a bewildering array of subject matter approaches to citizenship education and a limited research base from which to choose exemplary citizenship learning activities for secondary schools. One way to ensure exemplary citizenship education in schools is to enact collaborative and cooperative dialogues between the school and the community. Data gathered from community stakeholders and the school community can crystalize a school's definition of subject matter worth teaching and indicate pedagogical direction for operationalizing this definition. The following is a five-step recommendation for developing an action plan aimed at local development of exemplary citizenship education practices (see Fig. 3.1).

First, school leaders should survey the local and school communities in order to gauge stakeholders' visions of exemplary citizenship and to determine opinion on how citizenship education should manifest in the school's mission and curriculum. An example of one such survey was developed by Joyce, Alleman-Brooks, and Orimoloye (1982). Originally intended to gauge teachers', supervisors', and teacher educators' perceptions of social studies, this survey also reflects respondents' goals for citizenship education. Second, school leaders should tabulate the results and summarize them in a generally accessible form. Third, the results should be disseminated throughout the school and local community via press releases, radio and television broadcasts, and the school newspaper. Fourth, admin-

Step One
Conduct survey of community and school stakeholders

↓

Step Two
Tabulate and summarize results in an accessible form

↓

Step Three
Disseminate results throughout the school and community

↓

Step Four
Hold public hearings to solicit feedback on survey results

↓

Step Five
Incorporate findings into curriculum design for citizenship education

FIG. 3.1. Five step action plan for developing exemplary citizenship education practices.

istrators, curriculum supervisors, and the local school board should hold public hearings on the results with the intention of gathering feedback and uncovering ideas not revealed by the survey instrument. Fifth, school personnel, especially social studies educators, should discuss the results of the survey and hearings in order to: formulate an acceptable school and community-wide definition of citizenship, apply this definition as a criterion for identifying and assessing different subject matter and instructional approaches to citizenship education, and develop methods of evaluation that assess student progress toward realizing the goal of exemplary citizenship.

Conclusions

Unlike totalitarian societies, citizenship in a democratic society is a point for debate and, at times, contention. This review intended to bring together exemplary practices found in the research base of secondary school citizenship education. In so doing, it centered on the most commonly taught subject matter in citizenship education and research findings on learning activities that develop democratic citizenship in our youth. In both instances, the literature afforded a vast set of beliefs and suggestions, but few research findings. The bewildering array of subject matter possibilities and of virtually groundless self-proclamations of success with learning activities, coupled with the paucity of research findings, indicates that school leaders need to identify democratic citizenship through a whole-community endeavor and translate these findings into criteria for judging the most appropriate approach to democratic citizenship education for their community and their school.

References

Adelson, J. (1972). The political imagination of the young adolescent. In J. Kagan & R. Coles (Eds.), *Twelve to sixteen: Early adolescence* (pp. 106–144). New York: Norton.

Adelson, J. (1982). Rites of passage. *American Education, 62,* 6–13.

Alliance for Service-Learning in Education Reform. (1993). *Standards of quality for school-based service-learning.* Chester, VT: Author.

Anderson, C. C. (1994). *Global understandings: A framework for teaching and learning.* Washington, DC: Association for Supervision and Curriculum Development.

Anderson, F. J., & Palmer, J. (1988). The jigsaw approach: Students motivating students. *Education, 109*(1), 59–62.

Araboglou, A. (1996). The challenge of multicultural education: Prospects for school social studies. In B. G. Massialas & R. F. Allen (Eds.), *Critical issues in teaching social studies: K–12* (pp. 253–284). Belmont, CA: Wadsworth.

Atwood, V. A., & Wilen, W. W. (1991). Wait time and effective social studies instruction: What can research in science education tell us? *Social Education, 55*(3), 179–181.

Banaszak, R. A. (1991). The economic perspective: Economic literacy and citizenship education. In R. E. Gross & T. L. Dynneson (Eds.), *Social science perspectives on citizenship education* (pp. 88–115). New York: Teacher's College Press.

Banks, J. A., & Clegg, A. A., Jr. (1990). *Teaching strategies for the social studies: Inquiry, valuing, and decision-making* (4th ed.). White Plains, NY: Longman.

Benenson, W., Braun, J. A., & Klass, P. H. (1992). Did you ever have to make up your mind? Decision making in a social studies classroom. *Illinois School Research and Development, 29*(2), 8–10.

Bennett, C. E. (1990). *Comprehensive multicultural education: Theory and practice* (2nd ed.). Needham Heights, MA: Allyn & Bacon.

Bennett, W. (1993). *The book of virtues.* New York: Simon & Schuster.

Berliner, D. (1984). The half-full glass: A review of research on teaching. In P. L. Hosford (Ed.), *Using what we know about teaching* (pp. 51–84). Washington, DC: Association for Supervision and Curriculum Development.

Berson, M. J. (1996). Effectiveness of computer technology in the social studies: A review of the literature. *Journal of Research on Computing in Education, 28*(4), 486–499.

Beyer, B. K. (1985). Critical thinking: What is it? *Social Education, 49,* 270–276.

Beyer, B. K. (1987). *Practical strategies for the teaching of thinking.* Boston: Allyn & Bacon.

Beyer, B. K. (1988). *Developing a thinking skills program.* Boston: Allyn & Bacon.

Bloom, B. S. (Ed.). (1956). *Taxonomy of educational objectives, the classification of educational goals: Handbook I. The cognitive domain.* New York: David McKay.

Boocock, S. S., & Schild, E. O. (Eds.). (1968). *Simulation games in learning.* Beverly Hills, CA: Sage.

Bowers, C. A. (1988). *The cultural dimensions of educational computing: Understanding the non-neutrality of technology.* New York: Teacher's College Press.

Boyer, E. L. (1987). Service: Linking school to life. *Community Education Journal, 15*(1), 7–9.

Brandhorst, A. (1991). The social psychological perspective: Social contexts, processes, and civil ideologies. In R. E. Gross & T. L. Dynneson (Eds.), *Social science perspectives on citizenship education* (pp. 161–183). New York: Teacher's College Press.

Brophy, J., & Good, T. (1986). Teacher effects. In M. C. Wittrock (Ed.), *Handbook of research on teaching* (3rd ed., pp. 328–375). New York: Macmillan.

Burch, H. R., & Patterson, S. H. (1918). *Problems of American democracy: Political, economic, social.* New York: Macmillan.

Burstyn, J. N. (Ed.). (1996). *Educating tomorrow's valuable citizen.* Albany: State University of New York Press.

Carter, G. R. (1997). Service learning in curriculum reform. In J. Schine (Ed.), *Service Learning: Ninety-sixth yearbook of the National Society for the Study of Education* (pp. 69–78). Chicago: National Society for the Study of Education.

Center for Civic Education. (1994). *National standards for civics and government.* Calabasas, CA: Author.

Cherryholmes, C. H. (1966). Some current research on effectiveness of educational simulations: Implications for alternative strategies. *American Behavioral Scientist, 10,* 4–7.

Chilcott, J. H. (1986). *Anthropological perspectives on citizenship education* (Report No. SO 017 533). Palo Alto, CA: Annual Conference of the Social Science Education Consortium. (ERIC Document Reproduction Service No. ED 274 579)

Chilcott, J. H. (1991). The anthropological perspective: Anthropological insights for civic education. In R. E. Gross & T. L. Dynneson (Eds.), *Social science perspectives on citizenship education* (pp. 184–194). New York: Teacher's College Press.

Clegg, A. A., Jr. (1991). Games and simulations in social studies education. In J. P. Shaver (Ed.), *Handbook of research on social studies teaching and learning* (pp. 523–529). New York: Macmillan.

Colby, A., & Damon, W. (1992). *Some do care: Contemporary lives of moral commitment.* New York: The Free Press.

Connell, R. (1971). *The child's construction of politics.* Carleton, Australia: Melbourne University Press.

Conrad, B. D. (1988). Cooperative learning and prejudice reduction. *Social Education, 52*(4), 283–286.

Conrad, D. (1991). School-community participation for social studies. In J. P. Shaver (Ed.), *Handbook of research on social studies teaching and learning* (pp. 540–548). New York: MacMillan.

Costa, A. (1985). Teacher behaviors that enable student thinking. In A. Costa (Ed.), *Developing minds* (pp. 125–137). Alexandria, VA: Association for Supervision and Curriculum Development.

Crisman, F., & Mackey, J. (1990). A comparison of oral and written techniques of concept instruction. *Theory and Research in Social Education, 18*(2), 139–155.

Czarra, F., & Smith, A. (1992). *A survey of state international education co-ordinators.* Washington, DC: Council of Chief State School Officers.

Dantonio, M. (1990). *How can we create thinkers? Questioning strategies that work for teachers.* Bloomington, IN: National Education Service.

Dewey, J. (1902). *The child and the curriculum.* Chicago: University of Chicago Press.

Dewey, J. (1916). *Democracy and education.* New York: Macmillan.

Dewey, J. (1933). *How we think.* Lexington, MA: Heath.

Dillon, J. T. (1982). Cognitive correspondence between question/state and response. *American Educational Research Journal, 19,* 540–551.

Dunn, W. W. (Comp.). (1916). *The social studies in secondary education* (Bulletin No. 28). Washington, DC: U.S. Bureau of Education.

Dynneson, T. L., & Gross, R. E. (1991). The educational perspective: Citizenship education in American society. In R. E. Gross & T. L. Dynneson (Eds.), *Social science perspectives on citizenship education* (pp. 1–42). New York: Teacher's College Press.

Ehman, L. H., & Glenn, A. D. (1991). Interactive technology in the social studies. In J. P. Shaver (Ed.), *Handbook of research on social studies teaching and learning* (pp. 513–522). New York: Macmillan.

Ehman, L. H., Glenn, A. D., Johnson, V., & White, C. S. (1992). Using computer databases in student problem solving: A study of eight social studies teachers' classrooms. *Theory and Research in Social Education, 20,* 179–206.

Ehman, L. H., Mehlinger, H., & Patrick, J. (1974). *Toward effective instruction in secondary social studies.* Boston: Houghton Mifflin.

Engle, S. H., & Ochoa, A. S. (1988). *Education for democratic citizenship: Decision making in the social studies.* New York: Teacher's College Press.

Evans, R. W. (1997). Teaching social issues: Implementing an issues-centered curriculum. In E. W. Ross (Ed.), *The social studies curriculum: Purposes, problems, and possibilities* (pp. 197–212). Albany: State University of New York Press.

Frech, W. (1974). An analysis of the effect of the anthropology curriculum project material, *The Concept of Culture,* on the ethnocentric attitudes of fourth grade students (Doctoral dissertation, University of Georgia, 1973). *Dissertation Abstracts International, 34,* 3830A–3831A.

Gagnon, P. (1988, November). Why study history? *Atlantic Monthly, 262*(5), 43–66.

Gall, M. D. (1985). Discussion methods of teaching. In T. Husen & T. N. Postlethwaite (Eds.), *International encyclopedia of education* (Vol. 3, pp. 1423–1427). Oxford, England: Pergamon.

Gall, M. D., & Rhody, T. (1987). Review of research on questioning techniques. In W. W. Wilen (Ed.), *Questions, questioning techniques, and effective teaching* (pp. 23–48). Washington, DC: National Education Association.

Geography Education Standards Project. (1994). *Geography for life.* Washington, DC: National Geographic Research and Exploration.

Gilligan, C. (1982). *In a different voice.* Cambridge, MA: Harvard University Press.

Gilliom, M. E. (Ed.). (1977). *Practical methods for the social studies.* Belmont, CA: Wadsworth.

Goodlad, J. I. (1984). *A place called school.* New York: McGraw-Hill.

Goodman, J. (1992). *Elementary schooling for critical democracy.* Albany: State University of New York Press.

Griffin, A. F. (1992). *Alan F. Griffin on reflective teaching: A philosophical approach to the subject matter preparation of teachers of history.* Washington, DC: National Council for the Social Studies.

Hanvey, R. G. (1976). *An attainable global perspective.* Denver, CO: Center for Teaching International Relations.

Hartshorne, H., & May, M. (1928). *Studies in the nature of character: Vol. 1. Studies in deceit.* New York: Macmillan.

Helburn, N. (1991). The geographical perspective: Geography's role in citizenship education. In R. E. Gross & T. L. Dynneson (Eds.), *Social science perspectives on citizenship education* (pp. 116–140). New York: Teacher's College Press.

Higgins, K., & Boone, R. (1992). Hypermedia computer study guides for social studies: Adapting a Canadian history text. *Social Education, 56,* 154–159.

Hunt, M. P., & Metcalf, L. E. (1968). *Teaching high school social studies: Problems in reflective thinking and social understanding* (2nd ed.). New York: Harper & Row.

Hurd, P. D. (1991). Why we must transform science education. *Educational Leadership, 49*(2), 33–35.

Hursh, D. (1997). Multicultural social studies: Schools as places for examining and challenging inequality. In E. W. Ross (Ed.), *The social studies curriculum: Purposes, problems, and possibilities* (pp. 107–119). Albany: State University of New York Press.

Johnson, D. W., & Johnson, R. T. (1986). Mainstreaming and cooperative learning strategies. *Exceptional Children, 52*(6), 553–561.

Johnson, D. W., & Johnson, R. T. (1996). Cooperative learning and traditional American values: An appreciation. *NASSP Bulletin, 80*(579), 63–65.

Joyce, W. W., Alleman-Brooks, J. E., & Orimoloye, P. S. (1982). *Social Education, 45*(6), 357–360.

Kennedy, K. J. (1991). The historical perspective: The contribution of history to citizenship education. In R. E. Gross & T. L. Dynneson (Eds.), *Social science perspectives on citizenship education* (pp. 66–87). New York: Teacher's College Press.

Kennedy, K. J. (Ed.). (1997). *Citizenship education and the modern state.* London: Falmer.

Kirschenbaum, H. (1992). A comprehensive model for values education and moral education. *Phi Delta Kappan, 73*(10), 771–776.

Kohlberg, L. (1966). Moral education in the school. *School Review, 74,* 1–30.

Kohlberg, L. (1975). Moral education for a society in moral transition. *Educational Leadership, 33*(1), 46–54.

Kohlberg, L. (1976). The cognitive-developmental approach to moral education. In P. H. Martorella (Ed.), *Social studies strategies: Theory into practice* (pp. 127–142). New York: Harper & Row.

Kohlberg, L. (1980). Educating for a just society: An updated and revised statement. In B. Munsey (Ed.), *Moral development, moral education, and Kohlberg* (pp. 455–470). Birmingham, AL: Religious Education Press.

Lane, R. E. (1972). *Political man.* New York: The Free Press.

Leming, J. S. (1985). Research on social studies curriculum and instruction. Interventions and outcomes in the socio-moral domain. In W. B. Stanley (Ed.), *Review of research in social studies education: 1976–1983* (pp. 123–213). Washington, DC: National Council for the Social Studies and the Social Science Education Consortium.

Leming, J. S. (1996). Teaching values in social studies education: Past practices and current trends. In B. G. Massialas & R. F. Allen (Eds.), *Critical issues in teaching social studies: K–12* (pp. 145–180). Belmont, CA: Wadsworth.

Levy, S. (1994, December). E-Money—That's what I want. *WIRED,* 174–179.

Lickona, T. (1991). *Educating for character: How our schools can teach respect and responsibility.* New York: Bantam.

Lindblom, K. J. (1991). Civic consciousness and cooperative learning: Critically viewing mass media. *English Journal, 80*(5), 53–59.

Lipka, R. P., Beane, J. A., & O'Connell, B. E. (1985). *Community service projects: Citizenship in action.* Bloomington, IN: Phi Delta Kappa Educational Foundation.

Livingston, S. A., & Stoll, C. S. (1973). *Simulation games: An introduction for the social studies teacher.* New York: The Free Press.

Mackey, J. A. (1991). Adolescents' social, cognitive, and moral development and secondary school social studies. In J. P. Shaver (Ed.), *Handbook of research on social studies teaching and learning* (pp. 134–143). New York: Macmillan.

Margolis, H., McCabe, P. O., & Schwartz, E. (1990). Using cooperative learning to facilitate mainstreaming in the social studies. *Social Education, 54*(2), 111–114, 120.

Martorella, P. H. (1991). Knowledge and concept development in social studies. In J. P. Shaver (Ed.), *Handbook of research on social studies teaching and learning* (pp. 370–384). New York: Macmillan.

Martorella, P. H. (1996). *Teaching social studies in middle and secondary schools* (2nd ed.). Englewood Cliffs, NJ: Prentice-Hall.

Marzano, R. M., Brandt, R. S., Hughes, C. S., Jones, B. F., Presseisen, B. Z., Rankin, S. C., & Suhor, C. (1988). *Dimensions of thinking.* Alexandria, VA: Association for Supervision and Curriculum Development.

McBrien, J. L., & Brandt, R. S. (1997). *The language of learning: A guide to education terms.* Alexandria, VA: Association for Supervision and Curriculum Development.

Merriam, C. (1934). *Civic education in the United States.* New York: Scribner's.

Merryfield, M. M. (1997). Infusing global perspectives into the social studies curriculum. In E. W. Ross (Ed.), *The social studies curriculum: Purposes, problems, and possibilities* (pp. 183–195). Albany: State University of New York Press.

Miller, S. L. (1996). Essential economics for civic education in former communist countries of central and eastern Europe. In R. C. Remy & J. Strzemieczny (Eds.), *Building civic education for democracy in Poland* (pp. 23–40). Washington, DC: National Council for the Social Studies and ERIC Clearinghouse for Social Studies/Social Science Education.

Mills, S., Rice, C. T., Berliner, C. C., & Rousseau, W. W. (1980). The correspondence between teacher questions and student answers in classroom discourse. *Journal of Experimental Education, 48*, 194–204.

Mosher, R., Kenny, R. A., Jr., & Garrod, A. (1994). *Preparing for citizenship: Teaching youth to live democratically.* Westport, CT: Praeger.

National Center for History in the Schools. (1996). *National standards for history.* Los Angeles: Author.

National Council for the Social Studies (NCSS) Task Force on Ethnic Studies Curriculum Guidelines. (1992). Curriculum guidelines for multicultural education. *Social Education, 56*(5), 274–294.

National Council for the Social Studies (NCSS) Task Force. (1994). *Curriculum standards for the social studies: Expectations for Excellence.* Washington, DC: NCSS.

National Council on Economic Education. (1997). *Voluntary national content standards in economics.* New York: Author.

Newmann, F. M., Bertocci, T. A., & Landsness, R. M. (1977). *Skills in citizen action.* Madison, WI: Citizen Participation Curriculum Project, University of Wisconsin.

Ogle, D. (1986). KWL: A teaching model that develops active reading of expository text. *The Reading Teacher, 39*, 564–570.

Oldenquist, A. (Ed.). (1996). *Can democracy be taught?: Perspectives on education for democracy in the United States, central and eastern Europe, Russia, South Africa, and Japan.* Bloomington, IN: Phi Delta Kappa Educational Foundation.

Owen, R. C., & Zevin, J. (1996). Studying and teaching anthropology. In Social Science Education Consortium (Eds.), *Teaching the social sciences and history in secondary schools* (pp. 203–236). Belmont, CA: Wadsworth.

Pahl, R. H. (1996). Digital technology and social studies. In B. G. Massialas & R. F. Allen (Eds.), *Critical issues in teaching social studies: K–12* (pp. 341–386). Belmont, CA: Wadsworth.

Palincsar, A. S., & Brown, A. L. (1984). Reciprocal teaching of comprehension-fostering and comprehension-monitoring activities. *Cognition and Instruction, 1*, 117–175.

Parker, W. C. (1991). Achieving thinking and decision-making objectives in social studies. In J. P. Shaver (Ed.), *Handbook of research on social studies teaching and learning* (pp. 345–356). New York: Macmillan.

Peck, K. L., & Dorricott, D. (1994). Why use technology? *Educational Leadership, 51*(7), 11–14.

Raths, L. E., Harmin, M., & Simon, S. B. (1966). *Values and teaching.* Columbus, OH: Merrill.

Remy, R. C. (1980). *Handbook of basic citizenship competencies.* Alexandria, VA: Association for Supervision and Curriculum Development.

Reyes, D. J., & Smith, R. B. (1983). The role of concept learning in social studies textbook comprehension: A brief analysis. *The Social Studies, 74*(4), 85–88.

Roedding, G. R. (1990). *Using computer-assisted instruction to improve students' performance skills in social studies.* Fort Lauderdale, FL: Nova University. (ERIC Document Reproduction Service No. ED 332 950)

Ross, E. W. (1997). The struggle for the social studies curriculum. In E. W. Ross (Ed.), *The social studies curriculum: Purposes, problems, and possibilities* (pp. 3–19). Albany: State University of New York Press.

Rossi, J. A. (1996). Creating strategies and conditions for civil discourse about controversial issues. *Social Education, 60*(1), 15–21.

Rowe, M. B. (1986). Wait time: Slowing down may be a way of speeding up! *Journal of Teacher Education, 37*(1), 43–50.

Schechter, S. L., & Weil, J. (1996). Studying and teaching political science. In Social Science Education Consortium (Eds.), *Teaching the social sciences and history in secondary schools* (pp.137–170). Belmont, CA: Wadsworth.

Schine, J. (1997a). Editor's preface. In J. Schine (Ed.), *Service learning: Ninety-sixth yearbook of the National Society for the Study of Education* (pp. vii–ix). Chicago: National Society for the Study of Education.

Schine, J. (1997b). Looking ahead: Issues and challenges. In J. Schine (Ed.), *Service learning: Ninety-sixth yearbook of the National Society for the Study of Education* (pp. 186–199). Chicago: National Society for the Study of Education.

Schultz, J. B. (1989). AHEA's survey of American teens. *Journal of Home Economics, 81*, 27–38.

Seldes, G. (Comp.). (1985). *The great thoughts.* New York: Ballantine.

Simon, S. B., Howe, L., & Kirschenbaum, H. (1972). *Values clarification: A handbook of practical strategies.* New York: Hart.

Slavin, R. (1983). *Cooperative learning.* New York: Longman.

Slavin, R. E. (1989–1990). Research on cooperative learning: Consensus and controversy. *Educational Leadership, 47*(4), 52–54.

Social Science Education Consortium. (1996). *Teaching the social sciences and history in secondary schools: A methods book.* Belmont, CA: Wadsworth.

Stevens, L. (1993). A social studies computer lab. *Social Education, 57*(1), 8–10.

Swartz, R. J., & Perkins, D. N. (1990). *Teaching thinking: Issues and approaches.* Pacific Grove, CA: Midwest Publications.

Taba, H. (1969). *Teaching strategies and cognitive functioning in elementary school children* (Cooperative Research Project No. 2404). Washington, DC: U.S. Office of Education.

Thompson, D. F. (1970). *The democratic citizen.* New York: Cambridge University Press.

Tobin, K. G. (1987). The role of wait time in high cognitive level learning. *Review of Educational Research, 57*(1), 69–95.

VanSickle, R. L. (1986). A quantitative review of research on instructional simulation gaming: A twenty-year perspective. *Theory and Research in Social Education, 14,* 245–264.

Vars, G. F. (1996). The effects of interdisciplinary curriculum and instruction. In P. S. Hlebowitsh & W. G. Wraga (Eds.), *Annual review of research for school leaders* (pp. 147–164). New York: Scholastic.

Verba, S. (1969). Political participation and strategies of influence: A comparative study. In J. D. Barber (Ed.), *Readings in citizen politics* (pp. 3–26). Berkeley: University of California Press.

Vocke, D. E. (1992). American history and cooperative learning: A rationale and sample lesson for the secondary level. *The Social Studies, 83*(5), 212–215.

Vockell, E. L. (1992). Computers and social studies skills. *Social Education, 56*(7), 366–369.

Vockell, E. L., & Brown, W. (1992). *The computer in the social studies curriculum.* Santa Cruz, CA: Mitchell/McGraw-Hill.

Wade, R. C., & Saxe, D. W. (1996). Community service learning in the social studies: Historical roots, empirical evidence, critical issues. *Theory and Research in Social Education, 24*(4), 331–359.

Weil, M., & Murphy, J. (1982). Instructional processes. In *Encyclopedia of educational research* (5th ed., Vol. 2, pp. 890–916). New York: Macmillan.

Wertheimer, M., Yeager, T., & Jones, V. L. (1996). Studying and teaching psychology. In Social Science Education Consortium (Eds.), *Teaching the social sciences and history in secondary schools* (pp. 72–104). Belmont, CA: Wadsworth.

Wexler, P., Grosshans, R. R., Zhang, Q. H., & Kim, B-U. (1991). The cultural perspective: Citizenship education in culture and society. In R. E. Gross & T. L. Dynneson (Eds.), *Social science perspectives on citizenship education* (pp. 141–160). New York: Teacher's College Press.

Wilen, W. W. (1985). Questioning, thinking and effective citizenship. *Social Science Record, 22*, 4–6.

Wilen, W. W. (1996). Thinking skills instruction in social studies classrooms. In B. G. Massialas & R. F. Allen (Eds.), *Crucial issues in teaching social studies: K–12* (pp. 111–144). Belmont, CA: Wadsworth.

Wilen, W. W., & Clegg, A. A., Jr. (1986). Effective questions and questioning: A research review. *Theory and Research in Social Education, 14*(2), 153–161.

Windrim, R. J. (1990). Co-operative learning as an agent of inquiry. *History and Social Science Teacher, 25*(4), 193–196.

Woyach, R. B. (1991). The political perspective: Civic participation and the public good. In R. E. Gross & T. L. Dynneson (Eds.), *Social science perspectives on citizenship education* (pp. 43–65). New York: Teacher's College Press.

Wynne, E., & Ryan, K. (1993). *Reclaiming our schools: A handbook on teaching character, academics, and discipline.* New York: Merrill.

Yeager, E. A., & Morris, J. W., Jr. (1995). History and computers: The views from selected social studies journals. *Social Studies, 86*(6), 277–282.

Zeldin, S., & Tarlov, S. (1997). Service learning as a vehicle for youth development. In J. Schine (Ed.), *Service learning: Ninety-sixth yearbook of the National Society for the Study of Education* (pp. 173–185). Chicago: National Society for the Study of Education.

PART II

Multicultural Education

THE TASK OF ARRIVING AT A SENSE of social cohesion has long been a fundamental ideal of public education in the United States. With the ever-increasing diversity of the American people, effective ways and means of fostering social solidarity while simultaneously protecting and enhancing the integrity of individuals and cultures remain imperatives. This social and educational challenge is renewed virtually each generation as the sources of immigration to the United States continue to vary. Chapters in this section recount the history of multicultural education in the United States, review contemporary research and professional literature about multicultural education, and identify effective practices based on research and experience. John J. Patrick places multicultural education squarely in the context of the civic mission of public schools. Patrick provides readers with a decidedly critical yet thoroughly constructive examination of the assumptions of some variations on the multiculturalism theme, identifying crucial shortcomings of some proposals for multicultural education practice. Patrick also offers practical suggestions for developing a multicultural and democratic approach to civic education. Carl A. Grant and Kim Wieczorek offer a comprehensive review of the variegated literature in the field of multicultural education. Their discussion of the literature both illuminates the realities of conventional school practice and identifies promising multicultural education practices.

Chapter 4

MULTICULTURAL EDUCATION AND THE CIVIC MISSION OF SCHOOLS

John J. Patrick
Indiana University, Bloomington

A LONG-STANDING AND DEEPLY ROOTED MISSION IN American schools stresses common education for citizenship in a government based on consent of the governed and rights of individuals. Advocates of this traditional civic mission of schools assume that without effective education for democratic citizenship neither popular sovereignty nor the personal and political rights of individuals are secure. Furthermore, proponents claim that national unity is at risk unless the socially and culturally diverse people of the United States are educated to know and support in common certain civic principles that define them as a distinct people and polity.

A recent and emphatically expressed challenge to the traditional civic mission of schools in the United States highlights social and cultural diversity between different groups. This new multicultural mission is necessary, according to its leading advocates, to improve the old civic mission through recognition of long-neglected groups that have suffered inequitable discrimination. Most proponents claim they want to democratize and legitimize civic education for all groups in the United States, not to overturn and replace it with a radical alternative.

This chapter briefly treats the traditional civic mission of American schools. Then it discusses key elements of current multicultural challenges of the traditional civic mission of schools. It next appraises these challenges to suggest their strengths and weaknesses—contributions and pitfalls—with regard to the fundamental principles of U.S. democracy, which are endorsed by both multicultural challengers and traditional civic educators. Finally, it suggests how multicultural education and civic education can be conjoined in the mission and core curriculum of schools to support genuinely the principles and practices of democratic citizenship.

THE TRADITIONAL CIVIC MISSION OF AMERICAN SCHOOLS

During the founding and early national eras of U.S. history, there was agreement among leaders with different political agendas that there must be common education for citizenship if their new republic would endure. John Adams and Thomas Jefferson, for example, led opposing political parties while agreeing about the necessity of pervasive education for citizenship to transmit common civic knowledge and commitment to core principles and practices of government in a republic. Jefferson no doubt concurred when Adams wrote, "Children should be educated and instructed in the principles of freedom.... It is not too much to say that schools for the [civic] education of all should be placed at convenient distances and maintained at the public expense" (L. S. Pangle & T. L. Pangle, 1993, p. 96).

The major goal of Thomas Jefferson's proposals for the education of citizens was derived directly from the principal founding document, the Declaration of Independence, which proclaimed "that to secure these Rights [to Life, Liberty, and the Pursuit of Happiness] Governments are instituted among men, deriving their just powers from the Consent of the Governed" (Center for Civic Education., 1997, p. 6). In line with these principles of good government, Jefferson recommended education of citizens "to enable every man to judge for himself what will secure or endanger his freedom" (L. S. Pangle & T. L. Pangle, 1993, p. 108).

Jefferson, Adams, and other leaders of the founding era understood, however, that individual rights to liberty would be secure only in a healthy community with an effective popular government. So they wanted the education of citizens to stress both individual rights and responsibility for the common good, the general welfare of civil society. L. S. Pangle and T. L. Pangle (1993) emphasized, "The paramount educational challenge of the founding generation was that of preparing future generations to become democratic citizens who would sustain a regime of individual freedoms as well as responsible self-rule" (p. 11).

The "paramount educational challenge" of the founders became the civic mission of public schools in the 19th and 20th centuries. It generated virtually unchallenged components of the core curriculum that pertained to "explicit and continuing study of the basic concepts and values underlying our democratic political community and constitutional order" (Butts, 1989, p. 308). And it aimed to build a common national identity and loyalty (Feinberg, 1998, pp. 1–12). Current indicators of the enduring civic mission schools are the 1998 National Assessment of Educational Progress in Civics, which emphasizes knowledge of the principles and practices of government and citizenship in U.S. constitutional democracy (NAEP Civics Consensus Project, 1996), and the *National Standards for Civics and Government* on which the national assessment is based (Center for Civic Education, 1994).

Civic educators today recognize and emphasize the striking social pluralism and cultural diversity in the United States, as did their counterparts of the past. Civic educators of yesterday and today have understood that Americans have been and are a people bound primarily by common civic principles rather than common kinship, ethnicity, or religion—the ties that have bound most other nations in the world. A main point of civic education in the United States, therefore, has been to develop among diverse people a common commitment to principles and values expressed in such founding documents as the 1776 Declaration of Independence, the 1787 Constitution, and the 1791 Bill of Rights. The imperative of building and maintaining national unity from social and cultural diversity has pervaded the traditional civic mission of the schools.

An emphatic contemporary endorsement of the traditional civic mission is presented by the U.S. Commission on Immigration Reform, which was led by Barbara Jordan until her death in 1996 and by Shirley Hufstedler until completion of the commission's final report in 1997. The commission strongly recommended "the renewal and emphasis on instruction of all kindergarten through grade twelve students in the common civic culture that is essential to citizenship." Further, the commission assumed, "An understanding of the history of the United States and the principles and practices of our government are essential for all students, immigrants and natives alike." Finally, the Commission urged "a renewed emphasis on the common core of civic culture that unites individuals from many ethnic and social groups" (U.S. Commission on Immigration Reform, 1997, pp. 39–40).

Multicultural Challenges of the Civic Mission of Schools

Multicultural educators tend to be critical and skeptical of the recommendations and claims of traditional civic educators. And they have challenged the long-standing civic mission of schools. Multicultural challengers of this traditional civic education contend that the needs of diverse minority groups in the United States have been slighted by the long-standing and overarching concern with civic unity at the expense of cultural diversity. Banks (1997), for example, argued, "Citizenship education in the United States historically reinforced dominant-group hegemony and student inaction" (p. 4).

Unlike traditional civic educators who stress cultural unity to bind diverse individuals and groups, multicultural educators emphasize differences between groups. And they extol cultural pluralism as "an ideal state of societal conditions characterized by equity and mutual respect among existing cultural groups. It contrasts sharply with cultural assimilation, or 'melting pot' images where ethnic minorities are expected to give up their traditions and blend in or be absorbed by the mainstream society or predominant culture" (Bennett, 1995, p. 13).

Multicultural educators uniformly applaud principles of democracy at the core of the traditional civic mission. "Almost every discussion of multiculturalism and multicultural education is placed in the context of democracy and citizen participation" (Ladson-Billings, 1992, p. 308). Gay (1994) stressed education for democracy in concert with multicultural education in order to maximize the likelihood of developing genuine democratic citizenship among students of all cultural groups. Like many others who push for a multicultural mission, she maintained it will contribute greatly to the necessary narrowing of the great gap between grand ideals and flawed practices of democracy in the United States. She wrote, "Multicultural interpretations of citizenship act as a critical voice, a civic conscience, and a reality filter for general education values and goals for democracy" (p. 103).

Banks (1999) agreed with traditional civic educators that "an important goal of the schools in a democratic society is to help students acquire the knowledge, values, and skills needed to participate effectively in public communities" (p. 1). This statement concurs exactly with mainline documents in civic education (Center for Civic Education, 1994; NAEP Civics Consensus Project, 1996). But Banks (1997) and other multicultural educators concerned about the civic mission of schools maintained that this mission will be unfulfilled, as in the past, unless it is transformed by multicultural means and ends (pp. 10–17). Bennett (1995) expressed a widely shared view of these means and ends in her textbook for students in teacher education programs: "Multicultural education is an approach to teaching and learning that is based upon democratic values and beliefs, and seeks to foster cultural pluralism" (p. 13).

Multicultural educators would "foster cultural pluralism" through a school curriculum and classroom instruction that favors inclusion and accurate recognition of groups previously neglected or stereotyped, exclusion of civic myths that falsify the history of democracy in the United States and foster monocultural assimilation, preservation of minority group identities and cultures in the United States, and promotion of cultural democracy. These four categories are not presented as the exclusive or total multicultural agenda for reform of civic education. And they certainly are not intended to address a broader range of multicultural education reforms that extend far beyond the scope of civic education. Rather, they are emphasized as especially important general concerns about education for democratic citizenship shared by multicultural educators, regardless of various philosophical differences that otherwise separate them. Further, they point to particular and pervasive criticisms among various kinds of multicultural educators of the civic mission and directions for transforming it to serve multicultural goals.

INCLUSION AND ACCURATE RECOGNITION OF MINORITY GROUP ACHIEVEMENTS

Multicultural educators affirm their commitment to cultural pluralism through advocacy of inclusion and accurate recognition of women and certain ethnic and racial groups in the curriculum. And they would expose all students to multiple perspectives on particular events in history that reflect the diverse values of different cultural groups. They agree with Takaki (1993): "Through their narratives and circumstances, the people of America's diverse groups are able to see themselves and each other in our common past.... By sharing their stories, they invite us to see ourselves in a different mirror" (pp. 16–17). This "different mirror"—a symbol of multiple perspectives on the past and present of different cultural groups in the United States—can be used to reflect various multicultural meanings in classrooms from which some groups have been excluded.

Content analyses of widely used social studies textbooks and curriculum frameworks during the past half century provide ample evidence in support of multicultural educators' claims that certain groups (e.g., African Americans, Hispanics, and indigenous peoples of America) have been marginally and inaccurately treated. A work titled provocatively, *Lies My Teacher Told Me: Everything Your American History Textbook Got Wrong*, offers many examples of stereotypes and other distortions of minority groups (Loewen, 1995).

Comparisons of textbooks and curriculum frameworks of the 1980s and 1990s with those of previous 20th-century decades show great changes desired by multicultural educators (Lerner, Nagai, & Rothman, 1995; Patrick & White, 1992; Ueda, 1994). High school U.S. history textbooks, for example, "have substantially increased their coverage of blacks, both absolutely and proportionally" during the past 40 years. Further, "They present blacks positively far more frequently than the whites" (Lerner et al., 1995, p. 70). Similar trends have been noted on inclusive and positive recognition of women and indigenous peoples of America.

Despite documented improvements in textbooks and other curricular materials, multicultural educators have continued their calls for elimination in social studies and civic education of inaccurate, biased, stereotypical, and unfair treatment of minority groups in the United States. They have relentlessly claimed that the people of the United States constitute the world's most multicultural society. And they have demanded, therefore, that the curriculum of schools continue to become more inclusive and respectful of cultural diversity that is transforming the United States (Landry, 1997, pp. 41–61; Loewen, 1995, pp. 307–312).

EXCLUSION OF CIVIC MYTHS

If multicultural educators would include long-muted voices of culturally diverse persons and groups, they adamantly would exclude from the curriculum distorted, biased, or otherwise inaccurate treatments that mask inequities and falsely glorify heroes in the history of democracy in the United States. Banks (1997) argued:

> In a democratic curriculum, students need to be taught about and have opportunities to acquire American democratic values while at the same time learning about American realities that challenge these ideals, such as discrimination based on race, gender, and social class.... [B]y emphasizing ways in which American history had actualized American democratic ideals—as we have often done in the past—students are likely to conclude that we have already attained these ideals and that, consequently, little work is needed to maintain a just and democratic society. (p. 9)

The tendency toward civic mythmaking—unwarranted "heroification" and glossed-over inequities suffered by various disadvantaged groups—is thoroughly documented in many content analyses of widely used civics and history textbooks. *Lies My Teacher Told Me: Everything Your American History Textbook*

Got Wrong is full of striking examples of distortions and omissions in best-selling textbooks that falsify the story of American democracy through one-sided emphasis on glorious achievements (Loewen, 1995).

A particular target of multicultural opponents of civic mythmaking and proponents of a transformed civic education is typical textbook treatment of the American founding era, 1760–1800, when fundamental principles of government were established. Most multicultural educators laud the founding documents and civic principles and values embedded in them (Banks, 1997; Ladson-Billings, 1992). But they fault instructional guides and textbooks for being insufficiently critical of shortcomings in the institutions and actions of the founders. J. Banks and C. A. M. Banks (1995), for instance, charged the founders with denial of rights and privileges of citizenship to African Americans, indigenous peoples of America, and women, and thereby contradiction of the grand civic ideals of the founding documents. "One of its [multicultural education] major aims is to actualize for all the ideals that the founding fathers intended for only an elite few at the nation's birth" (p. xi). According to multicultural educators, such unpalatable facts must be emphasized if the civic mission of the schools would be true to its democratic ideals.

Multicultural educators assert that traditional civic myths in the curriculum of schools have been used to foster "Americanization" or assimilation of diverse racial and cultural groups in the United States to monocultural unity. They claim, however, that assimilation has been falsely overemphasized to mask the persistent and growing cultural pluralism in the United States. Further, they equate the growth of social and cultural diversity with the growth of democracy. Thus, they denigrate civic education in support of assimilation as outmoded and antidemocratic (Bennett, 1995, pp. 84–86; Pai & Adler, 1997, pp. 61–66).

PRESERVATION OF MINORITY GROUP IDENTITIES AND CULTURES

Multicultural educators believe that equitable treatment of diverse minority groups involves more than tolerance of differences. It also requires respect and security for the rights of minority groups to maintain their members and sustain their cultural integrity. Thus, multicultural educators tend to promote protected and preserved identities for certain minority cultural or racial groups in the United States. And they advocate teaching and learning in schools that favors particular rights and privileges for certain minority groups (L. Davidman & P. T. Davidman, 1997, pp. 13–27).

Multicultural educators reject the "melting pot" symbol of American unity and favor maintenance of official group identities, such as African American, Hispanic, Asian American, and Native American (Hollinger, 1995, pp. 19–49; Ueda, 1994, pp. 137–144). They use the stained glass window, tapestry, and mosaic to project images of cultural pluralism in opposition to the monocultural tendencies of the traditional civic mission of schools (Bennett, 1995, p. 86).

Ueda (1994) described how multicultural education in schools has begun to transform the traditional civic mission toward the preservationist goal of cultural pluralism:

> Whereas schools for most of the twentieth century endeavored to build a supra-ethnic identity, in the late twentieth century schools gave priority to the preservation and inculcation of group identities and cultures. The schools still taught about the shared values that underlay American national identity, but they also cultivated alternative identities and cultures. (pp. 140–141)

PROMOTION OF CULTURAL DEMOCRACY

Advocacy for preservation of cultural pluralism and group rights, at the center of the multicultural mission in schools, leads directly to civic education for cultural democracy. Banks (1997) pointed out that "a central tenet of cultural democracy is that individuals and groups must have cultural freedom in a democratic nation-state, just as they have political freedom" (p. 123).

Current conceptions of cultural democracy are anchored in the work of early 20th-century cultural pluralists. Kallen (1924), a precursor of current multiculturalist thought, was the most influential and articulate of these early opponents of the melting pot and monocultural unity. He urged preservation of cultural groups and viewed the United States as a "federation of cultures"—a cultural democracy composed of unmeltable ethnic groups:

> The outlines of a great and truly democratic commonwealth become discernible. Its form is that of the federal republic; its substance a democracy of nationalities, cooperating voluntarily and autonomously in the enterprise of self-realization through the perfection of men according to their kind.... The political and economic life of the commonwealth is ... the foundation and background for the realization of the distinctive individuality of each *nation* that composes it.... Thus "American civilization" may come to mean ... a multiplicity in a unity, an orchestration of mankind. (p. 124)

Kallen believed that ancestry is destiny, that people's genetic inheritance determines their fundamental behavioral characteristics or culture. He asserted, "What is unalienable in the life of mankind is its ... psycho-physical inheritance. Men ... cannot change their grandfathers.... The selfhood which is inalienable in them ... is ancestrally determined, and the happiness which they pursue has its form implied in ancestral endowment. This is what, actually, democracy in operation assumes" (Kallen, 1924, pp. 122–123).

Kallen believed that certain human differences are immutable and that all human beings are not fundamentally alike and potentially transformable in their ethnic identities and cultures. Thus, basic human differences could not dissolve in any "melting pot." Rather, they must be identified, protected, and perpetuated (Higham, 1984, pp. 200–214). According to Hollinger (1995), Kallen's doctrine "of enduring ethno-racial groups located him at the proto-separatist extreme of cultural pluralism" (p. 93).

Kallen portended key ideas of late 20th-century multicultural educators. They currently recommend that their idea of cultural democracy, an expansive adaptation of Kallen's concept to fit contemporary conditions and agendas, should be infused into the civic mission of schools (Banks, 1997, pp. 122–139; Parker, 1996b, pp. 192–206). Thus, multicultural education would be a means to "empowerment" for groups long oppressed or marginalized. Unless this happens, they contend, the civic mission of schools will not attend fully to the goals of democracy, which they link to rights for diverse minority groups to preserve and promote their cultures and to receive public resources based on group identity.

AN APPRAISAL OF MULTICULTURAL CHALLENGES

Many indicators point to the success of multicultural challenges of the civic mission of schools: professional association proclamations in support of multicultural education, courses on multicultural education that professional schools of education require for the certification of teachers, state curriculum frameworks and guides that emphasize cultural diversity in terms of the multicultural education agenda, and the many programs of professional association meetings that feature prominent multicultural educators in discussions of the trends and issues of their burgeoning academic field. The central theme of the 1998 meeting of the American Educational Research Association—"Diversity and Citizenship in Multicultural Societies"—is further evidence of the high status of multicultural education among professional educators.

In the title of his latest and hottest book, Glazer (1997) proclaimed that *We Are All Multiculturalists Now*. "Multiculturalism of some kind there is, and there will be. The fight is over how much, what kind, for whom, at what ages, under what standards" (p. 19). In his acknowledgment of multiculturalism's success in the education establishment, Glazer raised a disturbing question: "Will multiculturalism undermine what is still, on balance, a success in world history, a diverse society that continues to welcome further diversity, with a distinctive and common culture of some merit?" (p. 20).

Critics of multiculturalism and multicultural education have sounded alarms in response to disturbing questions like that raised by Glazer. Consider the following titles published during the 1990s that criticize various aspects of multiculturalism and multicultural education in the United States: *The Disuniting of America: Reflections on a Multicultural Society* (Schlesinger, 1992); *The Twilight of Common Dreams: Why America Is Wracked by Culture Wars* (Gitlin, 1995); *Postethnic America: Beyond Multiculturalism* (Hollinger, 1995); *The Menace of Multiculturalism* (Schmidt, 1997); *Against the Multicultural Agenda*

(Webster, 1997); *One Nation Indivisible: How Ethnic Separatism Threatens America* (Wilkinson, 1997); *The Unmaking of Americans: How Multiculturalism Has Undermined America's Assimilation Ethic* (Miller, 1998); and *Losing Our Language: How Multicultural Classroom Instruction Is Undermining Our Children's Ability to Read, Write, and Reason* (Stotsky, 1999). Three of these books are written by prominent scholars of long-standing orientation toward the political left (Gitlin, 1995; Hollinger, 1995; Schlesinger, 1992), who usually have been associated with progressive or liberal causes. The misgivings of these scholars and like-minded colleagues about certain elements of the multicultural agenda are "red flags" in the pathway of multicultural challenges of the civic mission of schools.

What strengths and weaknesses of the multicultural mission in schools are revealed by the literature of scholarly criticism? What elements of the multicultural education literature should be incorporated into the civic mission of schools? And which elements should be rejected? The following responses to these questions are directed to the needs of elementary and secondary school educators in their roles as developers of curriculum and deliverers of instruction. Thus, they might be assisted in screening the multicultural education literature to sort sense from nonsense, the warranted from the unjustified or insupportable statements and viewpoints. The following appraisal of the literature of multicultural education pertains to three categories: conceptions of culture, democracy, and identity; treatments of diversity and unity; and pursuit of inclusion and recognition.

CONCEPTIONS OF CULTURE, DEMOCRACY, AND IDENTITY

Multicultural educators profess support for the fundamental principles and values of U.S. democracy, such as freedom, equality, and popular sovereignty. They especially emphasize freedom and fault traditional civic education for inadequate treatment of this core value of democracy (L. Davidman & P. T. Davidman, 1997, p. 49). "The goal of multicultural education in the broader sense is an education for freedom" (Banks, 1994, p. 6).

Some conceptions of culture and identity in the literature of multicultural education, however, are less compatible than others with the democratic value of freedom. For example, Kallen's conception of cultural pluralism, in its deterministic implications for personal identity, is inimical to individual freedom of choice. When Kallen (1924) asserted that "Jews or Poles or Anglo-Saxons, in order to cease being Jews or Poles or Anglo-Saxons, would have to cease to be," he implied cultural determinism as an inhibiter of personal freedom to choose or modify a person's identity (pp. 122–123). Later he wrote "that people are irreducibly different from one another and that this difference is an inalienable right" (Kallen, 1971, p. 147).

Kallen and other current multicultural educators in agreement with him practically reify the idea of culture as if it were an immutable entity beyond their power to modify. For example, "Ethnicity and culture are key determinants of individuality" (Gay, 1994, p. 80). Certainly these factors influence individuality, but if they determine it, then individuals' degrees of freedom to choose, develop, or modify their identity and personality are grossly diminished or nonexistent.

Other examples of determinism in the literature of multicultural education pertain to the confounding of culture and race, which is revealed in such expressions as "Black Culture" or "White Culture." These terms, which suggest that biological inheritance determines culture and behavior, appear in highly regarded publications of multicultural educators (Bennett, 1995; Howard, 1996; Sleeter, 1995). This kind of conflation of race and culture was typically expressed in 19th- and early 20th-century publications by White supremacists such as Arthur de Gobineau and Madison Grant (Herman, 1997, pp. 45–75; Higham, 1963, pp. 156–157). However, social scientists of the 20th century clearly and compellingly have rejected the reactionary view that human behavior is determined by a person's "race" (Cohen, 1998, pp. 11–59). "In its most general sense within the social sciences, culture refers to the socially inherited body of learning characteristic of human societies" (D'Andrade, 1996, p. 161). And Harris (1999) pointed out that "a culture is the socially learned ways of living found in human societies" (p. 19). Culture has nothing to do with "race"—an idea totally discredited by biological scientists (Rex, 1993, pp. 536–530).

Biologists and social scientists concur, "Culture is not directly associated with race; men of different biological stocks participate in the same culture, men of the same biological stock have different cultures" (Berelson & Steiner, 1964, p. 648). So, as Huggins wrote, "An Afro-American and the grandson of a Polish immigrant will be able to take more for granted between themselves than the former could with a Nigerian or the latter with a Warsaw worker" (Schlesinger, 1992, p. 87). Appiah (1998), the Ghanaian-born philosopher at Harvard, rejected the racially determined concept of culture "because it proposes as a basis for common action the illusion that black (and white and yellow) people are fundamentally allied by nature" (p. 41). And Higham warned that "multiculturalists in general see group identities as fixed and in that way they can resemble racists" (Hackney, 1994, p. 8).

Deterministic expressions about cultural pluralism and human behavior, especially those that confound the concepts of race and culture, deserve rejection by designers of curriculum and instruction for elementary and secondary schools. They contradict consensual knowledge among biologists and social scientists and civic traditions of freedom in the United States. And they can be detrimental to individual rights by unyieldingly elevating cultural group identity, continuity, and solidarity above and beyond the various needs and interests of group members.

Some prominent, current multicultural and democratic educators recognize and criticize deterministic thinking among colleagues. Parker (1996a), for example, warned that the "identity politics that inevitably comes with pluralism" sometimes brings about "a new politics of excessive group-interest" that is inimical to democracy. He also argued against conceptions of culture and identity "that would make group identity into something natural, etched in primordial stone. Not only are ethnic identities not inborn, they are circumstantial and even voluntary to some extent" (p. 119). These are worthy criticisms and warnings by an advocate of cultural pluralism and democracy against unworthy ideas of some colleagues.

The individual's right to liberty has been an overarching principle and aspiration of most Americans from the founding of the republic until today. This right to liberty includes people's freedom to choose, within broad natural and physical limits, who they are or might become. Any conception of personal or group identity in the United States that threatens this basic liberty opposes deeply rooted civic traditions and public opinions that favor fluidity and free choice against any kind of determinism or coercion. This sentiment against an illiberal cultural determinism in the education of Americans is expressed emphatically by Elshtain (1995): "My democratic dream was nurtured by a presumption that none of us is stuck inside our own skins; our identities and ideas are not reducible to our membership in a race, or ethnic group, or a sex.... [E]ducation is about opening the world up, not imprisoning us in terms of race, gender, or ethnicity" (pp. 85–86).

Another questionable idea in the multicultural education literature is cultural democracy. Expressed originally by Kallen and repeated currently in a modified form by prominent multicultural advocates, it implies cultural group rights and privileges. Parker (1996a), for example, presented his conception of cultural pluralism and democracy in response to debates about what *e pluribus unum* should mean. To him, this American motto "means the political one alongside the cultural many," rather than cultural diversity within an overriding civic and political unity (p. 121). To Parker (1996a), this formulation represented "advanced ideas about democracy" and required commitment to some type of protected and preserved autonomy for many separate ethnic and cultural groups within the United States (pp. 105–125). Would it also require subordination of an overarching American national identity and culture to the primacy of multicultural identities?

Parker's "advanced ideas" promote cultural democracy with its stress on group rights. He also recognized the importance of traditional individual rights at the core of liberal democracy. But can these two types of rights easily coexist? In inevitable cases of conflict between them, would group rights tend to trump individual rights and thereby raise cultural democracy above liberal democracy? If so, would the freedom of individuals to choose or shape their identities be diminished or foreclosed in favor of group-based ancestral claims on them, treated as if they were immutable or "etched in stone"? Is the concept of cultural democracy, which in certain instances may promote a group's rights to the detriment of an individual's rights, a compelling guide to the future of the United States?

Many multicultural educators would respond to these questions with a strong preference for group rights. If so, they are likely to ignore or dismiss a compelling reason for the primacy of individual rights, which is the possibility of extensive variations in attitudes and behavior among the individuals of a group. For example, variations within some so-called cultural groups (e.g., Hispanics, Asian Americans, African Americans, or Native Americans) are large. Sometimes they are even larger or more significant than differences between cultural groups, which may prevent a group from adequately representing the interests or protecting the rights of individuals within it. The dignity and worth of each person, a primary principle of the U.S. civic tradition, will be at risk unless the individual, and not the group, is the fundamental unit of analysis and concern with regard to human rights.

A final weakness of the cultural democracy concept is its flawed assumptions about the type and extent of cultural diversity in society, which suggest that no country in the world is more multicultural than the United States. However, India, Russia, South Africa, and Nigeria are much more multicultural than the United States by such criteria as the number and variety of extensively and enduringly used primary languages and long-standing, territorially based ethnic identities. Both the federal republics of India and Russia, furthermore, are federations of national or cultural groups, which occupy distinct territories that historically have been their own. Some multiculturalists might wish to reconstruct radically the United States into a federation or union of many cultures or nations with inviolable group rights, but this country neither is nor has been such a multicultural or multinational federation.

Educators who adhere to scholarly standards of accuracy must reject certain statements in the multicultural literature, which if applied to curriculum development and classroom instruction would lead to gross distortions of reality. And educators with firm commitments to certain values in the U.S. civic tradition, such as the worth and dignity of each person and the right of individuals to choose or modify their identities as freely as possible, must be wary of curricular prescriptions that contradict these values.

TREATMENTS OF DIVERSITY AND UNITY

The persistent claim of multicultural educators that the United States is the most multicultural country in the world is used to buttress their opposition to assimilation and its melting pot metaphor. They would teach students in U.S. history and civics courses that assimilation is a declining phenomenon, and its demise is desirable.

Does the evidence support claims of multicultural educators about the decline and likely demise of assimilation and any kind of national cultural unity? "No," is the recent answer of prominent sociologists and social historians (Alba, 1990; Glazer, 1998; Higham, 1993; Lieberson & Waters, 1988; Ueda, 1994; Waters, 1998). They marshal data persuasively to conclude that the process of assimilation continues to be a dynamic force for the integration of culturally different minorities into an American civic life and national culture. "Assimilation, properly understood, is neither a dead hope nor a demeaning concept" (Glazer, 1998, p. 16).

Most citizens of the United States today see themselves primarily as Americans and only secondarily, if at all, as something else. In answer to the question in the national census about one's ancestry, millions of Americans express "multiple ancestries" (Glazer, 1998, p. 33). Their ancestry is too mixed and/or remote from "old world" antecedents to sustain any sense of ethnic or national identity other than identification with the United States. If pressed to find their "roots," most people in the United States would discover two or more ethnic strains in their ancestry. Such mixtures may lead to identification primarily as an "American" (Alba, 1990, p. 315; Lieberson & Waters, 1988, p. 45; Miller, 1998, pp. 142–146; Waters, 1998, pp. 43–44).

Ethnic mixture or amalgamation, which yields a mixed or an American identity, results from intermarriages. Sowell (1981) reported, "More than half of all marriages of Americans of German, Irish, British, or Polish ancestry are with people of different ethnicity, and Italian and Japanese Americans are not far behind" (pp. 286–287). The rates of intermarriage among all European ethnic groups have been very high during the 1980s and 1990s. Today, most non-Hispanic Whites born in the United States are of mixed ancestry (Miller, 1998, p. 143). Hispanic intermarriage rates are also significant. In 1990, for example, it was 28% for marriages involving Mexican Americans, 35% for Puerto Ricans, 26% for Cubans, and 44% for marriages involving other Hispanic groups (Miller, 1998, p. 144). Interracial marriages and thus mixed race children, too, have increased greatly, although the percentage of Black–White marriages is still minuscule in comparison to the overall rate of intermarriages (Glazer, 1998, p. 33; Hollinger, 1995, p. 166; Lieberson & Waters, 1988, p. 182; Waters, 1998, pp. 32–39). However, in 1990, the interracial marriage rate for Asian Americans was 30%. And today 50% of Japanese Americans marry someone outside their ethnic group (Miller, 1998, p. 144).

According to Waters (1998), "The increasing intermarriage rates reported here are the result of the success of American pluralism." She concluded that "we are facing a situation where growing numbers of Americans no longer fit the categories we currently use to define Americans." And boundaries between groups are becoming "much more permeable" (p. 44).

There is little doubt, when referring to the evidence, that 20th-century trends on interethnic and interracial marriages have blurred and broken down group differences in favor of a more mixed or unified American identity. Further, Higham (1993) used the evidence on intermarriage and ethnic identity to conclude, "Americans are a people molded by processes of assimilation. An adequate theory of American culture will have to address the reality of assimilation as well as the persistence of differences" (p. 209).

Assimilation in the United States tends to be a reciprocal process involving many culturally diverse groups, which produces a fluid, dynamic, compound national culture. The Northern and Western European component of this unfinished, evolving American national culture (especially the Anglo-Saxon strain) is and will be very significant. But the complex and multifaceted American national culture and identity neither was nor is the product of only one heritage representing a single civilization or region of the world. Rather, Ueda (1994) concluded, "A world melting pot is forming in the United States in which the question 'whose identity and culture?' is increasingly irrelevant" (p. 153). It is relevant, however, to recognize the continuing reality of assimilation, reciprocal and otherwise, and the increasingly inclusive American national culture and identity that it synthetically produces. "In the sharing of our varied stories," said Takaki (1998), "we can create a community of 'a larger memory'" (p. 353).

Glazer (1998) argued from compelling evidence that assimilation is "still the most powerful force affecting the ethnic and racial elements of the United States" (p. 33). The process may be different today from what it was during the early years of the 20th century, especially in its growing reciprocity and inclusiveness, but it still affects, more or less strongly, many different persons and groups. Some persons and groups in the United States freely reject or resist assimilation and responsibly accept the particularistic consequences of their choice. People have this freedom in an open society. They also have the freedom to seek and accept assimilation to a larger community, which most people in the United States have done, some more than others. Both assimilation to a common American culture and ethnic group cohesion are recognized as worthy goals, which different individuals will freely choose in different degrees. Thus, it is misleading and miseducative for multicultural educators to claim in their proposals and materials for curriculum and instruction in schools that assimilation is dead or undesirable. Clearly, assimilation is not defunct and its desirability should be open to debate and inquiry in classrooms and public forums.

Glazer (1998) explained the reluctance among multicultural educators and their supporters to recognize the continuing reality in the United States of assimilation and its melting pot metaphor. "Our problem in recognizing this has to do with one great failure of assimilation in American life, the incorporation of the African American, a failure that has led in its turn to a more general counterattack on the ideology of assimilation" (p. 16). Hollinger (1998) concurred with Glazer about "America's national failure to act on its universalist aspirations" about equality and rights, especially in regard to Black Americans. Nonetheless, based on current evidence and trends, he predicted a postethnic future in which individual Americans will be "as free as possible from the consequences of social distinctions visited upon them by others" (pp. 47–48).

PURSUIT OF INCLUSION AND RECOGNITION

Taylor explained that multiculturalism, whether advanced by African Americans or other advocates, is primarily about the "politics of recognition." According to Taylor (1994):

The thesis is that our identity is partly shaped by recognition or its absence ... and so a person or group of people can suffer real damage, real distortion, if the people or society around them mirror back to them a confining or demeaning or contemptible picture of themselves. Nonrecognition or misrecognition can inflict harm, can be a form of oppression, imprisoning someone in a false, distorted, and reduced mode of being. (p. 25)

The multicultural movement for accurate inclusion and recognition in the school curriculum of previously ignored or marginalized groups is justified aptly by Taylor. Further warrants for this kind of inclusive recognition of persons and groups can be found in the civic culture of the United States, which stresses respect for minority rights. Civic education certainly is flawed if it fails to promote tolerance of differences that contributes to recognition and respect for the rights of everyone. Finally, it is plausible that emphatic expressions of recognition and respect for different cultural and racial groups in the school curriculum will decrease social and political alienation among these groups and increase positive identification with the American civic culture.

These justifiable accolades for the educational strategy of "inclusion and recognition" should, however, be accompanied by a warning against overzealous pursuit of this good idea. Promotion through curriculum and instruction in schools of inaccurate, biased, or otherwise unwarranted statements about persons or groups is wrong, regardless of the benign motives that may have impelled this effort. Certainly, inclusion in the curriculum of a multicultural mythology is just as objectionable as the civic mythology and "heroification" decried by multicultural educators. In the interest of sound civic education, it must be avoided.

Regrettably, however, careless and uncritical pursuit of inclusion and recognition of certain cultural groups has produced some notable errors and distortions of reality in textbooks and instructional guides used extensively in schools. Three representative examples are presented to alert educators in elementary and secondary schools to the ever-present need for critical vigilance in their evaluation and adoption of curricular materials for use by students. These examples are not presented to discredit the potentially worthy goal of accurate, warranted inclusion and recognition in the school curriculum of women and different minority groups in the United States. Rather, the following three examples are presented as representative of a general problem in the literature of multicultural education, which should be noted and fixed.

The first example pertains to hypotheses of archeologists about the original peopling of ancient America that occurred thousands of years ago. The standard explanation is that nomads from Siberia crossed the "Bering land bridge" into the part of North America known as Alaska. From these long-ago beginnings, groups of wanderers eventually spread to all parts of the continent. Abundant evidence to support this hypothesis is synthesized cogently in *The Great Journey: The Peopling of Ancient America*, a book favorably reviewed by scholars (Fagan, 1987). Recent archeological investigations, however, have uncovered concrete evidence for new, alternative hypotheses about various avenues of entry into North and South America along the Pacific coastlines of these continents, which may have occurred thousands of years before the far northern migration into Alaska. Thus, the "Bering land bridge" theory appears to be one of a few tenable explanations about when, where, and how the Americas originally were populated (Petit, 1998).

Disregarding the evidence, some prominent multicultural educators reject the archeology-based migration theories in favor of an explanation presumably more sensitive to the feelings of today's descendants of the indigenous peoples of the United States. For example, the following commentary appears in a leading textbook on multicultural education used by undergraduate students in teacher education programs throughout the United States:

> What is the native perspective that should become part of the revised curriculum? The Bering Straits migration theory should be treated with great skepticism since there is absolutely no evidence (except logic) to support it. Indian people generally believe that they evolved or were created in the Americas. This viewpoint should be respected although it is acceptable to discuss the possibility of migration as an alternative explanation. The point is that there is no empirical evidence to support any particular migration theory. (Bennett, 1995, p. 307)

On the contrary, the point is that integrity and veracity in education require recognition and serious study of credible theories and empirical evidence offered by experts, not facile dismissal of them.

A second notable example of overzealous pursuit of inclusion and recognition pertains to textbook treatments of African Americans. It certainly is good that African Americans are more inclusively and accurately presented in textbooks today. But it is miseducative and wrong for textbook publishers to inaccurately glorify African Americans. Yet this kind of multicultural mythmaking occurs in schools. Consider the following example about treatments of Crispus Attucks in widely used secondary school U.S. history textbooks.

Franklin reported that Crispus Attucks was a fugitive slave living freely in Boston when he died in the "Boston Massacre"—one of five American men shot and martyred by British troops in an event that presaged the American Revolution (Franklin & Moss, 1988, pp. 65–66). The names of the other martyrs to the Revolution are not commonly known. But Attucks, who also was a little-known figure, has emerged in textbooks of the late 20th-century as a "bonafide hero" of the founding era. Examination of several secondary school U.S. history textbooks reveals that Attucks, once a rather obscure person, is treated more extensively than many others whose accomplishments were vastly more significant in the causes, conduct, and consequences of the War of Independence (Lerner, Nagai, & Rothman, 1995, pp. 81–84).

A concluding factual note on the relative significance of Crispus Attucks in the American Revolution is that his name does not appear in such well-researched reference works on persons in American history as the *Dictionary of American Biography*, the *Oxford Companion to American History*, and the *Concise Dictionary of American History*. The *Reader's Companion to American History* includes one very brief mention of Attucks within the entry on the Boston Massacre: "Among the victims was Crispus Attucks, a man of black or Indian heritage" (Foner & Garraty, 1991, p. 124). Does this meager historical record justify the "heroification" of Attucks? Has it happened only in excessive pursuit of the new multicultural mission of schools?

A third example of a suspect or fraudulent interpretation of history by multicultural educators concerns the Iroquois Confederation. This highly creative and effective political structure brought commendable unity to the governance of the five nations of indigenous peoples that founded it.

The Iroquois Confederation was discussed admiringly, if briefly, at the Albany Congress in 1754, when representatives of seven colonies of British North Americans met to discuss unified action for their mutual defense after the outbreak of war between Britain and France. Benjamin Franklin, the leading representative of Pennsylvania, proposed the Albany Plan of Union, a confederation of colonies under the British Crown. In his unsuccessful attempt to win formal approval of his plan, Franklin pointed approvingly to the Iroquois Confederation and challenged his colleagues to do as well as the Iroquois peoples had done in providing politically for their mutual defense and well-being.

Franklin's dream of confederal unity among the British American colonies became reality eventually through the Continental Congress that represented the United States during the War of Independence against the British. Franklin's Albany Plan of Union influenced the new nation's first constitution, the Articles of Confederation. And remember that in his original advocacy of the Albany Plan of Union, Franklin spoke admiringly of the Iroquois Confederation. Does this justify current proposals by multicultural educators to teach students that the federal government framed by Americans in 1787 was heavily influenced by the Iroquois peoples and their confederation?

Consider this claim in a recently published book on multicultural education:

> Most Americans are aware of the fact that our United States government was based on the English view of rights derived from the Magna Carta and the eighteenth-century political philosophy of natural rights, but the form of our government may, in fact, also be modeled after an alliance of tribes that had been formed by a group of Native Americans before the Europeans landed in the Western Hemisphere. This alliance, known as the *Iroquois Confederation*, was based on the idea of cooperation among diverse nations.... (Timm, 1996, p. 19)

Another example from a prominent multicultural education publication more strongly and broadly claims that indigenous peoples of North America influenced the design of the U.S. Constitution and federal government:

> Native peoples, particularly those who lived in the northeastern part of the continent, provided the model for many aspects of American democracy that differed from what was known in Europe: a federal system of government, the separation of civil from military authorities, the concept of impeachment, admission of new territories as states ... the caucus, an egalitarianism that disallowed slavery, and a political voice for women. Most of this has been left out of the history books, which is typical of the fate of a colonized people. (Bennett, 1995, p. 91)

"Most of this has been left out of the history books," it might be argued, because it is false. And the few curricular materials that have included this kind of misinformation deserve scholarly criticism and condemnation, not praise.

The Iroquois Confederation is a worthy achievement on its own terms and within its own context. Its worth does not depend on claims that it influenced the form and function of constitutional government in the United States. These claims, however, appear to have little or no validity. For example, Tooker (1994) concluded her study of "The United States Constitution and the Iroquois League" with this disclaimer: "The evidence presently available, then, offers little support for the notion that the framers of the Constitution borrowed from the Iroquois ideas respecting the proper form of government, ideas that were, in fact, radically different from those familiar in Western civilization that were subsequently incorporated into the Constitution" (p. 115). Further, the four-volume *Encyclopedia of the American Constitution*, an authoritative work of scholarship by the world's leading experts on U.S. government, includes no mention of the Iroquois Confederation (Levy, Karst, & Mahoney, 1986). One will search in vain among the works of prominent founding-era scholars (e.g., Bernard Bailyn, Pauline Maier, Forrest McDonald, Gordon Wood, etc.) for any discussion of the supposed impact of the Iroquois Confederation or other political ideas of the indigenous peoples of the United States on the federal republic and U.S. Constitution.

Hertzberg (1966), an authority on the culture of the Iroquois, made no claims for the influence of the Iroquois Confederation on the U.S. federal government. Rather, she offered these words of caution:

> We know a great deal about the political organization of the Confederacy, from both Iroquois sources and the accounts of observers. But in seeking to describe its form and functioning, it is important to use our own political terms carefully so that we do not transfer our meanings to theirs and thus distort the facts. For example, while the Confederacy was representative government, its method of decision-making was different from ours, being based not on a majority but on unanimity. (p. 109)

Confirmed knowledge of the Iroquois Confederation indicates that it was more like the ill-fated Articles of Confederation than the Constitution of 1787, which according to both its supporters and critics in the ratification debates of 1787–1788 offered a brand new or unprecedented concept of federalism. When reasoning by analogy, it is clear that the logical connection of the Iroquois Confederation is to the Articles of Confederation (hardly a concept of federalism that "differed from what was known in Europe") and not to the 1787 U.S. Constitution.

Once more, it is important to laud multicultural educators for their efforts to include and recognize in the school curriculum notable achievements of minority groups, especially groups previously ignored or stereotyped. It is equally important, however, to evaluate carefully these well-intentioned proposals for inclusion and recognition to prevent the miseducation of students that results from inaccurate information or unwarranted interpretations of people, ideas, and events in history.

CURRICULAR RESPONSES TO MULTICULTURAL CHALLENGES

Civic education unmodified by multicultural education is flawed in its failure to recognize and respect cultural diversity and dissent by various minorities in response to civic injustices. In the absence of multicultural challenges, lessons in civics typically have glossed over maltreatment of minorities and glorified the deeds of some Americans while neglecting or even denigrating the positive contributions of "others." Civic education is undemocratic, unjust, and untrue when it disdains or disrespects the participation and achievements of women and minority groups in the common history and culture of the United States.

Gutmann (1996) proposed a multicultural remedy to some unacceptable traditions in civic education. She would teach students "to understand and appreciate the social contributions and life experiences of the various groups that constitute society. Such understanding and appreciation define one common conception of multicultural education, a conception compatible with the principles of democratic education" (p. 158).

Gutmann recognized appropriately that not all conceptions of multicultural education are equal in merit or fit with principles of democracy at the center of the school's civic mission. Certain multicultural challenges of the civic mission of schools are unwarranted and thereby deserve rejection by curriculum developers and teachers, as revealed by the preceding discussion in this chapter. Other challenges, however, as noted by Gutmann, are warranted and should be accepted into the core curriculum. Civic education can only be improved by incorporation of the following elements of multicultural education:

> Accurate inclusion and recognition in the school curriculum of long-neglected or negatively stereotyped minority groups who have contributed significantly to U.S. history and civic life.

Warranted curricular emphasis on cultural diversity in conjunction with civic unity in the past and present of the United States.

Inquiry by students on discrepancies between civic ideals and realities and efforts, both successful and failed, to narrow the gap that has separated the promises from the practices of civic life.

Affirmation of core principles of U.S. constitutional democracy that constitute a unifying civic culture for a culturally diverse society.

The preceding list is a coherent educational agenda for conjoining multiculturalism with civism (i.e., the principles and practices of democratic citizenship) in the mission of American schools. The primary curricular response should be practical integration of these compatible elements of multiculturalism and civism in the core curriculum, the common lessons required of all students in elementary and secondary schools.

CONJOINING MULTICULTURALISM AND CIVISM IN THE CORE CURRICULUM

A necessary characteristic of education for democratic citizenship is a common core of knowledge, cognitive processes, and attitudes, which all students are expected to learn regardless of their race, ethnicity, gender, socioeconomic class, or vocational prospects. In a country distinguished by its social and cultural diversity, such as the United States, a core curriculum serves the civic mission of schools by fostering reasoned, knowledge-based commitment among all citizens, regardless of differences, to fundamental principles, values, practices, and dispositions of constitutional democracy. This body of basic ideas on democratic citizenship is embedded in the founding documents and in documents of subsequent periods of U.S. history that stem directly from the principles and issues of late 18th-century seedbed of constitutional democracy (Center for Civic Education, 1995, 1997). The pedagogical problem is to select a few of the very best documents available, and to organize them effectively for teaching and learning in the classroom.

A worthy list of core documents on democracy suitable for the core curriculum certainly includes the traditional texts of the founding era, such as the Declaration of Independence, the Constitution, the Federalist Papers, and the Antifederalist Papers (Patrick, 1995). But it also includes pieces by women, African Americans, indigenous peoples, and others that broaden a student's understanding of multiple perspectives and interpretations of key founding-era events. A few examples of nontraditional founding-era documents worthy of inclusion in the core curriculum are a petition against slavery to the General Court of Massachusetts by free African Americans, 1777, which used principles of the Declaration of Independence in arguments for freedom; a letter from three Seneca leaders to President

Washington, 1790, which expressed critical opinions about the effects of the American Revolution on indigenous peoples; letters exchanged by Abigail Adams and Mercy Otis Warren on political and social issues of the 1770s; a sermon against slavery by the Reverend James Dana, 1791; and a letter to Thomas Jefferson from Benjamin Banneker, 1791, which included discussion of severe discrepancies between civic ideals of the American Revolution and the condition of Black people in the United States (Patrick, 1995, pp. 73–107).

Ideas and controversies about constitutional democracy and the rights and responsibilities of citizenship, rooted in the founding era, have permeated U.S. history from the 1770s through the 1990s. Thus, documents in subsequent periods of the country's history, which fit the American civic tradition, should be part of the core curriculum. And they should reflect various voices, diverse perspectives, and multiple interpretations of fundamental ideas, issues, and events in the development of American constitutional democracy (Patrick, 1996, pp. 98–99). A few illustrative examples of the kinds of documents subsequent to the founding era that might be included in the core curriculum are the Declaration of Sentiments and Resolutions at Seneca Falls, NY, 1848; the Independence Day Speech by Frederick Douglass at Rochester, NY, 1852; the Gettysburg Address, 1863, and Second Inaugural Address, 1865, by Abraham Lincoln; the Four Freedoms Speech by Franklin D. Roosevelt, 1941; and Letter from Birmingham Jail and the I Have a Dream Speech by Martin Luther King, Jr., 1963 (Center for Civic Education, 1995, 1997).

Excerpts from certain landmark Supreme Court decisions, which apply fundamental principles of democracy to key constitutional issues, should also be included in any collection of core documents for secondary school students (Patrick, 1994). Many of these court cases involve issues of majority rule and minority rights, liberty and equality, diversity and unity, which significantly have affected the civic life of diverse individuals and groups in the United States.

A core curriculum of schools that conjoins civism and multiculturalism emphasizes diverse perspectives and interpretations of the key turning points in the history of constitutional democracy, such as the American Revolution and War of Independence, the Framing of the Constitution and Bill of Rights, the Civil War and Reconstruction, the Great Depression and New Deal, and the Civil Rights Movement. Education about these critical turning points should address both consensus and conflicts, the common ideas that have bound Americans as one nation and the controversies that have challenged their sense of national unity and community. "In sum, our national constitutional tradition is one of perpetual struggle to balance multiple competing concerns" (Massaro, 1993, p. 127). Thus, multicultural challenges and perspectives on critical issues in the past and present must be part of the civic mission of American schools if it is to remain faithful to the history of constitutional democracy in the United States.

Massaro, a professor of constitutional law, conceived a brilliant design for a core curriculum in elementary and secondary schools that conjoins civism and multiculturalism through analyses and critical appraisal of constitutional principles and issues in U.S. history. Her position on curriculum and instruction is succinctly and cogently expressed in the following quotation from her laudable publication, *Constitutional Literacy: A Core Curriculum for a Multicultural Nation* (1993):

> Any national curriculum should stress, among other things, the kind of national knowledge that will enable our children to assume the complex duties of American citizenship. This includes not only baseline literacy and historical knowledge but also a rich appreciation of our conflicts and pluralism.... Democratic life depends, in part, on having this framework, [which] should include constitutional literacy ... recognition of constitutional terms, constitutional dilemmas, and historical assumptions upon which the Constitution arguably rests ... and its multiple contested interpretations.... Any national curriculum must be true to our national experience, but "our" must be defined pluralistically. (p. 153)

In its emphatic concern with both civic unity and diversity, Massaro's core curriculum has the potential to bring multicultural challenges coherently into the civic mission of schools.

HOW TO TREAT THE FOUNDING ERA IN THE CORE CURRICULUM

Massaro's core curriculum requires emphasis on the founding of the republic, a great turning point in both U.S. history and world history with continuing significance for Americans and various peoples around the world. Curricular treatments of founding era events, personalities, and ideas, however, must be accurate, balanced, unbiased, and inclusive of various perspectives, if they would avoid the unwarranted mythmaking, "heroification," and other distortions of reality discussed in previous parts of this chapter.

In their pursuit of curricular integrity, educators in elementary and secondary schools must recognize that threats to accurate and warranted treatments of the founding era, and other historical periods or themes, may come from both unreconstructed, traditional civic educators and overzealous, ideologically driven multiculturalists. Bland, uncritical, and unrealistic portrayals of the "founding fathers" certainly are unacceptable. So are similarly flawed interpretations of founding-era people, ideas, and events put forward by multicultural educators more interested in promoting preferred social causes than sound social education.

Many prominent multicultural educators extremely and unconditionally fault the founders and their era for grievous offenses against freedom, equality, and justice in contradiction of their proclaimed ideals (Banks, 1997, pp. 3–9). Certainly, the constitutional rights guaranteed to most adult White males were not equally applicable to women, Black people, and various indigenous peoples. But it is also true that the proportion of Americans with the right to vote or otherwise participate in their governance was unparalleled in the world of the 1780s. Further, constitutional provisions for certain personal rights that are taken for granted today, such as freedom of conscience and speech, security against unwarranted seizures of property or invasions of privacy, and due process of law for persons accused of crimes, were rare or nonexistent outside the United States.

Maier (1996), a founding-era historian, advised assessing social conditions of the founding era contextually and comparatively. If so, the quality of judgments may be transformed. She explained:

> Accustomed as we are to emphasizing the continuing problems of gender and race, we are inclined to emphasize the restrictions on early republican citizenship. But against the example of the ancient world, where civic participation was limited to an elite, or indeed, compared to any other nation of the time, American citizenship was extraordinarily comprehensive and has evolved over time toward greater inclusiveness. (p. 56)

Slavery, of course, was a cruel contradiction of the founders' ideas about individual rights and dignity. But slavery in the United States, if awful, was not unique in the world of the 1780s. Pronouncements of the American founders about the universality of individual rights, however, were quite unusual, and they became irrepressible standards to which both Black and White abolitionists appealed in their successful crusade against slavery (West, 1997, pp. 1–36). Further, Lewis pointed out that although slavery was a common phenomenon in the world since ancient times, abolition of slavery was exceptional. Black and White Americans, therefore, who founded and led 19th-century abolitionist movements against slavery were doing something unusual in behalf of human freedom. Lewis (1998) revealed, "Alone among the [slaveholding peoples] of the world, West Europeans and later Americans proceeded not just to the emancipation of their slaves but to the abolition of the institution of slavery—first in their own countries, then in their colonies, finally in the rest of the world wherever peoples of European culture lived or ruled" (p. 24).

An antidote to narrow and excessively critical interpretations of the founding era are three interrelated methods of inquiry used by Maier and Lewis to reach their aforementioned conclusions: *contextual analysis*, *comparative analysis*, and *global perspectives*. If students would accurately comprehend people, events, and ideas of the founding era, then their lessons must be anchored in the social and cultural context of that time. If students would fairly assess and appraise the founding-era ideas and practices, then they should begin by comparing conditions in the United States with those of other countries at that time in various regions of the world. Some concepts of free government and citizenship of the founding era were daring and practically unique in the late 18th-century world. By today's standards, the liberty, equality, and justice of the founding era seem stunted and flawed. But by the world-class standards of their own times, the founders had broken new ground and planted new seeds for an exceptional growth and development of individual rights during the next two centuries.

Classroom studies of the founding era, which involve the educational methods of contextual and comparative analysis with a global perspective, may be used to conjoin multiculturalism and civism in the core curriculum. These methods are congruent with multicultural concerns about inclusion and recognition of culturally diverse peoples and wide-ranging perspectives. They also are compatible with the civic mission of schools to develop deep comprehension and justified acceptance of the core principles and values of constitutional democracy rooted in the founding era. These methods, however, may lead to judgments about the relative worth of particular cultures in responding more or less effectively to certain human problems and needs. This kind of transcultural judgment is anathema to some multicultural educators with extreme commitments to cultural relativism, which compels them to view all cultures as equally worthy. But an unqualified acceptance of cultural relativism is arguable and should be subject to inquiry and debate in free-wheeling, open, and democratic classrooms—the only kind compatible with the civic mission of schools rightly understood.

EDUCATION OF CITIZENS FOR FREEDOM IN THE OPEN SOCIETY

Education for citizenship in the free and open society, the genuine modern democracy, develops individuals with capacities and dispositions for critical thinking, reflective inquiry, and free choice about public issues, including controversies about cultural pluralism, assimilation, group membership, and personal identity. It favors free and open competition of ideas in public forums. It encourages a diversity of voices, a multiplicity of perspectives, in the free marketplace of democratic debate. And, it guarantees the right of individuals to choose the extent to which they and their groups will preserve traditional ways of living or seek new ones. Thus, an open society and its culture or cultures are fluid, dynamic, and changeable by the free choices of individuals. By contrast, the oppressive and closed society is static and resistant to changes in culture, group membership, and personal identity.

Civic education in the free and open society is charged with a paradoxical mission. Like its opposite, the oppressive and closed society, the open society must, if it would survive, bring about "conscious social reproduction"—the transmission of hallowed civic traditions from one generation to the next (Gutmann, 1987, pp. 34–46). Unlike the oppressive and closed society, however, it must also encourage individuals' right to freely question and criticize the traditions that are being transmitted to them. As students mature, development of their capacities for critical thinking and independent decision making should become a more prominent part of education for democratic citizenship. If so, then civic education is true to a core principle in the tradition of modern democracy, the individual's right to liberty.

Civic education in the free and open society necessarily involves both conscious social reproduction and deliberate development of personal liberty. Social reproduction is necessary to buttress social order that thwarts nihilism and anarchy, inevitable enemies of security for individual liberty. And disciplined critical thinking for choices that bring positive social change is necessary to oppose dysfunctional cultural stagnation associated with an oppressive and closed society (Magee, 1985; Popper, 1966; Shearmur, 1996, pp. 175–178).

Schools that support the free and open society through education for democratic citizenship, then, enable and encourage students to think effectively, responsibly, and independently about important personal and public issues and choices concerning the extent and significance of cultural pluralism and unity in the United States. Thus, these students will be prepared for the inescapable challenges of ongoing controversies about citizenship, identity, assimilation, and rights—about the very meaning of constitutional democracy—that Americans will confront in the 21st century.

Conclusions

From the 1770s to the 1990s, Americans have been concerned and sometimes confounded about cultural diversity, national unity, and personal identity and the civic commitments they entail. According to Cremin (1988), "Two hundred years after they had made their Revolution, Americans were still in the process of defining what it meant to be an American and hence what they were prepared to teach themselves and their children" (p. 14). In this controversial quest, Americans continue to argue about the proper treatment of civic unity and cultural diversity, civism and multiculturalism, in their educational institutions, especially elementary and secondary schools.

Americans tend to agree that civic education in schools should emphasize core civic principles and values in their country's founding documents, which sociologists have labeled "the American Creed" (Lipset, 1996, p. 31). Sociological surveys of public opinions and attitudes, from the 1950s through the 1990s, reveal strong and abiding support among most Americans for civic principles and values on which their nation was founded. In 1995, for example, 75% of a nationally representative sample of adult respondents said "they are proud to be Americans" (Lipset, 1996, p. 51). And 91% of respondents in a nationwide survey by Public Agenda said that "the United States is a better country than most other countries in the world" (Manzo, 1998, p. 5).

Attachment to civic principles and values of "the American Creed" (e.g., liberty, equality of opportunity, popular sovereignty, the rule of law, and individual rights and responsibilities) signifies an individual's Americaness. And most Americans want these commonly accepted principles and values to be included emphatically in the school curriculum. Many of these Americans also demand that their schools teach positively about cultural pluralism in the United States and recognize inclusively the contributions of diverse minorities to the common national history and culture of the United States. However, in a recent survey by Public Agenda, 89% of a nationally representative sample said that "there's too much attention paid these days to what separates different ethnic and racial groups and not enough to what they have in common" (Manzo, 1998, p. 5). By contrast, however, some extreme proponents of multicultural education would have the schools promote "a new 'cultural democracy' and even assert a 'right' to cultural diversity" (Pangle, 1998, p. 174).

Educators in U.S. elementary and secondary schools face the critical challenge of how to blend and balance the competing and sometimes conflicting curricular aims of civism and multiculturalism. Their choices collectively will shape curriculum and instruction about civic unity and multicultural diversity and thereby have a profound impact on the civic knowledge and values of the next generation of citizens.

Will these students be educated more or less effectively for democratic citizenship in a racially and culturally diverse nation? Can the civic mission of American schools be directed successfully to meet the multicultural challenges of the United States in the 21st century? Will we continue our quest to be one American nation distinguished by its capacity somehow to accommodate the complexities, ambiguities, and controversies of conjoining civic and cultural unity with multicultural diversity? The future of the American republic will turn on how well people respond as responsible citizens and civic educators to the ongoing paradoxical problem of how simultaneously and compatibly to treat civism and multiculturalism in the core curriculum of the schools and the fabric of the polity.

REFERENCES

Alba, R. D. (1990). *Ethnic identity: The transformation of white America.* New Haven, CT: Yale University Press.

Appiah, K. A. (1998). The limits of pluralism. In A. M. Melzer, J. Weinberger, & M. R. Zinman (Eds.), *Multiculturalism and American democracy* (pp. 37–54). Lawrence: University Press of Kansas.

Banks, J. A. (1994). *An introduction to multicultural education.* Boston: Allyn & Bacon.

Banks, J. A. (1997). *Educating citizens in a multicultural society.* New York: Teacher's College Press.

Banks, J. A., & Banks, C. A. M. (1995). Introduction. In J. A. Banks & C. A. McGee Banks (Eds.), *Handbook on research on multicultural education* (pp. xi–xiv). New York: Macmillan.

Bennett, C. L. (1995). *Comprehensive multicultural education: Theory and practice.* Boston: Allyn & Bacon.

Berelson, B., & Steiner, G. A. (1964). *Human behavior: An inventory of scientific findings.* New York: Harcourt, Brace & World.

Butts, R. F. (1989). *The civic mission in educational reform.* Stanford: Hoover Institution Press.

Center for Civic Education. (1994). *National standards for civics and government.* Calabasas, CA: Center for Civic Education.

Center for Civic Education. (1995). *We the People: The Citizen and the Constitution.* Calabasas, CA: Center for Civic Education.

Center for Civic Education. (1997). *American legacy: The United States Constitution and other essential documents of American democracy.* Calabasas, CA: Center for Civic Education.

Cohen, M. N. (1998). *Culture of intolerance: Chauvinism, class, and racism in the United States.* New Haven, CT: Yale University Press.

Cremin, L. A. (1988). *American education: The metropolitan experience, 1876–1980.* New York: Harper & Row.

D'Andrade, R. (1996). Culture. In A. Kuper & J. Kuper (Eds.), *The social science encyclopedia* (pp. 161–163). London: Routledge.

Davidman, L., & Davidman, P. T. (1997). *Teaching with a multicultural perspective: A practical guide.* New York: Longman.

Elshtain, J. B. (1995). *Democracy on trial.* New York: Basic Books.

Fagan, B. M. (1987). *The great journey: The peopling of ancient America.* London: Thames & Hudson.

Feinberg, W. (1998). *Common schools/uncommon identities: National unity and cultural differences.* New Haven, CT: Yale University Press.

Foner, E. F., & Garraty, J. A. (1991). *The reader's companion to American history.* Boston: Houghton Mifflin.

Franklin, J. H., & Moss, A. A., Jr. (1988). *From slavery to freedom.* New York: McGraw-Hill.

Gay, G. (1994). *At the essence of learning: Multicultural education.* West Lafayette, IN: Kappa Delta Pi.

Gitlin, T. (1995). *The twilight of common dreams: Why America is wracked by culture wars.* New York: Henry Holt.

Glazer, N. (1997). *We are all multiculturalists now.* Cambridge, MA: Harvard University Press.

Glazer, N. (1998). Is assimilation dead? In A. M. Melzer, J. Weinberger, & M. R. Zinman (Eds.), *Multiculturalism and American democracy* (pp. 15–36). Lawrence: University Press of Kansas.

Gutmann, A. (1987). *Democratic education.* Princeton, NJ: Princeton University Press.

Gutmann, A. (1996). Challenges of multiculturalism in democratic education. In R. K. Fullinwider (Ed.), *Public education in a multicultural society: Policy, theory, critique* (pp. 159–176). Cambridge, England: Cambridge University Press.

Hackney, S. (1994). A conversation with John Higham. *Humanities, 15*(1), 6–9, 40–41.

Harris, M. (1999). *Theories of culture in postmodern times.* Walnut Creek, CA: AltiMira Press.

Herman, A. (1997). *The idea of decline in western history.* New York: The Free Press.

Hertzberg, H. W. (1966). *The great tree and the longhouse: The culture of the Iroquois.* New York: Macmillan.

Higham, J. (1963). *Strangers in the land: Patterns of American nationalism.* New York: Atheneum.

Higham, J. (1984). *Send these to me: Immigrants in urban America.* Baltimore: Johns Hopkins University Press.

Higham, J. (1993). Multiculturalism and universalism. *American Quarterly, 45*(2), 197–218.

Hollinger, D. A. (1995). *Postethnic America: Beyond multiculturalism.* New York: Basic Books.

Hollinger, D. A. (1998). Postethnic America. In W. F. Katkin, N. Landsman, & A. Tyree (Eds.), *Beyond pluralism: The conception of groups and group identities in America* (pp. 47–62). Urbana: University of Illinois Press.

Howard, G. (1996). Whites in multicultural education: Rethinking our role. In J. A. Banks (Ed.), *Multicultural education, transformative knowledge, and action* (pp. 323–334). New York: Teacher's College Press.

Kallen, H. (1924). *Culture and democracy in the United States.* New York: Boni & Liveright.

Kallen, H. M. (1971). *What I believe and why—maybe: Essays for the modern world.* New York: Horizon Press.

Ladson-Billings, G. (1992). The multicultural mission: Unity and diversity. *Social Education, 56*(5), 308–311.

Landry, B. (1997). Education in a multicultural society. In P. M. Hall (Ed.), *Race, ethnicity, and multiculturalism* (pp. 41–62). New York: Garland.

Lerner, R., Nagai, A. K., & Rothman, S. (1995). *Moulding the good citizen: The politics of high school history texts.* Westport, CT: Praeger.

Levy, L. W., Karst, K. L., & Mahoney, D. J. (1986). *Encyclopedia of the American constitution.* New York: Macmillan.

Lewis, B. (1998). The historical roots of racism. *The American Scholar, 67*(1), 17–25.

Lieberson, S., & Waters, M. (1988). *From many strands: Ethnic and racial groups in contemporary America.* New York: Russell Sage Press.

Lipset, S. M. (1996). *American exceptionalism: A double-edged sword.* New York: Norton.

Loewen, J. W. (1995). *Lies my teacher told me: Everything your American history textbook got wrong.* New York: The New Press.

Magee, B. (1985). *Philosophy and the real world: An introduction to Karl Popper.* LaSalle, IL: Open Court.

Maier, P. (1996). Nationhood and citizenship: What difference did the American revolution make? In G. J. Jacobsohn & S. Dunn (Eds.), *Diversity and citizenship: Rediscovering American nationhood* (pp. 45–62). Lanham, MD: Rowman & Littlefield.

Manzo, K. K. (1998). Parents say schools should imbue patriotism, teach English. *Education Week, 18*(12), 5.

Massaro, T. M. (1993). *Constitutional literacy: A core curriculum for a multicultural nation.* Durham, NC: Duke University Press.

Miller, J. J. (1998). *The unmaking of Americans: How multiculturalism has undermined America's assimilation ethic.* New York: The Free Press.

NAEP Civics Consensus Project. (1996). *Civics framework for the 1998 national assessment of educational progress.* Washington, DC: National Assessment Governing Board.

Pai, Y. & Adler, S. A. (1997). *Cultural foundations of education.* Columbus, OH: Merrill.

Pangle, L. S. (1998). Multiculturalism and civic education. In A. M. Melzer, J. Weinberger, & M. R. Zinman (Eds.). *Multiculturalism and American democracy* (pp. 173–197). Lawrence: University Press of Kansas.

Pangle, L. S., & Pangle, T. L. (1993). *The learning of liberty: The educational ideas of the American founders.* Lawrence: University Press of Kansas.

Parker, W. C. (1996a). Advanced ideas about democracy: Toward a pluralist conception of citizen education. *Teachers College Record, 98*(1), 104–119.

Parker, W. C. (1996b). Curriculum for democracy. In R. Soder (Ed.), *Democracy, education, and the schools* (pp. 182–210). San Francisco: Jossey-Bass.

Patrick, J. J. (1994). *The young Oxford companion to the supreme court of the United States.* New York: Oxford University Press.

Patrick, J. J. (1995). *Founding the republic: A documentary history.* Westport, CT: Greenwood Press.

Patrick, J. J. (1996). Constitutionalism in education for democracy. In A. Oldenquist (Ed.), *Can democracy be taught?* (pp. 91–107). Bloomington, IN: Phi Delta Kappa.

Patrick, J. J., & White, C. S. (1992). Social studies education, secondary schools. In M. C. Alkin (Ed.), *Encyclopedia of educational research* (pp. 1236–1245). New York: Macmillan.

Petit, C. W. (1998). Rediscovering America. *U.S. News & World Report, 125*(14), 56–64.

Popper, K. R. (1966). *The open society and its enemies* (5th ed., rev.). Princeton, NJ: Princeton University Press.

Rex, J. (1993). Race. In W. Outhwaite & T. Bottomme (Eds.), *Twentieth-century social thought* (pp. 536–538). Oxford, England: Blackwell.

Schlesinger, A. M., Jr. (1992). *The disuniting of America: Reflections on a multicultural society.* New York: Norton.

Schmidt, A. J. (1997). *The menace of multiculturalism: Trojan horse in America.* Westport, CT: Praeger.

Shearmur, J. (1996). *The political thought of Karl Popper.* London: Routledge.

Sleeter, C. E. (1995). White preservice students and multicultural education coursework. In J. M. Larkin & C. E. Sleeter (Eds.), *Developing multicultural teacher education curricula* (pp. 17–29). Albany: State University of New York Press.

Sowell, T. (1981). *Ethnic America.* New York: Basic Books.

Stotsky, S. (1999). *Losing our language: How multicultural classroom instruction is undermining our children's ability to read, write, and reason.* New York: The Free Press.

Takaki, R. (1993). *A different mirror: A history of multicultural America.* Boston: Little, Brown.

Takaki, R. (1998). *A larger memory: A history of our diversity with voices.* Boston: Little, Brown.

Taylor, C. (1994). The politics of recognition. In A. Gutmann (Ed.), *Multiculturalism: Examining the politics of recognition* (pp. 25–74). Princeton, NJ: Princeton University Press.

Timm, J. T. (1996). *Four perspectives in multicultural education.* Belmont, CA: Wadsworth.

Tooker, E. (1994). The United States Constitution and the Iroquois League. In J. A. Clifton (Ed.), *The invented Indian: Cultural fictions & government policies* (pp. 107–128). New Brunswick, NJ: Transaction Publishers.

Ueda, R. (1994). *Postwar immigrant America: A social history.* Boston: St. Martin's Press.

U.S. Commission on Immigration Reform (1997). *Becoming an American: Immigration and immigrant policy.* Washington, DC: U.S. Government Printing Office.

Waters, M. C. (1998). Multiple ethnic identity choices. In W. F. Katkin, N. Landsman, & A. Tyree (Eds.), *Beyond pluralism: The conception of groups and group identities in America* (pp. 28–46). Urbana: University of Illinois Press.

Webster, Y. O. (1997). *Against the multicultural agenda: A critical thinking alternative.* Westport, CT: Praeger.

West, T. G. (1997). *Vindicating the founders: Race, sex, class, and justice in the origins of America.* Lanham, MD: Rowman & Littlefield.

Wilkinson, J. H. (1997). *One nation indivisible: How ethnic separation threatens America.* Reading, MA: Addison-Wesley.

CHAPTER 5

BEST PRACTICES IN MULTICULTURAL EDUCATION: RECOMMENDATIONS TO SCHOOL LEADERS

Carl A. Grant
Kim Wieczorek
University of Wisconsin, Madison

Compared to life at home, schools are like cross-roads, marketplaces, village squares, and cities themselves.
— *Walter C. Parker (1997)*

PICTURE THE FOLLOWING CLASS: OF ITS TOTAL OF 30 STUdents (15 girls and 15 boys), 21 are White, 5 are African American, 3 are Latinos (2 Mexican Americans and 1 Cuban American), and 1 is second-generation Asian American. Two of the African American students, 1 Latino student, and 4 White students come from families who live below the poverty line, and another 4 White students are from upper-income homes. These socioeconomic status distinctions are not readily visible, however, because most students are clad in jeans and cotton shirts or T-shirts. Nevertheless, a glance at home addresses and at the free-lunch roster suggests the students' socioeconomic status. The students' families vary widely: Whereas only 2 students come from families in which the father but not the mother works outside the home, 8 are from single-parent families (6 of which live below the poverty line), and both parents of the remaining 19 students hold or have recently held jobs (at least part-time). One is from a family with two lesbian mothers. Most of the students grew up speaking English, but 2 of the Latino students speak Spanish at home, and 1 White student speaks French at home. The students' academic skills vary widely: Two spend part of the day in an outside resource room with a teacher of students with learning disabilities, 1 is labeled with a cognitive disability and receives curricular support from the resource room teacher, 1 is in a gifted program, and 1 is in a speech therapy pull-out program.

This picture is one that can be found in many U.S. schools (National Center for Education Statistics, 1990). However, there are many other pictures in the nation's schools: classrooms in rural communities where recent immigrants from Southeast Asia and Mexico are just now entering the schools, and classrooms in smaller communities where African American and Latino students are entering the schools. There are also many communities that still appear and think of themselves as monocultural in that most students seem to be from the same backgrounds. Nevertheless, there is much diversity in all of these classrooms.

Consider the following questions: How do school leaders and teachers in these schools work with such a diverse population of students? Is the curriculum culturally responsive to the students? What instructional strategies are appropriate? What connections are made between the school, home, and community? How are classroom language and discourse affecting students' learning? What is the role of school leaders in providing leadership in culturally diverse schools?

Can educational literature help school leaders to answer these and other questions? This chapter reviews the multicultural education literature and reports what research and the literature on best practices claim about teaching all the students in schools. It explores the aforementioned questions through a multicultural framework using a particular lens. Each and every school leader has to make a similar decision when making choices about multicultural education. The typology from Grant and Sleeter's (1998) *Turning on Learning* and Sleeter and Grant's (1994) *Making Choices for Multicultural Education* is helpful in examining the literature on multicultural education.

Grant and Sleeter (1998) identified the following five different teaching approaches that address human diversity: race, ethnicity, gender, social class, sexual orientation, and disability:

1. *Teaching the Exceptional and Culturally Different* focuses on helping students of color, from low-income families, and with disabilities, to succeed in schools and society; it is teaching those who are considered outside of the mainstream how to better fit into the mainstream.
2. *Human Relations* helps students learn to appreciate each other's similarities and differences and to improve intercultural relations; teaching everyone to "just get along."
3. *Single-Group Studies* focuses on a particular group such as Native Americans, women, gays and lesbians, and low-income populations and examines issues of structural inequalities and discusses social ideas and educational concepts from the group's perspective.
4. *Multicultural Education* is a combination of the first three approaches. According to Grant and Sleeter (1989), "It [multicultural education] suggests changes to most existing school practices for all students so that the school and classroom may become more concerned with human diversity, choice, and equal opportunity. It is hoped that such changes will bring about greater cultural pluralism and equal opportunity in society at large as today's students become tomorrow's citizens" (p. 7) or, teaching about multiple perspectives within the curriculum.
5. *Education That is Multicultural and Social Reconstructionist* (EMCSR) addresses social inequities in society: "The primary goals of this approach are to prepare students to work actively in groups and individually, to deal constructively with social problems, and to take charge of their own futures," (Sleeter & Grant, 1989, p. 7) teaching not only the many perspectives from different points of view, but also about the structural, institutional effects of inequalities which exist.

This chapter employs Grant and Sleeter's (1998) framework because it is often used by scholars in the field to analyze and discuss theories and practices of multicultural education. It is also used by teachers in making decisions about curriculum and instruction practices in their classrooms.

History and Conceptualizations of Multicultural Education

Banks (1995a) wrote that multicultural education "emerged out of the civil rights movement of the 1960s and 1970s" and pointed to how the demands by African Americans for "symbolic and structural changes" (p. xi) were often focused on changes in this country's schools, colleges, and universities. Supporters of the demands for change came from many different ethnic and racial groups who also participated in the struggles for change.

Sleeter and Grant (1994) also referred to the 1960s and the efforts to desegregate schools as a time when White educators had to recognize the presence of students of color, although they often saw them as culturally deprived. Other views contested this "deficit model" (Portes, 1996) and said that students were different, not deficient, and their differences should be accepted by the school. This was paralleled by special educators' views who saw students' different abilities as something to build on. The first approach from the Grant and Sleeter typology (1998), *teaching the exceptional and culturally different*, illustrates this history.

Another movement that sparked an approach to multicultural education was the post-World War II intercultural education movement, which argued that respect, getting along, and more effective communication should be developed to bring people who differ closer together in schools. Respect and regard for others are the dominant themes in the *human relations* approach.

Also occurring during the 1960s was the movement in ethnic, women, and labor studies. These programs of study developed in an effort to focus attention on a specific group: to raise consciousness about the group's oppression and marginalization; to examine social issues from the perspective of the group; and to mobilize the group toward social action to change structural inequalities. Examples from this movement in the 1960s and early 1970s were the establishment of ethnic studies and women's studies departments. Also, during the 1960s, a number of high schools across the country added courses in Afro-American history and/or ethnic studies to their curriculum. Additionally, in many K–12 schools, staff development sessions increasingly addressed issues of multicultural education and antibias curriculum. The *single-group studies* approach reflects much of this history.

During the mid-1970s, what Sleeter and Grant (1994) called the *multicultural education* approach emerged as educators grew disenchanted with earlier approaches and began to conceptualize more complete and complex plans for reforming education. This approach sought to include diverse curriculum materials and content, multiple perspectives, instructional strategies adapted to different learning styles, an acknowledgment of language diversity, the use of authentic assessment, heterogeneous groupings of students, close home and school relationships, and nonstereotypical extracurricular activities.

During the late 1970s and into the 1980s, there was a growth in what Sleeter and Grant (1994) called the *education that is multicultural and social reconstructionist* approach. Grant (1978) claimed that this approach is more what schools need. He argued that the entire educational program (staffing, testing, curriculum, instruction) should be redesigned to reflect the concerns of diverse cultural groups (race, class, gender, sexual orientation, language). Sleeter and Grant (1994) argued that reconstruction in a Brameldian (1956) sense is needed because it offers philosophical guidelines that educators can use to give direction to how people should go about reconstructing society so that all groups are better served.

As educational leaders examine the history of multicultural education over the last 30 years, they will discover that school leaders have played at best a small role in its intellectual and practical development. As they prepare students for the 21st century, a question with which they must contend is: What is the role of school leaders in shaping the history and direction of multicultural education in schools for the next 30 years?

In order to implement multicultural education in schools, Geneva Gay (1995b) believed it needs to be "a *process* instead of a product. As a process, it is a way of thinking, a decision-making style, and a way of behaving in educational settings that is pervasive and ongoing (Banks, 1993). It requires long-term investments of time and resources, and carefully planned and monitored actions" (p. 29). Gay argued that Grant (1978) "captures the essence" of this conception of multicultural education as process instead of product when he explained why he preferred to use education that is multicultural to identify the enterprise instead of just multicultural education. "Rather than a specific, discrete education program (such as social studies, bilingual, or science education), he sees multicultural education as a different approach to the entire educational enterprise in all its forms and functions" (Gay, 1995b, p. 29).

Banks (1995b) provided school leaders with such a process for "doing." His typology of dimensions of multicultural education includes *content integration*, the *knowledge construction process*, *prejudice reduction*, an *equity pedagogy*, and an *empowering school culture and social structure*. *Content Integration* is illustrated by the practice of including examples and data from various cultures and groups to illustrate concepts and theories in a subject area or discipline. The *knowledge construction* dimension is illustrated by procedures by which "teachers help students to understand how knowledge is created and how it is influenced by the racial, ethnic, and social-class positions of individuals and groups" (p. 4). The *prejudice reduction* dimension describes practices that attempt to talk about children's racial attitudes and suggest strategies that can be used "to help students develop more democratic attitudes and values" (p. 4). The *equity pedagogy* dimension exists "when teachers use techniques and methods that facilitate the academic achievement of students from diverse racial, ethnic, and social-class groups" (p. 4). The dimension that describes an empowering school culture describes the "process of restructuring the culture and organization of the school so that students from diverse racial, ethnic, and social-class groups will experience education equality and cultural empowerment (Cummins, 1986)" (Banks, 1995b, p. 5).

Banks (1995b) argued that several serious problems result when multicultural education is conceptualized only or primarily as content integration. Teachers in subjects such as mathematics and science perceive multicultural education, when it is conceptualized only as content integration, as appropriate for social studies and language arts teachers but not for them (p. 19). Banks went on to warn that when multicultural education is "narrowly conceptualized, it is often confined to activities for special days and occasions, such as Martin Luther King's birthday and Cinco de Mayo. It may also be viewed as a special unit, an additional book by an African American or a Mexican American writer, or a few additional lessons" (p. 19).

School leaders and teachers often ask which typology they should use: Grant and Sleeter (1998) or Banks (1995b)? Reports from the best practice literature suggest that both models are widely used in K–12 education and universities, and both provide an excellent and user-friendly way for educators to consider the theory and practice of multicultural education.

In searching for research and best practices information on multicultural education, educational leaders should be aware that some of the names used for definitions for reforms dealing with diversity are *multicultural education*, *nonsexist education*, *human relations*, *gender fair education*, *multiethnic education*, *ethnic studies*, *sex equity*, *bilingual/bicultural education*, *anti-racist teaching*, and *inclusive education*. However, multicultural education has emerged as the "umbrella concept" that deals with race, culture, language, social class, gender, sexual orientation, and disability.

CRITIQUES AND MYTHS OF MULTICULTURAL EDUCATION

There are two major critiques of multicultural education that can be described as conservative and radical:

CONSERVATIVE CRITIQUE

Sleeter (1995) pointed out that whereas multicultural education has been the "subject of occasional conservative critiques since its inception (Broudy, 1975; Glazer, 1981; Ivie, 1979; M.D. Thomas, 1981), the early 1990s saw a barrage of these critiques. They are written primarily for a popular audience" (p. 82). The conservative critiques first emerged in the form of conservative articulations of what children should be taught, for example, in Hirsch's (1987) *Cultural Literacy: What Every American Needs to Know*, then quickly escalated into a broad attack on multicultural curricula. For example, their targets are "curricular changes and policies being instituted in schools and universities on a wide scale, particularly New York State's *A Curriculum of Inclusion* (1989) (a framework written by a task force to guide the development of new K–12 multicultural curricula), Portland, Oregon's, *African American Baseline Essays* (1989) (a series of essays that explicates six disciplines from an Afrocentric perspective, designed to help K–12 teachers reconceptualize their own curriculum), Afrocentrism in general, and revisions of core curricula on several university campuses" (Sleeter, p. 83).

Conservative critics regard education in the United States as largely politically neutral and fair to all children (e.g., Balch, 1992). Ravitch (1991–1992) insisted that the curriculum already is multicultural because "the common culture is multicultural" (p. 10). Stotsky (1991) optimistically explained that reasonable citizens "should applaud the integration of non-Western cultures and the histories of various minorities—women, Hispanics, blacks, native Indian communities—into our schools' curricula (p. 26)" (p. 83). Sleeter (1995) pointed out that the point of contention is not whether or not the curriculum should be multicultural but what that means to different conservative critics.

RADICAL CRITIQUE

Sleeter (1995) also outlined how those called radicals do not see multicultural education as radical enough. They argued that multicultural scholars are weak in their interrogation of structural inequalities (racism, White supremacy, capitalism). Sleeter (1995) argued that "radical left critiques of multicultural education have been written mainly by theorists for an audience of theorists (Giroux, 1992; Mattai, 1992; McCarthy, 1988, 1990a, 1990b; Ogbu, 1992; Olneck, 1990; Popkewitz, 1988). Their purpose is not to mobilize public opinion, but rather to influence scholarly debate and, in some cases, influence multicultural education theorists" (p. 89).

In sum, Sleeter (1995) purported that after having experienced "considerable conceptual growth and some limited gains in affecting schools," the field of multicultural education is currently "buffeted by critiques." Those who work in multicultural education find themselves "walking a tightrope between naming issues accurately and antagonizing potential supporters" (p. 92). Additionally, there is some critique of the field by multicultural scholars. Most multicultural scholars, after some years of debate, now accept race, class, gender, and ability under the multicultural umbrella. However, the acceptance of sexual orientation is being contested by some. The final outcome of this debate, in part, can be influenced by school leaders as they offer direction in curriculum and instruction to their teachers and staff members.

MYTHS OF MULTICULTURAL EDUCATION

There are several myths about multicultural education, including: It is divisive; it is the same thing as "political correctness"; it rejects a common culture; it will impede the teaching of the basics and preparation of students to live in a global technological society; and the one that is most frequently heard is that multicultural education is "for minorities only." Grant (1994b) pointed out that many teachers and school leaders see multicultural education as a "minority thing." They see it as related to the school experience of students of color, who are assumed to have a negative self-image, as a plan to help manage the behavior of these students, and as a curricular adaptation to include underrepresented groups. Conversely, it is not seen as necessary for Whites. According to this view, the focus of multicultural education is race and race is perceived narrowly as a Black or Brown problem, something Black and Brown people have to overcome (Omi & Winant, 1986). Often forgotten is the U.S. history of slavery and discrimination and the need for Whites to understand how they contribute to everyday racism (Essed, 1990).

When race is seen as the only foundational pillar of multicultural education, the attention scholars in the field give to discussions of socioeconomic class, gender, disability, and sexual orientation are ignored. Also, when multicultural education is seen as only a minority thing, Whites are miseducated. They are inclined to develop ethnocentric and prejudicial attitudes toward people of color when they are deprived of the opportunity to learn about the sociocultural, economic, and psychological factors that produce conditions of ethnic polarization, racial unrest, and hate crimes. Additionally, they are inclined to be put off by ongoing, multilayered discussions of multicultural education, arguing that they have "heard it all before." Further, when multicultural education is seen as a minority thing, the importance of analyzing the impact of race, class, and gender interactions, which are important to multicultural education research, is ignored or understated.

STUDENTS

The picture described at the beginning of the chapter, although from the 1990 census, does not include other important demographic considerations. Orfield (1993) reported, ironically, that schools have become increasingly segregated, in many regions, along race and social class lines between the time the Supreme Court declared school segregation unconstitutional in 1954 to the present. In a study providing national data to show the relation of segregation to poverty, Orfield showed that both African American and Latino students "are much more likely than white students to find themselves in schools of concentrated poverty" and that segregation by race "is strongly related to segregation by poverty" (p. 1). Orfield's study points out that minority students are more likely to be in high poverty schools; that segregation "remains high in big cities and serious in mid-sized central cities"; and there are also segregated schools in the suburbs of the largest metropolitan areas. Orfield stated that "rural areas and small towns, small metropolitan areas, and the suburbs of the mid-size metro areas are far more integrated" (p. 1). He explained how court cases have limited the possibility of desegregating cities (e.g., *Milliken v. Bradley*, 418 U.S. 717 [1974]) by limiting desegregation to a single district unless the court found that suburban or state action had caused segregation in the city. Orfield maintained that such decisions are the "basic reason why Illinois, New York, Boston, Michigan, and New Jersey ... have been the most segregated states for black students for more than a decade" (p. 2). At the conclusion of the study, Orfield stated that "the country and its schools are going through vast changes without any strategy" and the "civil rights impulse from the 1960s is dead in the water and the ship is floating backward toward the shoals of racial segregation" (p. 2).

Mesa-Bains (1993) explained how the changing demographics affect students and educators in schools, referring to a great wave of immigration, escalating birth rates, a society with no distinct majority, and one with "multicultural enclaves in many areas, urban and rural." One of the most alarming statistics reported from Mesa-Bains about the United States' changing demographics is that the poorest 20% of the population is able to earn and use only 4.5% of the nation's wealth. This group's struggles for social and economic equality is linked to how students fare in school, and that, in turn, is influenced both by teacher perceptions and students' own expectations (Mesa-Bains, 1993). She argued that educators face multiple and complex issues that challenge many of their educational practices and assumptions (Mesa-Bains, 1993).

The student population is enormously mixed, encompassing an array of races, cultures, and languages never before seen in single schools or classrooms. Mesa-Bains (1993) also observed that there are powerful interpenetrations of race and class that have created among some a sense of disenfranchisement. Because schools perpetuate the myth of a classless society, students' socioeconomic class is rarely acknowledged as a factor in educational achievement.

Other dilemmas are rooted in the problems faced by newly arrived immigrant families. Many Mexican and Central American children are coming from areas so rural or so torn by civil strife that no consistent, ongoing education has been provided in over a generation. This is coupled with extreme economic deprivation, affecting health and well-being. Ironically, even the journey of escape and migration to a better life brings more difficulties for many students. Separation, culture shock, loss, exposure to violence, and limited English proficiency often combine to create a kind of posttraumatic stress syndrome. Some children exhibit a lack of interest or low affect as a result of overwhelming circumstances (Mesa-Bains, 1993).

Clearly, many incoming students are not school-ready. According to the best practice literature, school leaders must be careful about how they view Asian American students. The "model minority" (Lee, 1996) notion associated with Asian Americans is an incorrect stereotype. Many Asian students struggle against barriers to learning. Although established economic improvement networks often make the Asian socioeconomic situation different from that of many

Latin Americans, many Indochinese students entering schools are also beset by posttraumatic stress, limited English proficiency, and culture shock (Mesa-Bains, 1993).

Stern (1994) addressed increasingly diverse rural schools where just 6% of the school teachers and principals are Native American, Asian, Black, or Latino, as compared to 13% in nonrural schools. She explained how rural students envisioned themselves more often in lower level, less skilled positions than did nonrural youth. Thus, rural youth expected to complete their full-time education at lower levels of attainment than did either urban or suburban students.

Additionally, another rationale for the importance of multicultural education and the discussion of the multiple factors affecting students includes the report about gender equity in schools today. The National Coalition for Women and Girls in Education (1997) reported that true gender equity remains elusive, despite 25 years of Title IX, and gave multiple examples of unequal opportunities and results within their report. Research about same-sex classes and the progress of female students in the areas of math and science still offer few conclusions or solutions that school leaders can use with certainty. Banks (1995b) believed an important goal of multicultural education "is to give male and female students an equal chance to experience educational success and mobility (Klein, 1985; Sadker & Sadker, 1982)" (p. 3).

THE TEACHING FORCE

WHO ARE THEY?

The average public school teacher is a White woman in her early 40s, who is married with children and has a spouse who is employed (National Education Association [NEA], 1992). Using years of teaching experience as a gauge, it is estimated that in the public school sector Hispanic teachers are younger than teachers in all groups other than White, with 48.8% having less than 10 years of experience and only 17.1% with more than 20 years of experience. On the other hand, African American teachers are older than their counterparts, with 29.4% having less than 10 years of experience and 35.3% with more than 20 years experience. In regard to educational attainment, a greater proportion of African American, Hispanic, and Asian or Pacific Islander teachers hold doctorates than White or Native American teachers. A greater percentage of African American teachers hold master's degrees than any other group. Asian American teachers lead all groups in education specialist certificates (Snyder & Hoffman, 1995, p. 77).

In 1993–1994 the K–12 U.S. teaching force was approximately 2.6 million. Of this number, approximately 13% were teachers of color. In 1993–1994, of the K–12 public school teacher workforce, 7.0% of the teachers were African American, as compared to an African American student population of up to 16.1% of all public school students; 4.0% of the teachers were Hispanic, as compared to a Hispanic student population of 12.7%; 1.0% were Asian/Pacific Islander, as compared to 3.6%; and fewer than 1.0% of teachers were Native American, as compared to just over 1% of students. Overall, 87.0% of public school teachers were White, as compared with 66.1% of public school students (Snyder & Hoffman, 1995, pp. 60, 77).

WHAT WILL THE FORCE LOOK LIKE IN THE FUTURE?

Eighty-one percent of prospective teachers are female (near 90% if in elementary education); 92% are White; less than 3% know a language other than English; and only 9% report they would choose to teach in urban or multicultural settings (*21st Century*, 1991). The number of people of color entering colleges and universities is decreasing, with fewer of them entering teaching. Currently, only 4% of teachers come from culturally different populations (p. 38)

TEACHER PREPARATION

What is happening in the majority of teacher education institutions in relation to the multicultural education preparation of teachers? Whereas the current literature supports the need for excellent teachers to teach children of diverse backgrounds (Haberman, 1987; McCormick, 1990; Stallings, Bossun, & Martin, 1990), and provides some direction on how to train teachers to work with diverse groups of students, few teacher education institutions are reported to take up and implement the full range of coursework, field placements, and other experiences necessary to provide a quality multicultural teacher education program (Buttery, Haberman, & Houston, 1990; Grant & Secada, 1990; Grant & Tate, 1995).

Studies indicate that many teachers do not desire to work in urban areas. According to an AACTE (1987) report, approximately 80% of the new teaching force grew up in suburban and rural settings and strongly desires to teach in those kinds of environments (see also AACTE, 1988, 1989, 1990; Zempher & Ashburn, 1992). Teachers most often come from isolated ethnic groups, with professional preparation that does not generally include much direct interaction with different cultures (p. 38).

Mesa-Bains (1993) revealed that many teachers have had no sustained contact with individuals of another race prior to entering the inner-city and multicultural classrooms. Not only do they lack familiarity, most are fearful of confronting the issue of race, as well as issues of class, sexual orientation, and ability. In college, as much through the hidden curriculum as the overt curriculum, they are taught that Blacks are really the same as White people, except perhaps they are culturally deprived; that all Asians are the "model minority" (Lee, 1996); and that education is neutral, with no class bias. Additionally, the issues of sexual orientation and ability are often invisible in teacher education programs. Furthermore, few have been taught to work with the students with disabilities who are now included in their classrooms. This is, in part, because courses in special education are kept separate from "regular education" and content and practice about students with disabilities is not usually infused into traditional education programs.

RETENTION AND CULTURE SHOCK

Limited experiences with cultural diversity virtually guarantee classroom culture shock (Bowman, 1989; Mock, 1981). Mock (1981) referred to culture shock for a child when the individual feels trapped between two sets of values and beliefs. The individual feels powerless, helpless, and isolated. Teachers (pre-service or in-service) can experience this same discrepancy. They may view children through their own cultural prism (Bowman, 1989), resulting in feelings of alienation for both the teacher and the pupils in the class (p. 38). This culture shock leads to low retention rates in certain areas. The literature reveals that teachers going to urban areas are unprepared for the demands of the urban environment. As a result, retention rates of teachers in urban school districts are extremely low, in stark contrast to retention in suburban school districts. According to research findings compiled by Haberman (1987), the dropout rate of new teachers assigned to inner-city schools is double that of other teachers (approximately 40% in the largest metropolitan centers). In California, for example, more than 50% of all newly hired teachers leave the profession within 5 years (Estes, Stansbury, & Long, 1990). For urban school districts, the percentage is often higher.

Classroom teachers agree and express concern about not being prepared to work in multicultural settings. Cultural differences are threatening and intercultural communications are awkward for those who have not had diverse experiences (Banks, 1991, 1994; Gollnick & Chinn, 1986).

TEACHER TRACKING

Addressing tracking of teachers, a concept most often noted in discussions about students, Darling-Hammond (1995) reported that evidence suggests that "teachers themselves are tracked, with those judged to be the most competent, experienced, or with the highest status assigned to the top tracks (Oakes, 1986; Davis, 1986; Finley, 1984; Rosenbaum, 1976; Talbert, 1990)" (p. 473).

Darling-Hammond (1995) observed:

> Expert, experienced teachers who are in great demand are rewarded with opportunities to teach the students who already know a lot. New teachers, unprepared teachers, and those teaching outside their field of preparation are often assigned to the students and the classes that others do not care to teach, which leaves them practicing on the students who would benefit most from the skills of the expert, experienced teachers. (p. 473)

Darling-Hammond (1995) stated that a

> major reason for the persistence of this practice is the kind of preparation teachers receive generally. Managing a heterogeneous classroom requires preparation that relatively few teachers receive and skills that relatively few of them acquire (Darling-Hammond, 1990; Wheelock, 1992). It requires refined diagnostic ability, a broad repertoire of teaching strategies, and the ability to match strategies to varied learning styles and prior levels of knowledge. Managing heterogeneous classrooms require skill in using inquiry and cooperative learning strategies, as well as skills in classroom management even more considerable than those required in a homogeneous classroom. Since relatively few teachers are prepared to manage heterogeneous classrooms effectively, tracking persists. (pp. 473–474)

MULTICULTURAL EDUCATION IN CLASSROOMS AND SCHOOLS

CURRICULUM

School leaders will find numerous discussions on both the overt and hidden curriculum. Curriculum development is perhaps the area of multicultural education that has received the most attention over the past 30 years. This is especially so with instructional materials, including textbooks. Recent studies of text materials report an improvement in the portrayals of African Americans and White women (Grant & Sleeter, 1991). However, Native Americans, Latinos, and Asian Americans are still very much marginalized. For example, Native Americans are still portrayed as the "noble savage" and in stories set in the time period of the Western movement. Mexican Americans are mostly portrayed through conflicts between the United States and Mexico over southwest territory in the 1800s. Asian Americans are usually portrayed in the building of the transcontinental railroad and always as "foreigners" or "strangers from a different shore" (Takaki, 1989). Discussions of sexual orientation and disability are rarely seen in text materials. Texts still are centered around the dates and famous people orientation to social life and what one does not see is a multilayered discussion of events. For example, many textbooks will feature Martin Luther King, Jr., characterizing him as a civil rights leader and a person who used nonviolence, along with a few lines from his speech on the March on Washington. These books usually neglect to mention that King was fighting against everyday and institutionalized racism and the impact of poverty on poor people. This example illustrates that discussions in textbooks often offer an artificial view of history and people. How such discussions become texts in books for schools is discussed in *The Great Speckled Bird* (1995) by Cornbleth and Waugh. They provided an insightful and provocative analysis of how the educational policy making surrounding curriculum decisions concerning multicultural materials for K–12 classrooms is often hotly contested, using examples from California and New York debates.

Pang's (1995) writing on curriculum recommended to school leaders that K–12 curriculum must be multicultural and, as diverse populations enter their schools, it is important for them to use materials that relate to their backgrounds in realistic ways and represent their experiences to show the complexities of their cultural history (p. 422). Lomawaima (1995) supported Pang's notion and claims that curriculum content is the important issue. She responded to how some research often looks for the one way (the magic bullet) different groups of students learn. Relating this point to Native Americans as an example, she asserted that how children are taught, and how they learn, should not obscure the critical nature of what they are being taught. She reported that research findings from the Rough Rock Demonstration School on the Navajo reservation argue that, when an experimental social studies curriculum based on local values and ideas was introduced, children blossomed from silent "concrete" learners into talkative, analytical students (Benally, Lynch, McCarty, & Wallace, 1991, p. 341).

Two curriculum models that school leaders will find useful in helping their staff to implement a multicultural curriculum are the Gay (1995a) and the Banks (1993) models. Gay (1995a) wrote about empowering practice through four "developmental stages" of multicultural education theory and implementation. She described the *inclusion* level as one where students are introduced to a "a host of ethnic individuals who have made major contributions to their own cultural groups, as well as to United States society and humankind" (p. 8). She believed this approach requires teachers to choose authentic ethnic individuals and artifacts through understanding what is a cultural hero or heroine according to the standards of different ethnic groups. The *infusion* level is implemented by demonstrating how the typical components of curriculum development and regular instruction can be culturally diversified. Here Gay suggested that the concepts the teacher is planning every day be infused with multicultural ideas and notions. For example, if teachers are teaching measurement, they would have students measure the height of the water fountain to see if it is wheelchair accessible, and record the difference in restrooms between stalls that are and are not wheelchair accessible. The level of *deconstruction* includes "critique, interrogation, and knowledge reconstruction." Students are encouraged to become skeptics and to question claims of social and academic truths and accuracy. Gay's *transformative* level is what she called the "action response" to the deconstruction level and processes, and is an approach that focuses on constructing new realities, new systems, and new possibilities after critiquing what the present curriculum offers (pp. 8–9).

Banks' (1993) contribution to the multicultural curriculum discussion is to conceptualize four different approaches used to integrate content from different cultural and ethnic groups into curriculum: the *contributions approach*, focusing on "heroes and heroines," holidays, and other "discrete cultural elements";

the *additive approach*, where material from different groups is added on to the curriculum without changing the basic structure of the curriculum; the *transformation approach*, which is designed to help students learn how knowledge is constructed and where the structure of the curriculum can be changed to enable students to view concepts from perspectives of various cultural groups; and the *social action approach*, which extends the transformation approach and encourages students to make decisions on important social issues and take action to help solve them (p. 12). King (1995) provided an example of Banks' transformation approach with an explanation of the "Algebra Project." This curriculum development project made algebra, traditionally a "gatekeeping" course, accessible to middle school students in inner-city and southern schools by building on African American cultural knowledge to teach math concepts (M. Moses, personal communication, August 20, 1993).

Media as Curriculum. Increasingly, there are discussions among governmental leaders, scholars, and the public in general about the media's role in shaping the identities and behaviors of students. Whereas school leaders may frequently hear this debate in the teachers' lounge and at conferences, there are two educators that provide insights that school leaders may wish to consider (Cortes, 1995; McCarthy, 1998). Cortes (1995) stated that whereas students learn in schools, they also learn outside of schools through the "'societal curriculum'—that massive, ongoing, informal curriculum of families, peer groups, neighborhoods, churches, organizations, institutions, mass media, and other socializing forces that educate all of us throughout our lives (Berry, 1980; Cortes, 1981; Leifer, Gordon, & Graves, 1974; Leiss, Line, & Jhally, 1986; Spring, 1992)" (p. 169).

Cortes (1995) argued that a major element of societal multicultural education is the mass media. He explained that it works through such avenues as newspapers, magazines, motion pictures, television, and radio. These media disseminate information, images, and ideas concerning race, ethnicity, culture, and foreignness. Media educate both for better and for worse (p. 169).

The mass media play a critical role in the social construction of knowledge concerning diverse groups of people. This involves not only knowledge about specific groups, but also a broader way of thinking about race and ethnicity, sexual orientation, class and disability, as well as about relations between and among these groups. Cortes (1995) claimed that this critical role of the mass media in the social construction of knowledge (as well as attitudes and perceptions) about race and ethnicity, and also about disability, sexual orientation, and gender roles, has significant implications for school multicultural education. Teachers, administrators, students, parents, and others involved in school education are exposed to the media, including intended and unintended focuses on multicultural issues (p. 180)

McCarthy (1998) extended this discussion of the social construction of knowledge in the media in his attention on the role of Hollywood film and television in the coordination of the identities of the middle-class inhabitants of the suburbs and the disorganization of the identities of the dwellers of the inner city (p. 31).

McCarthy argued that the electronic media play a critical role in the production and channeling of suburban anxieties and retributive morality onto its central target: the depressed inner city (p. 32). According to McCarthy, increasingly the underclass or working-class subject is contemporaneously being placed on the outside of the arena of the public sphere and the middle-class subject of history moves in to occupy and to appropriate the identity of the oppressed. "The center becomes the margin" (p. 37).

McCarthy referred to how the mainstream news media address Black and Latino America and how "Black and Latino youth appear metonymically" (represented partially and not as complete beings) in the discussion of problems: "kids of violence, kids of welfare moms, car jackers, the kids without fathers, kids of illegal aliens, kids who don't speak 'American.'" The inner city is used as a signifier of danger and the unknown that at the same time narrows the complexity of urban working-class life. Watch the network evening news and it is possible to predict when Black and Latino bodies will enter and when they will exit. "The overwhelming metaphor of crime and violence saturates the dominant gaze on the inner city" (p. 39).

McCarthy made an additional point that school leaders should consider about films. He argued that the portrayals of the inner city in films like *Boys 'n the Hood* and *Falling Down* illustrate what he called the "discourse of resentment," and not only have powerful rhetorical, or persuasive, effects, but also devastating material effects. Inner-city Black school youth are surrounded by this powerful discourse of crime and violence in which they are the constructed other—social objects who grapple with the reality code projected from the popular media culture. Their experience of the reality code is grounded in material practices such as police harassment. Black and Latino youth experience the reality code as a "problem of representation." In other words, they are represented in particular ways by the media, and people in society expect these youth to live up to that image portrayed in the media. Thus, this representation affects their access to opportunities and life choices (p. 42).

INSTRUCTION

Cultural Responsiveness. A concept that is becoming increasingly popular under the multicultural umbrella is the notion of being "culturally responsive." However, culturally responsive means different things to different educators. To some, for example, it means using the first Grant and Sleeter (1998) approach, that is, teaching the exceptional and culturally different, helping students not from middle-class, European American, heterosexual, non-disabled backgrounds to "fit in." What many multicultural education scholars have in mind when speaking of culturally responsive classrooms and schools points not to just "helping" some students fit into the formulas already offered in schools, but to thinking in more complex terms about what educators need to do to change in order to meet the academic and social needs of every student. For example, a growing body of recent work in the area of culturally responsive classrooms and schools suggests that effective teachers of students of color form and maintain connections with their students within their social contexts. They do not shy away from issues of race and culture; they are familiar with the common vernacular even though they instruct in standard English; and they celebrate their students as individuals and as members of specific cultures (Cochran Smith, 1995; Garcia, 1993; Irvine, 1992; Ladson-Billing, 1994; Murrell, 1991; Nieto, 1996; Strickland, 1995). There is a significant level of cultural synchronization between teachers and students (Irvine, 1995).

Some proponents of culturally responsive teaching (Au, 1980; Calderon & Diaz, 1993; Delpit, 1988; Foster, 1995; Hale-Benson, 1986; Hilliard, 1997; Irvine, 1992, Kunjufu, 1989; Ladson-Billings, 1994; Nieto, 1994, Waters, 1989) argue that essential to this idea are teachers who are consciously responsive to their students' cultural backgrounds and learning styles.

Garcia (1995) and others related culturally responsive classrooms to social, cultural, and linguistic development. Garcia maintained that, for culturally responsive classrooms, it is important to understand

> that language, culture, and their accompanying values are acquired in the home and community environment (Cummins, 1986; Goldman & Trueba, 1987; Heath, 1981); that children come to school with some knowledge about what language is, how it works, and what it is used for (Hall, 1987; Goodman, 1980; Smith, 1971); that children learn higher-level cognitive and communicative skills as they engage in socially meaningful activities (Duran, 1987); and that children's development and learning is best understood as the interaction of linguistic, sociocultural, and cognitive knowledge and experiences (Trueba, 1988). A more appropriate perspective of learning, then, is one that recognizes that learning is enhanced when it occurs in contexts that are both socioculturally and linguistically meaningful for the learner (Diaz, Moll, & Mehan, 1986; Heath, 1986; Scribner & Cole, 1981; Wertsch, 1985). (p. 382)

Nieto (1995) and Pang (1995) offered some reasons for culturally responsive pedagogy. Nieto (1995) observed that many schools focus on students or their families as "the problem." She argued that schools need to look at their own policies and practices in order to improve the education of Puerto Rican and other children rather than to focus on issues about which they can do "precious little," such as poverty, low parental educational levels, or single-parent family structure (p. 107). Pang (1995) pointed out that schools often stereotype students. She revealed the inaccuracies of the "model minority" myth and belief in the homogeneity of the Asian Pacific American student population. She believed that educators need to examine their attitudes toward and knowledge of Asian Pacific American and other marginalized students (p. 421) as an important part of pedagogy that is culturally responsive.

Successful Pedagogy. There are many educators and scholars who write about how to teach successfully (Collins, 1990; Foster, 1995; Kohl, 1967, 1998; Ladson-Billings,1994). Whereas some are directing their recommendations to a particular group of students, for example, Eugene Garcia's writings on Mexican Americans, a great deal of what is reported for successful instruction with one particular group is often reported by authors for other groups. Garcia's (1995) review of research on successful practices with Mexican American students is a case in point. It provides excellent suggestions for teaching students from diverse groups.

Garcia (1995) maintained that successful pedagogy requires a redefinition of the instructor's role. This redefinition requires instructors to become familiar with the different dimensions of learning; how to recognize the ways different forms of instruction and assessment affect learning; classroom curriculum, its purposes, and the extent of its implementation; setting up a classroom so it is socially and instructionally compatible to the students and concepts to be learned; the nature of interactions between students and teachers and students and students; as well as how to help students display what they know and demonstrate they are competent learners and language users (p. 383).

Garcia (1995) reported that the common attributes found in successful classrooms are the following: (a) the emphasis of high expectations; (b) a high degree of functional communication between teachers and students, making sure assignments and students' roles are clear; (c) student collaboration on small-group projects organized around "learning centers," where individualized work tasks and "worksheet" exercises are minimal; (d) a very informal family-like social setting where the teacher works with small groups of students or travels around the room; (e) a very small amount of large-group instruction usually confined to start-up activities in the morning; (f) instruction of basic skills and academic content consistently organized around thematic units such as "bears," "butterflies," and "dinosaurs" in the early grades, and "pop music," "gardens," "pesticides," and "peace/war" in the higher grades, themes often chosen by students in consultation with the teacher (p. 383).

Garcia (1995) concluded his review by asking and answering the following questions regarding effective academic environments:

1. *What role did native-language instruction play?* These "effective" schools considered native-language instruction key in the early grades (K–3).
2. *Was there one best curriculum?* No common curriculum was identified. However, a well-trained instructional staff implementing an integrated "student-centered" curriculum, with literacy pervasive in all aspects of instruc-

tion, was consistently observed across grade levels. Basals were utilized sparingly and usually as resource material.

3. *What instructional strategies were effective?* Consistently, teachers organized so as to ensure small collaborative academic activities requiring a high degree of heterogeneously grouped student-to-student social (and particularly linguistic) interaction. Individual instructional activity such as worksheets/workbooks was limited, as was individual competition as a classroom motivational ingredient.

4. *Who were the key players in this effective schooling drama?* School administrators and parents played important roles. However, teachers were the key players. They achieved the educational confidence of their peers and supervisors. They worked to organize instruction, create new instructional environments, assess effectiveness, and advocate for their students. They were proud of their students, academically reassuring but consistently demanding. They rejected any notion of academic, linguistic, cultural, or intellectual inferiority regarding their students (E. Garcia, 1991, p. 8). (p. 384)

Important Instructional Features. Moran and Hakuta (1995) supported Garcia's characteristics of successful pedagogy with their findings. They identified, much like Garcia, ideas that are important for successful instruction. They described how, despite great diversity in districts, programs, and classrooms, the following "five instructional features were found to be significant, appearing frequently, consistently, and with high quality":

1. Successful teachers utilized active teaching strategies, including: (a) emphasizing clear communications during instruction, clear descriptions of tasks, and appropriate strategies for explaining, clarifying, and organizing information; (b) maintaining students' engagement in instructional tasks, keeping students focused, pacing instruction appropriately, and communicating expectations clearly; and (c) monitoring students' progress and providing immediate feedback to students.

2. Successful teachers used both primary and second language to mediate instruction, alternating between the languages to increase student understanding of the instruction.

3. Successful teachers integrated English-language development with academic skills even when students' primary language was used for some of the instruction.

4. Successful teachers incorporated the home culture into the classroom, including references to the culture, building on cultural discourse modes, and observing the values and norms of the Limited English Proficient (L.E.P.) students' home culture while the majority culture norms were being taught.

5. Successful teachers had congruency among their instructional goals, organization and delivery of lessons, and student outcomes. They communicated high expectations for L.E.P. students and had confidence in their ability to teach all students (see Tikunoff, 1985). (p. 451)

Learning Styles. School leaders will find the research on learning styles helpful in that it reminds educators that students learn in different ways. Irvine and York (1995) believed the learning styles research has significant possibilities for enhancing the achievement of culturally diverse students as it reminds teachers to be attentive not only to individual students' learning styles but to their own actions, instructional goals, methods, and materials in reference to their students' cultural experiences and preferred learning environments (p. 484).

Reminders of what the learning styles research tells educators include understanding and appreciating students' personal cultural knowledge, using students' prior knowledge and culture in teaching, and the importance of affect in teaching culturally diverse students. Learning styles and the theories that surround them show the significance of teacher–student interactions that include eye contact, facial expressions, body posture, physical space, use of silence, and interpersonal touching (Longstreet, 1978).

Irvine and York (1995) described learning styles research as "based on the theory that individuals respond to learning situations with consistent patterns of behavior. When applied to culturally diverse students, learning-styles research proposes to explain why children of the same culture and ethnicity often employ similar strategies for learning" (p. 490).

However, school leaders should attend to the fact that Irvine and York (1995), when reviewing the research on learning styles, say that the applicability of the learning styles research is limited. Understanding this limitation is particularly important in the education of children of color. One core assumption inherent in the learning styles research is that children outside of mainstream culture learn better when teaching matches their preferred style. However, research on learning styles using culturally diverse students fails to support the premise that members of a given cultural group exhibit a distinctive style. Hence, the issue is not the identification of a style for a particular ethnic or gender group, but rather the way instruction should be arranged to meet the instructional needs of the individual students who are present in the classroom. Teachers who understand the preferred style of a student can use that knowledge to design and plan instruction and to encourage students to experiment with a wider repertoire of learning approaches. Clearly, learning styles research is a useful beginning point in designing appropriate instruction for culturally diverse students, but not an end in itself (p. 490).

Cooperative Groups. Although there is a great deal of discussion and use of cooperative group instruction in classrooms, the research on cooperative groups from a multicultural perspective is somewhat thin. There is, however, a general belief among educators that cooperative group work is good for all students. L. Cooper, D. W. Johnson, and Wilderson (1980) found greater friendship across race lines in a cooperative treatment than in an individualized method in which students were not permitted to interact. D. W. Johnson and R. T. Johnson (1981) found more cross-racial interaction in cooperative than in individualized classes during free time (pp. 632). Slavin (1977) and Slavin and Oickle (1981) found that African American students appear to achieve at higher levels when cooperative learning instructional strategies are used.

Tracking. It has been said that a child's college education starts in kindergarten. For a traditionally underserved child, however, tracking weaves a different story. Categorizing students into slow learners and fast learners tracks has been shown to be a form of institutionalized racism against Native Americans, Hispanics, African Americans, and low income students (Grant & Sleeter, 1986; Oakes, Ormseth, & Campbell, 1990; Sleeter, 1994). People do not need to go farther than their own neighborhood schools to see how tracking has created a form of segregated schools within schools.

Wells and Serma (1996) conducted a 3-year study of 10 ethnically and socioeconomically diverse schools engaged in detracking reform. They discovered that many Anglo-European and middle- and upper-class parents implemented four types of strategies to undermine detracking initiatives at their respective schools. These strategies, for example, included threatening flight ("White Flight"), making sure the teachers with the best reputations taught their children, garnering support from parents whose students may not be in the honors classes by promising them their children would not be placed in classes with a large number of low tracked students, and accepting detracking bribes, like the offer from administrators to make sure there are gifted and talented programs in place for their children (p. 23).

Finally, Oakes (1985) has been arguing for over a decade that there is a disproportionate representation of poor and minority youth who get placements in lower track and non college bound classes with too little representation in gifted and talented programs.

Tests and Social Inequality. Over many decades,

> ... standardized tests have been used to define both teaching goals and students' opportunities to learn. As a tool for tracking students into different courses, levels, and kinds of instructional programs, testing has been a primary means for limiting or expanding students' life choices and their avenues for demonstrating competence. Increasingly, the use of tests are recognized as having the un intended consequence of limiting students' access to further learning opportunities (Darling-Hammond, 1991; Oakes, 1985; Glaser, 1990). Testing proved a convenient instrument of social control for those late 19th-century su-

> perintendents who sought to create the "one best system" of education (Tyack, 1974). It also proved enormously useful as a means of determining how to slot students for either more or less rigorous (and costly) curricula when public funding of education and compulsory attendance vastly increased access to schools in the early 20th century. (Darling-Hammond, 1995, p. 475)

Much of this legacy remains in place today, and Darling-Hammond (1991) argued that the use of tests for placements and promotions ultimately reduces the amount of learning achieved by students placed in lower tracks or held back in grade. Students of color are disproportionately subject to both of these outcomes of testing. Neither outcome ultimately improves achievement. Students who are retained in grade fall consistently behind on both achievement and social-emotional measures when compared with students of equivalent achievement levels who are promoted (Holmes & Matthews, 1984; Shephard & M. L. Smith, 1986). Furthermore, the practice of retaining students is a major contributor to increased dropout rates (Carnegie Council on Adolescent Development, 1989; Mann, 1987; Massachusetts Advocacy Center, 1988; Wehlage, Rutter, G. A. Smith, Lesko, & Fernandez, 1990).

Additionally, many studies have found that students placed in the lowest tracks or in remedial programs with disproportionately low income and students of color are most apt to experience instruction geared only to multiple choice tests,

> ... working at a low cognitive level on test-oriented tasks that are profoundly disconnected from the skills they need to learn. Rarely are they given the opportunity to talk about what they know, to read real books, to write, or to construct and solve problems in mathematics, science, or other subjects (Oakes, 1985; Cooper & Sherk, 1989; Davis, 1986; Trimble & Sinclair, 1986). In short, they have been denied the opportunity to develop the capacities they will need for the future, in large part because commonly used tests are so firmly pointed at educational goals of the past. (Darling-Hammond, 1995, p. 475).

Authentic Assessment. In recent years, the school reform movement has engendered widespread efforts to transform the ways in which students' work and learning are organized and assessed in schools. These alternatives are frequently called performance-based, or "authentic," assessments because they engage students in real-world tasks rather than multiple choice tests, and evaluate them according to criteria that are important for actual performance in that field (Wiggins, 1989). Such assessments include oral presentations or exhibitions, along with collections of students' written products and their solutions to problems, experiments, debates, constructions and models, videotapes of performances and other learning occasions, and results of scientific and other inquiries (Archbald & Newman, 1988).

> Much of the rationale for these initiatives is based on growing evidence that traditional norm-referenced, multiple-choice tests fail to measure complex cogni-

tive and performance abilities. Furthermore, when used for decision making, such tests encourage instruction that tends to emphasize decontextualized, rote-oriented tasks imposing low cognitive demands rather than meaningful learning. Thus efforts to raise standards of learning and performance must rest in part on efforts to transform assessment practices.

If performance-based assessments that are currently being developed point at more challenging learning goals for all students, they may ameliorate some of the current test-induced sources of inequality that often are the result of not taking into account the diverse student populations and are also the result of basing the standards and measurements on white, middle-class norms (Darling-Hammond, 1994; Glaser, 1990). However, this will be true only to the extent that teachers are able to teach in the ways demanded by these assessments—that is, in ways that support the development of higher-order thinking and performance skills and in ways that diagnose and build upon individual learners' strengths and needs. Equalization of educational opportunities must rest as much on improving the caliber of teaching encountered by low-income and minority students as it does on changing the testing instrument or other technologies of schooling to which they are subject. (Darling-Hammond, 1995, p. 476)

LANGUAGE AND DISCOURSE

Scholars are arguing that language and discourse form the medium through which everything, in and out of schools, passes. People know their realities and identities through what they say and the ways they speak. Minami and Ovando (1995) described how most educational discourse and learning environments to date have tended primarily to reflect the discourse practices of mainstream society, with often unfortunate results for nonmainstream students, including many language minority students (Cazden, 1988, Cazden, Michaels, & Tabors, 1985; Gee, 1990, 1991; Michaels, 1981, 1991; Michaels & Collins, 1984). Using the term "match–mismatch," some linguists (e.g., Cook-Gumperz & Gumperz, 1982; Erickson & Mohatt, 1982; Heath, 1982; Mehan, 1991; Philips, 1982) have postulated that language-minority students do not prosper academically in such contexts (mismatch) because the discursive practices of their homes do not match the discursive practices of the school environment. In turn, such a mismatch between the discursive practices of the students' home and school impedes access to and participation in higher educational and occupational opportunities (Spener, 1988). In other words, whereas children from middle- and upper-class cultural and speech communities are sociolinguistically advantaged in the school environment, children from poor, non-English, and nonstandard English speech communities are more likely to be disadvantaged and even at risk of being marginalized in school environments (p. 435)

Minami and Ovando (1995) also described how more than half a million immigrants from nearly 100 different countries and cultures enter the United States every year,

> ... most speaking languages other than English (Crawford, 1989). To help them master the new language, immigrant children who speak little or no English are placed in a variety of programs, such as Maintenance Bilingual Education (MBE) (or additive/late-exit), Transitional Bilingual Education (TBE) (or early- exit), or English as a Second Language (ESL). Researchers, policymakers, administrators, the public, and those actively involved in bilingual and ESL programs have been engaged for the past 25 years in heated debates for and against bilingual education. For example, Baker and de Kanters (1981, 1983) evaluation studies generally concluded that bilingual programs are no more effective in promoting language and academic skills than alternative programs, such as structured immersion programs in which content-area instruction is provided through a monolingual English approach with modified use of ESL techniques. In contrast to Baker and de Kanter (1983), Willig (1985), Ramires, Yuen, and Ramey (1991), and Rosier and Holm (1980) found evidence supporting the efficacy of bilingual programs; that is, bilingual education promotes the learning processes of bilingual children and, moreover, programs with substantial native-language components seem effective in promoting education achievement by minority students. (p. 435)

With the recent passage of Proposition 209 in California, which moves to end bilingual education, and which is expected to cause national debate, school leaders will be put in positions to argue what is best for the non-native English-speaking students in their schools.

Mehan, Lintz, Okamoto, and Wills (1995) stated that the language teachers use with students is constitutive, or establishes the boundaries of students' opportunities to learn. The way in which teachers ask questions and engage in discourse with students both constrains and enables the ways in which they can display what they know. Because of the concurrence relation that operates in conversation, what students can say in lessons depends on the frames established by what teachers say, and the questions they ask (p. 129).

Scholars and students of language use in homes and schools (Cazden, 1988; Heath, 1982, 1986; Laosa, 1973; Mehan, 1979; Philips, 1982) have suggested that "recitation-type lessons in school may be compatible with the discourse patterns in Anglo families but may be incompatible with the discourse patterns of certain families of color. This discontinuity, in turn, may contribute to the lower achievement and higher drop-out rate among students of color" (p. 130). These observations regarding home–school discontinuity spurred attempts to rearrange classroom discourse for compatibility with home-based discourse. When the discourse structure of the classroom takes into account the discourse pattern of students living at or below the poverty level, students' academic performance improves (Mehan et al., 1995, p. 130).

When addressing the language needs of African American students, Lee and Slaughter-Defoe (1995) saw language as an

> essential tool through which we not only communicate, but through which we construct knowledge or think through new problems. Thus any discussion of

> factors influencing the learning of African American children, adolescents, and adults must take into account the variable of language use. This variable becomes particularly problematic in a society, such as the United States, in which language varieties are valued hierarchically. The conditions under which there are low- and high-prestige language varieties in a society have been labeled *diglossia* by Saville-Troike (1989). (p. 357)

According to Foster (1989), Marva Collins, the well-known teacher from Chicago's Westside Prep School, had success with her students because of the "congruence between her interactional style and the children's cultural experience. Familiar language and participation structures, including rhythmic language, call and response, repetition, and deliberate body motions, comprise the interactional pattern" (Mehan et al., 1995, p. 131).

Lucas, Henze, and Donato (1990) identified the following factors that are related to successful outcomes with language-minority students:

> (a) Value is placed on the students' languages and cultures; (b) High expectations of language minority students are made concrete; (c) School leaders make the education of language-minority students a priority; (d) Staff development is explicitly designed to help teachers and other staff serve language-minority students more effectively; (e) A variety of courses and programs for language-minority students is offered; (f) A counseling program gives special attention to language-minority students through counselors who understand those students linguistically as well as culturally; (g) Parents of language-minority students are encouraged to become involved in their children's education; and (h) School staff members share a strong commitment to empower language-minority students through education. (pp. 324–325, as quoted in Mehan et al., 1995, p. 439)

This section began with the observation that people know their realities and identities through discourse, that is, what people say and the way they speak. Much of the discussion in the literature on language relates to different models of bilingual education and/or the question of whether there should be bilingual education. When the discourse is presented in this way, it limits school leaders' thinking to only a few questions about language and culture. There are other questions regarding language and discourse: What is the relation between language learning and ethnocentrism?; How is it that within some cultures, most members are able to learn and use two or more languages?; Do we not need to provide opportunities for students to learn more languages in an increasingly global society? Why not use the skills of other language speakers within our country to teach us their languages?

HOME AND COMMUNITY

> Families do not come to schools alone, as blank slates to be inscribed with school knowledge. They come as part of social networks that provide an array

of information and resources that shape their actions and relationships. (Graue, 1993, p. 488)

There is a growing awareness that cultural forces shape the definitions that schools and families have about adult–child interaction and participation in various activities. Through extensive sociolinguistic analysis, Heath (1983) described how communities develop locally specific ideas about childhood, with proscribed roles for parents and their children. The tasks undertaken by parents to prepare their children for school, their ideas about what their children should know, and parceling of responsibility to family and community members were much the same within a community and varied between communities. Heath attributes mismatch between home and school for certain children to sociolinguistic differences that shape interactional patterns and the roles taken by individuals.

Lareau (1989) picked up the thread of the community orientation to home–school relations in her study of parent involvement in working-class and upper-middle-class elementary schools. Arguing that styles of home–school interaction are related to social class and cultural capital, Lareau described relations between schools and families that mirrored their relations between work and home life. Working-class parents played out relations characterized as separation—the home had roles and responsibilities that were quite distinct from those of the school. In contrast, middle-class parents blurred the boundaries between home and school, extending their domain from care of children to their education. Parental roles in the educational process, parents' relationships with school professionals, and their efficacy as advocates for their children set the stage for the emerging home–school relation (p. 467).

Beaulieu, Israel, and M. H. Smith (1990) discussed how, taken separately, family and community elements showed varying but significant influences on student dropout behaviors. In combination, however, they exerted a powerful force. When family and community influences were weak, the dropout rate exceeded 50%, when both were strong, students were virtually assured of completing their high school studies (p. 64).

Hidalgo, Bright, Siu, Swap, and Epstein (1995) stated the following about the involvement of families in educational practices: "The similarities and differences among families within and between cultural groups and the common and unique practices that schools must implement to involve families identify new directions for research and practice that link the fields of school and family partnership and multicultural education" (p. 516). Epstein (1991) wrote about family/school connections that are, ultimately, a school-by-school story. The literature on home and community relations with schools supports Epstein's final analysis. She argued it is the hard work of principals, teachers, and other staff members in each school that will determine whether families understand the schools and how their children are doing as well as what influence the families themselves continue to have in their children's learning and development. Also, the research and best practices literature supports the notion that all parents are very supportive of their children receiving a good education and are willing to participate, to the best of their ability, in helping their children to achieve that end. The multicultural literature debugs the myth that parents of color and poor parents are not concerned or supportive of their children's education.

PRACTICES OF SUCCESSFUL SCHOOL LEADERS

Among the few studies that give explicit recommendations to school leaders for how to develop successful instructional programs for multicultural populations, Lee and Slaughter-Defoe (1995) reviewed a synopsis of Sizemore's (1985, 1987, 1988) analyses of administrative programs for schools in African American communities. Sizemore (1988) documented organizational features, academic routines, qualities of leadership, and staff support that result in sustained academic achievement. Among the features identified by Sizemore (1988) that the literature suggests are applicable to most schools are the following:

1. The use of staff and teacher expertise, skills, information, and knowledge to conduct problem-directed searches for the resolution of school concerns and dilemmas.
2. The involvement of parents in some participatory and meaningful way in the school's program.
3. The prompt evaluation of teacher and staff performances and the provision of assistance, help, and in-service where necessary; the rating of performances as unsatisfactory where warranted, including persuading such teachers to transfer in spite of central office resistance.
4. The demand for the use of materials which prove functional for elevating achievement when such are not approved by the Board of Education, especially in the areas of phonics, African American History and Culture, and mathematics problem solving.
5. The denial of student placement in Educable Mentally Retarded divisions unless all strategies for regular learning had occurred and had been exhausted.
6. The refusal to accept system programs which consumed administration and supervision time normally given to the regular program unless such programs increased the school day. (pp. 244–245)

Lee and Slaughter-Defoe (1995) pointed out that whereas it may not be evident on the surface, "Sizemore's analysis includes *both cultural and political dimen-*

sions [emphasis added]. She emphasized the need for leaders at the school level who are willing to confront bureaucratic restrictions and struggle to institute curriculum, academic routines, and staff necessary to bring about academic achievement in underachieving African American public schools. She also emphasized the need to include African American history and culture as a foundational component of the academic curriculum" (pp. 363–364).

Sizemore (1988) concluded:

> While there is much in the literature citing teacher leadership and parent involvement as important crit eria for high achievement, our findings do not confirm these notions. It may be that the African American school needs a different mix of ingredients for a successful recipe. Since there has never been a consensus among the American polity around full citizenship for the African American, and since the institutional value of white superiority still dominates the social reality, strong leadership may continue to emerge as the most important factor in the elevation of achievement in African American schools until the education of teachers comes to include content which reflects the true history and condition of African Americans so that they are enlightened and better prepared to teach African American children. (p. 265)

Lee and Slaughter-Defoe (1995) suggested that strong consideration must be given to Sizemore's analysis, "as her work demonstrates evidence of sustained high academic achievement" (pp. 363–364).

Similarly, Garcia (1995) described the work of principals in a successful set of schools serving Mexican American students:

> Principals (average administrative experience of 11.7 years) tended to be highly articulate regarding the curriculum and instructional strategies undertaken in their schools. They were also highly supportive of their instructional staff, taking pride in their accomplishments. They reported their support of teacher autonomy, although they were quite aware of the potential problems regarding the pressure to conform strictly to district policies concerning standardization of curriculum and the need for academic accountability (testing). (p. 384)

CONCLUSIONS

School leaders may wish to consider the following points:

- Multicultural education has a history and presence that is evolving. According to the research, it is not a temporary fad or reform effort but is both a theoretical and practical educational movement that will be with schools both nationally and internationally for years to come.
- Multicultural education is like most educational movements in that, as it gains popularity, critiques and myths abound. The critiques about multicultural education must be carefully examined to know whether they are insightful and helpful and can lead to improvement, or if their real purpose is to fracture or mystify the potential power of this multicultural effort to reform schools and classrooms.

"Students" are increasingly addressed as demographics, which are used to make many educational arguments. For example, the number of Spanish-speaking students in a school often determines considerations for ESL or bilingual programs. Although this use of demographics is important, a reading of the multicultural literature argues for students to be treated not as a demographic, but as unique individuals who want to and can succeed academically. The literature also suggests students need to be taught how to take charge of their life circumstances, challenge structural inequalities, and accept and appreciate the diversity that surrounds them.

The literature on teacher demographics argues that for the next two to three decades, the teaching force will be mainly White and female. The pre-service teaching force preparation for working with diverse student populations according to all reports continues to be incomplete. Also, noticeably absent from this literature are studies showing that school districts have instituted successful, ongoing staff development programs to help teachers and other school staff to work with diverse populations. Incidents of culture shock, teacher burn out, and teacher's holding low expectations of diverse students have become concerns to which school leaders must give serious attention.

Throughout educational history, curriculum has been described as the lifeblood of the school. The multicultural research and best practices literature offers several ideas or models (Banks, 1993; Gay, 1995; Grant & Sleeter, 1998) for how to plan and write curriculum so that narratives are framed in such a way that students from all backgrounds will feel that the curriculum content addresses their cultural backgrounds and academic needs.

There is no silver bullet, one way, or one best practice for teaching all members of a particular ethnic group. Whereas the research reports the importance of recognizing different learning and teaching styles, there are still cautions for teachers and school leaders to acknowledge there is no one formula. Culturally responsive instruction is suggested as a recommended approach for teaching and working with diverse groups of students. This approach, which takes advantage of students' cultural backgrounds, languages, life experiences, and learning potential works very well with the movement toward authentic assessment. Both teacher and student come together to plan instruction and assessment around tasks that are real to students and important to their learning needs.

There is a mismatch between the language and discourse of the schools and the language and discourse of some students' homes and communities. Although there have been considerable debates over the last 25 or more years about bilingual education, many researchers do report a favorable response for students when they are able to utilize their home languages in schools and are placed in a maintenance model of bilingual instruction. At the very least, schools need to acknowledge the value of home languages and ways of speaking and to offer opportunities for students to be proud of their diverse language backgrounds.

Excellent home/community–school interactions take place when parents and community members serve in active ways, not just assigned as spectators or as monitors asked to continually perform low involvement, passive tasks. Best practices literature suggests that schools need to recognize parent and community diversity and to reach out to parents in ways that acknowledge and accept their ethnic and cultural backgrounds. Some schools with a record of success send correspondence home in the parents' native languages, have staff members fluent in the native languages, make certain that parents feel welcome and proud when they come to their children's schools, and assure that parents are highly regarded members of the wider school community.

As schools are not neutral sites, school leaders must be politically minded. In other words, they have to recognize the politics inherent in their position of leadership. They need to know what is going on, to be supportive of their staff and, when teachers and other school personnel are not acting in the best interests of their students, school leaders need to act to get such staff out of their schools. School leaders need to establish and work in partnership with parents and community members as well as with teachers and school personnel. The educational literature reports that school leaders who take the initiative and stand up for their students are usually rewarded with higher student achievement and a more cooperative and engaging school environment.

It must be acknowledged that, of the studies and materials found, the conceptualization of multicultural education is much further along than the practice of multicultural education. Very few of the studies were more than isolated accounts and were written without the benefits of financial support and a thorough and ongoing chain of inquiry. Very little of the research and best practices literature dealt with gender and social class from a multicultural perspective. Also, it was not possible to locate materials dealing with the intersections of race, class, and gender. As far as ability is concerned, there is a body of literature about individuals with disabilities, but most often it is not written from a multicultural perspective. Additionally, in the research and best practices literature reviewed, material connecting sexual orientation to educational practices is just now emerging and the works of Sears and Williams (1997), Harbeck (1992), and Woodson (1995) are recommended as places to begin reading about such connections (along with the Gay, Lesbian, Straight Education Network website: GLSTNAlert@aol.com).

Although it has been noted that many scholars in the field of multicultural education like to use Grant and Sleeter's (1998) fifth approach—education that is multicultural and social reconstructionist (EMCSR)—to interrogate issues of structured inequality within schools, these scholars, between their offering of the purposes, or intent, of their studies and their recommendations, narrow their results from an EMCSR perspective to one that considers only one or at most two factors in students' education (e.g., language, or ethnicity). The interconnections between these and other factors such as race, ability, and gender are not often considered. Few studies offer school leaders suggestions that take into account race, ethnicity, social class, gender, sexual orientation, and language, all together.

Over the last three decades, school leaders have been presented with discourses that describe diverse students as culturally deprived, or at-risk, within language minorities, kids of violence, kids of single-parent families, and/or as culturally different, kids from homes of same-sex parents, of different religious backgrounds, of different abilities. These descriptions do more to offer a way of thinking about some students in the schools than providing educational discourse to facilitate discussions between professionals. In other words, these descriptions work to do more than just label students.

If schools are like "crossroads, marketplaces, village squares, and cities themselves," then the different studies only point to small corners of the more complex intersections that exist within every school. It is important that school leaders play a significant role in shaping the direction of research and best practices in multicultural education if their intent is to prepare all students for the challenges they will face in the new millennium. Finally, it is believed the research and best practices literature reported in this chapter offer a good beginning.

REFERENCES

American Association of College for Teacher Education. (1987). *RATE I. Teaching teachers: Facts and figures.* Washington, DC: American Association of College for Teacher Education.

American Association of College for Teacher Education. (1988). *RATE II. Teaching teachers: Facts and figures.* Washington, DC: American Association of College for Teacher Education.

American Association of Colleges for Teacher Education. (1989). *RATE III. Teaching teachers: Facts and figures.* Washington, DC: American Association of College for Teacher Education.

American Association of College for Teacher Education (1990). *RATE IV. Teaching teachers: Facts and figures.* Washington, DC: American Association of College for teacher Education.

Archbald, D. A., & Newman, F. M. (1988). *Beyond standardized testing: Assessing authentic academic achievement in the secondary school.* Reston, VA: National Association of Secondary School Principals.

Au, K. H. (1980). Participation structures in a reading lesson with Hawaiian children: Analysis of a culturally appropriate instructional event. *Anthropology and Education Quarterly, 1*(2), 91–115.

Baker, K. A., & de Kanter, A. A. (1981). *Effectiveness of bilingual education: A review of the literature.* Washington, DC: Office of Planning, Budget and Evaluation, U.S. Department of Education.

Baker, K. A., & de Kanter, A. A. (1983). Federal policy and the effectiveness of bilingual education. In K. A. Baker & A. A. de Kanter (Eds.), *Bilingual education* (pp. 33–86). Lexington, MA: Lexington Books.

Balch, S. A. (1992). Political correctness or public choice? *Educational Record, 73*(1), 21–24.

Banks, J. (1991). *Teaching strategies for ethnic studies.* Boston: Allyn & Bacon.

Banks, J. (1994). *Multiethnic education: Theory and practice.* Boston: Allyn & Bacon.

Banks, J. A. (1993). Multicultural education: Characteristics and goals. In J. A. Banks & C. A. McGee Banks (Eds.), *Multicultural education: Issues and perspectives* (2nd ed., pp. 2–26). Boston: Allyn & Bacon.

Banks, J. A. (1995a). Introduction. In J. A., Banks & C. A. McGee Banks (Eds.), *Handbook of research on multicultural education* (pp. xi–xiv). New York: Macmillan.

Banks, J. A. (1995b). Multicultural Education: Historical development, dimensions, and practice. In J. A., Banks & C. A. McGee Banks (Eds.), *Handbook of research on multicultural education* (pp. 3–24). New York: Macmillan.

Beaulieu, L. J., Israel, G. D., & Smith, M. H. (1990, April). *Community as social capital: The case of public high school drop-outs.* Paper presented at the annual meeting of the Rural Sociological Society, Norfolk, VA.

Bennally, A., Lynch, R., McCarty, T., & Wallace, S. (1991). Classroom inquiry and Navajo learning styles: A call for reassessment. *Anthropology and Education Quarterly, 22,* 42–59.

Berry, G. L. (1980). Children, television and social class roles: The media as an unplanned educational curriculum. In E. L. Palmer & A. Dorr (Eds.), *Children and the faces of television* (pp. 71–81). New York: Academic Press.

Bowman, B. (1989). Education language-minority children: Challenges and opportunities. *Phi Delta Kappan, 71*(3), 118–121.

Brameld, T. (1956). *Toward a reconstructed philosophy of education.* New York: Holt, Rinehart & Winston.

Broudy, H. S. (1975). Cultural pluralism: New wine in old bottles. *Educational Leadership, 33,* 173–175.

Buttery, T., Haberman, M., & Houston, R. (1990). *ATE: First annual survey of critical issues in teacher education.* Reston, VA: Association of Teacher Educators.

Calderon, M., & Diaz, E. (1993). Retooling teacher preparation programs to embrace Latino realities in schools. In R. E. Castro & Y. R. Ingle (Eds.), *Reshaping teacher education in the southwest: A response to the needs of latino students and teachers* (pp. 51–70). Claremont, CA: Tomas Rivera Center.

Carnegie Council on Adolescent Development. (1989). *Turning points: Preparing youth for the 21st century.* New York: Carnegie Corporation of New York.

Cazden, C. B. (1988). *Classroom discourse: The language of teaching and learning.* Portsmouth, NH: Heinemann.

Cazden, C. B., Michaels, S., & Tabors, P. (1985). Spontaneous repair in sharing time narratives: The interaction of metalinguistic awareness, speech event, and narrative style. In S. W. Freedman (Ed.), *The acquisition of written language* (pp. 51–64). Norwood, NJ: Ablex.

Cochran-Smith, M. (1995). Uncertain allies: Understanding the boundaries of race and teaching. *Harvard Educational Review, 65*(4), 541–570.

College Board. (1985). *Equality and excellence: The educational status of Black Americans.* New York: College Entrance Examination Board.

Collins, M. (1990). *Marva Collins' way.* Los Angeles: J. P. Tarcher.

Cook-Gumperz, J., & Gumperz, J. J. (1982). Communicative competence in educational perspective. In L. C. Wilkinson (Ed), *Communicating in the classroom* (pp. 13–24). New York: Academic Press.

Cooper, E., & Sherk, J. (1989). Addressing urban school reform: Issues and alliances. *Journal of Negro Education, 58*(3), 315–331.

Cooper, L., Johnson, D. W., & Wilderson, F. (1980). Effects of cooperative, competitive, and individualistic experiences on interpersonal attraction among heterogeneous peers. *Journal of Social Psychology, 111*, 243–252.

Cornbleth, C., & Waugh, D. (1995). *The great speckled bird: Multicultural politics and education policymaking.* New York: St. Martin's Press.

Cortes, C. E. (1981). The societal curriculum. Implications for multiethnic education. In J. A. Banks (Ed.), *Education in the 80's: Multiethnic education* (pp. 24–32). Washington, DC: National Education Association.

Cortes, C. E. (1995). Knowledge construction and popular culture: The media as multicultural educator. In J. A. Banks & C. A. McGee Banks (Eds.), *Handbook of research on multicultural education* (pp. 169–183). New York: Macmillan.

Crawford, J. (1989). *Bilingual education: History, politics, theory, and practice.* Trenton, NJ: Crane Publishing.

Cummins, J. (1986). Empowering minority students: A framework for intervention. *Harvard Educational Review, 54*, 18–36.

Darling-Hammond, L. (1990). Teacher professionalism: Why and how. In A. Lieberman (Ed.), *Schools as collaborative cultures: Creating the future now* (pp. 25–50). Philadelphia: Falmer.

Darling-Hammond, L. (1991). The implications of testing policy for quality and equality. *Phi Delta Kappan, 73*(3), 220–225.

Darling-Hammond, L. (1994). Performance-based assessment and educational equity. *Harvard Educational Review, 66*(1), 5–30.

Darling-Hammond, L. (1995). Inequality and access to knowledge. In J. A. Banks & C. A. McGee Banks (Eds.), *Handbook of research on multicultural education* (pp. 465–483). New York: Macmillan.

Davis, D. G. (1986, April). *A pilot study to assess equity in school curricular offerings across three diverse schools in a large urban school district.* Paper presented at the annual meeting of the American Education Research Association, San Francisco.

Delpit, L. D. (1988). The silenced dialogue: Power and pedagogy in educating other people's children. *Harvard Educational Review, 48*, 280–298.

Diaz, S., Moll, L. C., & Mehan, H. (1986). Sociocultural resources in instruction: A contextspecific approach. In *Beyond language: Social and cultural factors in schooling language minority students* (pp. 197–230). Sacramento: Bilingual Education Office, California State Department of Education.

Duran, R. (1987). Factors affecting development of second language literacy. In S. Goldman & H. Trueba (Eds.), *Becoming literate in English as a second language* (pp. 33–55). Norwood, NJ: Ablex.

Epstein, J. (1991). Paths to partnership: What we can learn from federal, state, district, and school initiatives. *Phi Delta Kappan, 72*(5), pp. 344–358.

Erickson, F. D., & Mohatt, G. (1982). Cultural organization of participation structures in two classrooms of Indian students. In G. D. Spindler (Ed.), *Doing the ethnography of schooling: Educational anthropology in action* (pp. 132–175). New York: Holt, Rinehart & Winston.

Essed, P. (1990). *Everyday racism.* Claremont, CA: Hunter House.

Estes, G., Stansbury, K., & Long, C. (1990). *Assessment component of the California New Teacher Project: First year report.* San Francisco, CA: Far West Laboratory for Educational Research and Development.

Finley, M. K. (1984). Teachers and tracking in a comprehensive high school. *Sociology of Education, 57*, 233–243.

Foster, M. (1989). "It's cookin' now": A performance analysis of the speech events of a Black teacher in an urban community college. *Language in Society, 13*(1), 1–29.

Foster, M. (1995). African American teachers and culturally relevant pedagogy. In J. A. Banks & C. A. McGee Banks (Eds.), *Handbook of research on multicultural education* (pp. 570–581). New York: Macmillan.

Garcia, E. E. (1991). *The education of linguistically and culturally diverse students: Effective instructional practices.* Washington, DC: Center for Applied Linguistics.

Garcia, E. E. (1993). Language, culture, and education. In L. DarlingHammond (Ed.), *Review of research in education* (Vol. 19, pp. 51–98). Washington, DC: American Educational Research Association.

Garcia, E. E. (1995). Educating Mexican American students: Past treatment and recent developments in theory, research, policy, and practice. In J. A. Banks & C. A. McGee Banks (Eds.), *Handbook of research on multicultural education* (pp. 372–387). New York: Macmillan.

Gay, G. (1995a). Bridging multicultural theory and practice. *Multicultural Education*, Fall, pp. 4–9.

Gay, G. (1995b). Curriculum theory and multicultural education. In J. A. Banks & C. A. McGee Banks (Eds.), *Handbook of research on multicultural education* (pp. 25–43). New York: Macmillan.

Gee, J. P. (1990). *Social linguistics and literacies: Ideologies in discourse.* Bristol, PA: Falmer.

Gee, J. P. (1991). Memory and myth: A perspective on narrative. In A. McCabe & C. Peterson (Eds.), *Developing narrative structure* (pp. 1–25). Hillsdale, NJ: Lawrence Erlbaum Associates.

Giroux, H. A. (1992). Postcolonial ruptures and democratic possibilities: Multiculturalism as antiracist pedagogy. *Cultural Critique, 21*, 5–40.

Glaser, R. (1990). *Testing and assessment: O tempora! O mores!* Pittsburgh: University of Pittsburgh, Learning Research and Development Center.

Glazer, N. (1981). Pluralism and the new immigrants. *Society, 19*, 31–36.

Goldman, S., & Trueba, H. (Eds.). (1987). *Becoming literate in English as a second language: Advances in research and theory.* Norwood, NJ: Ablex.

Gollnick, D., & Chinn, P. (1986). *Multicultural education in a pluralistic society.* Columbus, OH: Merrill.

Goodman, Y. (1980). The roots of literacy. In M.P. Douglass (Ed.), *Reading: A humanizing experience* (pp. 286–301). Claremont, CA: Claremont Graduate School.

Grant, C. A. (1978). Education that is multicultural—Isn't that what we mean? *Journal of Teacher Education, 29*, 45–49.

Grant, C. A. (1994a). Best practices in teacher preparation for urban schools: Lessons from the multicultural teacher education literature. *Action in Teacher Education, 16*(3), 1–18.

Grant, C. A. (1994b). Challenging the myths about multicultural education. *Multicultural Education*, Winter, 4–9.

Grant, C. A., & Secada, W. G. (1990). Preparing teachers for diversity. In W.R. Houston (Ed.), *Handbook of research on teacher education* (pp. 403–422). New York: Macmillan.

Grant, C. A., & Sleeter, C. E. (1986). *After the school bell rings*. Barcombe, England: Falmer.

Grant, C. A., & Sleeter, C. E. (1989). *Turning on learning: Five approaches for multicultrual teaching plans for race, class, gender, and disability.* New York: Merrill.

Grant, C. A., & Sleeter, C. E. (1991). Race, class, gender and disability in current textbooks. In M. W. Apple and L. K. Christian-Smith (Eds.), *The politics of the textbook.* New York: Routledge.

Grant, C. A., & Sleeter, C. E. (1998). *Turning on learning: Five approaches for multicultural teaching plans for race, class, gender, and disability.* New York: Merrill.

Grant, C. A. & Tate, W. F. (1995). Multicultural education through the lens of the multicultural education research literature. In J. A. Banks & C. A. McGee Banks (Eds.), *Handbook of research on multicultural education* (pp.145–166). New York: Macmillan.

Graue, M. E. (1993). Social networks and home-school relations. *Educational Policy, 7*(4), 466–490.

Haberman, M. (1987). *Recruiting and selecting teachers for Urban schools.* Urban Diversity Series Number 95. New York: ERIC Clearing House on Urban Education.

Hale-Benson, J. E. (1986). *Black children: Their roots, culture and learning styles.* Baltimore: Johns Hopkins University Press.

Hall, N. (1987). *The emergence of literacy.* Portsmouth, NH: Heinemann.

Harbeck, K. M. (Ed.). (1992). *Coming out of the classroom closet: Gay and lesbian students, teachers and curricula.* New York: Haworth.

Heath, S. B. (1981). Towards an ethnohistory of writing in American education. In M. Farr-Whitman (Ed.), *Writing: The nature, development and teaching of written communication: Vol. 1. Variation in writing: Functional and linguisticcultural differences* (pp. 225–246). Hillsdale, NJ: Lawrence Erlbaum Associates.

Heath, S. B. (1982a). Questioning at home and at school: A comparative study. In G. Spindler (Ed.), *Doing the ethnography of schooling* (pp. 102–131). New York: Holt, Rinehart & Winston.

Heath, S. B. (1983). *Ways with words: Language, life and work in communities and classrooms.* New York: Cambridge University Press.

Heath, S. B. (1986). Sociocultural contexts of language development. In *Beyond language: Social and cultural factors in schooling language minority students* (pp. 143–186). Sacramento: Bilingual Education Office, California State Department of Education.

Hidalgo, N. M., Bright, J. A., Siu, S. F., Swap, S. M., & Epstein, J. L. (1995). Research on families, schools, and communities: A multicultural perspective. In J. A. Banks & C. A.

McGee Banks (Eds.), *Handbook of research on multicultural education* (pp. 498–524). New York: Macmillan.

Hilliard, A. G. (1997). *Critical knowledge for diverse teachers and learners.* Washington, DC: American Association of College Teacher Educators.

Hirsch, Jr., E. D. (1987). *Cultural literacy: What every American needs to know.* New York: Houghton-Mifflin.

Holmes, C. T., & Matthews, K. M. (1984). The effects of nonpromotion on elementary and junior high school pupils: A meta-analysis. *Review of Educational Research, 54*, 225–236.

Irvine, J .J. (1992). Making teacher education culturally responsive. In M. E. Dilworth (Ed.), *Diversity in teacher education* (pp. 79–92). San Francisco: Jossey-Bass.

Irvine, J. J., & York, D. E. (1995). Learning styles and culturally diverse students: A literature review. In J. A. Banks & C. A. McGee Banks (Eds.), *Handbook of research on multicultural education* (pp. 484–497). New York: Macmillan.

Ivie, S. D. (1979). Multicultural education: Boon or boondoggle? *Journal of Teacher Education, 30*, 23–25.

Johnson, D. W., & Johnson, R. T. (1981). Effects of cooperative and individualistic learning experiences on interethnic interaction. *Journal of Educational Psychology, 73*, 444–449.

King, J. E. (1995). Culture-centered knowledge: Black studies, curriculum transformation, and social action. In J. A. Banks & C. A. McGee Banks (Eds.), *Handbook of research on multicultural education* (pp. 265–290). New York: Macmillan.

Klein, S. S. (Ed.). (1985). *Handbook for achieving sex equity through education.* Baltimore: Johns Hopkins University Press.

Kohl, H. (1967). *36 children.* New York: Signet.

Kohl, H. (1998). *The discipline of hope: Learning from a lifetime of teaching.* New York: Simon & Schuster.

Kunjufu, J. (1989). *A talk with Jawanzaa: Critical issues in educating African American youth.* Chicago: African American Images.

Laosa, L. M. (1973). Reform in educational and psychological assessment: Cultural and linguistic issues. *Journal of the Association of Mexican-American Educators, 1*, 19–24.

Ladson-Billings, G. (1994). *The dreamkeepers: Successful teachers of African-American children.* San Francisco: Jossey-Bass.

Lareau, A. (1989). *Home advantage.* New York: Falmer.

Lee, C. D., & Slaughter-Defoe, D. T. (1995). Historical and sociocultural influences on African American education. In J. A. Banks & C. A. McGee Banks (Eds.), *Handbook of research on multicultural education* (pp. 348–371). New York: Macmillan.

Lee, S. J. (1996). *Unraveling the "model minority" stereotype: Listening to Asian American youth.* New York: Teacher's College Press.

Leifer, A. D., Gordon, N. J., & Graves, S. B. (1974). Children's television more than mere entertainment. *Harvard Educational Review, 44*(2), 213–245.

Leiss, W., Kline, S., & Jhally, S. (1986). *Social communication in advertising.* Toronto: Methuen.

Lomawaima, K. T. (1995). Educating Native Americans. In J. A. Banks & C. A. McGee Banks (Eds.), *Handbook of research on multicultural education* (pp. 331–347). New York: Macmillan.

Longstreet, W. C. (1978). *Aspects of ethnicity.* New York: Teacher's College Press.

Lucas, T., Henze, R., & Donato, R. (1990). Promoting the success of Latino language minority students: An exploratory study of six high schools. *Harvard Educational Review, 60*(3), 315–334.

Massachusetts Advocacy Center and the Center for Early Adolescence. (1988). *Before it's too late: Dropout prevention in the middle grades.* Boston: Author.

Mattai, P. R. (1992). Rethinking multicultural education: Has it lost its focus or is it being misused? *Journal of Negro Education, 61*(1), 65–77.

McCarthy, C. (1990a). *Race and curriculum.* London: Falmer.

McCarthy, C. (1990b). Race and education in the United States: The multicultural solution. *Interchange, 21*(3), 45–55.

McCarthy, C. (1998). Educating the American popular: Suburban resentment and the representation of the inner city in contemporary film and television. *Race, Ethnicity and Education, 1*(1), pp. 31–48.

McCormick, T. E. (1990). Collaboration works! Preparing teachers for urban realities. *Contemporary Education, 61,* 420–426.

Mehan, H. (1979). *Learning lessons.* Cambridge, MA: Harvard University Press.

Mehan, H. (1991). *Sociological foundations supporting the study of cultural diversity* (Research Report 1). Santa Cruz, CA: National Center for Research on Cultural Diversity and Second Language Learning.

Mehan, H., Lintz, A., Okamoto, D., & Wills, J. S. (1995). Ethnographic studies of multicultural education in classrooms and schools. In J. A. Banks & C. A. McGee Banks (Eds.), *Handbook of research on multicultural education* (pp. 129–144). New York: Macmillan.

Mesa-Bains, A. (1993). Introduction. In J. H. Shulman, Amalia Mesa-Bains (Eds.), *Diversity in the classroom: A casebook for teachers and teacher educators* (pp. 1–4). Hillsdale, NJ: Research for Better Schools and Lawrence Erlbaum Associates.

Michaels, S. (1981). "Sharing time": Children's narrative styles and differential access to literacy. *Language in Society, 10*, 423–442.

Michaels, S. (1991). The dismantling of narrative. In A. McCabe & C. Peterson (Eds.), *Developing narrative structure* (pp. 303–351). Hillsdale, NJ: Lawrence Erlbaum Associates.

Michaels, S., & Collins, J. (1984). Oral discourse styles. Classroom interaction and the acquisition of literacy. In D. Tannen (Ed.), *Coherence in spoken and written discourse* (pp. 219–244). Norwood, NJ: Ablex.

Minami, M. & Ovando, C. J. (1995). Language issues in multicultural contexts. In J. A. Banks & C. A. McGee Banks (Eds.), *Handbook of research on multicultural education* (pp. 427–444). New York: Macmillan.

Mock, K. (1981, November). *Multicultural education in early childhood: A developmental rationale.* Paper presented at the National Conference on Multicultural Education, Winnipeg, Canada.

Moran, C. E. & Hakuta, K. (1995). Bilingual education: Broadening research perspectives. In J. A. Banks & C. A. McGee Banks (Eds.), *Handbook of research on multicultural education* (pp. 445–462). New York: Macmillan.

Murrell, P. (1991). Cultural politics in teacher education: What's missing in the preparation of minority teachers? In M. Foster (Ed.), *Qualitative investigations into schools and schooling* (pp. 205–225). New York: AMS Press.

National Center for Education Statistics. (1985). *The condition of education.* Washington, DC: U.S. Department of Education.

National Center for Education Statistics. (1990). *The condition of education.* Washington, DC: U.S. Department of Education.

National Coalition for Women and Girls in Education. (1997, June). *Title IX at 25: Report Card on Gender Equity.* Washington, DC: National Coalition for Women and Girls in Education c/o National Women's Law Center.

National Education Association. (1992). *Status of the American public school teacher 1990–91.* Washington, DC: Author.

Nieto, S. (1994). Lessons from students on creating a chance to dream. *Harvard Educational Review, 64*(4), 392–426.

Nieto, S. (1995). A history of the education of Puerto Rican students in U.S. mainland schools: "Losers," "outsiders," or "leaders"? In J. A. Banks & C. A. McGee Banks (Eds.), *Handbook of research on multicultural education* (pp. 388–411). New York: Macmillan.

Nieto, S. (1996). *Affirming diversity: The sociopolitical context of multicultural education.* White Plains, NY: Longman.

Oakes, J. (1985). *Keeping track.* New Haven, CT: Yale University Press.

Oakes, J. (1986, June). Tracking in secondary schools: A contextual perspective. *Educational Psychologist, 22*, 129–154.

Oakes, J., Ormseth, R., & Campbell, P. (1990). *Multiplying inequalities: The effects of race, social class, and tracking opportunities to learn mathematics and science (NSF)*. Santa Monica, CA: RAND Corporation.

Ogbu, J. U. (1992). Understanding cultural diversity and learning. *Educational Researcher, 21*(8), 5–14.

Olneck, M. (1990). The recurring dream: Symbolism and ideology in intercultural and multicultural education. *American Journal of Education, 98*(2), 147–174.

Omi, M., & Winant, H. (1986). *Racial formation in the Unites States: From the 1960s to the 1980s*. New York: Routledge.

Orfield, G. (1993). *The growth of segregation in American schools: Changing patterns of separation and poverty since 1968*. A report of the Harvard Project on School Desegregation to the National School Boards Association.

Pang, V. O. (1995). Asian Pacific American students: A diverse and complex population. In J. A. Banks & C. A. McGee Banks (Eds.), *Handbook of research on multicultural education* (pp. 412–424). New York: Macmillan.

Parker, W. C. (1997). The art of deliberation. *Educational Leadership, 54*(5), 18.

Philips, S. U. (1982). *The invisible culture: Communication in classroom and community on the Warm Springs Indian reservation*. New York: Longman.

Popkewitz, T. P. (1988). Culture, pedagogy, and power: Issues in the production of values and colonialization. *Journal of Education, 170*(2), 77–90.

Portes, P. R. (1996). Ethnicity and culture in educational psychology. In D. C. Berliner & R. C. Calfee (Eds.), *Handbook of educational psychology* (pp. 331–357). New York: Macmillan.

Ramirez, J. D., Yuen, S. D., & Ramey, D. R. (1991). *Longitudinal study of structured English immersion strategy, early-exit and late-exit transitional bilingual education programs for language-minority children. Final report to the U.S. Department of Education*. (Executive Summary and Vols. 1 & 2). San Mateo, CA: Aguirre International.

Ravitch, D. (1991–1992). A culture in common. *Educational Leadership, 49*(4), 3–11.

Rosenbaum, J. (1976). *Making inequality: The hidden curriculum of high school tracking*. New York: Wiley.

Rosenbaum, J. E. (1980). Social implications of educational grouping. In D. C. Berliner (Ed.), *Review of research in education* (Vol. 8, pp. 361–401). Washington, DC: American Educational Research Association.

Rosier, P., & Holm, W. (1980). *The Rock Point experience: A longitudinal study of a Navajo school program*. Washington, DC: Center for Applied Statistics.

Sadker, M. P., & Sadker, D. M. (1982). *Sex equity handbook for schools.* New York: Longman.

Saville-Troike, M. (1989). *The ethnography of communication.* New York: Basil Blackwell.

Scribner, S., & Cole, M. (1981). *The psychology of literacy.* Cambridge, MA: Harvard University Press.

Sears, J. T., & Williams, W. L. (Eds.). (1997). *Overcoming heterosexism and homophobia: Strategies that work.* New York: Columbia University Press.

Shephard, L., & Smith, M. L. (1986). Synthesis of research on school readiness and kindergarten retention. *Educational Leadership, 4*(3), 78–86.

Sizemore, B. A. (1985). Pitfalls and promises of effective school research. *Journal of Negro Education, 54,* 269–288.

Sizemore, B. A. (1987). The effective African American elementary school. In G. W. Noblit & W. T. Pink (Eds.), *Schooling in social context: Qualitative studies* (pp. 175–202). Norwood, NJ: Ablex.

Sizemore, B. A. (1988). The Madison elementary school: A turnaround case. *Journal of Negro Education, 57*(3), 243–266.

Slavin, R. E. (1977). *Student learning team techniques: Narrowing the achievement gap between the races* (Report no. 228). Baltimore, MD: Johns Hopkins University, Center for Social Organization of Schools.

Slavin, R. E., & Oickle, E. (1981). Effects of cooperative learning teams on student achievement and race relations: Treatment by race interactions. *Sociology of Education, 54,* 174–180.

Sleeter, C. E. (1994). White racism. *Multicultural Education, 1*(4), 5O8 & 39.

Sleeter, C.E. (1995). An analysis of the critiques of multicultural education. In J. A. Banks & C. A. McGee Banks (Eds.), *Handbook of research on multicultural education* (pp. 81–94). New York: Macmillan.

Sleeter, C. E., & Grant, C. A. (1994) *Making choices for multicultural education: Five approaches to race, class, and gender.* Englewood Cliffs, NJ: Merrill.

Smith, F. (1971). *Understanding reading.* New York: Holt, Rinehart & Winston.

Snyder, T. D., & Hoffman, C. M. (1995). *Digest of education statistics 1994.* Washington, DC: National Center for Education Statistics, U.S. Department of Education.

Spener, D. (1988). Transitional bilingual education and the socialization of immigrants. *Harvard Educational Review, 58*(2), 133–153.

Spring, J. (1992). *Images of American life: A history of ideological management in schools, movies, radio, and television.* Albany: State University of New York Press.

Stallings, J. S., Bossung, J., & Martin, A. (1990). Houston Teaching Academy: Partnership in developing teachers. *Teaching and Teacher Education, 6,* 355–365.

Stern, J. D. (1994, June). *The condition of education in rural schools.* U.S. Department of Education and the Office of Educational Research and Improvement Programs for the Improvement of practice.

Stotsky, S. (1991). Cultural politics. *American School Board Journal, 178*(10), 26–28.

Strickland, D. (1995). Early childhood development and reading instruction. In C. Brooks (Ed.), *Tapping potential: English and language arts for the Black learner* (pp. 88–101). Washington, DC: National Council of Teachers in English.

Takaki, R. (1989). *Strangers from a different shore: A history of Asian Americans.* Boston: Little, Brown.

Talbert, J. E. (1990). *Teacher tracking: Exacerbating inequalities in the high school.* Stanford, CA: Center for Research on the Context of Secondary Teaching, Stanford University.

Thomas, M. D. (1981). The limits of pluralism. *Phi Delta Kappan, 62,* 589–592.

Tikunoff, W. J. (1985). *Applying significant bilingual instructional features in the classroom* (Part C Bilingual Education Research Services). Josselyn, VA: National Clearinghouse for Bilingual Education.

Trimble, K., & Sinclair, R. L. (1986, April). *Ability grouping and differing conditions for learning: An analysis of content and instruction in ability-grouped classes.* Paper presented at the annual meeting of the American Education Research Association, San Francisco.

Trueba, H. (1988). *Rethinking learning disabilities: Cultural knowledge in literacy acquisition.* Unpublished manuscript, Office for Research on Educational Equity, Graduate School of Education, University of California, Santa Barbara.

21st Century: Restructuring the education of teachers. (1991). Reston, VA: Association of Teacher Educators.

Tyack, D. B. (1974). *The one best system.* Cambridge, MA: Harvard University Press.

Waters, M. M. (1989). An agenda for educating Black teachers. *The Educational Forum, 53*(3), 267–279.

Wehlage, G. G., Rutter, R. A., Smith, G. A., Lesko, N., & Fernandez, R. R. (1990). *Reducing the risk: Schools as communities of support.* New York: Falmer.

Wells, A. S., & Serma, I. (1996). The politics of culture: Understanding local political resistance to detracking in racially mixed schools. *Harvard Educational Review, 66*(1), 93–118.

Wertsch, J. V. (1985). *Vygotsky and the social formation of mind.* Cambridge, MA: Harvard University Press.

Wheelock, A. (1992). *Crossing the tracks.* New York: The New Press.

Wiggins, G. (1989). Teaching to the (authentic) test. *Educational Leadership, 46*(7), 41–47.

Willig, A. C. (1985). A meta-analysis of selected studies on the effectiveness of bilingual education. *Review of Education Research, 55*, 269–317.

Woodson, J. (1995). *From the notebooks of Melanin Sun.* New York: Scholastic.

Zempher, N., & Ashburn, E. (1992). Countering parochialism in teacher candidates. In M.D. Dilworth (Ed.), *Diversity in teacher education* (pp. 40–62). San Francisco: Jossey-Bass.

PART III

Gifted and Talented Education

*G*IFTED AND TALENTED EDUCA-*tion is generally motivated by a desire to attend to the individual differences of students and to be sure that particular student aptitudes, talents, and interests are optimized by the school experience. This is obviously an important and well-established objective in the school curriculum. But gifted and talented education is not as cut and dry, or as simple, as this important school objective might suggest. Decisions have to be made about the criteria used to determine "giftedness" and about the general process used to actualize or implement the criteria. Various issues related to fairness and to accuracy quickly emerge when these decisions are weighed. The curriculum response to the determination of giftedness also raises heady concerns. Such a response could range from comprehensive pullout programs, which include students believed to be generally high in academic aptitude, to idiosyncratic classroom accommodations. Clearly, the ways in which schools determine who belongs to the category of gifted and the means for serving them are fundamental concerns.*

Any time a categorical device is used to classify particular groups of students for the purposes of adjusting their education, questions have to be raised about how the category came into being and what it means to the education of all youth. To designate some students as "gifted" means simultaneously to designate the remaining population as "not gifted." To use achievement data as the basis for determining whether a student is "gifted" privileges those students who have enjoyed the widest home and community opportunities to learn. To equate "giftedness" with verbal and mathematical intelligence is to dismiss the place of other forms of intelligence in the curriculum. And if considerations of race, gender, and socioeconomic standings are injected into these efforts and disparities are found, then the issues for school leaders widen and become more severe.

The chapter in this section provides a comprehensive discussion of the many issues involved in the determination and the operation of gifted and talented programs. School leaders, who are often under state and community pressure to offer official programs for gifted and talented students, sometimes find themselves in the less than satisfactory position of arguing for a narrowly defined academic vision of giftedness manifested in programs that could probably be appropriate for the education of all youth. Or, they find that the gifted and talented programs used in their schools are really little more than high ability level tracks that educate the children of parents of financial and political means. Or, they find that their programs are really high ability experiences that fail to reach out to profoundly gifted children. The potential problems, and the potential promises, of the education of the gifted and talented are considerable. These are precisely the kinds of issues addressed in chapter 6.

CHAPTER 6

POLICY IMPLICATIONS OF CONTINUING CONTROVERSIES IN GIFTED EDUCATION

Nancy Ewald Jackson
Heidi L. Doellinger
The University of Iowa

*S*PECIAL EDUCATION FOR GIFTED STUDENTS IS AN ENTER-
prise that has struggled for decades to prove that it is effective for participants and equitable within the broader context of an educational system. Therefore, it is vital to consider how gifted education might be improved (Callahan, 1993; Passow & Rudinski, 1993). Our purpose here is to expose some of prominent logical and empirical flaws in the practice of gifted education. These flaws weaken the arguments that could be made for providing optimal programs to the most able students. We are not arguing that gifted education should be abolished, but that it should be reconceptualized.

> Some problems in gifted education are summarized, centering around the way giftedness is defined, identified, and accommodated in special programs. Gifted education exists within a broader system of categorical funding for special programs predicated on the assumption that students can be sorted out according to special instructional needs and that equitable education need not be the same for all children (Benbow & Stanley, 1996). In that context, several questions must be answered about the nature of equity and of giftedness, the effectiveness of gifted education programs, and the selection systems by which children are placed in them.

How Can Gifted Education Programs Be Equitable?

> Gifted education programs should be justifiable in principle if they are offered as equitable solutions to the problem of providing appropriately challenging learning opportunities for all students. This rationale does, however, require a particular definition of equity.
>
> Although the two terms sometimes are used interchangeably, it is important to distinguish between *equal*, meaning the same, and *equitable*, meaning fair, education. Within the professional community, most strong advocates of improving equity in the schools acknowledge that equity can be conceptualized in terms of comparable opportunity to learn (Guiton & Oakes, 1995). For example, Pendarvis and Howley (1996) argued that no group of students has a right to a better quality education, but that all students deserve the opportunity to become engaged in challenging, meaningful learning. Therefore, gifted education programs can be equitable to the extent that they meet the criterion of providing ap-

propriate challenge, but inequitable to the extent that they enable some students to gain access to a better (i.e., more enriched, more expensive, more effective) education. At the same time, lack of access to appropriately challenging education may be inequitable to gifted students (Gallagher, 1996).

One difficulty encountered by advocates for gifted education is that members of one of their most relevant constituencies, the children themselves, are unlikely to distinguish between equal and equitable educational practices or to perceive differences in work adjusted to differences in ability as fair. Most children do not relate intelligence to effortful learning until age 10 (Nicholls, Patashnick, & Mettetal, 1986), and many regard any unequal allocation of work as unfair (Thorkildsen, 1989). The within-class accommodation to differences in ability that both gifted and average-ability children and adolescents most widely perceive as fair is peer tutoring (Thorkildsen, 1989, 1993).

Similarly, some adults treat equity as synonymous with equality, cooperative learning as the panacea for coping with individual differences, and differentiated education as a necessary evil (see Benbow & Stanley, 1996). The only way to counter such perceptions is to focus arguments for gifted education clearly on the issue of differentiating programs to provide equitable challenges and support for all students (Biemiller, 1993). Unfortunately, many in the field have lost this focus, becoming entangled in unmanageable conceptualizations of who gifted students are and how they should be taught.

How Should Giftedness Be Defined?

Special education as currently conceptualized and funded implies the existence of a category of students who are gifted. Who are these students?

The development of the first practical intelligence tests early in this century gave impetus to the study of giftedness in children, and some scholars have argued that giftedness is meaningful only as a synonym for intelligence (Humphreys, 1985). Furthermore, much of the research on the cognitive characteristics of gifted children consists of studies of groups selected for high IQs (Jackson, 1995). Nonetheless, the concept of *giftedness*, as used in educational programming, usually connotes something more, or at least different. A statement known as the Marland definition, set forth in a 1972 report to Congress by the then Commissioner of Education remains influential. It reads as follows:

> Gifted and talented children are those identified by professionally qualified persons [and] who by virtue of outstanding abilities are capable of high performance. These are children who require differentiated educational programs and services beyond those normally provided by the regular school program in order to realize their contribution to self and society.

Children capable of high performance include those with demonstrated achievement and/or potential ability in any of the following areas, singly or in combination:

(1) general intellectual ability
(2) specific academic aptitude
(3) creative or productive thinking
(4) leadership ability
(5) visual and performing arts
(6) psychomotor ability. (Passow, 1993, p. 30)

This bureaucratic creation set the standard for many years of gifted education despite its logical, psychological, and educational awkwardness.

The conceptualization of giftedness remained an unresolved issue in the 1990s (Cramer, 1991). In 1986, Sternberg and Davidson addressed this long-standing problem by bringing psychologists and educators to joint consideration of the question in an edited book. Their work helped specify some dimensions of the problem, but did not lead to any consensus. Indeed, things may be receding even further from conceptual clarity. The editors of a more recent international handbook begged the question by writing in their concluding summary that giftedness "is a multifaceted phenomenon, the nature of which is still at issue.... Thus, the gifted and the talented are clearly a very heterogeneous set of persons" (Passow, Monks, & Heller, 1993, pp. 886–887). Citing failures of past efforts to reach consensus and the argument that giftedness means different things in different contexts, they went on to suggest that "as the year 2000 approaches, the focus will no longer be on devising a single, comprehensive conception or construct of giftedness" (p. 888).

Indeed, some authorities have begun to refer to a subgroup of students whom they designate as exceptionally or profoundly gifted (Gross, 1993; Winner, 1996). For example, Winner (1996) maintained that

> we need, first of all, to recognize the striking differences between moderately and profoundly gifted children. Profoundly gifted children are years ahead of their peers. They learn rapidly and independently, and have an extraordinary rage to master the area in which they have exceptional ability. These are the children who read voraciously (often nonfiction) before entering kindergarten, who turn everyday experiences into math challenges to solve, or who induce by themselves the rules of algebra or phonics. Moderately gifted children, in contrast, are more appropriately described as bright children. (p. 34)

The merit of this portrait of the exceptionally gifted does not concern us here, although it could be questioned. What matters for our present purposes is that it illustrates the drawing of yet another boundary to set off a category of students as even more gifted than others.

Winner went on to suggest that resources are wasted on programs for the moderately gifted, who should be served adequately by any good educational program. Her views contrast dramatically with a much more broadly inclusive approach to gifted education put forth by Renzulli (e.g., Renzulli & Reis, 1996). Should gifted education, then, be concerned about programming for 20%, for 3%, or for a minuscule fraction of the population of schoolchildren? Clearly, there is not even agreement on this point.

Scholars in the field are comfortable with giftedness as a socially constructed category, acceptable because it is perceived as useful (Gallagher, 1996; Tannenbaum, 1993). However, those who make practical decisions on the basis of definitions of giftedness seem to act like positivists. Constructivism and fuzzy set boundaries do not fit well in educational policies geared toward categorical funding. Despite the plurality and ambiguity of scientific and educational conceptualizations of giftedness, teachers asked to identify gifted students speak and act as if they are certain they know what giftedness is (Peterson & Margolin, 1997), and that curriculum needs to be differentiated based on "the unique characteristics of gifted children" (Cramer, 1991, p. 89).

One can see specialists' confidence that they know what giftedness is in their formal statements. In one study, most of a panel of 29 people designated as experts in the field agreed that "giftedness is the potential for exceptional development of specific abilities as well as the demonstration of performance at the upper end of a talent continuum: it is not limited by age, gender, race, socioeconomic status, or ethnicity" (Cramer, 1991, p. 8).

Everyday decisions about gifted education are made with the same degree of certainty, but may not reflect the same principles as the experts' statements. When some Iowa teachers were asked to select students for a gifted education program, their comments and decisions reflected values consistent with their own cultural backgrounds and at odds with some values that may have been different in some ethnic groups represented by the applicants. Elements mentioned by teachers as aspects of giftedness included good behavior, competitiveness, being well rounded, and perfectionism. Social skills and compliance also mattered. For instance, one teacher volunteered, "Talented and gifted isn't necessarily IQ alone. It's more. I think teachers think of not only those who achieve in their classes, but also get along and are not a problem" (Peterson & Margolin, 1997, p. 93). The teachers in this study sample also made remarks that seemed to treat factors such as a family's socioeconomic status as relevant to interpreting a child's performance.

The educational community has been placed in the position of providing a clearcut definition of giftedness, even though doing so is scientifically dubious (e.g., Tannenbaum, 1993). Practical decisions do not reflect the socially constructed nature of the designation and therefore create, rather than reflect, absolute categories.

Should Gifted Children Receive Special Education Because They Are Tomorrow's Leaders?

Rationales for gifted education or other special education programs can and should be based on children's current educational needs. However, arguments to justify spending extra tax dollars on gifted education typically are based on the assumption that these children will be exceptionally valuable adults, that "they are going to be our future leaders. They are the people who are going to cure diseases" (Belcastro, cited in Siebert, 1998, p. 1). The idea that society can justify spending more money on the education of gifted children now because doing so is a good long-term investment is one manifestation of the complexity of the assumptions that often are made about children who have been labeled as gifted. Most of these assumptions have little or no empirical support.

Giftedness is a term that comes to its current educational usage with a great deal of excess baggage. Some parts of this baggage, such as the idea that superior abilities are gifts of special favor from a deity, play little overt role in current usage, but may lurk in the collective subconscious. Critical theorists also have argued that labeling some students as gifted, and others, usually implicitly, as nongifted, implies global judgments of moral worth (Margolin, 1994). Major sources in the field, such as Terman's *Genetic Studies of Genius* (1925), justify this concern.

Whatever its source and moral implications, giftedness throughout most of the past century has been treated as an enduring, even lifelong, trait (e.g., Terman, 1925). Even in the 1990s, it remained politically acceptable to use "gifted" to modify "child" or "student" without putting the person first (Jackson, 1993). One speaks of "a gifted child with a reading disability," but not of "a reading-disabled child with a gift." Perhaps this nomenclature is accepted because people wish a positive label to be broadly and permanently applied.

Although giftedness is presumed by most to be enduring, the term is used most often to describe children and adolescents (Jackson, 1994). When used in reference to adults, it typically modifies a professional label, as in "gifted pianist," or is otherwise domain restricted, as in "mathematically gifted." Indeed, the generic giftedness of the schoolhouse may have relatively little connection with giftedness in adult life (Siegler & Kotovsky, 1986).

Individual differences in some aspects of intellectual functioning and personality are moderately stable from the elementary school years into adulthood (Sternberg, 1982). Also, at least during the early years of the past century, boys identified in childhood as being well above average in intelligence were likely to have successful adult careers, especially if they came from relatively affluent families (Terman & Oden, 1947). However, the evidence on continuity in superior achievement from childhood to adulthood stops short of showing that those children who are identified as gifted in elementary school are likely to make more worthwhile contributions to society than those who are not so identified (Jackson, 1993; Subotnik, Kassen, Summers, & Wasser, 1993). A substantial amount of discontinuity in gifted performance is likely because statistical regression toward the mean operates strongly at extremes of distributions, because the definition and demands of excellence change as expertise develops (Csikszentmihalyi & Robinson, 1986; Jackson & Klein, 1997) and because unpredictable life events and an individual's responses to them continue to influence development throughout life.

Given the indeterminacy of development over years and decades, identifying children for gifted education programs on the basis of their potential for superior adult accomplishment seems ill advised, perhaps unethical. Nonetheless, a long-standing tradition (e.g., Terman & Oden, 1947) calls attention to gifted students as those who have more potential than others for significant adult accomplishment, and who therefore are a special economic resource for their society, as noted in the Marland definition. This premise has been translated into rationales for extra funding to support gifted education by suggesting that the costs will be paid back to society by the recipients in their supposedly exceptionally productive adult years. However, as Pendarvis and Howley (1996) pointed out, "a rationale and definitions that rely on highly problematic inferences about children's futures do not represent an adequate basis for instruction" (p. 218).

How Can Selection of Children for Gifted Education Be Empirically Defensible?

Systems developed over the years to identify children for gifted education programs reflect the breadth and fuzziness of the Marland and subsequent definitions. Much effort has been devoted to moving away from exclusive or even primary reliance on criteria such as standard academic achievement or intelligence test scores or grades. Rating forms for parents and teachers and peers, tests of productive (supposedly creative) thinking, portfolios, and elaborate combinations of indices have been used in efforts to identify students as qualified for gifted education on the basis of potential for either immediate or long-term future accomplishment (Renzulli & Reis, 1997).

The laudable goal of such diversified identification efforts is to make gifted education more inclusive of those who might be left out if only the more traditional achievement and intelligence scores were used: students from ethnic minority or bilingual backgrounds or those with learning disabilities or a history of underachievement. Some advocate multidimensional, multimodal identification systems as especially appropriate for minority students (Ford, 1996). However, these efforts to make gifted education more inclusive may, in fact, make programs less equitable. Identification of children for gifted education programs by psychometrically weak measures geared toward potential rather than performance increases opportunities for inequitable selections.

Guiton and Oakes (1995) reported data from recent San Jose, California, Rockford, Illinois, and Wilmington, Delaware, court cases showing that fewer Latino and African American ninth-graders were placed in an accelerated math class than White or Asian students with the same test scores. For example, only 56% of Latino students with normal-curve-equivalent scores in the highest range (between 90 and 99) were placed in accelerated math classes in San Jose, as compared with 93% of Whites and 97% of Asians with these scores. Apparently, whatever selection system was used exacerbated rather than corrected for tendencies for African American and Latino students in these districts, on the whole, to earn lower test scores.

Pendarvis and Howley (1996) suggested that the best way to compensate for the likelihood that fewer children from disadvantaged minority groups will be identified for gifted education programs by traditional measures such as intelligence and achievement tests is to compensate mathematically for test bias or establish local norms, rather than weaken the identification system by including measures of dubious validity and reliability. Their concern is warranted because of data such as that reported by Guiton and Oakes (1995) and observations of teachers' behaviors like those made by Peterson and Margolin (1997) and reported earlier in this review. Poorly designed selection systems open up abundant opportunities for ethnocentric and irrelevant judgments to be made. Standard tests need not be the only components of good identification systems, but measures such as portfolio assessments should also be subject to scrutiny regarding their reliability and validity for selecting the participants who are most appropriate for particular programs.

IS GIFTED EDUCATION DIFFERENTIALLY EFFECTIVE FOR GIFTED CHILDREN?

Dividing public school students into groups who receive different kinds of education can be equitable if each program better serves the abilities, interests, and needs of the participating students than it does those of students who are not included. Programs are not equitable if they give some students more opportunities for appropriate learning than others receive (Guiton & Oakes, 1995). The argument that gifted children constitute a class of qualitatively different learners who require a curriculum that is differentiated in some (usually unspecified) way cannot be defended within this context.

Much emphasis in gifted education over the past few decades has been given to developing or adopting curriculum that focuses on general thinking and problem-solving skills or higher order thought. Rationales for such curricula have included arguments that gifted students are in special need of such skills because they are the leaders of tomorrow, they can master basic skills in less time and therefore can devote time to more reflective education, and their high intelligence or other abilities make them predisposed to higher level thought. None of these arguments is sound.

The first argument can be dismissed quickly. It already has been argued that gifted education cannot be justified on the basis of students' hypothetical promise of adult accomplishment. Even if, on the average, more able students are likely to pay more taxes, make more medical breakthroughs, or negotiate more corporate takeovers than less able students, the possibility of such future outcomes does not entitle them to a better public education.

The "time available" rationale might seem to have some merit, and it is a favorite of advocates for gifted education (e.g., Gallagher, 1996; Renzulli & Reis, 1997). However, it is justifiable only to the extent that the experiences made available to students who have mastered the basic curriculum quickly are less valuable than the core curriculum to "nongifted" students and are specially suited to the abilities and interests of the students selected for the program. There is no psychological justification for the argument that only gifted students have the time to learn to think reflectively, at higher levels, or about important problems that require connections across bodies of knowledge.

Little is known about any special characteristics of gifted children defined according to the eclectic criteria often used to select children for special programs. When giftedness is defined as high IQ, then it is known that highly intelligent students are indeed more widely, and often deeply, knowledgeable as well as more capable of spontaneously planning and monitoring their problem solving, making connections between old and new learning, and reasoning abstractly (e.g., Jackson & Butterfield, 1986; Perleth, Lehwald, & Browder, 1993). However, calling these differences "qualitative" adds no information (Jackson & Butterfield, 1986; Pendarvis & Howley, 1996). Furthermore, there is no reason to infer from these data that the thinking, problem-solving, and abstract reasoning skills of less intelligent students should be neglected. Indeed, the least able learners are likely to need the most help in order to be able to synthesize, evaluate, and apply what they have learned in the classroom. Do educators wish to work for a society in which only the most able students are encouraged to think well or to use what they have learned?

Much of the education of teachers of the gifted is devoted to teaching them how to teach general-purpose thinking skills, rather than increasing their knowledge of and ability to teach specific subject matter. This instruction of teachers influences what happens in programs for the gifted. As Gallagher (1996) put it, "Teachers do not teach things for which they have not been prepared, and teachers of the gifted have not been prepared to teach significant content" (p. 243).

This focus is unfortunate. Those programs for the gifted that are likely to be most equitable are those firmly grounded in challenging content. Pendarvis and

Howley (1986) and cognitive developmentalists such as Bruner (1973), Piaget (1964–1967), and Vygotsky (1978) believed that all children learn best when they are challenged with, and are supported in the attempt to master, material that stretches their current understanding. Gifted education is justifiable to the extent that it contributes to efforts to provide a range of educational challenges appropriate for all students. Many of the concepts employed in gifted education classrooms constitute good educational practices that have a place in all classrooms (Sapon-Shevin, 1996). "Gifted children should not simply be exempted from a poor curriculum. To do so privileges gifted children, miseducating them by teaching them that they deserve a better education than other children" (Pendarvis & Howley, 1996, p. 222).

Gifted education programs should focus on educational content appropriate to the achievements and interests of the children served. Funding for public gifted education programs that involve selection of some students and exclusion of others should rest in evidence that these programs are selectively effective.

Unfortunately, few programs for gifted students have been evaluated adequately. Program evaluation has been more often suggested than required for state funding or accreditation, and some states have reduced evaluation to become synonymous with identification of students (Passow & Rudnitski, 1993). There is evidence that acceleration and enrichment programs that make substantial curricular adjustments for talented learners can have large positive effects on their learning (C. C. Kulik & J. A. Kulik, 1982; J. A. Kulik, 1992). However, many programs in gifted education are not of this type.

Even when funds, time, and technical support are available, gifted education programs may be difficult to evaluate because their goals may be complex and long-term and the services offered may be integrated with the regular school curriculum (Borlund, 1997; Callahan, 1993; Passow & Rudnitski, 1993; Rogers, 1991). Evaluation designs are likely to be quasi-experimental at best. However, the difficulties inherent in the evaluation of gifted education are no excuse for continued public investment in, and commitment of students' time to, special programs of unproven merit.

Furthermore, even the most comprehensive and thoughtful evaluations of gifted education programs generally have failed to address a question that is central to issues of equity. Would this program be beneficial only for the students selected, and not for other students? If a program is likely to benefit all or most students, the only reason to restrict access to some elite group is on the basis that these "leaders of tomorrow" deserve a better education than others do. We already have shown the flaws in this argument. The question of the specific, differential effectiveness of gifted education for students identified as gifted is especially pertinent to evaluation of the programs likely to be least effective for their selected populations (i.e., those that do not involve especially advanced or challenging curricular content; Kulik, 1992).

Conclusion

It is likely that decisions about gifted students and gifted education could be logically and empirically defensible if grounded in specific educationally relevant measures that are appropriate in particular sociocultural contexts. Appropriately challenging programs for the most able students can be both cost effective and equitable. They do not necessarily require smaller student–teacher ratios or special equipment.

Most of the concerns we have raised about gifted education do not apply to programs such as those developed by Stanley, Benbow, and others to provide appropriately challenging accelerated education to students identified as qualified for advanced instruction (e.g., Benbow & Stanley, 1996; Swiatek & Benbow, 1991). The specificity of the conceptualization of gifted performance that underlies these accelerated programs and the clear match they offer between that conceptualization and the educational program offered are a model for the field. Because they are likely to be a good match to the needs of the children served and specifically appropriate for those children only, accelerated programs for advanced students are often recognized as the most defensible in terms of both equity and demonstrated educational outcomes (C. C. Kulik & J. A. Kulik, 1982; J. A. Kulik, 1992; Pendarvis & Howley, 1996).

In contrast, much of the budget for many gifted education programs currently is devoted to the design and implementation of elaborate identification systems (Gallagher, 1996). At the same time, virtually no resources have been devoted to evaluations that could demonstrate that these programs were good for the students who participated and would not have been good for those who did not. Our modest proposal for the future posits that the selection of children for gifted education programs should become routine only when those two criteria can be met.

Acknowledgments

A preliminary version of this chapter was presented at the November 23, 1996, meeting of the Iowa Academy of Education in Ames. The second author's contributions were supported by a University of Iowa Fellowship and an Iowa Measurement Foundation Special Graduate Assistantship.

References

Benbow, C. P., & Stanley, J. C. (1996). Inequity in equity: How "equity" can lead to inequity for high-potential students. *Psychology, Public Policy, and Law, 2*(2), 249–292.

Biemiller, A. J. (1993). Lake Wobegon revisited: On diversity and education. *Educational Researcher, 22*(9), 7–12.

Borland, J. H. (1997). Evaluating gifted programs. In N. Colangelo & G. A. Davis (Eds.), *Handbook of gifted education* (pp. 253–266). Boston: Allyn & Bacon.

Bruner, J. S. (1973). *Beyond the information given: Studies in the psychology of knowing.* New York: Norton.

Callahan, C. M. (1993). Evaluation programs and procedures for gifted education: International problems and solutions. In K. A. Heller, F. J. Monks, & A. H. Passow (Eds.), *International handbook of research and development of giftedness and talent* (pp. 605–618). Oxford, England: Pergamon.

Cramer, R. H. (1991). The education of gifted children in the United States: A delphi study. *Gifted Child Quarterly, 35*, 84–91.

Csikszentmihalyi, M., & Robinson, R. (1986). Culture, time, and the development of talent. In R. J. Sternberg & J. E. Davidson (Eds.), *Conceptions of giftedness* (264–284). New York: Cambridge University Press.

Fetterman, D. M. (1993). Evaluate yourself. *The National Research Center on the Gifted and Talented: Research-Based Decision Making Series* (No. 9304).

Ford, D. Y. (1996). *Reversing underachievement among gifted Black students.* New York: Teacher's College Press.

Gallagher, J. J. (1996). A critique of critiques of gifted education. *Journal for the Education of the Gifted, 19*, 234–249.

Gross, M. U. M. (1993). Nurturing the talents of exceptionally gifted individuals. In K. A. Heller, F. J. Monks, & A. H. Passow (Eds.), *International handbook of research and development of giftedness and talent* (pp. 473–490). Oxford, England: Pergamon.

Guiton, G., & Oakes, J. (1995). Opportunity to learn and conceptions of educational equity. *Educational Evaluation and Policy Analysis, 17*, 323–336.

Humphreys, L. G. (1985). A conceptualization of intellectual giftedness. In F. D. Horowitz & M. O'Brien (Eds.), *The gifted and talented: Developmental perspectives* (pp. 331–360). Washington, DC: American Psychological Association.

Jackson, N. E. (1993). Moving into the mainstream? Reflections on the study of giftedness. *Gifted Child Quarterly, 37*, 46–50.

Jackson, N. E. (1994). Genius, eminence, and giftedness. In *Encyclopedia of human behavior* (Vol. 2, pp. 407–414). New York: Academic Press.

Jackson, N. E. (1995). A collection of current perspectives on giftedness. *Contemporary Psychology, 40*, 1150–1151.

Jackson, N. E., & Butterfield, E. C. (1986). A conception of giftedness designed to promote research. In R. J. Sternberg & J. E. Davidson (Eds.), *Conception of giftedness* (pp. 151–181). New York: Cambridge University Press.

Jackson, N. E., & Klein, E. J. (1997). Gifted performance in young children. In N. Colangelo & G. A. Davis (Eds.), *Handbook of gifted education* (2nd ed., pp. 460–474). Boston: Allyn & Bacon.

Janos, P. M., & Robinson, N. M. (1985). Psychosocial development in intellectually gifted children. In F. D. Horowitz & M. O'Brien (Eds.), *The gifted and talented: Developmental perspectives* (pp. 149–195). Washington, DC: American Psychological Association.

Kulik, C. C. & Kulik, J. A. (1982). Effects of ability grouping on secondary school students: A meta-analysis of evaluation findings. *American Educational Research Journal, 19*, 415–428.

Kulik, J. A. (1992). An analysis of the research on ability grouping: Historical and contemporary perspectives. *The National Research Center on the Gifted and Talented: Research-Based Decision Making Series* (No. 9204).

Margolin, L. (1994). *Goodness personified: The emergence of gifted children.* New York: de Gruyter.

Nicholls, J. G., Patashnick, M., & Mettetal, G. (1986). Conceptions of ability and intelligence. *Child Development, 57*, 636–645.

Passow, A. J. (1993). National/state policies regarding education of the gifted. In K. A. Heller, F. J. Monks, & A. H. Passow (Eds.), *International handbook of research and development of giftedness and talent* (pp. 29–46). Oxford, England: Pergamon.

Passow, A. H., Monks, F. J., & Heller, K. A. (1993). Research and education of the gifted in the year 2000 and beyond. In K. A. Heller, F. J. Monks, & A. H. Passow (Eds.), *International handbook of research and development of giftedness and talent* (pp. 883–904). Oxford, England: Pergamon.

Passow, A. H. & Rudnitski, R. A. (1993). State policies regarding education of the gifted as reflected in legislation and regulation. *The National Research Center on the Gifted and Talented: Collaborative Research Study* (No. CRS93302).

Pendarvis, E., & Howley, A. (1996). Playing fair: The possibilities of gifted education. *Journal for the Education of the Gifted, 19*, 215–233.

Perleth, C., Lehwald, G., & Browder, C. S. (1993). Indicators of high ability in young children. In K. A. Heller, F. J. Monks, & A. H. Passow (Eds.), *International handbook of research and development of giftedness and talent* (pp. 283–310). New York: Pergamon.

Peterson, J., & Margolin, L. (1997). Naming gifted children: An example of unintended reproduction. *Journal for the Education of the Gifted, 21*, 82–100.

Piaget, J. (1964–1967). *Six psychological studies.* New York: Random House.

Renzulli, J. S., & Reis, S. M. (1997). The schoolwide enrichment model: New directions for developing high-end learning. In N. Colangelo & G. A. Davis (Eds.), *Handbook of gifted education* (2nd ed., pp. 136–154). Boston: Allyn & Bacon.

Renzulli, J. S., & Smith, L. H. (1979). Issues and procedures in evaluating programs. In A. H. Passow (Ed.), *The gifted and the talented: Their education and development* (pp. 289–307). Chicago: The University of Chicago Press,

Rogers, K. B. (1991). The relationship of grouping practices to the education of the gifted and talented learner. *The National Research Center on the Gifted and Talented: Research-Based Decision Making Series* (No. 9101).

Sapon-Shevin, M. (1996). Beyond gifted education: Building a shared agenda for school reform. *Journal for the Education of the Gifted, 19*, 194–214.

Siebert, M. (1998, Feb. 21). Short shrift for the gifted. *Des Moines Register*, pp. 1A, 4A.

Siegler, R., & Kotovsky, K. (1986). Two levels of giftedness: Shall ever the twain meet? In R. J. Sternberg & J. E. Davidson (Eds.), *Conceptions of giftedness* (pp. 417–436). New York: Cambridge University Press.

Sternberg, R. J. (Ed.). (1982). *Handbook of human intelligence.* Cambridge, England: Cambridge University Press.

Sternberg, R. J., & Davidson, J. E. (Eds.). (1986). *Conceptions of giftedness.* New York: Cambridge University Press.

Subotnik, R., Kassen, L., Summers, E., & Wesser, A. (1993). *Genius revisited: High IQ children grow up.* Norwood, NJ: Ablex.

Swiatek, M. A., & Benbow, C. P. (1991). A ten-year longitudinal follow-up of participants in a fast-paced mathematics course. *Journal for Research in Mathematical Education, 22*, 138–150.

Tannenbaum, A. (1993). Giftedness: A psychosocial approach. In K. A. Heller, F. J. Monks, & A. H. Passow (Eds.), *International handbook of research and development of giftedness and talent* (pp. 21–52). Oxford, England: Pergamon.

Terman, L. M. (1925). *Mental and physical traits of a thousand gifted children. Genetic studies of genius* (Vol. 1). Palo Alto, CA: Stanford University Press.

Terman, L. M., & Oden, M. H. (1947). *The gifted child grows up. Genetic studies of genius* (Vol. 4). Palo Alto, CA: Stanford University Press.

Thorkildsen, T. A. (1989). Justice in the classroom: The student's view. *Child Development, 60*, 323–334.

Thorkildsen, T. A. (1993). Those who can, tutor: High ability students' conceptions of fair ways to organize learning. *Journal of Educational Psychology, 85*, 182–190.

Vygotsky, L. S. (1978). *Mind in society: The development of higher psychological processes.* Cambridge, MA: Harvard University Press.

Winner, E. (1996). The miseducation of our gifted children. *Education Week*, 34–35.

Part IV

Classroom Assessment

To assess the school experience is to problematize it, to ask questions, and to gather evidence about the nature of the experience as it relates to the professed mission and goals of the school. Assessment, in this sense, is a vital part of a school's curriculum development strategy. It demands the collection and representation of a body of evidence that speaks for or against the attainment of any number of essential educational purposes. Any one particular method of assessment has value only to the extent that it makes a contribution to understanding whether a particular objective (or set of objectives) has been attained. Generally speaking, educators believe that certain standardized measurements are helpful in gauging achievement in reading, writing, language arts, and mathematics. Also, achievement measures may be taken in more discipline-centered areas, such as science and social studies. But the act of assessment is also carried out in very important ways in the world of the classroom. Using observations, interviews, questionnaires, the representation of student products, various self-made exams, and any number of other methods, teachers assess the skills, attitudes, values, and competencies of schoolchildren virtually on a daily basis.

In 1929, Tyler coined the term evaluation (Madaus & Stufflebeam, 1989). The use of this term represented an important turn for those interested in the appraisal of school education. Wanting to focus attention away from pencil-and-paper tests that contained largely restricted-response items, Tyler argued that evaluation should aim to find and demonstrate the things of value that students might be deriving from their education. Thus, to think about evaluation meant to open up the appraisal process and to get serious about determining how teachers might demonstrate whether educational objectives related to thinking skills, communication skills, inquiry skills, study skills, and various sociopersonal and sociocivic values were actually being met. This meant that the very notion of appraisal had to be widened to include the place of various locally devised appraisal methods specifically attuned to local learning and teaching priorities.

This is precisely the flavor of the chapters in this section. Focusing largely on classroom assessment issues, these chapters collectively represent a kind of conceptual landscape of views that school leaders might reflect in their own professional lives. The role of high stakes testing, the place of reflective portfolio assessment, the vast range of assessment activities that principals can encourage, and the increasing role of computer assessment mechanisms in the curriculum all make their way into the discussion. The section emphasizes the idea of evaluation, as Tyler originally constructed it, by making it clear that assessment can examine a wide assemblage of values, attitudes, skills, and behaviors. This is important because, in the end, decisions on what and how to assess will be decisions that will say a lot about what is valued in the school experience.

REFERENCE

Madaus, G. F., & Stufflebeam, D. (Eds.). (1989). *Educational evaluation: Classic works of Ralph Tyler.* Boston: Kluwer.

CHAPTER 7

THE PRINCIPAL'S ASSESSMENT RESPONSIBILITIES

Richard J. Stiggins
Assessment Training Institute, Portland, Oregon

THE TROUBLING FACT IS THAT MOST TEACHERS ARE UNPREpared to meet the increasingly complex assessment challenges they face in the classroom today. Teacher training programs have been notorious over the decades for their lack of relevant assessment training at both graduate and undergraduate levels. State certification standards typically do not require competence in assessment as a condition for teacher licensure. The commonly used certification examinations include virtually no exercises verifying assessment competence. Yet typical teachers can spend as much as a third to a half of their available professional time involved in assessment-related activities (Stiggins & Conklin, 1992). Thus, a fundamental mismatch is uncovered between professional competencies and the requirements of the job.

Assessment is one important key to school effectiveness. If classroom assessments are of high quality (i.e., if they produce accurate information about student achievement), then sound decisions can result and students can prosper. But if classroom assessments are of poor quality, then instruction cannot be effective. The fact is, over the decades, teachers have not been prepared to assess accurately. Even in 2000, the accuracy of teachers' classroom assessments cannot be guaranteed.

To make matters even more troubling, teachers typically cannot turn to their principals for assistance on assessment matters. Only 3 of the 50 states require that principals be competent in assessment as a condition of licensure (Trevisan, 1999). A review of assessment training in preparation programs reveals that it is essentially nonexistent (Schafer & Lissitz, 1987). Under these conditions, how can principals effectively supervise the assessment practices of their teachers? How can they help teachers learn to do a better assessment job? How can they serve as the primary interpreter of achievement test results to the local school community?

And to top off this deeply troubling state of affairs, how can school and district administrators who lack assessment literacy offer sound advice to policy making groups (e.g., on-site councils, school boards, and state and national legislatures) regarding sound assessment policies and regulations?

Is it any wonder, therefore, that the relation between assessment and effective schools continues to be as troubling in 2000 as it has been for decades at all levels of educational practice? The state of assessment practices in American education is as unhealthy as ever and educators remain unwilling or unable to attend to its health.

THE SOLUTION

The principal must play a key role in finding a solution to this problem. If assessment is ever to reach its potential, principals across the country must fulfill their leadership responsibilities. Specific roles are examined herein by exploring the following:

- The forces that have mitigated against the effective use of quality assessment in the past and the principal's role in removing them.
- How principals can help teachers tap the full potential of assessment in the service of maximum student achievement.
- The standards of professional competence that frame the principal's assessment responsibilities.
- The understandings, attitudes, and conditions that must be in place in schools to harness the true power of assessment and the principal's responsibilities in making sure those conditions are met.

CONFRONTING THE OPPOSING FORCES

There are powerful barriers to achieving excellence in assessment. One barrier has been our long-standing belief as a nation that the path to school improvement is paved with standardized tests. This belief was manifested in its earliest form in the 1930s with the development of the College Boards, a college admissions test that quickly turned into a national school accountability measure, with upward and downward score trends serving as the basis for judging school effectiveness. Then, in the 1950s and 1960s, commercially developed norm-referenced, districtwide tests began to be used extensively nationwide for local accountability programs. The 1970s was the decade of the statewide testing program—the decade began with 3 and ended with 37. The count is now up to 48. In the 1970s and 1980s, a national assessment program was added. In the 1980s and 1990s, international assessments became popular. Looking to the 21st century, can interplanetary assessment be far behind?

Thus, assessment history reveals layer upon layer of tests at immense costs with scant evidence of positive impact on student success. For some reason, policymakers and educational leaders became mesmerized by the belief that each new layer of testing would accomplish what prior layers had failed to do, that is, to stimulate school improvement. The problem is that the high accumulated costs of such annual assessments have left nothing to help teachers become assessment literate in order to effectively manage the other 99.9% of the assessments that happen in a student's life (i.e., those conducted day to day in the classroom).

Moreover, how can teachers institute sound assessment practices if they have no opportunity to learn what they are?

The principal's role in this scenario is to advocate on behalf of balanced development and use of assessments. In order for schools to improve, both standardized tests and classroom assessments must be of high quality and be effectively used. Unfortunately, assessment history has not permitted the attainment of such balance.

Another barrier related to excellence in assessment and in the classroom is a collective reticence to be held accountable for student learning. Lest communities discover a potentially troubling truth about student learning in local schools, educators try to keep people believing what they want people to believe about that learning. Because there is still uncertainty about how much students are learning and about the effectiveness of teachers, a detailed examination of student achievement is risky for educators. Communities are allowed to believe they can judge school quality based on the narrowest possible definition of student success, scores on norm-referenced tests (including college admissions test scores). Yet, few practicing educators at any level of schooling know or understand the achievement targets reflected in the exercises on the standardized tests they administer, nor can they explain the meaning of scores in terms that the citizenry is likely to understand. In general, open public discussion of these issues is not encouraged.

To counter this, principals must become assessment literate and promote the open and honest analysis of student success. Illusions of accountability do not help students become the lifelong learners they must be, nor do they encourage communities to invest the resources needed to enhance school quality.

A third barrier to the effective use of quality assessments in schools can be parents and communities who define sound assessment practices in terms of their own personal experiences during their youth. Sometimes, parents try to set the standards of assessment excellence by saying, in effect, anything new—that is, that was not done when they were in school—represents unsound practices. If parents or communities, therefore, hold the schools accountable for carrying out what educators know to be unsound practices, then they create a barrier to quality.

In this case, the principal's responsibility must be to understand standards of sound assessment practice and to help the community come to understand those standards also. As the spokesperson for the school, the principal must take the lead in helping the whole community become assessment literate.

A fourth barrier to quality assessment is a lack of clarity about what students are expected to achieve and be able to do. Historically, academic success has been defined in terms of seat time or credits earned, not in terms of competencies attained. As a result, there has been a failure to define the ascending levels of academic competence across grade levels that would help students achieve ultimate success. Consequently, there is no continuous progress curriculum defining each teacher's assigned instructional responsibilities in terms of achievement targets. How are teachers to provide dependable information about student achievement if targets are not defined?

In this case, instructional leadership includes advocating on behalf of developing a continuous progress curriculum districtwide. And it includes making sure every teacher in each school building is a competent confident master of the achievement targets that students are to hit.

Finally, with respect to barriers, there is a long tradition of making naïve assumptions about the relation between assessment and student motivation. There has been a total reliance on behavior management through the manipulation of rewards and punishments to motivate students to want to learn. Yet, this does not work for many (perhaps most) students (Covington, 1992; Kohn, 1993). If bribery and intimidation are not effective in promoting the pursuit of academic excellence, then what will work? It is the principal's responsibility to know the answer to this question and to know how to promote the professional development needed to tap the internal motivation that will turn students on to learning.

These assessment problems in school buildings and classrooms did not arise by chance alone. Many forces conspired to create them. It will take a major investment in counter forces to extricate the system. And primary among those forces must be assertive leadership from principals.

TAPPING THE FULL POWER OF ASSESSMENT

Principal leadership can bring the full force of assessment to bear for student success only if there is agreement on what that means for developing an "effective school" and how assessment fits into attaining this goal.

WHAT IS AN EFFECTIVE SCHOOL?

Citizens hold widely varying views of what a good school looks like and what it should do for its community. As it turns out, proponents of each view evaluate their schools differently.

For example, some parents regard a school as effective if they can put their kids there and not deal with them all day. They simply want their children watched so they can continue their adult activities, with low cost child-care service. For these parents, a good school is open and in session all day, everyday.

Other parents believe that a good school is primarily a safe place. If they can put their kids there and be confident that they will not be attacked, hit on by drug dealers, or otherwise placed in harm's way, then their school is effective. They want a child-care center free of concern for the well-being of their children.

Yet other parents want their children to "self-actualize" in school—that is, to find their way confidently in life. They want an unstructured school environment that frees their child to explore the world around them and to come to terms with it in their own way.

Some parents want school to impart the religious values espoused by the particular church with which their family is affiliated. For example, some favor teaching creation rather than evolution in science. They want their children to learn to pray and see their lives as being connected to their family's image of God.

Other parents hope that schools will impart the sense of discipline in their children that they have failed to impart at home. They look to educators to force their children to walk the straight and narrow, to stop breaking society's rules. A good school demands compliance.

Still others regard school as a social institution intended to instill the values needed to participate in a highly competitive free enterprise economy. There should be winners and losers, the way it was when they were in school. Schools should sort students along a continuum of achievement from valedictorian to the bottom. "My child should win," they say, "if others lose, that's life."

More recently, another vision of school effectiveness has emerged. In this case, an effective school is seen as one that maximizes the achievement of the largest possible proportion of its student population. This definition of excellence began to appear in the 1950s, with discussions of "mastery learning models." Rather than following traditions of holding the amount of the time available to learn constant (one year per grade level) and permitting the amount learned by the end of that time to vary across students (thus allowing schools to rank students), the time available to learn varies and the amount to be learned is held constant (all or most students should meet mastery standards given enough time).

In the 1960s, this same idea reappeared in the form of behavioral objectives detailing the specific proficiencies that all students would be expected to master. In the 1970s, those achievement expectations were relabeled as "minimum competencies." In the 1980s, the language was changed once again, this time referring to "outcomes-based education." In the 1990s, those essential learnings have been referred to as high achievement standards.

The different labels express the same central idea. Each version made it clear that a fundamental shift was taking place in the mission of education. Schools that merely rank a group of relatively low achieving students would no longer be considered effective. Excellence would be defined in terms of the proportion of students who met academic standards.

Further, each version of this vision of effective schools, from the 1950s to the present, attracted new followers. A school that merely ranks a group of self-actualized but incompetent writers, readers, math problem solvers, and so on, would no longer be permitted to call itself effective. The pursuit of high standards of academic excellence for all students would become the mission of the day for schools.

With this transformation of schools from a place of ranking students to a place where students must become competent, has the role of assessment also changed?

HOW DOES ASSESSMENT HELP?

This adjustment in mission places an entirely new set of demands on assessment, giving it far greater potential power for helping students to succeed than ever before. For instance, in achievement-driven schools, assessment becomes a more powerful political tool than ever before. Once communities understand and endorse a set of achievement expectations for their students, they demand understandable evidence of student mastery of those standards.

In addition, assessment becomes a much more powerful instructional tool. When communities merely asked for a dependable rank order at the end of high school, a 4-year long series of potentially unreliable classroom assessments including numerous errors of measurement could work. Some teachers would over estimate achievement, while others would underestimate. Thus the errors of measurement would often cancel each other out. The result was a relatively dependable grade point average and rank in class at the end of high school.

But in a system in which students are expected, for example, to ascend through ever higher levels of writing competence until they finally are judged competent writers, any undependable assessments create barriers. They lead to misdiagnosis of students' needs, failure to find the most effective instructional interventions, and inaccurate feedback to students. In short, inaccurate day-to-day classroom assessments (which were not as problematic when simply accumulated into a long-term grade point average) become barriers to the development of academic competence.

In an environment driven by a desire for competence, the quality and accuracy of day to day assessment become critical to promoting learning. To assure the accuracy of these classroom assessments and to tap the full potential of assessment for student success, every teacher in every classroom must be assessment literate. This is a professional development challenge that has been systematically avoided in the past. If schools continue to avoid it, then academic excellence will continue to allude them.

Yet another way to tap the full power of assessment in the service of effective schools is to realize that students are the most important assessment users. Educators virtually always think of students as playing a passive role in the assessment process. The importance of the way students use assessment results is almost never acknowledged. Yet, one excellent way to turn assessment into a powerfully focused instructional intervention is to open up the assessment development and application processes by bringing students in as full partners. Potential assessment power can be tapped through student-involved assessment design and use, student involved record keeping, and student-involved communication about their success as learners.

In short, a transformation of the relation between assessment and effective schools is taking place in American education. There is movement away from the obsessive belief that schools can be made effective merely by instituting another standardized test and demanding accountability by reporting test scores to the media. Although this kind of accountability definitely will continue to be a powerful motivator for change, it has become apparent that it is insufficient to be the catalyst.

Such accountability meets the information needs of some important policy-level decision makers, but it does not begin to meet other key stakeholders' assessment needs. Once-a-year accountability-oriented standardized tests do not, indeed cannot, meet the information needs of students, teachers, and parents. To make the moment-to-moment, day-to-day, and week-to-week decisions they face, these users must have access to accurate, useful, and dependable classroom assessment-based evidence of student achievement.

But the dependability of classroom assessments cannot be guaranteed because of a consistent failure to invest in the assessment literacy of practicing teachers. Unless there can be assurance that high quality standardized tests will be administered by users who know what they are doing and that high quality classroom assessments will be developed and used by assessment-literate teachers, then the desired excellence in American education can never be achieved.

Here then is a primary leadership responsibility for principals: Principals need to develop a plan for determining their own current level of assessment literacy and for establishing the assessment literacy training needs of their staff. Then, they need to plan how to address the results of such a needs assessment, first building a personal base of proficiency and then a staff training plan.

This foundational challenge is explored here from a variety of different perspectives.

Assessment Competencies for Principals

Two independent efforts have framed assessment competencies for building administrators. One set of competencies was established by the National Policy Board for Educational Administration in 1993. The second was framed in 1997 by a joint commission of representatives from the American Association of School Administrators, the National Association of Elementary School Principals, the National Association of Secondary School Principals, and the National Council on Measurement in Education. These latter standards attend to assessment competencies for school administrators in general. The former defines competencies specifically for the school building principal.

The joint commission's work divides administrator competencies into three groups. One includes those related to supporting teachers as they face the challenges of classroom assessment, another focuses on setting and implementing sound assessment policies, and the third addresses the proper interpretation and use of assessment results. Twelve essential competencies are included in the following categories:

Assist teachers:
- Develop a working level of competence in the *Standards for Teacher Competence in the Educational Assessment of Students* (developed jointly by the American Federation of Teachers, the National Education Association, and the National Council on Measurement in Education to guide teacher preparation and licensure).
- Know the appropriate and useful mechanics of constructing various assessments.

(Note that these first two lead to the inference that administrators are expected to master all classroom assessment competencies expected of teachers.)

Provide leadership in setting policy:
- Understand and be able to apply basic measurement principles to assessments conducted in school settings.
- Understand the purposes (e.g., description, diagnosis, placement) of different kinds of assessment (e.g., achievement, aptitude, attitude) and the appropriate assessment strategies to obtain the assessment data needed for the intended purpose.
- Understand the need for clear and consistent building and district-level policies on student assessment.

Ensure proper assessment use:
- Understand and explain technical assessment concepts and terminology to others correctly, but in nontechnical ways.
- Understand and follow ethical and technical guidelines for assessment.
- Reconcile conflicting assessment results appropriately.
- Recognize the importance, appropriateness, and complexity of interpreting assessment results in light of students' linguistic and cultural backgrounds and in making accommodations for individual differences, including disabilities; help ensure the valid use of assessment results for all students.

- Ensure that assessment and information technology are employed appropriately to conduct student assessment.
- Use available technology appropriately to integrate assessment results and other student data to facilitate student learning, instruction, and performance.
- Judge the quality of an assessment strategy or program used for decision making within their jurisdiction. (adapted from AASA, NAESP, NASSP, NCME, 1997, p. 6)

The National Policy Board work (Thompson, 1993), entitled *Principals for Our Changing Schools: The Knowledge and Skill Base*, takes a different approach to defining principal competence in assessment. It also establishes three roles within which to categorize competencies. But, in this case, the principal is cast as instructional leader, building manager, and communicator with the school community. In addition, this framework adds a set of principal competencies common to all three roles. Each competency is explained in terms of key behaviors of effective principals:

Instructional Leader Competencies:
- Develop and implement assessment policies that contribute to sound assessment practices.
- Assist staff in integrating assessment into the teaching and learning process.
- Evaluate teachers' classroom assessment competencies.
- Plan and coordinate staff development activities that expand teachers' classroom assessment competencies.
- Use assessment results for building-level instructional planning.

Building Manager Competencies:
- Accurately analyze and interpret building-level standardized test results.
- Understand how to use assessment results for building-level decision making.

Communicator Role Competencies:
- Create conditions within the school and the community that promote appropriate uses of assessment information.
- Communicate effectively with community members about assessment results and their implications for instruction.

Assessment Competencies Underpinning All Three Roles:
- Understand and be able to differentiate between sound and unsound assessment practices.

- Understand how to make various assessment systems operating within a school work together.
- Maintain standards of ethical and appropriate assessment use to protect the best interests of students and staff.

These competencies were articulated for the purpose of guiding the preparation of administrators to fulfill their responsibilities. Yet few currently practicing principals have had the opportunity to master them. That means individual building administrators must take personal responsibility for evaluating their own preparedness to manage assessment effectively and for monitoring their own growth and development in this arena of professional practice. A later section discusses ways to accomplish these goals.

LEADERSHIP AS AN ASSESSMENT COMPETENCE

But first, one more competence issue must be addressed. In order to promote the development of school and classroom assessment environments that use assessment to promote student success, principals must approach this topic with the desire and ability to provide assertive leadership. Merely managing assessment will not suffice. Consider the differences.

Managers strive to keep assessment and grading issues as they always have been. This means there are rules to be followed, and procedures to be implemented that are spelled out in the policy manual. Teachers who innovate in assessment and grading, try to stretch classroom assessment practice, or strive to learn and experiment outside the lines are sources of anxiety. Change is discouraged. Participants (teachers and students) are expected to adapt to the system. Fear forms the basis of strong discipline. The goal is to raise test scores, and it is the end result that counts. Furthermore, this is the way parents want things to be.

In today's school environment in which assessment and grading practices are nowhere near where they need to be, it should be clear that mere management of the status quo will not suffice.

Leaders, on the other hand, explore new ways to weave assessment and communication into the schooling process. The principal who is fulfilling important leadership responsibilities might say, "Let's rethink our procedures to try to find better ways. Our policy on grading simply isn't meeting our needs. Let's rethink it to see if we can do a better job. Teachers who think outside of the lines (within limits) are learning and will be able to teach the rest of us lessons soon. Change might help us help kids more." Leaders think like this: The system must be adapted to meet the needs of learners (young and adult). Fear inhibits growth—evidence of success spurs growth. Build confidence. The goal is to prepare good readers and writers. Do this, and the test scores will take care of themselves. "We need to be accountable, but for real learning. If we succeed, our students will handle any standardized test."

In an environment in which assessment and grading practices are nowhere near what they need to be, leadership for improvement is the key to school success. In this context, principals must be competent not just in managing, but also in facilitating, assessment change.

THE CONDITIONS UNDERPINNING SUCCESS

From a practical point of view, if principals are to lead the efforts to integrate assessment deeply into the teaching and learning process, five specific conditions must be in place:

1. Achievement expectations must be clearly articulated.
2. A commitment must be made to provide dependable assessment results to all who need access to them.
3. A program must be implemented for the development of an assessment literate school and community.
4. A policy environment must be put in place that demands and supports quality assessment at all levels.
5. A priority must be placed on the effective management of information about student achievement. (Assessment Training Institute, n.d.)

In fact, these conditions must be put in place at the school district level. That is, there needs to be consistency in achievement expectations across school buildings within a district. There needs to be a districtwide commitment to meeting the information needs of all assessment users. Typically, the need for assessment literacy usually pervades the organization, not just some schools in the district. Assessment policy is set for the district by the school board, not for each building by its site council. And plans for the management of information about student achievement must facilitate communication both within and between buildings. So clearly, the five conditions listed must be coordinated by the district.

But assessment work that is coordinated at the district level must be implemented, evaluated, and reworked as needed within the schools of that district. That is where the principal's leadership comes in. The next section explores that role within each condition.

CONDITION 1: ACHIEVEMENT TARGETS

To assess student achievement accurately, teachers and administrators must know and understand the achievement targets their students are to master. It is not possible to assess (or teach!) achievement that has not been defined. To reach the goal of establishing clear and appropriate achievement expectations, three critical steps must be taken.

First, the community must agree on the meaning of academic success within its schools by asking: What are successful graduates of the local educational system expected to know and be able to do?

Second, district curriculum directors and building faculties across grade levels must meet to decide how that general vision of success can be realized within the local curriculum. The result of their deliberations must be a continuous progress curriculum that specifies how students move along a path to competence—how they succeed from kindergarten through high school.

Third, a careful audit must be conducted to be sure all teachers are confident, competent masters of the achievement targets assigned as their instructional responsibility. Although no major problems are anticipated here, districts or communities should not simply assume that all teachers are prepared to deliver their part of the big picture.

Principals must be key players in the completion of all three steps. Consider why.

High School Graduation Requirements. As mentioned previously, members of a school community do not always agree on the definition of an "effective school." To review briefly, in some quarters, an effective school is a safe place to house children while their families fulfill their adult responsibilities. Thus, effective schools serve a custodial function. In other quarters, schools are effective when they rank students from the highest to the lowest achiever. In this case, schools serve a sorting function. And in still other quarters, schools serve the purpose of producing competent students. Here the most effective schools are those that help the largest proportion of students attain their highest levels of achievement.

These purposes for schooling need not be mutually exclusive. Parents demand safe schools because the law requires placing children there. Further, in a competitive society where resources for postsecondary education and job opportunities are limited, society asks that students be ranked. But ultimately, an increasingly complex, technically sophisticated society demands that its graduates master the academic competencies needed in order to be productive contributors.

For this reason, from here on, it is assumed that effective schools maximize the achievement of the largest possible number of students. They are achievement-driven institutions: The more students who succeed in meeting achievement standards, the better the school. The more sophisticated the achievement targets they hit, the better the school.

This does not mean that all students will experience the same level of academic success. In the end, there will be variation in the amount students have learned. But schools cannot be considered effective merely because they sort students according to achievement, if the result is a rank order of students who have in fact learned very little. Thus, the purpose of this guide is to offer a plan for using quality assessment processes and results to maximize student achievement.

To be achievement driven, schools must work with their communities to define their local vision of academic success. The place to start is with the articulation of achievement expectations for high school graduation.

There are also divergent opinions about what those targets should be. To succeed, schools must find strategies for blending the views of at least four segments of the community. Without question, schools should solicit the opinions of the "family community"—the parents who entrust their children to schools and the taxpayers who support the social institution. In addition, input must be derived from the "business community"—future employers of those successful graduates. Still other advice must come from the "higher education community"—the other destination for successful graduates. And, finally, careful consideration should be given to the opinions of those in the "school community"—the teachers who are masters of the disciplines students are to learn.

In tapping segments of community opinion, schools bring a wide range of background and experience to bear on the question of essential learnings for students. For instance, the family community may bring input from the church. The business community will bring a sense of the future development of a technological society. The higher education community will balance that with a sense of intellectual foundations. And the school community will bring the best current thinking about academic standards from within their particular disciplines as well as any state-level academic standards that must be woven into the picture.

The process most school districts use to achieve this synthesis of community values is a combination of community meetings or forums and community surveys of public opinion. Principals should be leading those discussions within their school community, through PTA discussions, site council deliberations, and structured and unstructured surveys of community opinion. Often several iterations of each are needed to reach a consensus on the sense of the community and to work through heated arguments about differences of opinion.

Many school districts have succeeded in assembling these diverse sets of educational values into composite portraits of their successful graduates. An example is provided in Fig. 7.1. Although this particular statement of valued achievement expectations is quite general, it encompasses many essential ingredients. Principals should be prime players in the formulations of such statements.

A Continuous Progress Curriculum. Once the school community's vision of ultimate success is completed, the community of professional educators must take over to add the next ingredient. They must work collaboratively across school buildings and grade levels to back those end-of-high-school achievement targets down into the curriculum so as to map out the routes that students will take from kindergarten to high school to achieve success.

The result of this work must be a carefully planned and completely integrated continuous progress curriculum. That means teachers from primary grades, ele-

> It is our expectation that students exiting South Kitsap School District will demonstrate a core of basic knowledge in order to be:
>
> *Creative thinkers* who develop and use a variety of resources to identify, assess, integrate, and apply a basic core of knowledge to effectively make decisions and solve problems.
>
> *Self-directed learners* who set priorities, establish goals, and take responsibility for pursuing and evaluating those goals in an ever changing society.
>
> *Active citizens* who take the initiative to contribute time, energy, and talent to improve the quality of life for themselves and others in their local, national, and global environments.
>
> *Effective communicators* who receive information in a variety of forms and present information in various ways to a wide range of audiences.
>
> *Quality producers* who create innovative, artistic, and practical products that reflect originality, high standards, and the use of appropriate technologies.
>
> *Collaborative workers* who use effective group skills to manage interpersonal relationships within diverse settings.

FIG. 7.1. One school district's vision of academic success: South Kitsap (WA).

mentary grades, middle schools or junior highs, and high schools within the district must meet and divide up responsibility for helping students progress grade by grade through higher levels of academic attainment. It means that teachers must interact with one another and plan for the contributions to be made by each K–12 team member.

To illustrate, if students are to become competent writers, educators must specify what writing foundations primary grade teachers will need to help their students master. How will elementary teachers then build on that foundation? What forms of writing competence will middle school or junior high teachers contribute? And how will high school teachers top off writing competence that launches confident writers into work or college? Not only must each question be thoughtfully answered, each teacher must know how their contribution fits into this big picture.

This same planning process must be carried out in science, math, reading, social studies, and other disciplines. There must be a plan for student mastery of content knowledge, specific patterns of reasoning, performance skills, and product development capabilities as they play out within and across disciplines. Planning teams must decide who will take what responsibility for which forms of student growth. If students are to master scientific knowledge, what knowledge must be acquired in early grades? And how will later teachers reinforce and build on prior foundations? These questions must be answered to coordinate and integrate curriculum across grade levels and school buildings within a school district.

Many districts have found it useful to work in cross-grade-level teams to generate answers. These planning teams can tap into state standards and grade-level benchmarks to assist in finding appropriate divisions of content. They can also consult the standards being developed by national teams working within the professional associations of teachers, like the National Council of Teachers of Mathematics, the International Reading Association, or the National Council of Teachers of English.

A continuous progress curriculum is the foundation of quality assessment, because it tells educators what they should be assessing to track student progress. To create such a program, teachers must meet across grade levels within a local school district and work together as teams.

Principals have several roles to play with respect to the development of these road maps to student success. They all have to do with removing barriers to the completion of this work.

Their first role is to promote teamwork—that is, a sense of team membership among faculty members. The development of this kind of integrated curriculum can be tricky for several reasons. For instance, teaching has historically been something teachers do alone. Within general curricular guidelines, teachers select their own educational objectives and design instruction to achieve those objectives. Given this history, the concept of collaborative planning can be difficult to achieve.

In addition, educators do not have an outstanding track record over the years of mutual respect across grade levels. Elementary teachers sometimes find high school faculty controlling, and high school faculty sometimes fail to respect the discipline-based expertise of primary and elementary counterparts. Given this history, it can be difficult to blend into a team.

Besides, the history of academic freedom has entitled teachers to tailor their own instructional priorities to topics that interest them or that represent their strengths. Those who have established these personal priorities may be reluctant to reevaluate their emphasis as part of the process of compromising that leads to an integrated curriculum.

For all these reasons, it may be productive to precede curriculum-building activities with organizational development in the form of school building and district team-building activities conducted under the leadership of principals.

Another barrier to progress in constructing a continuous progress curriculum is that it can pose some challenging community relations problems. Many who view education from afar assume that there already is a curriculum that is integrated across grade levels. After all, the grade level numbers run in consecutive order and each subject is identified as important in each grade. People hear and make common reference to subsets of this curriculum—"third-grade math," "a sixth-grade reading level," "eighth-grade science," and the like. Parents naturally assume that these labels must mean that a well-planned and articulated sequence of instruction (and therefore assessment) has been laid out for children, with each grade building thoughtfully on those that preceded it. Unless the community understands that such a curriculum has not been developed, they will not know or understand what resources are needed to do it.

Principals have traditionally been the primary communicator with the local school community, and they should continue to play that role here too. They must diplomatically but firmly inform the community that schools are being retooled for a new achievement-driven system of schools. As a result, a new and better foundation of quality assessment must be put in place. Part of that foundation is a reexamination of the grade-level achievement expectations. Principals must help communities understand that a good deal of resources must be allocated to this effort in order to maximize student achievement. This is a critically important public relations role that only principals can play.

Teachers Who Are Ready to Guide Students to Success. With the development of a vision of academic success and a continuous progress curriculum, expectations for students are established. The next necessary condition for success is that all teachers be masters of the targets students are expected to master. This is part three of the scope of work to be completed under Condition 1.

Teachers can neither teach nor accurately assess learning that they themselves have not mastered. A school district cannot afford even one classroom where teachers are inadequately prepared. If just one teacher is incapable of helping students master essential achievement targets, then that teacher becomes a weak link in a continuous chain that will cause some students to fail later because they will not have mastered prerequisites.

Consequently, once achievement target responsibilities are divided across grade levels, principals must be sure their teachers are prepared to help students succeed. One challenging part of this is helping teachers conduct the open and honest internal self-reflection needed to evaluate their own preparedness. Most people did not grow up in an environment where it was safe to admit their inadequacies, nor has the adversarial tone that often characterizes teacher/supervisor relations made it easy for a teacher to be frank about the need for improvement. It takes a special kind of principal to establish a professional development environment in a school building that permits teachers to take the risk of being honest about their own preparedness to perform in the classroom.

It is essential that principals strive to establish supervisory and professional development environments devoted to excellence—not just minimum competence—in teaching. This takes a kind of collaboration, trust, and confidence that will permit teachers to go to their supervisors in the spirit of professional growth, and ask for help in gaining greater mastery of their discipline. Teachers must believe they can get the help they need without being penalized for asking the next time a staff evaluation comes along. This kind of environment is essential in helping teachers gain the knowledge and skills they need to be confident, competent classroom assessors.

Then it takes a special kind of principal to be sure the resources are allocated and opportunities are readily available to help teachers grow professionally. Responsibility for growing is the teacher's. Responsibility for encouraging and supporting that effort is the principal's.

CONDITION 2: A COMMITMENT TO ALL USERS

By definition, an assessment produces results that reflect a student's performance with respect to a specified set of achievement targets at a single point in time. Standardized test results provide achievement data summarized across large numbers of students on multiple targets. These targets are broadly defined for a particular grade level at a given stage during the school year. These tests are most useful in providing periodic status reports necessary for the program-planning level of decision making.

Classroom assessments, on the other hand, are focused on individual student attainment of narrowly defined targets throughout a particular course of study. As teachers use repeated assessments over time, each reflective of the achievement of fewer students, they can see and manage the development of students' achievement.

Educational decision makers who need only once-a-year access to achievement information reflecting group performance can effectively use standardized test results to satisfy those needs. Teachers, students, and parents who need continuous access to the high resolution portraits of individual student achievement are provided that information by classroom assessments.

Because decision makers at different levels have such diverse information needs, no single assessment can meet all their needs. If educators are to administer and use assessments with maximum effectiveness and efficiency, then they must plan carefully for their use and understand what information is actually needed.

Principals stand in a unique place in this array of assessment users. They are decision makers themselves, with certain information needs of their own. Because of the schoolwide implications of some of those decisions, principals often need test results that are comparable across classrooms. That requires standardized testing. But principals also need to be champions of high quality classroom assessment, so their teachers, students, and parents receive the information they need. The result is the need for a big picture perspective along with effective classroom assessment, which requires a careful balancing act.

Understanding Who the Users Are. First consider the big picture. In schools, there are three levels of assessment users: classroom, instructional support, and policy. The first column in Table 7.1 describes these categories. Column 2 identifies key questions to be answered based on interpretation of assessment results of some kind. A school district committed to meeting the needs of all assessment users must develop plans for conducting the assessments needed to provide the required information—at all levels.

TABLE 7.1
Sample Users and Uses of Assessment

At the Classroom Level

Assessment User	Sample Questions/Answers With Assessment Results
Student	Am I succeeding? Am I improving overt time? Do I know what it means to succeed here? What should I do next to succeed? What help do I need to succeed? Do I feel in control of my own success? Do I think I'm capable of success? Is the learning worth the effort? How am I doing in relation to my classmates? Where do I want all of this to take me?
Teacher	Are my students improving? Is it because of me? What does this student need? Is this student capable of learning this? What do these students need? What are their strengths that we can build on? How should I group my students? Am I going too fast, too slow, too far, not far enough? Am I improving as a teacher? How can I improve? Did that teaching strategy work? What do I say at parent–teacher conferences? What grade do I put on the report card?
Parent	Is my child learning new things—growing? Is my child succeeding? Is my child keeping up? Are we doing enough at home to support the teacher? What does my child need to succeed? Does the teacher know what my child needs? Is this teacher doing a good job? Is this a good school? District?

At the Instructional Support Level

Assessment User	Sample Questions
Principal	How do we define success in terms of student learning? Is this teacher producing results in the form of student learning? How can I help this teach improve? Is instruction in our building producing results? Is instruction at each grade level producing results? Are our students qualifying for college? Are our students prepared for the workplace? Do we need professional development as a faculty to improve? How shall we allocate building resources to achieve success?
Mentor Teacher	Is this new teacher producing results? What does this new teacher need to improve?
Curriculum Director	How do we define success in terms of student achievement? Is our program of instruction working? What adjustments do we need to make in our curriculum?

continued on next page

Special Services	Who needs (qualifies for) special educational services? Is our program of services helping students? What advice does this student need to succeed?

At the Policy Level

Assessment User	Sample Questions
Superintendent	Are our programs of instruction producing results in terms of student learning? Is each building principal producing results? Which schools deserve or need more or fewer resources?
School Board	Are our students learning and succeeding? Is the superintendent producing results?
State Department of Education	Are programs across the state producing results? Are individual school districts producing results?
Citizen/Legislature	Are our students achieving in ways that prepare them to become productive citizens?

Note: From *Student-Involved Classroom Assessment* (3rd ed.) by R. J. Stiggins, in press. Copyright by Merrill. Reprinted with permission.

A thoughtful analysis of the information needs of the first category of users—instructional staff—reveals they will obtain the information they need from the teacher's day-to-day classroom assessments. User needs at the other two levels will be served by standardized assessments.

From the principal's perspective, the essential planning question is: How is it possible to be sure all building and classroom level users receive relevant student achievement information in a timely and understandable form? At the classroom level, each individual teacher must develop a plan for answering this question. Principals must support that effort. At the level of building instructional support, the leadership team also needs a plan. The principal must lead that effort.

Planning for Classroom Assessment. To monitor student achievement effectively and efficiently, all classroom teachers must begin each unit of instruction or course of study with a clear vision of the specific achievement targets their students are to hit in that context. Beginning with the foundational instructional targets, teachers must understand how their students will progress over time to higher levels of academic proficiency. In what order will they master more advanced levels of content knowledge? How will they use that knowledge productively to reason and solve problems? What performance skills will they master, and in what sequence? What kinds of achievement products will they be called on to create? In short, at the classroom level, the continuous progress curriculum must be mapped.

With this in mind, then, teachers must start their instruction with a predetermined plan for assessing to what extent each student has reached the required goals. The next section explores the range of assessment methods available to teachers for this purpose. But for now, on request, teachers should be able to provide their written plan of targets, written plan for the sequence of assessments planned to track student progress, and a status report on the completion of those assessments and student results.

Further, teachers need to weave into their plans a description of how the results are to be clearly delivered to students and parents (i.e., how results evaluated specific targets) and delivered in time to use for the decision-making process. Because students, like teachers, make decisions of the sorts identified in Table 7.1 on a continuous basis, the feedback plan should also reflect ways to keep students continually in touch with their own progress.

Again, this classroom level of assessment planning completed by each teacher at the beginning of each program of study asks: What targets will be assessed, when, and how will the results be used?

The formulation of these plans and their implementation requires that teachers work from a foundation of understanding of their achievement targets and of the principles of sound classroom assessment. They must be assessment literate. It is the principal's job to be sure those prerequisites are in place by conducting careful staff evaluations and implementing necessary professional development programs.

Planning for Standardized Testing. Because standardized testing is most often coordinated at the school district level, there is less of a role for the principal in designing assessment systems that connect the assessments to their intended users. But one role that principals can play in the planning process is to advocate on behalf of balanced perspectives regarding standardized testing. These tests only serve certain limited purposes. They are not the key to effective schools. Although these tests must be used carefully to help certain decision makers do their job, they must be kept in balance with classroom assessment in contributing to the attainment of educational excellence.

Another advocacy position that principals should take is to urge policy and instructional support level users to develop their own assessment literacy. Sound standardized test planning requires that all users understand the assessment implications of these tests. All who participate at any level in the standardized testing program should be held accountable for meeting a rigorous standard of assessment literacy.

Beyond this, the principal's role is to see to the implementation of standardized testing plans at the building level. That means letting school and community know what targets are assessed for what students, when the assessments are administered, and what specific information/decision-making needs are served. If standardized tests are used for selection of students for special services, users must also know which targets are assessed, when are they assessed, and precisely how the results are being used. If the district participates in a statewide assessment, school and community must understand what targets are being tested, at what levels, and for whose purposes. Each assessment fills in part of the district's big assessment picture. By keeping track of the overall plan, principals can and should identify both overlaps and gaps in the assessments conducted.

CONDITION 3: ASSESSMENT LITERACY

If decision makers are to fulfill the various roles spelled out earlier, they must have access to dependable information about student achievement. Quality assessments are a must. Educators can develop and use high quality assessments only if they adhere to rigorous standards of quality. To meet those standards consistently, teachers and administrators must have the opportunity to learn about and practice applying them. In short, they must become assessment literate.

Assessment literacy includes two parts. The first is the ability to gather dependable information about student achievement. The second is the ability to use that information to advantage in the process of maximizing student achievement.

Assessments that help educators gather dependable information about student achievement meet the following specific standards of quality (Stiggins, in press).

Standard 1. Quality assessments arise from and accurately reflect clearly specified and appropriate achievement expectations for students. Knowing precisely what students are being asked to master is important because different targets require the application of different assessment methods. In any assessment context, the assessment development process begins by defining a clear vision of what it means to succeed. Are students expected to:

- Master subject matter content, meaning to know and understand? Does this mean they must know it outright? Or, does it mean they must know where and how to find it, using references?
- Use knowledge to reason and solve problems?
- Demonstrate mastery of specific performance skills, where it is the doing that is important?
- Use their knowledge, reasoning, and skills to create products that meet standards of quality?

Because there is no single assessment method capable of assessing all these various forms of achievement, a proper method cannot be selected without a sharp focus on which of these expectations is to be assessed.

Standard 2. Sound assessments are specifically designed to serve instructional purposes. Assessments cannot be designed without asking who will use the results and how. Recall that Table 7.1 lists the important users of assessment in schools, each of whom needs different information at different times to answer different questions. To provide quality information for teacher, student, and parent at the classroom level, sound classroom assessments are necessary. To provide useful information at the levels of policy or instructional support, there must be quality standardized tests. Because of the differences in information needs, each assessment event must begin with a clear sense of whose needs are being met. Otherwise these assessments are without purpose.

Standard 3. Quality assessments accurately reflect the intended target and serve the intended purpose. Because there are several different kinds of achievement to assess, and no single assessment method will reflect them all, educators must rely on a variety of methods. The options include *selected response tests* (multiple choice, true/false, matching, and fill-in), *essay assessments, performance assessments* (based on observation and judgment), and assessment based on direct *personal communication* with the student. The educator's assessment challenge is to match a method with an intended target, as depicted in Table 7.2. The professional development challenge is to be sure all concerned with quality assessment know and understand how the various pieces of this puzzle fit together.

Standard 4. Quality assessments provide a representative sample of student performance that is sufficient in its scope to permit confident conclusions about student achievement. All assessments rely on a relatively small number of exercises to permit the user to draw inferences about a student's mastery of larger domains of achievement. A sound assessment offers a representative sample of all those possibilities that is large enough to yield dependable conclusions about how the respondent would have done if given all possible exercises. Each assessment context places its own special constraints on the sampling procedures. Each assessment method carries with it a specific set of rules of evidence for using it to sample well. The quality control challenge is to know how to adjust the sampling strategies in each context to produce results of maximum quality at minimum cost in time and effort.

Standard 5. Sound assessments are designed, developed, and used in such a manner as to minimize sources of bias or distortion that interfere with the accuracy of results. Even if clear achievement targets are devised, they are transformed into proper assessment methods, and student performance is sampled appropriately, there are still factors that can cause students' scores on a test to misrepresent their real achievement. Problems can arise from the test, the student, or the environment where the test is administered.

For example, tests can consist of poorly worded questions, place reading or writing demands on respondents that are confounded with mastery of the material being tested, have more than one correct response, be incorrectly scored, or contain racial or ethnic bias. The student can experience extreme evaluation anxiety or interpret test items differently from the author's intent, as well as cheat, guess, or

TABLE 7.2
Aligning Achievement Targets to Assessment Methods

Target to Be Assessed	Assessment Method			
	Selected Response	*Essay*	*Performance Assessment*	*Personal Communication*
KNOWLEDGE MASTERY	Multiple choice, true–false, matching, and fill-in can sample mastery of elements of knowledge	Essay exercises can tap understanding of relations among elements of knowledge	Not a good choice for this target—three other options preferred	Can ask questions, evaluate answers and infer mastery—but a time-consuming option
REASONING PROFICIENCY	Can assess understanding of basic patterns of reasoning	Written descriptions of complex problem solutions can provide a window into reasoning proficiency	Can watch student solve some problems and infer about reasoning proficiency	Can ask student to "think aloud" or can ask follow-up questions to probe reasoning
SKILLS	Can assess mastery of the prerequisites of skillful performance—but cannot tap the skill itself	Can assess mastery of the prerequisites of skillful performance—but cannot tap the skill itself	Can observe and evaluate skills as they are being performed	Strong match when skill is oral communication proficiency; also can assess mastery of knowledge prerequisite to skillful performance
ABILITY TO CREATE PRODUCTS	Can assess mastery of knowledge prerequisite to the ability to create quality products—but cannot assess the quality of products themselves	Can assess mastery of knowledge prerequisite to the ability to create quality products—but cannot assess the quality of products themselves	A strong match can assess: (a) proficiency in carrying out steps in product development, and (b) attributes of the product itself	Can probe procedural knowledge and knowledge of attributes of quality products—but not product quality

Note: From *Student-Involved Classroom Assessment* (3rd ed.) by R. J. Stiggins, in press. Copyright by Merrill. Reprinted with permission.

lack motivation. Any of these could give rise to inaccurate test results. Or, the assessment environment could be uncomfortable, poorly lighted, noisy, or otherwise distracting.

Part of the challenge of becoming assessment literate is to be aware of the potential sources of bias and to know how to devise assessments, prepare students, and plan assessment environments to deflect these problems before they ever impact results.

The Standard of Effective Use.

Meeting these standards of sound assessment practice maximizes the dependability of the assessments. However, the most accurate assessment available is wasted if it is not used to maximum advantage. Effective use includes two parts.

To begin with, results must be communicated effectively. People communicate well when those intending to deliver information about student achievement and those who are to receive and act on that information understand the symbols used to deliver the message to mean the same thing. If test scores are used to deliver that message, both sender and receiver must understand a consistent meaning for those scores. If report card grades are used, again, sender and receiver must know precisely what the letter grade represents by way of achievement. Other ways to communicate effectively include portfolios, narrative reports, and conferences of various sorts. In short, there are options to choose from in deciding how to communicate. But people can only choose intelligently if they understand the principles of effective communication.

In addition, assessments are used effectively when we use the assessment development and application processes are used as instructional interventions. Assessment literacy includes understanding how to open up the performance assessment design steps so that students can be part of that process. In this way, assessment may be used to reveal to students precisely what it is that is expected of them. Students can hit any achievement target that they see and that holds still for them. Student-involved assessment, record keeping, and communication represent ways to help them feel in control of the level of academic success they attain.

The Principal's Role.

Principals have two critically important responsibilities regarding assessment literacy. The first is to become assessment literate themselves. Without this basis of professional expertise, principals will remain unable to provide the support teachers need to develop and use assessments productively in their classrooms.

The second role is to remove all barriers to the development of teachers' assessment literacy. These include personal, institutional, and community barriers. For teachers, the personal barriers can include the anxiety that accompanies trying a new assessment when they are not sure it will work. The principal needs to give teachers the confidence that failure to assess dependably or to use assessment effectively *initially* will not lead to a directive to stop trying. But teachers must also understand that they are expected to keep improving. From an institutional perspective, barriers can include a lack of time to learn and to experiment with new assessment ideas. Teachers need to know that school resources will be allocated for these purposes. And then principals need to make sure they are. Community barriers can include parents who question changes in assessment and communication procedures. Principals need to be sufficiently assessment literate to be able to ease community concerns in this regard.

In the next section, after an examination of the remaining conditions of effective assessment use is completed, an effective and efficient professional development strategy is detailed that principals can use to become assessment literate themselves and to help their teachers do the same.

CONDITION 4: A SUPPORTIVE POLICY ENVIRONMENT

One very important part of a quality assessment program is a statement of commitment to quality from those in leadership positions. This would take the form of district policy, making the standards of sound assessment practice clear and understandable. Such school board-endorsed policy also should spell out accountability for meeting those standards. In that way, it sets professional competence standards that support professional development and assure communities of sound assessment practices in their schools. Although sound assessment policies do not ensure sound practices, they can contribute by reaffirming a commitment to quality.

Because this typically is a school district matter, the policy setting responsibility does not fall to the building principal. However, the principal can play a key role in establishing such an assessment policy environment.

Preparing School Boards and Communities for Sound Assessment.

Before taking the critical step of reevaluating assessment policies, school board members and the community should be prepared to address some important issues. Apprising the school board of the need to reconsider assessment policies is the responsibility of the district leadership team. But informing the local school community is the charge of each school building principal. First, the community should be made aware of the problem being addressed. This can be risky business if not handled in a diplomatic manner, because it involves dispelling some common assumptions about the status of assessment in classrooms. Some in the community may be startled and troubled when they realize, for example, that some educators may not be accurately assessing student achievement. For this reason, the principal absolutely must bring to this conversation an appropriate understanding of the differences between sound and unsound assessment practices. In addition, both the district and building leadership teams should have in hand a specific plan for dealing with the problem before this conversation ever begins.

In addition, building-level leadership can contribute to the process of drafting for school board review a district assessment philosophy that articulates the assessment responsibilities for all who contribute to the effectiveness of schools. As a point of departure for local district policy discussions, a few sample entries for such a policy are offered in the next section. Principals can contribute much to the development of these local policies. But without question, they will be the driving force behind the implementation of such policies in their school buildings.

A Sample District Assessment Policy. A district assessment policy should establish the criteria by which quality assessment will be judged (as described previously). Further, it should assert an expectation that staff will apply standards of quality in all assessment contexts. For example, this kind of policy might be worded as follows:

> Because effective instruction depends on high quality assessment, this district expects all assessments to provide accurate information about student achievement. Each assessment must meet five standards of quality. It must arise from a clearly articulated set of achievement expectations, serve an instructionally relevant purpose, rely on a proper method, sample student achievement in an appropriate manner, and control for all relevant sources of bias and distortion that can lead to inaccurate assessment. Any assessments not meeting these standards are to be discarded.

This statement encourages all who are not conversant with the standards of quality or are uncertain of their ability to develop assessments that meet those standards to seek professional development assistance.

The quality standards specified previously hold that assessments must serve clear purposes, reflect clear targets, and rely on proper methods, so the district policy might outline the full range of appropriate purposes, kinds of targets, and acceptable methods as follows:

> It is the expectation of this school district that all assessments will be directly linked to specific instructional uses and thus to student academic well-being. Two types of use are considered appropriate: (a) assessment as a source of information for decision making and (b) assessment for the purpose of promoting higher levels of student achievement.

> With respect to the former, several levels of decision making and decision makers are considered important to student academic well-being: classroom level (students, teachers, and parents), instructional support level (principals, curriculum specialists, support teachers and guidance personnel), and policy level (superintendent, school board, citizens and taxpayers). The district as a whole and each school building will allocate assessment resources and devise assessment, evaluation, and communication programs to meet the information needs of all these users.

> With respect to the use of assessment in promoting high student achievement, the district acknowledges that assessment can serve as a powerful teaching tool. By involving students in the assessment and evaluation of their own achievement under direct supervision, teachers can use assessment to help students understand the meaning of academic success and meet the highest achievement expectations.

Any assessments that cannot be specifically linked to student academic well-being through effective decision making or instruction should be discarded.

Again, this sample policy statement shows an explicit expectation of assessment competence that encourages comprehensive professional development. Principals must lead that professional development effort.

Personnel Policy and Excellence in Assessment. Several dimensions of personnel policy may be in need of revision to ensure the long-term development of an assessment-literate staff. Beginning at the most general level, state licensing requirements should include explicit expectations of assessment competence as a condition for certification in a teacher or administrator role. As already mentioned, only a few states currently impose this licensing standard for teachers and administrators. This is why teacher and administrator training programs in higher education institutions should be encouraged to offer coursework that includes relevant assessment training. Over the decades, higher education has not delivered in this area of professional training. An adjunct responsibility of building administrators is to advocate on behalf of appropriate licensing standards through statewide professional associations.

However, admittedly, neither certification standards nor college course offerings are the responsibility of the principal. But the quality of teaching is. And principals cannot assure their communities of high quality until certain local personnel policies change. For example, the criteria that principals apply when screening and selecting new teachers should be adjusted to reflect an expectation of competence in assessment. The criteria used to evaluate ongoing teacher performance on the job might be adjusted to include evaluation of the quality of assessments and their use. Building staff-development priorities might be adjusted—at least on an interim basis—to reflect the strength of the need for assessment training, and assessment and professional development resources might be channeled in this direction.

In short, leadership is needed in creating a local personnel environment that expects and supports competence in assessment, as well as the effective application of that competence in the service of student academic well-being.

Effective leaders develop their own vision of excellence to guide the efforts of their organization. In schools, that vision takes the form of policies and regulations that guide everyday practice. Every school needs a vision of excellence in assessment to guide its practices, and this calls for a very carefully worded district assessment philosophy, codified as policy. The development of that vision is the responsibility of the principal.

The development of a vision of excellence in assessment that calls for the effective use of high quality standardized and classroom assessments is recommended. This policy should make standards of quality clear and explicit and should let all teachers understand that they will be held accountable for meeting standards of sound practice. Accountability for implementing such policies should rest squarely on the shoulders of the principal.

CONDITION 5: MANAGING INFORMATION ABOUT STUDENT ACHIEVEMENT

If schools are to help students progress in a continuous manner toward ever higher levels of academic proficiency with respect to a clearly defined progression of achievement targets, and if teachers are to track their development using classroom assessments, then academic record-keeping strategies will have to evolve rapidly. Educators must take advantage of modern information-processing technology for generating, storing, and retrieving information about student achievement.

In other words, a grade on a report card every 10 weeks based on a summary of hand written and often uninterpretable grade book notations cannot tell the student, teacher, or parent precisely where the student is at any point in time on the continuous progress path to becoming competent. Moreover, students charged with tracking and communicating their own improvement as achievers need continuous access to far greater detail about their own achievement than such records can provide. Teachers receiving new students at the beginning of the year or students who are coming from a different school, and who are expected to take students from where they are to new levels of competence, also require greater detail. Parents who desire and expect to see specific information about the progress of their children are not served by grades on a report card every 10 weeks. Further, the time required to enter, retrieve, and summarize records by hand, as teachers do with grade books, will prove too time consuming and labor intensive to be practical in a continuous progress curriculum.

For these reasons, school districts must begin to investigate, adopt, and then adapt electronic information management software systems for student achievement data. These systems can assist teachers and districts with essential assessment activities in a number of very efficient and effective ways. For example, they can organize the goals and objectives that comprise the curriculum in a continuous progress manner; generate assessments using a wide variety of exercise formats; assist teachers in the collection of classroom observational data; print assessments for administration or permit their administration online; permit instant scanning and scoring of selected response assessments; allow direct scanning of virtually any form of record desired, such as actual samples of student writing or videotapes of student performance; provide long-term dependable and efficient storage of that information and instant retrieval and summary as needed; and facilitate immediate access to records online by anyone authorized to see them, permitting teachers or parents to obtain instant information about the status of any student or any group of students for conferencing or planning purposes.

The time savings available to teachers and administrators through the use of these information management systems are immense. Every school district should form an ad hoc committee of teachers, principals, community representatives, and technology experts to review and evaluate these options. The building-level leadership role in this case is that of supporting professional development so staff understand the time and labor savings that can come with these systems, and to help them understand how to involve students in the use of such information management systems to their benefit. It also calls for principal leadership in helping teachers gain access to these technologies.

Retracing the PAth to Excellence in Assessment

For decades educators and policymakers have been searching for ways to use the power of assessment to achieve truly effective schools—schools that maximize the achievement of the largest possible proportion of their student populations. Success in reaching this goal remains contingent on the ability of those in leadership positions to see and embrace a vision that includes and extends far beyond the assessment traditions.

The barriers to quality assessment are significant. This is why it is difficult to tap the potential power of assessment in the service of effective schools. But the roadblocks can be removed if an assessment-literate school culture can be established. Those in school leadership positions can unlock and open the doors to excellence in assessment by ensuring that their leadership teams and faculties ask and answer the following questions in order to:

1. Develop a Clear Vision of Achievement Expectations
   A. Has the community established a set of expectations for successful graduates?
   B. Has the faculty worked as a team to take that vision to the classroom in a continuous progress curriculum?
   C. Have all teachers mastered the achievement targets they expect their students to master?
2. Commit to Quality Assessment Information for All Users
   A. What is the plan for meeting the information needs of students, teachers, and parents using classroom assessment?
   B. What is the plan for meeting the information needs of building and district administrators and the community with standardized tests?
3. Build an Assessment-Literate School Culture
   A. What is the plan for evaluating and then building the assessment literacy of the school building's faculty and staff?

B. What is the plan for developing assessment literacy within the community (parents, taxpayers, school board members)?
4. Develop a Supportive Assessment Policy Environment
   A. How will current policies and regulations be reviewed to see if they support the effective use of assessment?
   B. What is the plan for evaluating existing policies and for identifying new policy areas not currently addressed that will support and encourage the use of quality assessment?
5. Manage Student Achievement Information
   A. What new technologies are needed to effectively and efficiently collect, store, retrieve, and report information about student achievement?
   B. How can currently available information-processing systems be investigated in light of those needs?
   C. How shall staff, as well as the curriculum and instruction and assessment practices, be prepared to take full advantage of the efficiency of such systems?

The answers to these questions show how to develop quality schools through excellence in assessment, where excellence is defined as the balanced and effective use of high quality classroom and standardized assessments to promote student success.

Leadership in the pursuit of excellence in assessment begins with a vision. The building-level leadership team, under the direct supervision of the principal, must understand the importance of quality assessment at all levels and put forth the guiding standards for assessment practices throughout the building. The school board must establish the districtwide policy environment that underpins the pursuit of the assessment vision in every classroom and school within the district. Curriculum directors must contribute clear visions of achievement expectations, holding the entire team together to function as a unit across grade levels and disciplines.

Principals must also be prepared to use assessment to show the community how effective their schools are, while at the same time assisting their teachers in acquiring the levels of assessment literacy needed to develop and use high quality day-to-day classroom assessments with students. These are the essential keys to providing leadership for assessment excellence and building more effective schools.

Summarizing the Principal's Leadership Responsibility

As mentioned previously, there are an imposing array of personal and institutional roadblocks to quality assessment. This section summarizes those roadblocks, along with the principal's potential contribution to their removal.

REMOVING PERSONAL BARRIERS TO QUALITY ASSESSMENT

In a standards-driven educational system, educators are asked to be clear about targets, assess them well, and share the results with those who need access to them in order to fulfill their roles. But what if teachers administer rigorous assessments and the results reveal that students did not hit the target? And what if that failure was due to factors beyond the teacher's control—for example, students who failed to fulfill their responsibilities? If this happens, teachers or administrators may be unjustly blamed for students' lack of learning.

Under these circumstances, from the teacher's point of view, it may seem safer to remain vague about achievement expectations and to couch assessment results in such technically complex test scores and complicated grade book manipulations that no one could ever determine how much learning really took place in classrooms or schools. Again, from the teacher's perspective, such procedures appear to address accountability for student learning without risking real accountability.

But the following question must be asked: If educators preserve their own safety in these ways, then what are the implications of this behavior for student learning? Clearly, the implications will be far from positive. In this way, the sense of vulnerability about being evaluated in terms of student learning can lead the educator who lacks confidence to implement unsound practices.

But how can this pervasive fear be overcome? The only way is to establish a building-level supervision environment in which teachers are encouraged to take the risk of being honest about their current level of assessment literacy and to invest the time and energy needed to become a competent, confident classroom assessor.

REMOVING INSTITUTIONAL BARRIERS TO QUALITY

Another prominent barrier to quality assessment from the teacher's point of view is the lack of time to assess well. If teachers feel they do not have time to meet the standards of assessment quality, then they will not try. Several specific time issues trouble teachers deeply.

One concern is the broadening curriculum that leaves teachers needing to assess an ever expanding array of student achievement goals. The curriculum is growing to include more achievement targets such as important technology and health-related topics, more complexity within the "established" targets (for instance, an enhanced understanding of what it means to be a proficient reader or writer), and more complex ways of integrating the curriculum across disciplines. How can teachers assess even more when they already have too little time to assess current targets?

There is only one answer: Learn to assess smarter, not harder. Many teachers contend that the currently popular assessment methods are too labor intensive. The message many administrators and teachers are receiving is that performance assessment methodology—authentic exercises leading to observations and judgments of students—is the only acceptable way to assess student achievement. Advocates cite the richness of results they can derive from detailed observations of performance and judgment based on complex performance standards. Hidden between the lines for many teachers is the subliminal message "lots of hard work!" Some respond by digging in their heels. Few educators are actively looking for more work to do.

An obsession with performance assessment can throw the picture out of balance. Performance assessment is not always the best way. In fact, sometimes it is not even an acceptable way to assess. In certain instances, and with certain achievement targets, other methods such as multiple choice or true–false tests are better choices. When they fit, these are always more efficient options. And even when educators do turn to performance assessment, only those with a rich knowledge of the method know how to use it efficiently. Consequently, to tap assessment options with maximum efficiency, they must be assessment literate.

Another time problem is that, for many districts, the only acceptable way to store and communicate information about student achievement, according to the district policy manual, is the grade book and report card grades. That process eats huge amounts of time all by itself, leaving neither time nor opportunity to consider alternatives.

If record keeping is conceived of as a teacher-centered activity relying on turn-of-the-century grade book technology, then the time demands far outstrip anything a teacher or administrator can manage. Again, the solution to this problem lies in breaking an outdated mold. Information-processing technology of the 1920s will not—indeed cannot—meet the emerging new millennium. There must be a sharply focused vision of achievement targets, thoroughly developed assessment plans, highly efficient assessment methods, and strategies for record keeping that rely on many helpers and modern information management technology. But to tap this technology, educators need access to it and sufficient assessment literacy to take advantage of it. By creating this environment, the building supervisors remove this barrier to quality assessment.

REMOVING THE ULTIMATE BARRIER TO QUALITY

People cannot meet standards of quality if they do not know what those standards are or how to meet them. After reflecting on the barriers to quality—teachers' fear of accountability and a lack of time—it should be clear that their removal is contingent on the development of teachers' assessment literacy.

Assessment-literate educators are masters of the basic principles of sound assessment. They know and understand the five standards of assessment quality defined previously. But more importantly, they are able to apply those standards in their schools and classrooms routinely.

High quality professional development programs are needed to provide that foundation—especially given the long history of failing to train teachers and administrators in assessment. The objectives of a practitioner-centered professional development program in assessment, along with highly efficient training strategies, are outlined next. This is work that will not be completed unless and until principals lead building-level programs.

Both teachers and administrators are prepared to fulfill their ongoing assessment responsibilities when they understand essential differences between sound and unsound assessment practices and commit to meeting key quality standards; know how to meet standards of quality in all classroom, school, and district assessment contexts; and know how to use the assessment process as a teaching tool to motivate students to strive for excellence.

The achievement of these objectives requires the design, development, and implementation of professional development strategies that provide practical new assessment ideas and strategies in an efficient manner; offer classroom practice in applying those new strategies; give participants responsibility for managing their own development, and promote the sense of professionalism that comes from one's own pursuit of excellence; provide collegial support, where educators learn by sharing the lessons they have learned individually; deliver benefits very quickly to those who apply lessons learned in their classroom; and encourage a healthy concern for quality assessment by emphasizing its implications for student well-being and teacher effectiveness.

To satisfy these requirements, a professional development program is recommended that relies heavily on a blend of *learning teams* (also referred to as study groups or study teams) and *individual study* and experimentation by teachers as the basis of interaction and growth. In these teams, a small group of 5 to 10 teachers and administrators agree to meet regularly to share responsibility for their mutual professional development.

Between meetings, team members commit to completing assignments designed to advance their assessment literacy. They might, for example, study the same piece of professional literature and try the same assessment strategies, and then bring the lessons they have learned from that experience to share and discuss in the group meeting. Or team members might complete different assignments, learn different lessons, and meet to share a more diverse array of insights to the benefit of all.

Figure 7.2 provides a sample list of references that can help educators develop their assessment literacy across and within academic disciplines. They offer an excellent basis for learning team collaboration.

Some principals begin with a "leadership study team" comprised of a few key teachers from across the building. This team's mission is threefold: develop their own high levels of assessment literacy, devise a specific strategy for forming and offering support to multiple study groups throughout the building, and conduct an ongoing evaluation of the professional development effort to determine its impact.

Assessment Literacy:

Stiggins, R. (in press). *Student-involved classroom assessment* (3rd ed.). Columbus, OH: Merrill of Prentice-Hall. Distributed by the Assessment Training Institute, Portland, OR. A teacher's handbook on the development of quality assessments for use as teaching tools in the classroom; Learning Team Trainer's Guide also available. To order: 800-480-3060, ISBN 3-13-432931-7.

Assessment and Student Motivation:

Covington, M. (1992). *Making the grade: A self-worth perspective on motivation and school reform.* New York: Cambridge University Press. A comprehensive analysis of the relationship between our evaluations of students and their willingness to strive for excellence. To order: 914-937-9600, Order #34803X, ISBN 0-521-34261-9, $19.95.

Communicating About Student Achievement:

Austin, T. (1994). *Changing the view: Student-led conferences.* Portsmouth, NH: Heinemann. A teacher's handbook on setting up and conducting student-involved communications. To order: 800-541-2086, Order #08818, ISBN 0-435-08818-1, $14.50.

Davies, A., Cameron, C., Politano, C., & Gregory, K. (1992). *Together is better: Collaborative assessment, evaluation & reporting.* Courtenay, British Columbia: Classroom Connections International. A practical guide to the design and completion of student-involved communications. To order: 800-603-9888, ISBN 1-895411-54-8, $16.95.

Student-Involved Writing Assessment:

Spandel, V. (in press). *Creating writers: Linking assessment and writing instruction* (2nd ed.). New York: Addison-Wesley/Longman. A teacher's guide to the integration of student-involved writing assessment with the teaching and learning process. To order: 800-822-6339, ISBN 0-8013-1578-6.

FIG. 7.2 Resources for learning teams.

Obviously, learning teams can be configured in any of a variety of ways. Groups might be formed on the basis of grade level (within or across levels) or within or across discipline (math, science, arts, etc.). Learning teams might come into existence as opportunities arise, when, for example, an ad hoc committee is assembled to evaluate and consider revising report card grading or when a curriculum-development team decides to deal with some underlying assessment issues. All such instances represent opportunities for developing effective assessment strategies.

A principal might allocate released time or extended contract time to permit teachers to be involved in any or all of these efforts. The promise of time to concentrate on one important topic long enough to internalize some new and useful ideas can be a strong motivator. This, combined with time to talk with and learn from colleagues (both very rare commodities for most educators), may be incentive enough for some. In addition, an ongoing working relationship can be established with a higher education institution to offer graduate credit for competence in assessment attained through study group work.

Another internal source of motivation may include tapping into individuals' drive for excellence when they see themselves improving. One way to take advantage of this is to encourage all learning team members to build a portfolio of evidence of their own improvement as classroom assessors, including a journal of self-reflection about evolving assessment competence and examples of assessments collected over time, with written commentary on their increasing quality. Periodically, team members might present to the rest of the team their evidence of progress as an assessor.

This kind of principal leadership in professional development of assessment literacy sets students, teachers, schools, and school districts up for success. It balances classroom assessment with standardized tests in a manner that helps students feel confident. In addition, it promotes productive student/teacher team work, as well as strong building/staff relations.

REFERENCES

American Association of School Administrators, National Association of Elementary School Principals, National Association of Secondary School Principals, & National Council on Measurement in Education. (1997). *Standards for administrator competence in assessment.* Washington, DC: Authors.

American Federation of Teachers, National Education Association, & National Council on Measurement in Education. (1990). *Standards for teacher competence in educational assessment of students.* Washington, DC: Authors.

Assessment Training Institute. (n.d.). *Leadership for excellence in assessment: A school district planning guide.* Portland, OR: Author.

Covington, M. (1992). *Making the grade: A self-worth perspective on motivation and school reform.* New York: Cambridge University Press.

Kohn, A. (1993). *Punished by rewards.* New York: Houghton Mifflin.

Schafer, W. D., & Lissitz, R. W. (1987). Measurement training for school personnel: Recommendations and reality. *Journal of Teacher Education, 38*(3), 57–63.

Stiggins, R. (in press). *Student-involved classroom assessment* (3rd ed.). Columbus, OH: Merrill; Portland, OR: Assessment Training Institute.

Stiggins, R, & Conklin, N. (1992). *In teachers' hands: Investigating the practice of classroom assessment.* Albany: State University of New York Press.

Thompson, S. (Ed.). (1993). *Principals for our changing schools: The knowledge and skill base.* Washington, DC: National Policy Board for Educational Administration.

Trevisan, M. (1999). Administrator certification requirement for student assessment competence. *Applied Measurement in Education, 12*(1), 1–11.

Chapter 8

The Construction of Standardized Tests and Their Uses

Michelle A. Mengeling
The University of Iowa

WITH YET ANOTHER STANDARDIZED TEST CURRENTLY under development—the national voluntary test—Sacks (1997), an opponent of standardized testing, gained further support for his claim that "we are a nation of standardized-testing junkies" (p. 25). He expressed legitimate and passionate concerns in his writing concerning the use and misuse of standardized tests. Perhaps it is simple common sense that standardized tests do not provide and cannot be expected to provide all the information necessary to evaluate student development. However, in the haste to make comparisons among students, schools, districts, and even states, the purpose, and thus the limits of standardized testing, are often obscured by unrealistic expectations of the kind of information that can be obtained from standardized tests. It may be that the capacity of a standardized test to provide normative comparisons has overshadowed its primary purpose of improving student learning.

Standardized tests can be used as tools to improve student learning, rather than just as norm-referencing tools, if an appropriate test is chosen for the task at hand. Unlike tools used to measure concrete characteristics such as height or weight, the most appropriate tool to measure achievement is not easily discernible. For example, when testing the mathematics skills of a nonnative speaker, it may make sense to provide the text in the student's native language, rather than English, preventing students' mathematics achievement scores from being unduly influenced by their English language skills. However, many such math tests will likely be administered entirely in English, including the directions, test item, and response options. Decisions based solely on these results may be invalid for making inferences regarding this student's math achievement and thus can be potentially harmful to the student. In criticizing the validity of the results, the mismatch between test and student will most likely and perhaps mistakenly be attributed to the construction of the test rather than as a consequence of the decision to administer this test to this particular student.

The previous example illustrates an implicit assumption that many users of test results automatically make. Users often assume there is an inherent match between what they assume is being measured and what the test is actually measuring. An incorrect assumption can lead to incorrect interpretations and thus incorrect decisions. Therefore, these kinds of assumptions need to be brought to the foreground and made explicit so that assessment users can make meaningful and valid decisions using standardized test data.

This chapter explores the explicit and implicit assumptions regarding standardized tests. In order to do this, the entire standardized testing process is reviewed from the beginning, including specifying what to test, building the test, and finally interpreting and judging the quality of the data that result from testing. In order to facilitate this discussion, a basic review of common statistical terms used to communicate results and to judge the quality of the results is provided. The strengths and limitations of standardized testing are included throughout the discussion. Concluding remarks include a review of some of the most current literature regarding standardized tests, in which the major focus is on the criticisms of standardized test use.

Constructing a Standardized Test

For standardized tests, as well as classroom exams, the first task in the test development process is determining what to assess. For classroom assessments, there is a lot of variability among assessments, caused by classroom-to-classroom differences in what content to cover and emphasize, whether the test is formative or summative, whether the assessment will be used to gauge knowledge acquisition and understanding, or alternatively, evaluate creative processes such as writing and other behavioral objectives. Educators must use their expertise to match the appropriate assessment tool with the performance being assessed. In so doing, the educator's involvement with the design, administration, and scoring of the test allows for a deeper understanding of what the test is measuring.

Standardized tests serve a different function. They are not designed to assess the outcomes for any particular classroom but are to be used in multiple classrooms, school buildings, districts, states, and even nations. The tests used in the Third International Math and Science Study (TIMMS) were standardized tests. Standardized tests have been designed to assess general skills in content areas that are common across classrooms. Because the design, construction, and scoring of a standardized test are often removed from the classroom, and only the administration and test result interpretation are carried out in the classroom, it is important that what is being measured can be clearly explained to and understood by the users of standardized test data.

Determining What a Test Tests

An understanding of the information provided by a standardized test begins with knowing the purpose of the test. This information is a requirement of proper test use and can be found in the test's technical manual. It is specifically stated in the *Standards for Educational and Psychological Testing* that "test manuals should describe thoroughly the rationale for the test, state the recommended uses of the test, and provide a summary of the support for such uses" (American Educational Research Association [AERA], American Psychological Association [APA], and the National Council on Measurement in Education [NCME], 1985, p. 36). In the case of the *Iowa Test of Basic Skills* (ITBS), its primary design purpose is to provide information that can be used in improving instruction. However, the extent of this particular standardized measure is limited to what are referred to in the test manual as "fundamental or basic skills." The fundamental skills included in the ITBS batteries are listening, word analysis, vocabulary, reading, language, work study, and mathematics. However, there is much more detail provided by test manuals than just the content domain labels. Therefore, an illustrative example has been adapted from the ITBS *Interpretive Guide for School Administrators* (Hoover, Hieronymus, Frisbie, & Dunbar, 1994, pp. 14–50), which provides further analysis of what skills comprise each of these basic skills. For example, six subtests are included in the ITBS primary test battery used to test the achievement of students in kindergarten and first grade. The format of items at this level is pictorial, usually with three response options and the questions administered orally. Teachers read a statement and the students mark the circle under the picture that answers the question being asked or matches the situation being described.

One of the six subtests administered at this level is the Language subtest, which is further broken down into seven skill objectives. The following are the seven skill objectives listed in the manual:

Shared Characteristics Classification. Can the student group objects that belong together? For example, out of three objects pictured, such as a pair of scissors, a flashlight, and a saw, can the student determine two that perform similar tasks and the third that does something different?

Prepositions to Denote Relationships. Does the student understand the differences between a dog sitting "on" the chair, "under" the chair, and "next to" the chair?

Temporal Order. Can the student differentiate between verb tenses such as: the student "was taking" the exam, the student "will take" the exam, and the student "is taking" the exam?

Singular-Plural Usage. Is the student able to differentiate among the "women" washing the "car," the "woman" washing the "cars," and the "women" washing their "cars"?

Comparative and Superlative Adjectives. Can the student correctly identify the "tallest," "biggest," or "steepest" object?

Spatial-Directional Language. Does a student know directions? Can the student correctly identify the dog sitting to the right of the cat?

Developmental Oral Language. Is the student able to use language to make meaning for a particular situation? For example, if the student is told that Taylor is a tall girl with long hair and she is standing beside her friend that is just the opposite, will the student choose the appropriate picture that corresponds to this description?

The descriptions following each skill objective have been added for the purposes of this chapter in order to provide illustrative examples of the listed skill objectives. All items on the Language subtest are aligned with one of these seven skill objectives, so it is possible to examine the test items and determine which general skills are being assessed by each one. This level of differentiation allows a teacher to get a broader picture of a particular student's academic strengths and weakness in the area of cognitive development related to language. This level of detail, including the number of items for each skill objective, is provided for all six tests in the battery.

TEST ITEM DEVELOPMENT

The next stage in constructing a standardized test, after the skill objectives have been carefully articulated, is the item writing process. Many people are involved in this stage of test development, including item writers, teachers and other content area specialists, and measurement specialists. Many items are written, rewritten, and revised before a smaller subset of these items is selected. The item writing stage is very costly and time intensive due to the number of items needed to produce the smaller set of usable items. For example, in constructing the most recent edition of the 10 levels of the ITBS, approximately 14,800 items were developed and tried out, with only about 5,800 items being retained for the final version of the test (Hoover & Dunbar, in press).

According to the first criterion, the item should be a clear measure of a particular skill objective. For example, an item written for the Language subtest may be designed to measure understanding of prepositions. In this case, an item writer would not use different verb tenses in the item. Asking the student to mark the circle under the picture that shows the dog "on" the chair tests a student's understanding of the preposition "on." However, asking the student to fill in the circle under the picture of the dog "jumping on" the chair would unnecessarily confound the process of measuring understanding of prepositions with understanding of verb tense.

Another aspect of writing clear items is to try to make them as broadly representative and appropriate as possible. This requires an awareness, on the part of the item writers and item reviewers, of situations that may be geographically or situationally specific. For example, suppose an item was written for the early primary level and a grocery store was part of the context of that item. At the early primary level, the grocery store will be presented pictorially rather than as text; therefore, how the grocery store is drawn becomes relevant to the issue of presenting a "common" image of a grocery store, one that is not specific to a large or small community. Because the image that each person has of a grocery store may depend on the kind of community in which they live, it is necessary to determine how grocery stores appear in different locales. In this case, there may be no one picture that represents all grocery stores. In this case, the drawing may need to become more focused, such as picturing a grocery store shelf, rather than the entire store, in order to get a common idea across to a wide variety of examinees. The picture, like item text, should help clarify the context of the skill being measured.

The previous discussion of a common image of a grocery store may seem unnecessarily detailed, yet attention to these kinds of details helps to insure the validity of the measurement results. An item that causes students to answer incorrectly due to contextual features of the item, rather than due to a lack of knowledge or skill, is said to contain irrelevant difficulty or perhaps what has been called construct irrelevant variance (Messick, 1993, pp. 34–35). Irrelevant difficulty introduces error into the measurement results that may inaccurately lower a student's score, but this kind of error is invisible to all test result users. Another example where irrelevant difficulty may occur is in items that use sports concepts to test different skills. Examinees familiar with the sport may be able to answer the question due to their knowledge of the sport, rather than from a generalization of skills they learned in the classroom. On the other hand, students unfamiliar with the sport may be tripped-up by the context, thinking that their lack of knowledge about the sport prohibits them from correctly solving the problem. Both students, one knowing the sport and the other not, could potentially be mismeasured if the item is highly context dependent. In practice, items that cannot be revised sufficiently to be broadly representative and appropriate should be thrown out of the pool of potential items used in the final construction of a test.

Mismeasurement caused by irrelevant difficulty is one way that test results may be invalidated. In order to make valid interpretations using test results, inquiries must be made concerning whether "the test measures what we want to measure, all of what we want to measure, and nothing but what we want to measure" (R. M. Thorndike, Cunningham, R. L. Thorndike, & Hagen, 1991, p. 123). The evidence gathered through this inquiry helps to support appropriate inferences using test data. Because validity is a characteristic of test data inferences, and not the test alone, test scores may be valid for some uses and not valid for others. For example, a mathematics test composed of only addition and subtraction items could provide information over these two areas, but the levels of achievement displayed on this test would not generally indicate the level of achievement an examinee would obtain in other areas of mathematics. Although this example is overly simplified by using clearly distinct instructional areas, it should be emphasized that test validation is a process requiring multiple forms of evidence to support validity. Actual test validation requires accumulating evidence to support the validity of the inferences made from the data. A more in-depth discussion of validity, including types of validity evidence, is provided by Messick (1993).

TEST ITEM SELECTION

In the development of most standardized tests, many more items are written than are actually used and those that are chosen for final forms of the tests meet two criteria. The first is the previously stated criterion that each item is to be judged as a measure of one of the initial test specifications (skill objectives). Items are chosen to fulfill the content specifications that were articulated in the first stage—articulation of skill objectives, deciding what to test. When items have been selected that appropriately cover the content specifications, they are run through a "tryout." The tryout is the administration of these items to a large number of students who represent the age and mix of students that will eventually take the final version of the test. The tryout provides statistical measures that are used to judge the quality of each item.

The second criterion that items must satisfy relates to their technical characteristics. The items for a test administered under standard conditions must have certain statistical characteristics needed for a reliable test. To facilitate the selection of the subset of items for the final test version, each item is characterized by its content coverage as well as the statistical characteristics obtained during the item tryout. An example of how these criteria could be assembled for each item is shown in Fig. 8.1. The item is adapted from the ITBS *A Message to Parents* (Hoover, Hieronymus, Frisbie, & Dunbar, 1993, p. 2) pamphlet. The statistics associated with this item are for illustrative purposes only and do not reflect actual statistics for this item.

Vocabulary (adjective):
    1. A *hasty* decision
        A. difficult
        B. hurried
        C. wrong

		Experimental Unit 5436 SPRING, 1998 National Tryout					
1								
2	Item 1	LEVEL 7		N	A	B*	C	Omit
3	Upper 27%	U		53	6	94	0	0
4	Lower 27%	L		53	36	28	34	2
5	Total	DISC 66		196	22	61	16	1

FIG. 8.1. An illustration of an item and descriptive statistics collected from item tryout data. Adapted from the ITBS *A Message to Parents* pamphlet.

All the statistical information necessary for making item selections is shown in Fig. 8.1. Consider the following points:

The first row of information in the display contains identification information about the item data. In this example, this item was tried out on a nationally representative sample in Spring 1998.

The second row lists the item number in the test used for the tryout, the level, "N" for the number of examinees, and "A, B, C," which represent each response option, as well as "Omit" for the number of students that did not respond to the item.

The third row contains data from the top scoring 27% (the U group) of students in the sample. The data reported are the sample size and the percent of this group choosing each response option and the percent of omits. For this particular item, of the 27% of students who got the highest vocabulary score, 6% chose Option A, 94% chose Option B, the correct option, and no one chose Option C. In the upper group, the examinees have little difficulty choosing the correct answer to the question.

Row 4 shows the same response data for the lower 27% of students, the students who got the lowest scores on the vocabulary subtest. For this cohort (the L group), the most popular choice was Option A, whereas only 28% of this group chose the correct option, B, 34% chose Option C, and 2% did not answer this question. In the L group, each response option was selected by a substantial percent of the sample, indicating that the distracters for this item represent functional alternate responses. If a given distracter was selected by only a small percentage of students from this group, then it would probably be revised so that the item truly functions as a multiple choice item.

The total tryout sample consisted of 196 students and a breakdown of the percentage of students selecting each option is given for the entire group in the last row. In this case, when total group is referred to, the proportion of students choosing the correct response is referred to as the p value of the item. The p value for this item is .61. Each item will have a p value associated with it.

One additional piece of information that appears in the last row of Fig. 8.1 is the index of discrimination (DISC). The index of discrimination is a simple statistic used to gauge how well the item is functioning. In practical terms, is the U group of students, who do well on the test overall, more likely to answer this question correctly versus the L group of students, who do not do as well on the test overall? The index of discrimination, reported in the display as DISC 66, is calculated by taking the proportion of students in the U group that got the item correct and subtracting the proportion of students in the L group that got the item correct. In this scenario, the index of discrimination is $DISC = .94 - .28 = .66$. This index is actually an estimate of the correlation between the item and the total score on the test. Therefore, a high positive number indicates that students who do well on the test overall tend to get the item correct, whereas students who do not do well on the overall test tend to get the item wrong. What may not be initially obvious is that the index of discrimination can potentially range from −1.00 to +1.00. A negative discrimination value would indicate that more students in the L group were answering the item correctly than in the U group.

A common misperception regarding test development is that items are acceptable as long as their difficulty and discrimination statistics are acceptable. The reality is that the indexes of difficulty and discrimination are always secondary considerations in item selection. Content coverage always has the highest priority (Nitko, 1996, p. 317). The items chosen for the final version of a large-scale standardized test are selected because the collection satisfies demands for content coverage and statistical adequacy based on skill objectives and technical characteristics.

INTERPRETING DIFFERENT TYPES OF STANDARDIZED TEST DATA

NORM-REFERENCED INTERPRETATIONS

Although the standardized test has now been constructed, a frame of reference is needed in order to interpret the scores students will receive when they take the test. There are two common ways in which scores are given meaning. The first is when scores represent "how much" a student knows about a content domain. This represents a criterion-referenced interpretation. In this frame of reference, a score is tied to a detailed description that tells what a student knows or what skills the student has successfully demonstrated. Most published tests provide information in order to make criterion-referenced interpretations from student scores.

However, the frame of reference most commonly associated with standardized testing is norm referencing—comparing one score with the scores of many others. In order to make this kind of interpretation, normative information must be gathered from representatively sampled groups. In the case of nationally standardized achievement tests such as the Iowa Tests, the Standford Achievement Test, or the California Achievement Test, the norming sample contains students from all over the nation. However, there is not just one norm group. For example, the ITBS has a variety of norming groups, including a nationally representative group, a group of students representing just students from large cities, a group representing students who attend Catholic schools, and so on. Similar statistical information is obtained during the norming as was obtained during the tryout and used to develop norm-referenced statistics and tables. This kind of test data allows for comparisons across schools, districts, cities, and states, which is one of the distinctive features of standardized testing. The scores can be used to show how well students achieve relative to other students in their norm group who have been exposed to a different, but perhaps somewhat similar, curriculum.

The normative information associated with scores on standardized tests most often comes in the form of percentile ranks (PR). The PR for a score of interest is the percentage of examinees in the norm group who scored below that score of interest. For example, a person who is ranked 3rd out of a group of 10 scored better than 7 out of the 10 and would have a percentile rank equal to 70. The national norms for most commercially available standardized tests are developed using representative nationwide samples and are revised whenever new editions are published. In addition to national norms, many test publishers provide norms for localities as well as norms for specific populations, such as large enrollment districts or high SES districts. Many test publishers or state departments of education develop state norms for standardized tests. The normative information provides an indication of the rank of an individual compared to whichever norm group has been selected for the comparison. When the norms associated with a given edition of a standardized test do not change, achievement can be readily compared from year to year because the norms function as a "yardstick" that remains constant. This comparison of scores from year to year allows for measuring growth. Test publishers may also update the norms available with standardized tests, but when the norm base changes, year to year estimates of growth are not as easily calculated. Additional information from the test publisher is needed to make these kinds of comparisons.

STANDARD SCORE DATA

Normative statistics are often associated with percentile ranks (PR), which are useful in determining a student's relative strengths and weaknesses, but PRs are less helpful for estimating and monitoring growth. For this purpose, standard scores are more useful. Standard scores are developed to represent an achievement continuum that begins with the first level of the test and continues through the last level.

Each published standardized test has its own standard score scale, so direct comparisons of standard scores from different tests is not always possible. Also, published tests may have more than one standard score scale. For example, the ITBS uses two standard score scales. One is the Grade Equivalent (GE) scale and the other is the Developmental Standard Score (SS) scale. The difference between the two scales is that the GE scale shows equal average annual growth between any pair of grades. However, the SS scale shows that the average annual growth decreases as students move from one grade to the next. To illustrate this, the difference between average standard scores at grades 1 and 2 is 19 standard score points, but from grade 7 to 8, the difference in average standard scores is only 11 points (Hoover et al., 1994, p. 53). According to the authors of the ITBS, one reason for using developmental standard scores is because they better reflect the reality of achievement growth. However, developmental standard scores are not provided in a metric that is common to most educators. Educational researchers often use effect sizes, but many educators prefer the grade equivalent scores because they are expressed in terms of school grade levels and months, which provides the most useful information for individual classroom use. More information on these two score scales can be found in Hoover et al. (1994, pp. 51–63). An additional perspective on the most appropriate scores for measuring educational development is provided by Hoover (1984).

VARIABILITY IN EXAMINEE STANDARDIZED TEST SCORES

The fact that standardized test results are most frequently presented as a single score ignores many of the assumptions and fallibilities inherent in these kinds of measures. The previous discussion regarding the construction of a standardized test was devoted to discussing many of these assumptions. The assumptions implicit in interpreting test scores include an understanding of the objectives being measured, as well as how well the test is able to measure these objectives. However, even when constructs are carefully articulated and reliably measured, there is still a source of variability due to the examinee that cannot be explicitly communicated using a single score. The component of an individual score obtained from a single test administration, which is caused by unpredictable influences during test administration, is referred to as the standard error of measurement (SEM).

The SEM is an estimate of the variability associated with any one measure and provides an indication of examinee inconsistency. On any particular test date, students' test-taking abilities can be influenced by differing levels of motivation, attentiveness, health, and other such factors. Although there is no way to tell just how much an individual's score may have been under- or overestimated by the administration of a single test, it is possible to use the SEM to get reasonable estimates of the amount by which the abilities of students in a particular reference group have been mismeasured. The smaller the SEM, the smaller the chance variability in the scores, and the closer the measure is to the true, but unknown, achievement level. According to R. M. Thorndike et al. (1991),

> Another way to view the standard error of measurement is as an indication of how much a person's score might change on retesting. Each person's score on the first testing includes some amount of error. Most of the errors will be fairly small, but some will be quite large. About half of the errors will be positive (make the observed score too high) and about half will be negative (make the observed score too low). But we see only the observed score and have no way of knowing how large the error of measurement is for any individual or in what di-

rection.... When interpreting the test score of an individual, it is desirable to think in terms of the standard error of measurement and a band of uncertainty, and to be somewhat humble and tentative in drawing conclusions from that test score. (pp. 102–104)

Thorndike et al. referred to a "band of uncertainty." This band is usually referred to as a confidence region or confidence interval and can be found by adding and subtracting the SEM from the observed score. For example, the confidence region for a standard score of 160 with an SEM of 10 could be shown as the range from 150 to 170. This range would indicate that for about two thirds of the examinees, their unknown "true" standard score is between 150 and 170. Many standardized tests depict confidence regions using graphical representations. When confidence regions are presented graphically and viewed together over multiple content areas, they provide a picture of a student's relative strengths and weaknesses across the content areas tested that takes into account the SEM for each test. Using reports that include confidence regions in addition to the score may help promote a more accurate interpretation of standardized test results and when the confidence regions are displayed visually, they provide an instant sense of the variability of scores. Confidence regions also discourage overinterpretation of small differences in test performance across content areas and between individual examinees. Practical guidelines for the use of the SEM in interpreting standardized test scores are provided by Harvill (1991).

Concerns Regarding Standardized Test Administration

Most standardized tests include a wide variety of material related to the design and implementation of district testing programs. Basic to the design of any testing program is specifying the test purpose. Despite the recent emphasis placed on such tests as measures for accountability, the most prominent uses of standardized tests, according to the manuals that accompany them, have to do with their formative use in improving instruction and learning. For example, standardized tests are likely to be given in the fall or spring of the school year and are likely to be administered by classroom teachers. Many elementary school educators, possibly because they are involved in the administration but not the construction of the test, want all their students to do well. They therefore make requests for an "easy" test. Yet, if the standardized test is designed to be an informative diagnostic tool, its strength is its ability to differentiate among students. A standardized test can provide a diagnosis of specific qualitative strengths and weaknesses in a student's educational development in relation to themselves and in relation to a group broader than their own classroom only if appropriate levels are chosen for administration. If it is an effective measurement tool, then different measures for different individuals would be expected. A scale that said everybody weighed the same would be providing useless, as well as incorrect, information. A test that was too easy would provide this same useless information. And if it is made clear that the purpose of testing is to provide information to be used in conjunction with, not in place of, teacher judgment, then educators might view standardized tests as a beneficial addition, rather than an intrusion, to their classroom instruction.

Moreover, a test that is too easy for a particular group will not give an accurate picture of where students are in relation to their norm group. Students' scores may actually appear to be lower than their comparison groups. This can happen when the tested group knows more than what is being tested by the easier test, but the group is unable to demonstrate that on the given test. Only on a test that provides more difficult items can students differentiate themselves. For example, if an addition test of 10 items was given to a group of sixth-graders, most of the students would be able to solve all 10 items easily. However, due to haste, carelessness, or other such factors, students are likely to miss one or more questions. Consequently, their average scores may not be much better than a group of third-graders taking the same 10 items. However, if the sixth-graders were asked more developmentally appropriate math questions, it is likely that the average scores would be much higher in relation to the third-graders solving the same set of questions. This illustrates the importance of administrating a level-appropriate test, especially when comparisons are to be made with other groups.

Educators often worry about the affective outcomes that standardized testing will have on their students. But teachers have the power to mediate this effect because oftentimes they are the ones who communicate the results to students and their parents in a manner that is most beneficial to their learning. This is correct in that teachers will be better judges as to how the standardized test reflects what has been taught in the classroom. A low score in an area that students have not covered in the classroom would provide a source of validity of the standardized test. This result would show what was expected, which could only be identified as such by the classroom teacher. In order to make the best use of standardized test data, support in how to interpret results is usually offered to users by developers, because it is most often the user of the test (and not the developer) who must interpret and communicate the results to the test taker.

Test publishers attempt to produce a test that will be used for valid purposes by including the purpose in the technical manual. Further, test publishers seek to ensure reliability by testing the item characteristics in a tryout before developing a final version and then by publishing the final reliability statistics in the technical manual. But, in order for the tests to provide usable information, educators must understand the purposes of the test. By reviewing the skill objectives and the reliability statistics, the assumption of a match between the user's purpose and the test design's purpose can be explicitly verified by the test user. If these steps are carried out, then it is likely that educators will have another source of information that they can use to complement the information they gather during daily classroom instruction.

RESEARCH RESULTS USING STANDARDIZED TEST DATA

Although the primary purpose of standardized achievement tests is to help inform instruction, there are other audiences interested in the kind of information that only standardized tests provide. These audiences tend to be educational researchers that take advantage of the inherent characteristics of standardized test data in order to explore similarities and differences among groups. One of the most commonly used group distinctions is gender. One objective of this research has been to document the nature of differences between the test performance of representative samples of males and females. More ambitious objectives of this research have been to try to understand why these differences exist.

One of the most exciting aspects of current research regarding gender is that results have been found to depend on a wide variety of factors that are not easy for researchers to control in the context of any experimental design. The implications of such context dependent factors are that research contexts need to be carefully articulated when drawing conclusions. Further, broad generalizations that do not take into account these contextual differences may not hold for all potential comparisons between the test performances of males and females. Examples of contextual factors include ethnicity, SES status, achievement level, and course taking characteristics of students included in a particular study sample. In what follows, several studies are presented that look at gender differences, including a possible interacting factor that may influence results and thus inferences regarding gender differences in achievement.

Becker and Forsyth (1994) examined gender differences in mathematics problem solving and science using standardized test data from the *Iowa Tests of Educational Development* (Feldt, Forsyth, & Lindguist, 1979; Feldt, Forsyth, & Alnot, 1986). Theirs was a longitudinal study that continued with data originally analyzed by Martin and Hoover (1987). Martin and Hoover looked at grades 3 through 8, whereas Becker and Forsyth continued this for grades 9 through 12. Fig. 8.2 presents data taken from Becker and Forsyth (1990, p. 11). It shows the effect sizes across grades 3 through 12 for the same cohort of students for various content areas. Effect size is used to show the difference in male and female achievement while also taking into account the variability associated with both groups. The effect size is calculated by subtracting the average score for males from the average score for females and dividing by the sample standard deviation of the entire group. Fig. 8.2 also shows the effect sizes graphed for each content area in order to visualize the magnitude of differences between boys and girls across grades. An effect size of 0.00 occurs when there is no average difference between boys and girls. Positive differences mean that, on average, girls score higher than boys, whereas negative effect sizes show the opposite trend.

The content areas that show the greatest differences between males and females in Fig. 8.2 are Language and Math Problem Solving. Language effect sizes show females consistently performing above males, beginning with an effect size of .32 in grade 3 and increasing to .44 by grade 12. On the other hand, math problem solving shows males slightly ahead of females in grade 3 with an effect size of –.02. This lead is never relinquished and dramatically increases in grades 9 through 12, with the greatest difference appearing at grade 11 (where an effect size of –.42 is observed). The other three content areas show differences that grow or shrink across grades, but none show the large and apparently systematic effect sizes that appear in the Language and Math Problem Solving results.

The selection of various content areas highlight where differences do and do not exist between gender groups. This information leads to further questions such as why the differences in Language scores are so great, especially when students are taking the same classes. In mathematics, for example, why do problem-solving scores dramatically increase at the same time that students have more freedom in making their own course selections? This longitudinal data is useful in describing trends and supporting or contradicting personal intuition or observation. But it also leads to more questions.

Many studies agree that there is a difference in scores by gender for certain content areas. Most educators would probably tend to believe that females perform better on language-related tests and males tend to perform better on mathematical-related tests, relying on prior research evidence and commonly reported findings that have come to be common knowledge. However, often only the mean difference between males and females is reported. This merely gives an overall indication of gender differences and may not be appropriate at all achievement levels.

As another illustrative example using standardized test data, Han and Hoover (1994) analyzed the results of 15,000 students in grades 3 through 8. Instead of looking at the mean differences, their approach was to get a better understanding of gender differences in achievement by comparing the entire distributions for males and females. The Becker and Forsyth results presented here only compared the average scores of boys and girls, but Han and Hoover asked if introducing achievement level into the group characteristics might introduce an interaction between gender and achievement level in the findings of male and female achievement differences. Effect sizes are again used to compare the achievement of boys and girls; however, girls and boys are compared at like achievement levels. Table 8.1 shows the effect sizes at three achievement levels (90th, 50th, and 10th percentiles) for three grades (4, 8, and 11) for selected tests analyzed by Han and Hoover. Again, the results for the language tests show the girls outperforming the boys across all achievement levels and across grades. However, in the other content areas, the direction of the effect sizes were not consistent across achievement levels.

Subtest: Vocabulary

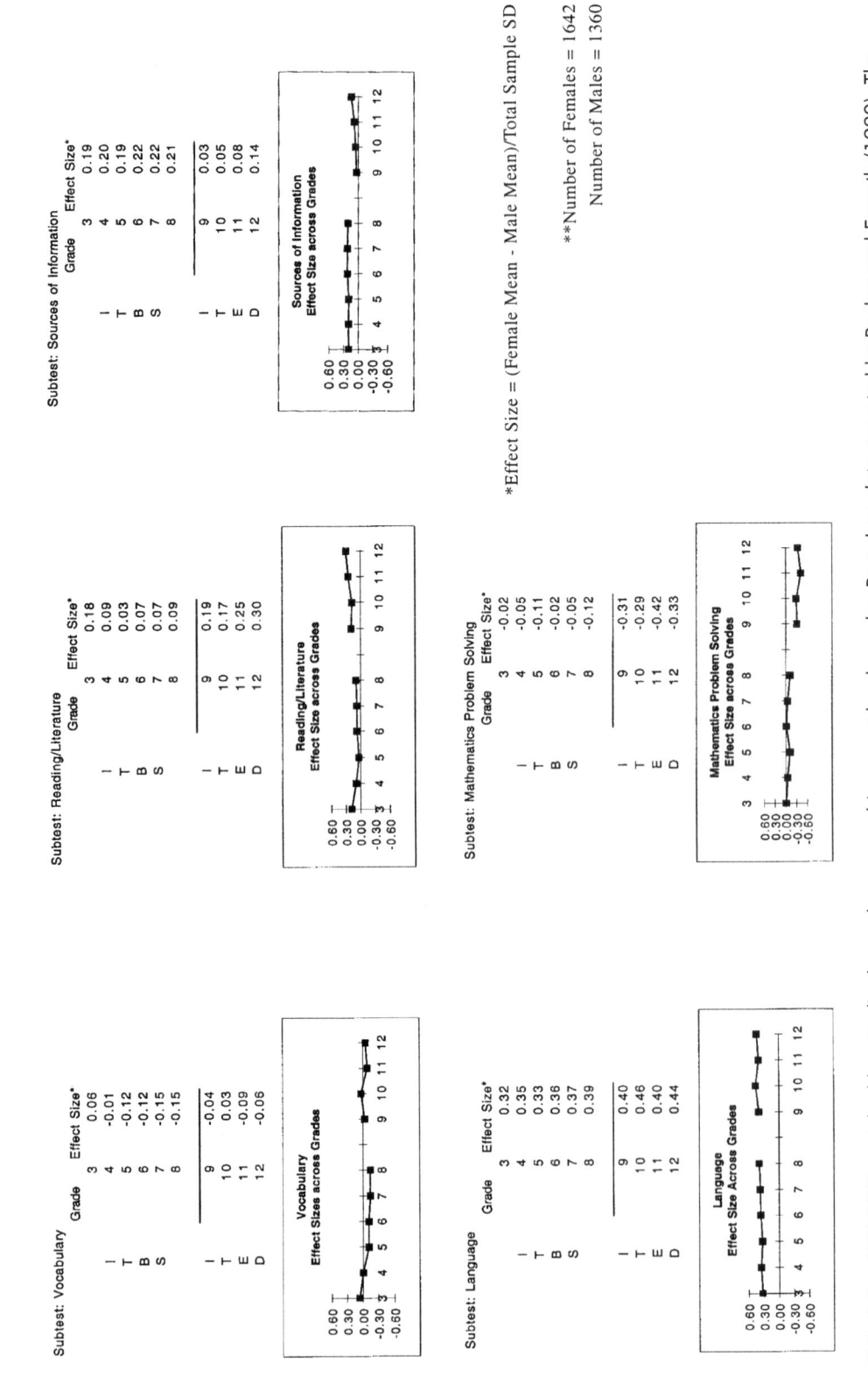

Grade	Effect Size*
3	0.06
4	-0.01
I T B S — 5	-0.12
6	-0.12
7	-0.15
8	-0.15
9	-0.04
10	0.03
I T E D — 11	-0.09
12	-0.06

Vocabulary
Effect Sizes across Grades

Subtest: Language

Grade	Effect Size*
3	0.32
4	0.35
I T B S — 5	0.33
6	0.36
7	0.37
8	0.39
9	0.40
10	0.46
I T E D — 11	0.40
12	0.44

Language
Effect Size Across Grades

Subtest: Reading/Literature

Grade	Effect Size*
3	0.18
4	0.09
I T B S — 5	0.03
6	0.07
7	0.07
8	0.09
9	0.19
10	0.17
I T E D — 11	0.25
12	0.30

Reading/Literature
Effect Size across Grades

Subtest: Mathematics Problem Solving

Grade	Effect Size*
3	-0.02
4	-0.05
I T B S — 5	-0.11
6	-0.02
7	-0.05
8	-0.12
9	-0.31
10	-0.29
I T E D — 11	-0.42
12	-0.33

Mathematics Problem Solving
Effect Size across Grades

Subtest: Sources of Information

Grade	Effect Size*
3	0.19
4	0.20
I T B S — 5	0.19
6	0.22
7	0.22
8	0.21
9	0.03
10	0.05
I T E D — 11	0.08
12	0.14

Sources of Information
Effect Size across Grades

*Effect Size = (Female Mean − Male Mean)/Total Sample SD

**Number of Females = 1642
Number of Males = 1360

FIG. 8.2. ITBS/ITED matched longitudinal sample mean achievement level graphs. Based on data reported by Becker and Forsyth (1990). The ITBS and ITED are on different developmental score scales. Therefore when looking at the means for the two tests, the ITBS means will be higher than the ITED means due to the score scale used.

Not apparent from the effect sizes, but also reported in Han and Hoover, is the fact that males tended to be more variable than females. The standard deviations associated with males were consistently larger than females across grades and content areas (Han & Hoover, 1994, p. 7). This means there were more boys scoring at the upper levels of the score scale, and there were also more boys scoring at the lower levels of the score scale. For example, in Math Concepts, Social Studies, and Science, males dramatically outperformed females in fourth and eighth grade only at the 90th percentile. This finding was reversed at the 10th percentile, where girls outperformed boys, although not as greatly.

It is also interesting to note that the effect size at the 10th percentile favored females in each content area. This finding may have been the impetus for what Becker and Forsyth (1994) concluded from their research: "Males generally performed better at the upper percentile levels of the score distributions in mathematics problem solving and science, while females closed the gap and, in some instances, out performed males at the lower percentile levels" (p. 407). Martin and Hoover (1987), finding similar results, suggested that "in view of the importance of reading and language skills in further academic achievement, it would not seem unwarranted to suggest that some of the emphasis in future research on the nature and causes of sex differences in achievement be focused on the language deficits of low achieving boys" (pp. 82–83). Han and Hoover (1994) expanded the suggestion to "include deficits of low achieving teen-age males in all subject matter areas" (p. 11).

TABLE 8.1
Gender Differences by Ability Level on the ITBS and TAP

Test and Grade	PR	Reading Total	Language Total	Math Concepts	Social Studies	Science	Sources of Information Total
ITBS 4	90	.04	.29	−.26	−.26	−.29	−.12
	50	.06	.30	−.11	−.14	−.07	.00
	10	.07	.28	.09	.10	.07	.21
ITBS 8	90	.03	.33	−.21	−.21	−.35	−.07
	50	.10	.52	−.10	−.06	−.01	.03
	10	.08	.40	.04	.09	.09	.14
TAP 11	90	−.02	.41		−.23	−.24	−.04
	50	.09	.64		.00	.03	.29
	10	.32	.55		.26	.32	.38

Note: Based on data reported by Han and Hoover (1994). Data is from a 1992 standardization and is therefore a cross-sectional comparison and not a longitudinal comparison. Table values are given as effect sizes. Effect size = (female mean score − male mean score)/average SD of males and females.

What is apparent from this data is that for the Language Usage subtests, females outperform males at every achievement level. However, in content areas where males performed better than females, the male lead tended to appear in the upper portion of the achievement scale. Females tended to be dominant at the median and the lower portions of the achievement scale. This may be a reflection of the variability differences seen in the gender groups. However, these results have a significant impact in practice through the assignment of different proportions of males and females to specific groups. If students are being assigned to "gifted" programs based only on standardized achievement test scores, then the group is likely to be made up of more males than females. Alternatively, if students are assigned to "remedial" groups based on these same scores, then males are more likely be assigned to this group too. Such occurrences can be explained by differences in variability between males and females.

Again, this data does not address every perspective. For example, the concern may not be determining if boys and girls achieve at the same rate, but that they eventually get to the same destination. Data used to answer this concern is more easily interpretable when provided in grade equivalent (GE) units because differences between male and female achievement can be expressed in months of the school year. Additional results taken from the Han and Hoover (1994) study are shown in Table 8.2. In Table 8.2, differences between males and females are expressed in GE units, that is, in months of the school year, where 10 months is equal to 1 school year. The GEs for three content areas are presented for grades K through 8 and for three achievement levels. A zero represents no difference be-

TABLE 8.2
1992 Gender Differences in Achievement

	\multicolumn{9}{c}{Grade}
	K	1	2	3	4	5	6	7	8
Vocabulary									
90th Percentile	0	0	0	0	−3	−3	−2	−1	−2
50th Percentile	1	0	0	0	−1	−1	0	0	−1
10th Percentile	1	0	1	1	0	−1	2	2	1
Total Language									
90th Percentile	2	3	2	2	2	3	4	6	5
50th Percentile	1	2	3	4	4	5	7	10	9
10th Percentile	1	1	2	3	4	7	7	8	10
Total Mathematics									
90th Percentile	0	0	−2	−1	−2	−1	−1	−1	−3
50th Percentile	0	0	0	0	0	1	2	2	0
10th Percentile	0	1	1	1	2	3	5	4	3

Note: From data reported by Han and Hoover (1994). Table values are in Grade Equivalent (GE) units, which are expressed in months. Positive differences favor females.

tween males and females. A "5" would mean that girls are 5 months ahead of boys in achievement or, in other words, half a school year ahead. Negative numbers indicate that boys are ahead of girls.

The overall results are consistent with the prior findings of Becker and Forsyth (1990). And the GE data are the same results reported for Language, in Table 8.1 for grade 4 and 8; however, Table 8.1 reported the differences in terms of effect size. For the Language subtest, the large effect sizes of .33, .52, and .40 at grade 8 translate into girls being half a year ahead of boys at the 90th percentile, and about a year ahead for girls at the 50th and 10th percentiles. Vocabulary, in comparison to Language, does not show large achievement differences between girls and boys.

In mathematics, by 8th grade, the boys are 3 months ahead of the girls at the 90th percentile. There was no difference in total mathematics achievement scores between boys and girls at the 50th percentile. At the 10th percentile, girls were 3 months ahead of the boys. Reasons for the male lead are not clear from this data, but recent literature does provide for speculative answers. A study published in the *Educational Researcher* (Fennema, Carpenter, Jacobs, Franke, & Levi, 1998a) addressed differences in mathematics problem-solving strategies employed by boys and girls in grades 1 through 3. Three accompanying articles provide various perspectives and speculations on reasons why differences were found in the initial study (Hyde & Jaffe, 1998, pp. 14–16; & Noddings, 1998, pp. 17–18; Sowder, 1998, pp. 12–13). However, reasons for the opposite result, with females performing better than the males at the lower achievement levels, are not common knowledge, nor is there current research underway to try to understand why this is occurring. However, these results may hint at different curricular experiences for these students of which no one is yet aware. The significance of the charts shown in Table 8.2 is their power to indicate trends. However, the ultimate goal of improving instruction, and therefore achievement, cannot be determined from the data alone. It is the data, appropriate interpretations, and contextual understanding that provide the basis for making sound educational decisions.

POLICY PERSPECTIVES ON ASSESSMENT: THE ROLE OF STANDARDIZED TESTING

Standardized tests have a role in the evaluation of student achievement, but a commonsense approach to assessment does not rely on a single measure but uses multiple measures, taking into account the strengths and limitations of each assessment method. The choice of a particular method should always be determined with regard to the purpose of testing. For example, performance assessments are often used when the purpose of testing is to inform instruction. When accountability and evaluation motivate testing, norm-referenced tests are most often used. Yet, the roles of specific assessment methods are not strictly defined. Kean (1996) reiterated this position when he pointed out that "it is important to realize, however, that performance assessment results can be used to evaluate programs and account for pupil progress, while traditional, multiple-choice tests also can provide valuable instructional information. Both types of tests continue to be in great demand as parents, the public, and policymakers seek to build better and more relevant measures into our education systems" (p. 14). Thus, rather than narrowing the types of assessments used, or expecting one assessment to provide all the information needed, multiple methods should be sought and employed by knowledgeable users.

Unfortunately, what tends to happen in discussions of specific assessment methods is that the purpose for using the method under discussion is not clearly articulated. This kind of misunderstanding occurred at the Third Annual Classroom Assessment Conference in Portland, Oregon (July 1997). Wiggins (1993), author of a recent book on performance assessment spoke about his assessment philosophy, focusing on the relationship formed between tester and examinee and the kind of information produced by this relationship. According to Wiggins, the worth of the information is judged in relation to how "it provides the performer with direct usable insights into current performance, based on tangible differences between current performance and hoped-for performance" (p. 182). But without clarifying his position, Wiggins made the statement that summative evaluations (e.g., final exams) were worthless and should not be done. What was missing from his language, which in turn caused confusion for his listeners, was that summative evaluations are not necessary for his purpose. He was focusing on assessment that informs the process of instruction and learning. Therefore, summative evaluations that cannot be followed-up with further instruction are not useful for his assessment purpose. Continuing the discussion of appropriate assessment, Wiggins expressed his belief that a rationale for standardized testing does not exist if the purpose of testing is to be "educative and authentic" (Wiggins, 1993, p. 94). Standardized tests that do not provide immediate and specific feedback are viewed by Wiggins as inappropriate for promoting student learning. With respect to appropriate test use, Wiggins matched the assessment method to his assessment purpose, which he defined as providing informative and timely feedback to the examinee. Any assessment does require this kind of match between purpose and instrument. However, all school administrators realize that a single assessment purpose or instrument will be unable to meet the broad assessment needs required by classrooms, buildings, districts, and states.

Yet the merits of all forms of assessment continue to be discussed and debated, especially with respect to standardized testing and its multiple purposes. Neill (1996), associate director of Fair Test, is concerned that the standardized test provides only normative information and therefore "does not tell us what a student knows, only whether she knows more or less than other students about whatever limited thing is measured" (p. 16). His comments emphasized the importance that should be placed on articulation and selection of the skill objectives, but they ignored the fact that the results of standardized tests are typically made available to users in a variety of descriptive frames of reference. Norms are one such frame of reference, but most test publishers offer score reports in terms of criterion-related objectives as well as performance standards. If meaningful objectives are articulated and the assessment reflects these objectives, then the information obtained from an assessment should provide meaningful data and may be limited only in the broadest sense that relevant reports are not widely disseminated by schools.

Neill (1996) continued by suggesting that "another instructional impact of the bell-curve is subtle but pernicious: it tells educators that only a few students can learn a lot and most will not learn very much, so they can settle for mediocre performance from their students" (p. 16). Neill was correct if it were true that standardized achievement tests measure something about a person's capability to learn, rather than what has been learned. The goal of instruction is to gradually move the mean of the distribution of student achievement up the scale and achievement data at local levels reflect such growth over time. Further, the variability that is seen in achievement test performance at any level is a general reflection of the variability in the population that will continue to exist as long as individuals have unique experiences that set them apart from one another. However, this does not mean that variability is constant. In understanding achievement measures, variability is used to help identify possible instructional and environmental differences among children. When differences among the correlates of achievement are discovered, this may help to reduce the variability that exists between high and low achieving students, or at least understand the reasons for it.

Additional concerns with student success, and how it is determined, were voiced by Henning-Stout (1994). She promoted "responsive assessment," which is "an approach to academic assessment that shifts the focus away from routine application of standardized assessment measures and toward understanding the immediate educational needs of learners" (p. 1). Henning-Stout advocated responsive assessment in place of standardized testing because she viewed standardized testing as an impediment to the learning experiences of students. In her discussion of student learning, she advocated an assessment model that provides information on how a student is thinking and learning. Her main concerns in this regard focus on understanding the life stressors of students, which may influence the formal assessment results. The criticisms of standardized tests stem from her view that standardized tests are used extensively and routinely to assess classroom problems without taking into account the home and school experiences specific to the child. Additionally, the assessments used address only a limited number of skills, which may not include areas in which the child is having success. The multiple purposes of assessment identified by Henning-Stout illustrate a case of high standards for the design of a comprehensive assessment model for individuals in the classroom setting. No single instrument will be able to meet the needs required by such a comprehensive assessment model. However, the expectations created by such a model can be met by using multiple assessment instruments.

Rotberg (1996) believed that expectations about what can be learned from testing students has become increasingly unrealistic: Tests "have been used effectively to measure student progress, predict future performance, diagnose learning problems, encourage changes in curriculum and teaching methods, and describe national trends. However, the current use of tests has gone well beyond the reality of what they can accomplish" (p. 30). Her observation regarding all tests is especially reflective of the reason for many of the criticisms aimed at standardized tests—unrealistic expectations.

In trying to measure the varied strengths and abilities of students, it is clear that not all that is valued will be measured by a single instrument. Standardized tests, for example, are concerned with those areas of instruction that are particularly amenable to objective measurement. In the final analysis, all assessment methods need to be viewed as having the same goal in mind, to enhance student learning. The extent to which multiple and varied measures of school achievement collectively accomplish this goal is largely the responsibility of informed users of all types of assessments.

Criticisms surrounding various forms of assessment will continue as long as the purposes of assessment remain vague. The purpose of assessment, when clearly articulated, revolves around matching assessments with appropriate interpretations and uses. And in this regard, standardized testing has a role to play in the assessment of student achievement. However, standardized testing does not claim to be the panacea for all of the ills of education, although recent focus on accountability may have done much to place it in that position. This chapter's intention was to provide a more realistic view of the role of standardized testing in student assessment. Through a better understanding of the design of standardized tests and the information that must be included in the interpretation of the numerical results, the users of these instruments will better understand appropriate and inappropriate interpretations, resulting in more valid test use.

Acknowledgment

I am indebted to Dr. Stephen B. Dunbar, who provided critical guidance throughout the writing of this chapter. Both his writing and measurement expertise were drawn upon to improve the quality of this paper.

REFERENCES

American Education Research Association (AERA), American Psychological Association (APA), and the National Council on Measurement in Education (NCME). (1985). *Standards for educational and psychological testing.* Washington, DC: American Psychological Association.

Becker, D. F., & Forsyth, R. A. (1990, April). *Gender differences in academic achievement in grades 3 through 12: A longitudinal analysis.* Paper presented at the annual meeting of the American Educational Research Association, Boston, MA.

Becker, D. F., & Forsyth, R. A. (1994). Gender differences in mathematics problem-solving and science: A longitudinal analysis. *International Journal of Education Research, 21*, 407–416.

Feldt, L. S., Forsyth, R. A., & Alnot, S. D. (1986). *Iowa tests of educational development, forms X-8 and Y-8.* Iowa City: University of Iowa.

Feldt, L. S., Forsyth, R. A., & Lindquist, E. F. (1979). *Iowa tests of educational development, forms X-7 and Y-7.* Iowa City: University of Iowa.

Fennema, E., Carpenter, T., Jacobs, V. R., Franke, M. L., & Levi, L. W. (1998). New perspectives on gender differences in mathematics: A reprise. *Educational Researcher, 27*(5), 19–21.

Han, L., & Hoover, H. D. (1994, April). *Gender differences in achievement test scores.* Paper presented at the annual meeting of the National Council on Measurement in Education, New Orleans, LA.

Harvill, L. M. (1991). Standard error of measurement. *Educational Measurement: Issues and Practice, 10*(2), 33–41.

Henning-Stout, M. (1994). Responsive academic assessment: Guidelines and potential barriers. *Special Services in the Schools, 9*(1), 1–23.

Hoover, H. D. (1984). The most appropriate scores for measuring educational development in the elementary schools. GE's. *Educational Measurement: Issues and Practice, 3*(4), 8–14.

Hoover, H. D., & Dunbar, S. B. (in press). *Research handbook for the Iowa Test of Basic Skills.* Chicago: Riverside.

Hoover, H. D., Hieronymus, D. A., Frisbie, D. A., & Dunbar, S. B. (1993). *A message to parents, ITBS Grades 3 through 8.* Chicago: Riverside.

Hoover, H. D., Hieronymus, D. A., Frisbie, D. A., & Dunbar, S. B. (1994). *Interpretive guide for school administrators Levels 5–14, ITBS Forms K/L.* Chicago: Riverside.

Hyde, J. S., & Jaffe, S. (1998). Perspectives from social and feminist psychology. *Educational Researcher, 27*(5), 14–16.

Kean, M. H. (1996). Multiple measures: The common-sense approach to education assessment. *The School Administrator, 53*(11), 14–16.

Martin, D. J., & Hoover, H. D. (1987). Sex differences in educational achievement: A longitudinal study. *Journal of Early Adolescence, 7,* 65–83.

Messick, S. (1993). Validity. In R. L. Linn (Ed.), *Educational measurement* (3rd ed., pp. 13–103). Phoenix, AZ: American Council on Education and the Oryx Press.

Neill, M. (1996). A response to Kean. *The School Administrator, 53*(11), 16.

Nitko, A. J. (1996). *Educational assessment of students* (2nd ed.). Englewood Cliffs, NJ: Merrill/ Prentice-Hall.

Noddings, N. (1998). Perspectives from feminist philosophy. *Educational Researcher, 27*(5), 17–18.

Rotberg, I. C. (1996). Five myths about test score comparisons. *The School Administrator, 53*(5), 30–31, 34–35.

Sacks, P. (1997). Standardized testing: Meritocracy's crooked yardstick. *Change, 29*(2), 24–31.

Sowder, J. T. (1998). Perspectives from mathematics education. *Educational Researcher, 27*(5), 12–13.

Thorndike, R. M., Cunningham, G. K., Thorndike, R. L., & Hagen, E. P. (1991). *Measurement and evaluation in psychology and education* (5th ed.). Englewood Cliffs, NJ: Macmillan.

Wiggins, G. (1993). *Assessing student performance: Exploring the purpose and limits of testing.* San Francisco, CA: Jossey-Bass.

CHAPTER 9

EXTERNAL PORTFOLIO ASSESSMENT: WHERE HAS THE REFLECTION GONE?

Julie Cheville

Elizabethtown College, Elizabethtown, Pennsylvania

Keeping track is a matter of reflective review and summarizing, in which there is both discrimination and record of the significant features of a developing experience. It is the heart of intellectual organization and of the disciplined mind.
—John Dewey (1938)

*F*OR NEARLY A DECADE, AS A TEACHER, AUTHOR, AND CON-
sultant, I have advocated the literacy portfolio as a tool for teaching students how to document and reflect on their histories and growth as readers and writers. A portfolio-keeper myself, I find that I am better able to reflect on my own professional development when I assume responsibility for collecting, organizing, and reflecting on the "artifacts" that testify to my growth as a teacher, writer, reader, and thinker. For my students and for me, these artifacts can take many multimedia (writing, artwork, photographs, video and audiotapes) and hypermedia forms. What matters most is assembling, revising, and displaying the portfolios together. We create our portfolios to inform and persuade an audience we know by face, by name, and by word. We write for each other.

As a teacher, I have come to rely on my students' literacy portfolios for the purposes of *evaluation* (both formative and summative), *communication* (with students, parents, and staff), and *curricular reform* (Murphy & Smith, 1992). I have discovered, as research suggests, that the literacy portfolios students create allow greater insights into their literate lives (Fu, 1992; Hansen, 1992; Herbert, 1992, Salvio, 1994). Displaying portfolios that document learning across communicative modes (writing, reading, speaking, and listening), across rhetorical contexts (school, home, and play), and across time, students provide the contextual information teachers need to teach well.

Despite cautionary warnings about linking portfolio-keeping to external assessment (Graves & Sunstein, 1992; Koretz, 1992; Wiggins, 1994; Zebroski, 1994), many states, organizations, and assessment companies have begun to mandate or market the portfolio as a quantifiable product. With the onset of external portfolio assessment, an evaluative context in which unknown assessors judge the portfolios of students they will never know, I believe the portfolio has been appropriated in troubling ways. In 1994, the New Standards Project began to assess students' portfolios for what they indicate about technical competence, range, and reflection in numerous content areas (see www.ncee.org). The National Board for Professional Teaching Standards now assesses teachers' professional portfolios for evidence of "quality teaching" (see www.nbpts.org). Numerous states and districts have begun to legislate their own portfolio mandates (Potts, 1996). And various testing companies that have built their reputations on standardized measurement now market their own portfolio projects. Currently, external portfolio assessment is used to gauge student performance, teacher development, and program evaluation. The assumption guiding many of these external assessments is that portfolios, fulfilling the demands of comparability, offer an accurate depiction of student performance across classrooms, districts, or states.

As the responsibility for portfolio assessment is legislated out of the hands and minds of students and teachers, the very principles and purposes that initially gave rise to portfolio-keeping are at risk. In many elementary and secondary classrooms, portfolio-keeping is no longer reflective, process oriented, or rhetorically viable. This chapter discusses how external portfolio assessment adulterates portfolio-keepers' experiences of purpose, ownership, and reflection. Educators can restore rhetorical integrity to their portfolio practice in specific ways. The discussion begins with attention to the circumstances underlying the shift from internal to external portfolio assessment.

FROM INTERNAL TO EXTERNAL PORTFOLIO ASSESSMENT: THE NEW STANDARDS PROJECT

During the 1980s, the portfolio made its way into writing classrooms, and later other content areas, as a pedagogical tool within an evolving process paradigm that privileged writing and reading as communicative processes composed of a series of sociocognitive stages. Literacy portfolios allowed students and teachers to collect artifacts attesting to their writing and reading and to understand these processes as interrelated. With sufficient time, guidance, and opportunities to share, students assembled portfolios in order to document the processes behind their products (Wolf, 1989). With authority to determine the contents of the portfolio, the nature and substance of reflection, and the manner of assessment, students experienced new opportunities for self-evaluation and goal setting.

In conjunction with the writing process movement, the portfolio was conceived as a text that students and teachers could rely on to monitor growth of skills, knowledge, and reflective maturity over time. Portfolio advocates maintained that what distinguished the portfolio from mere collection folders of student work was reflection. The International Reading Association and the National Council of Teachers of English urged their memberships to teach and model reflective thinking:

> Reflectiveness is not just an add on to instruction in reading and writing, it is an essential component of education. Students who have not learned to reflect on their own learning, who must depend on others to know how their learning is progressing or which learning strategies are working, are not well-prepared for survival in a democratic society saturated with choices and complex decisions. (Wolff, 1997, p. 16)

Research has indicated that engendering reflectiveness in students requires extensive teaching, modeling, and response. According to Tierney (1991), what often frustrates teachers and administrators, in some cases to the point of eliminating portfolios altogether, is that students' early attempts at reflection are superficial. Research indicates, however, that with sufficient instructional time, negotiation, and feedback, students begin to reflect with conceptual originality and depth (Elbow, 1994; Graves & Sunstein, 1992; Rief, 1990; Sunstein & Cheville, 1997). Three conceptual turns often characterize the portfolio process. First, when students are taught how to shift from prescribed reflective entry slips to personalized, free-form reflections, they frequently move beyond shallow assessments of their learning. Second, when teachers reserve frequent and consistent opportunities for portfolio sharing, as well as discussions of portfolio-keeping strategies, students begin to understand reflectiveness as a generative process. Finally, the opportunity to name the portfolio or to create the text in terms of a guiding metaphor encourages deep conceptual connections (Meyer, 1997).

In the early 1990s, the increasing call for educational standards led to assertions that the portfolio could serve as an object of external assessment. Although advocates differed on how best to achieve reliability and/or validity, they were attracted to the portfolio as a product. As White (1994) noted:

> Portfolios are traditionally collections of products, indeed, products selected to be the very best that have been made. Some make the assumption that since a fine product is clearly the result of a process, that process need not be exposed to view. The evaluator can intuit the process from examining the product. (p. 34)

Proponents of external portfolio assessment argued that the processes of reading and writing, although important to students and teachers, were not of particular relevance to the scoring of "best work" represented in the portfolio. What mattered was the product. Those students who best informed and/or persuaded external assessors were those who evidenced the rhetorical sensibility that warranted higher scores.

In 1990 the National Center on Education and the Economy, a not-for-profit organization based in Washington, DC, joined with the University of Pittsburgh's Learning Research and Development Center to create performance standards for students in English/language arts, math, science, and applied learning. The New Standards Project (1994), funded by the Pew Charitable Trust and the John D. and Catherine T. MacArthur Foundation, was one of the earliest nationwide portfolio assessment programs. The dimensions of the New Standards portfolio were conceived over the course of several years of national meetings, which included select teachers, researchers, and New Standards officials. By the 1994–1995 school year, students and teachers in participating New Standards Project sites were required to produce portfolios for the purposes of external assessment.

The New Standards portfolio, as well as other external portfolio assessments, has inspired considerable criticism from those who sense a fundamental ideological shift. Purves (1993) maintained that "the portfolio is not simply a device by which students can be sorted and ranked. It is a way of making school meaningful to each student as an individual.... The portfolio should not be subjected to the vagaries of large-scale assessment and to matters of validity, reliability, and comparability" (p. 10). What external assessments like the New Standards Project represent is a large-scale attempt to standardize the form and function of the portfolio, and in turn, to dehumanize the processes of reading and writing. What counts is only that which approximates the scale, the rubric, the standards. In effect, external portfolio assessments invade the authentic rhetorical communities students and teachers negotiate to prescribe practices and portfolio prototypes that often are confusing or, at worst, irrelevant (Potts, 1996).

The New Standards portfolio hinges on academic standards imposed on participating sites. An early student handbook prescribed the portfolio to participating students this way:

> A portfolio is a collection of your work that includes specific samples demonstrating high academic standards.... In order to create a portfolio that shows your work off to its best advantage, you need to understand the standards you are expected to meet, then use the work you've done—or do new work—as evidence, or proof, that you've met those standards. Your teachers will use your portfolio not only to judge, or assess, your level of achievement, but to understand what specific kinds of instruction, guidance, and support you may need in order to improve. (New Standards Project, 1994, p. 1)

Students and teachers, inundated with handbooks and reference documents, spent considerable instructional time interpreting the standards, approximating the ideal portfolio, and preparing for external assessment. Meyer (1997) recalled the struggle she and her fifth-grade students faced:

> As a group, we tried to hold on to the concept of the portfolio as a tool for formal assessment, but our own needs and purposes for keeping a portfolio kept nagging at us. Our reflections and our growing desire to set our own standards started to move us further and further away from the New Standard's notion of a portfolio. (p. 19)

The rhetorical tensions accompanying the transition from internal to external portfolio assessment are important because they signal a profound ideological shift in understanding of the relation of students to their reading and writing, to their teachers, and to their understanding of what constitutes knowledge. Fueyo (1997) was clear about what's at stake:

> Portfolios must be shaped by their creators. In order to understand what meanings students make of things, students need to find ways to represent their meanings. If the goals, contents, and criteria are imposed from outside, how much do we learn about students' conceptualizations of what things mean, of what matters, and of how these things connect for them? (p. 69)

In his ethnographic study of the 1994–1995 New Standards Project field trials in Iowa, Potts (1996) documented, in part, how teachers and students in three school districts accommodated external portfolio assessment. Most troubling is the extraordinary time students and teachers were forced to devote to interpreting external performance standards. New Standards reference materials describing the form and function of the portfolio befuddled students and teachers alike. Worse yet, teachers in New Standards sites who were previously uninterested in implementing portfolios were now obligated to do so. The imposition of portfolios, particularly in the classrooms of those teachers not inclined to teach them, had disastrous effects on student investment.

Across New Standards' sites, Potts (1996) discovered that students suddenly required by faceless external assessors to assemble portfolios often did so with minimal effort and interest. When it came to reflecting on a particular portfolio entry, Michael, a tenth-grader, admitted:

> Well, I really didn't know what to put down. I mean she told us but by the time everybody got around to doing it nobody really remembered. So I just kind of winged it. I spent just long enough to write a few sentences about it and I started recopying my stories. (Potts, 1996, p. 44)

In other cases, Potts found that students assumed the persona of the "suck up," an outcome-based identity apparent in Stephanie, another tenth-grader, who remarked of her portfolio:

> See, so I put one of those entry slips in there and wrote a reflective analysis about my paper. [*Reading aloud*] "The qualities of a friend was a paper that I really learned a lot from." Well, I didn't learn a lot from this. I didn't. I mean it was just about writing about a friend. I wrote this paper because he said write about a person, and I wrote this reflection because I wanted to make it look good. [*Reading aloud again*] "The most important thing that I learned is how I actually learned about the friend that I wrote about." I mean, give me a break. I already knew how I felt about her. This is all bullshit. I mean, all of this stuff is just bunk. I knew that he [Mr. Campbell] would want to hear this. This is what he wants to hear, so I wrote it. (Potts, 1996, p. 234)

Both Michael and Stephanie illustrated the consequences of assuming that portfolios and external assessment are compatible. Ethically, such assessments pose a dilemma to educators. To what extent do teachers corrupt students' reflectiveness when they ask them to evaluate their reading, writing, and learning for a grade, rank, or score? Certainly, they can only be expected to spit back exactly what assessors reward. Empirically, too, such assessments pose problems. Elbow (1994) argued the fundamental absurdity of forcing a qualitative instructional tool into a quantitative paradigm:

> When a portfolio gives us a pile of diverse pieces by each writer, and one writer's selection of pieces is different from that of another writer, it is vain to think we can trust a single holistic score that pretends to sum up this diversity of performances by each writer and compare all writers along a quantitative scale. (p. 45)

Given the ethical and empirical dilemmas, I have drawn nearer to the conclusion that external portfolio assessment is primarily a boon to bureaucrats. I have seen few assessment projects that encourage critical thinking, foster writing and reading processes, or reward genuine reflection. The most intriguing assessment projects are those that place the portfolio in an evaluative context that is qualitative in nature (Murphy & Smith, 1990).

RETURNING AUTHORITY TO TEACHERS: THE IOWA WRITING PROJECT

In 1994, with grant support from the Iowa-based Carver Foundation, the Iowa Writing Project (IWP) sought to develop a qualitative portfolio assessment project that would provide its membership formative instructional support. The IWP envisioned a descriptive assessment model designed by consulting assessors yet inherited soon after inception by its member teachers. The "writing to learn, learning to transform" initiative was introduced to Iowa Writing Project members in 1994 as an attempt to support teachers' implementation of portfolios. During the fall and spring of 1995–1996, the first year of the 3-year assessment, IWP teachers chosen to participate in the project were asked to either implement or continue portfolio-keeping in their classrooms. The IWP leadership resisted any attempt to mandate a particular form and/or function of the portfolio. They recommended only that project participants create teacher and student portfolios that most clearly represented their learning to outside assessors.

In summer 1996, fellow consultants Sandra Murphy (University of California, Davis), Terry Underwood (California State University, Fresno), and I met to devise an assessment model. Each of us seemed to take courage in Elbow's view (1994) that innovative external assessments might conceivably challenge existing projects, particularly those that alienated teachers, demanded students' "best work," and privileged interrater reliability. Sandra, Terry, and I had been hired by the IWP leadership to create a descriptive assessment model, one grounded on the anthropological principles of data collection and triangulated analysis. The primary obligation was to provide teachers with qualitative data about their portfolio practice. We did not wish to rank, score, or judge student and teacher portfolios. Instead, each assessor would document, or describe, the writing practices apparent within and across classroom collections. Of the representative portfolios, the assessment project would ask the basic anthropological question, what's happening here? The annual summer assessment sessions would be followed by IWP fall conferences, occasions when assessors and participating teachers would negotiate the project face to face.

Each assessment period Sandra, Terry, and I spent our days amidst stacks of portfolios created by students and their teachers. We entered into each classroom set by first reading the teacher's portfolio so that we might familiarize ourselves with students' philosophical intentions and instructional practices. From the teacher's portfolio, we passed to students' portfolios, documenting features each portfolio made evident. Our descriptive assessment was driven by various guiding questions:

1. What purposes does this particular learner seem to hold for portfolio keeping?
2. What textual patterns characterize the teacher's portfolio and students' within a single classroom?
3. To what extent is the teacher's portfolio congruent in theory and practice with students', and vice versa?
4. What features characterize portfolio-keeping across the a single classroom set? Across all classroom sets submitted for review?

Once data collection was completed, we had accumulated a significant store of information, which we began to analyze for various purposes. First, we intended to provide each teacher with formative response to the portfolio-keeping process and products of her classroom. To this end, each assessor wrote a collegial letter to participating teachers, identifying the distinguishing features they had documented across the teacher's classroom. In addition to the personal letter, participating teachers were presented with a list of features that assessors had recognized across sets of teacher and student portfolios. In varying degrees, most portfolios showed evidence of the six features described next:

Reflection. Evidence that teachers created opportunities for students to reflect on their work, their learning, and their growth and progress as writers. Evidence that teachers were reflective about their own practices and the impact of their practices on students.

Individualized Instruction. Evidence that teachers highlight students' individual growth as writers; that they compare their performances with earlier performances rather than the performances with other students; and that the prevailing expectation in the class is growth toward individual goals and potentials rather than an artificial standard.

Dialogic Emphasis. Evidence that reading and writing occur in a social context; that students have opportunities to exchange ideas and work with a variety of audiences: teacher, other students, parents, siblings, friends, and so on, at any stage of the reading or writing process.

Student Responsibility for Learning. Evidence that teachers encourage students to assume responsibility for documenting their learning; that teachers challenge students to set their own goals for writing and read-

EXTERNAL PORTFOLIO ASSESSMENT   269

ing, to assess their own work, to select pieces for their portfolios, and to experiment and take risks.

Process Approaches to Literacy. Evidence that students have opportunities to learn effective strategies for managing writing processes. This may include evidence of prewriting activities, drafting and revising, obtaining feedback from readers, reflecting across drafts, assignments, and other artifacts. Evidence that writing and reading processes vary by the task, avoiding formulaic stages.

Writing for Varied Audiences and Purposes in Varied Contexts. Evidence that students have opportunities to engage in writing of many different sorts; that their writing is directed to different audiences, both familiar and distant, and that they write for many different purposes, such as writing to learn, discover, and entertain, as well as writing to communicate knowledge or information. Evidence that students have opportunities to engage in writing over various time periods to write brief, informal pieces as well as engage in extended projects that may involve research, interviews, or collaborative work with peers.

Finally, assessors provided participating teachers with a cumulative document that identified, within the framework of the six defining features, all the instances when aims evident in a teacher's portfolio corresponded with practices evident in the portfolios of the students. In this way, teachers received elaborate documentation of the aims and congruent practices evident in classrooms besides their own, information that might facilitate their own portfolio instruction as well as create communicative links within the membership. A highly abbreviated version of this cumulative document follows:

THEME 1: REFLECTION

Across participating schools, assessors noted evidence that teachers and students reflected upon their work and growth.

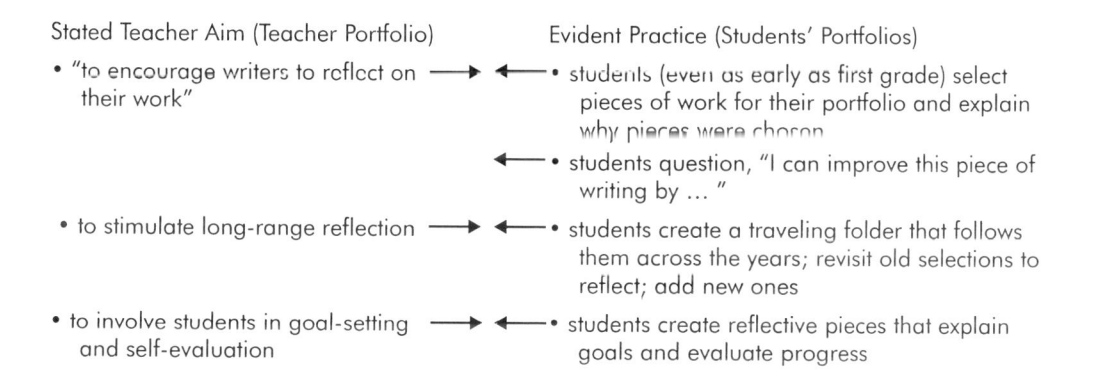

Stated Teacher Aim (Teacher Portfolio)	Evident Practice (Students' Portfolios)
• "to encourage writers to reflect on their work"	• students (even as early as first grade) select pieces of work for their portfolio and explain why pieces were chosen
	• students question, "I can improve this piece of writing by … "
• to stimulate long-range reflection	• students create a traveling folder that follows them across the years; revisit old selections to reflect; add new ones
• to involve students in goal-setting and self-evaluation	• students create reflective pieces that explain goals and evaluate progress

THEME 2: INDIVIDUALIZED INSTRUCTION

Assessors noted that teachers highlighted students' individual growth as writers, that they compared their performances with earlier performances rather than the performances of other students, and that they emphasized individual goals rather than an artificial standard.

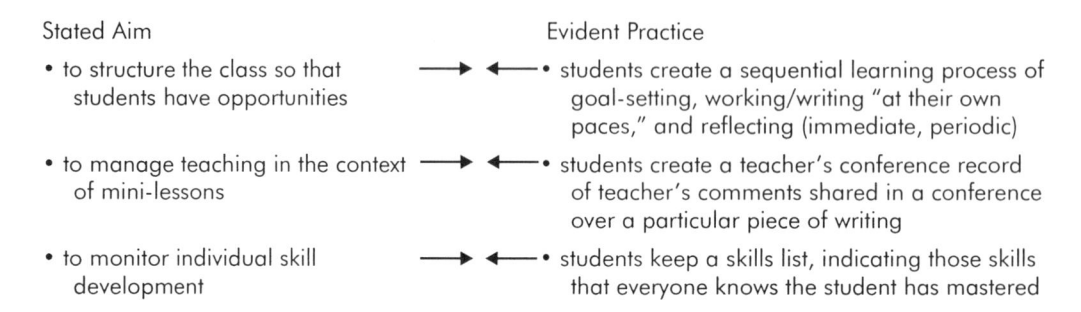

Stated Aim | Evident Practice
- to structure the class so that students have opportunities ⟶ ⟵ students create a sequential learning process of goal-setting, working/writing "at their own paces," and reflecting (immediate, periodic)
- to manage teaching in the context of mini-lessons ⟶ ⟵ students create a teacher's conference record of teacher's comments shared in a conference over a particular piece of writing
- to monitor individual skill development ⟶ ⟵ students keep a skills list, indicating those skills that everyone knows the student has mastered

THEME 3: DIALOGIC EMPHASIS

Assessors noted the ways in which teachers and students understand reading and writing as social activities and have opportunities to engage a live audience.

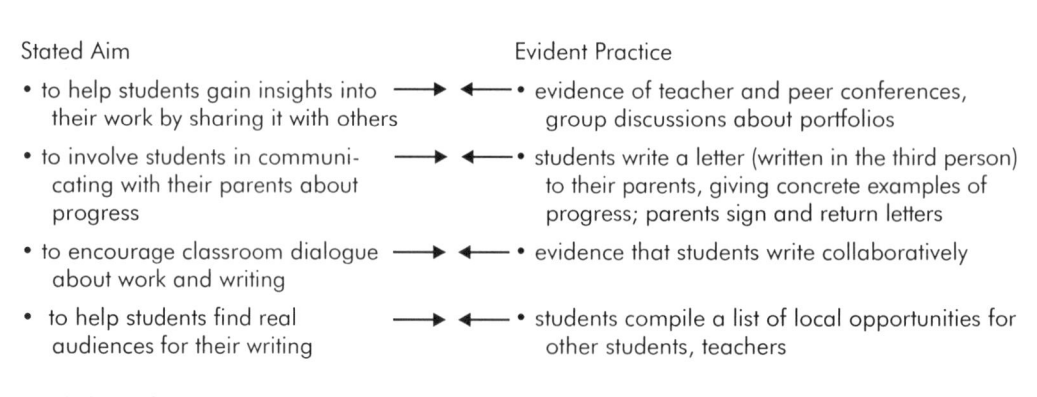

Stated Aim | Evident Practice
- to help students gain insights into their work by sharing it with others ⟶ ⟵ evidence of teacher and peer conferences, group discussions about portfolios
- to involve students in communicating with their parents about progress ⟶ ⟵ students write a letter (written in the third person) to their parents, giving concrete examples of progress; parents sign and return letters
- to encourage classroom dialogue about work and writing ⟶ ⟵ evidence that students write collaboratively
- to help students find real audiences for their writing ⟶ ⟵ students compile a list of local opportunities for other students, teachers

THEME 4: STUDENT RESPONSIBILITY FOR LEARNING

Assessors documented how teachers encourage students to assume responsibility for growth by setting goals, assessing their own work, selecting pieces for their portfolios, and taking risks.

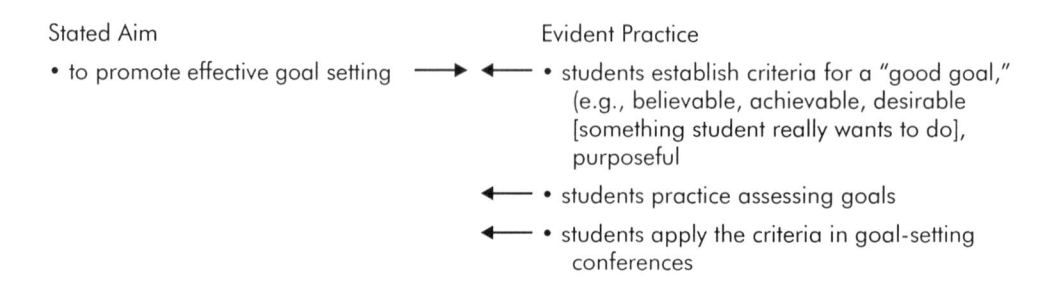

Stated Aim | Evident Practice
- to promote effective goal setting ⟶ ⟵ students establish criteria for a "good goal," (e.g., believable, achievable, desirable [something student really wants to do], purposeful
- ⟵ students practice assessing goals
- ⟵ students apply the criteria in goal-setting conferences

- to help students generate their   → ← • students keep a list of writing topic ideas
  own ideas for writing
- to help students learn how to   → ← • students use journals as places to periodically
  self-evaluate   self-evaluate (e.g., prior to parent conferences)

THEME 5: PROCESS APPROACHES

Assessors noted how students have opportunities to learn effective strategies for managing writing processes. They engage in prewriting activities, drafting and revising, obtaining feedback from peers and teachers and others, and reflecting.

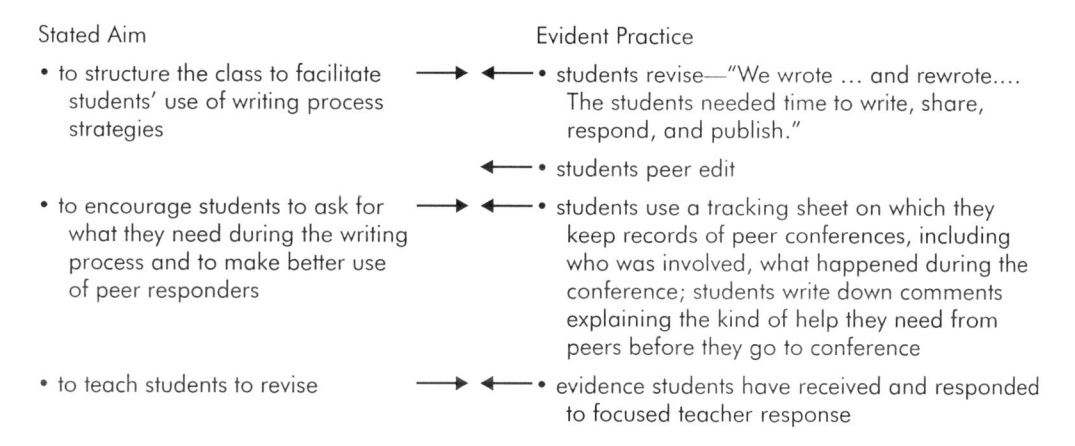

Stated Aim | Evident Practice

- to structure the class to facilitate   → ← • students revise—"We wrote ... and rewrote....
  students' use of writing process   The students needed time to write, share,
  strategies   respond, and publish."

                                         ← • students peer edit

- to encourage students to ask for   → ← • students use a tracking sheet on which they
  what they need during the writing   keep records of peer conferences, including
  process and to make better use   who was involved, what happened during the
  of peer responders   conference; students write down comments
                                                 explaining the kind of help they need from
                                                 peers before they go to conference

- to teach students to revise   → ← • evidence students have received and responded
                                                 to focused teacher response

THEME 6: WRITING FOR VARIED AUDIENCES AND PURPOSES IN VARIED CONTEXTS

Assessors noted that students have opportunities to engage in writing of many different sorts and in different disciplines; that their writing is directed to different audiences, both familiar and distant; and that they write for many different purposes, such as writing to learn, discover, and entertain, as well as writing to communicate knowledge. Assessors also found evidence that students engage in writing over various time periods—writing brief, informal pieces as well as extended projects that involve research, interviews, or collaborative writing.

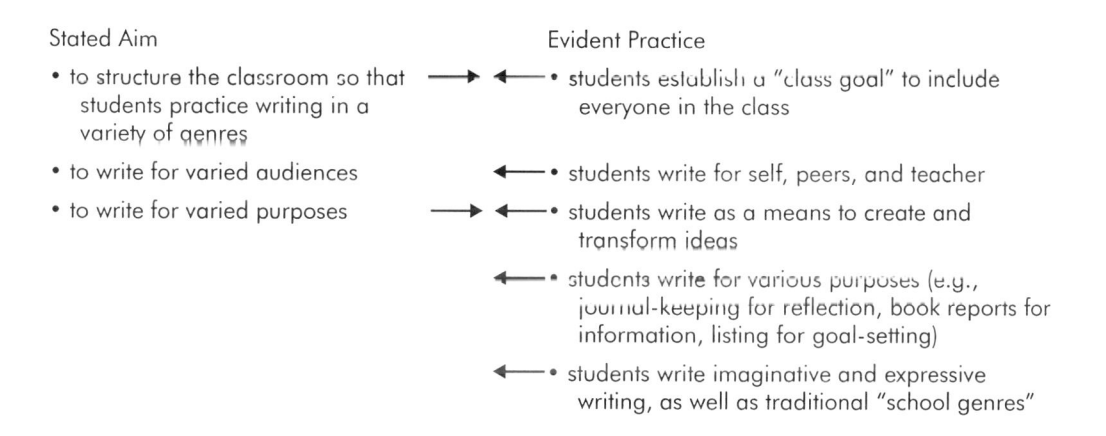

Stated Aim | Evident Practice

- to structure the classroom so that   → ← • students establish a "class goal" to include
  students practice writing in a   everyone in the class
  variety of genres

- to write for varied audiences   ← • students write for self, peers, and teacher

- to write for varied purposes   → ← • students write as a means to create and
                                                 transform ideas

                                         ← • students write for various purposes (e.g.,
                                                 journal-keeping for reflection, book reports for
                                                 information, listing for goal-setting)

                                         ← • students write imaginative and expressive
                                                 writing, as well as traditional "school genres"

As the Iowa Writing Project initiative concludes its third year, I must admit that I remain hesitant. Despite the fact that teachers will soon assume the responsibility for the IWP project, I worry about several issues. First, nearly all external assessments obligate teachers within a department, a school, or a district to participate. In the case of the IWP assessment, I encountered teachers who implied or expressed little interest in implementing portfolios but were required or felt pressured to do so. Not surprisingly, the portfolios represented in these classrooms evidenced, at best, stunted reflection.

I also share Fueyo's (1997) concern that external assessments, even those providing formative support, eventually precipitate the standardization they were created to defy. According to Fueyo (1997):

> The profession is not so much "doing portfolios" as doing them in. It's taken a potentially good thing and is specifying the life-force out of it. Why do I say this? The elementary classrooms I'm following are responding to school district directives to "do portfolios." This district has invited much input from classroom teachers and initially left many specifics open. Still ... the portfolios are becoming more and more prescribed as we come upon the third year of the initiative. (p. 69).

Inevitably, external portfolio assessments exert power over what teachers and students do. Even descriptive models reflect the authority of assessors, who distinguish and document according to what their own professional experiences have taught them to recognize. Once portfolios leave the context of a classroom, the risk of misinterpretation and misappropriation escalates. Perhaps the most painful story arising from the Iowa Writing Project assessment was the tale of a secretary in one school district's central office. In the course of preparing her district's portfolio sets for mailing, she had considered printing costs and thought it best to copy and mail only every fifth page of students' and teachers' portfolios. In one fell swoop, a single individual located beyond the context of the classroom had made literate lives incomprehensible.

Restoring Integrity to Portfolio Practice

Berlin (1994) remarked that elementary and secondary students who have passed through the 1990s are "victims of one of the most test-crazed eras in the history of our country" (p. 58). I agree, and I worry that in our dementia we disregard the implications for our students. Substantial research indicates that issues of reliability and validity in the assessment of portfolios have not been resolved (Despain & Hilgers, 1992; Greenberg, 1992; Hamp-Lyons & Condon, 1993; Huot, 1990). Nevertheless, these assessments continue to obligate students and teachers to prescribed standards, philosophies, and practices. White (1994) maintained that any intrusion on students' and teachers' purposes and autonomy is necessary for the greater good: "I argue that, even at its worst, intrusion is a small price to pay for the benefits that large-scale portfolio assessment can bring to us, our students, and American education" (p. 28).

Like many, White seemed unwilling to confront the fundamental paradox at work. Born of a qualitative interest in process, portfolios resist being wedged into a quantitative paradigm that demands standardization. What, in the end, is the purpose of adulterating portfolios when existing multiple choice and essay alternatives serve the purpose of scoring and ranking students' performances?

If portfolios are to engender the genuine reflection, self-knowledge, and rhetorical sensibility for which they were originally celebrated, they must reflect the choices and desires of the students and teachers who keep them. I believe, finally, that restoring integrity to the portfolio-keeping process requires administrators, teachers, and students to hold the following convictions:

> No educator or student must ever be forced to keep a portfolio.
>
> Portfolio-keeping must evolve within a legitimate rhetorical context, one in which students and educators assemble, share, and revise their portfolios on a regular basis.
>
> Educators who ask students to create portfolios must do so themselves.
>
> Portfolios require extensive time, display, and negotiation.
>
> Educators must teach, mentor, and model reflective strategies.

I have had the privilege of working and collaborating closely with K-college educators who share my enthusiasm for literacy portfolios. We have presented at national conferences with our students. And we have written together about our successes and failures (Sunstein & Cheville, 1997). Despite the realities and threats of external assessment, we continue to reserve a place for portfolios in our classrooms. Bouljon (1997) described how he confined his New Standards commitment so that his students might continue to take risks, to choose, and to reflect genuinely. Meyer (1997) acknowledged how, despite pressures of standardization in her district, she encouraged her students to think beyond dittoed entry slips and analysis sheets to free-form speculation about their literate lives as metaphors. She wrote of fifth-grader Abigail:

Abigail's portfolio *Through My Eyes* tells us that she wants the portfolio reader to know what her learning looks like from her point of view. She stated in a portfolio presentation that she chose not to put grades in her portfolio because grades are a teacher's view of her learning. Her portfolio is organized into sections named for different landscapes because she learns from landscapes. Her reading section is called "Summer Meadows" because she views reading as relaxing. Abigail calls her personal section "Mountains" because these entries represent the "peaks" in her life. Her section describing the presentations she has given is called "Jungles" because "you never quite know what you are going to find when you present. It's exciting." (Meyer, 1997, p. 23)

Within the context of single classrooms, portfolios are exciting. As an instructional tool, they continue to teach me much about what my students know and what they do not know. Portfolios allow me to integrate writing and reading, teach reflection, and facilitate students' critical awareness of audience. Most importantly, portfolios allow my students and me to affirm that intellectual activity involves the acceptance of difference, the freedom of choice, and the responsibility of reflection.

REFERENCES

Berlin, J. (1994). The subversions of the portfolio. In L. Black, D. Daiker, J. Sommers, & G. Stygall (Eds.), *New directions in portfolio assessment* (pp. 56–68). Portsmouth, NH: Boynton/Cook.

Bouljon, G. (1997). Personal and public portfolios: Striking a balance. In B. Sunstein & J. Cheville (Eds.), *Assessing portfolios: A portfolio* (pp. 100–101). Cedar Falls: Iowa Council of Teachers of English.

Despain, L., & Hilgers, T. L. (1992). Readers' responses to the rating of non-uniform portfolios: Are there limits on portfolios' utility? *WPA: Writing Program Administration, 16*, 24–37.

Dewey, J. (1938). *Experience and education.* New York: Collier-Macmillan.

Elbow, P. (1994). Will the virtues of portfolios blind us to their potential dangers? In L. Black, D. Daiker, J. Sommers, & G. Stygall (Eds.), *New directions in portfolio assessment* (pp. 40–55). Portsmouth, NH: Boynton/Cook.

Fu, D. (1992). One bilingual child talks about his portfolio. In D. Graves & B. Sunstein (Eds.), *Portfolio portraits* (pp. 17–20). Portsmouth, NH: Heinemann.

Fueyo, J. (1997). Dear portfolio explorers. In B. Sunstein & J. Cheville (Eds.), *Assessing portfolios: A portfolio* (pp. 68–71). Cedar Falls: Iowa Council of Teachers of English.

Graves, D., & Sunstein, B. (Eds.). (1992). *Portfolio portraits.* Portsmouth, NH: Heinemann.

Greenberg, K. (1992). Validity and reliability: Issues in the direct assessment of writing. *WPA: Writing Program Administration, 16*, 7–22.

Hamp-Lyons, L., & Condon, W. (1993). Questioning assumptions about portfolio-based assessment. *College Composition and Communication, 44*(2), 176–190.

Hansen, J. (1992, March). Evaluation: "My portfolio shows who I am." *Quarterly of the National Writing Project and the Center for the Study of Writing*, pp. 5–9.

Herbert, E. A. (1992). Portfolios invite reflection—from students and staff. *Educational Leadership, 49*(8), 58–61.

Huot, B. (1990, May). Reliability, validity, and holistic scoring: What we know and what we need to know. *College Composition and Communication, 41*(2), 201–213.

Koretz, D. (1992). *The reliability of scores from the 1992 Vermont portfolio assessment program, interim report.* Washington, DC: RAND Institute on Education and Training.

Meyer, K. (1997). Naming portfolios: An act of reflection. In *Assessing portfolios: A portfolio* (pp. 18–25). Urbana, IL: National Council of Teachers of English.

Murphy, S., & Smith, M. A. (1990). Talking about portfolios. *Quarterly of the National Writing Project and the Center for the Study of Writing, 12*(2), 1–26.

Murphy, S., & Smith, M. A. (1992). *Writing portfolios: A bridge from teaching to assessment.* Markham, Ontario: Pippin.

New Standards Project. (1994). *Student portfolio handbook: High school English portfolio.* Urbana, IL: National Council of Teachers of English.

Potts, J. (1996). *Assessing portfolios: A study of the New Standards Project 1994–95 field trial portfolios in three tenth-grade classrooms.* Unpublished doctoral dissertation, University of Iowa.

Purves, A. (1993). Oil and water: Some thoughts on the relationship of portfolios to large-scale assessment. *Portfolio News*, pp. 3–15.

Rief, L. (1990). Finding the value in evaluation: Self-assessment in a middle school classroom. *Educational Leadership, 47*, 24–29.

Salvio, P. M. (1994). Ninja warriors and vulcan logic: Using the cultural literacy portfolio as a curriculum script. *Language Arts, 71*, 419–424.

Sunstein, B., & Cheville, J. (1997). *Assessing portfolios: A portfolio.* Urbana, IL: National Council of Teachers of English.

Tierney, R. (1991). *Portfolio assessment in the reading–writing classroom.* Norwood, MA: Christopher-Gordon.

White, E. (1994). Portfolios as an assessment concept. In L. Black, D. Daiker, J. Sommers, & G. Stygall (Eds.), *New directions in portfolio assessment* (pp. 25–39). Portsmouth, NH: Boynton/Cook.

Wiggins, G. (1994). The constant danger of sacrificing validity to reliability: Making writing assessment serve writers. *Assessing Writing, 1*(2), 129–139.

Wolf, D. P. (1989). Portfolio assessment: Sampling student work. *Educational Leadership, 46*, 35–39.

Wolff, L. (1997). *An English department, portfolios, and the New Standards Project: A department chair's perspective.* Unpublished doctoral dissertation, University of Iowa.

Zebroski, J. T. (1994). *Thinking through theory.* Portsmouth, NH: Boynton/Cook.

Chapter 10

Computer Software Products for Classroom Assessment Purposes

Michelle A. Mengeling
The University of Iowa

COMPUTERS ARE USED EVERY DAY TO IMPROVE THE QUALITY and efficiency of day-to-day tasks in homes, businesses, and schools. Why not use computer technology to improve the quality and efficiency of tasks that occur every day in the classroom—specifically, classroom assessment tasks? This is a relevant question due to the growing number of products being introduced for classroom assessment purposes. Unfortunately, although the products are now available, there has not been a reference source that lists these products or tells what these products can offer. Consequently, the Assessment Training Institute—through newsletters, the Internet, and word of mouth—initiated a search for classroom assessment products. This search resulted in a variety of computer software products being identified and subsequently profiled.[1] A summary of this information is provided in this chapter.

The need for higher quality assessments and more efficient means to obtain them is fairly well established. Teachers spend as much as one third to one half of their time involved in assessment-related activities (Stiggins & Conklin, 1992). Research by Morine-Dershimer (1979), Joyce (1979a, 1979b), and Shulman (1980) found that teachers rely on their own assessments as the primary source for student achievement data. Dorr-Bremme (1983) and Yeh (1978) estimated that one third to three quarters of classroom assessments are developed by teachers. Because teachers create their own assessments and rely primarily on them, it is important to know what assessment techniques teachers are currently using. A study of teacher-made tests by Flemings and Chambers (1983) found the following: Teachers use short answer questions most frequently; all teachers, including English teachers, avoid essay questions; teachers use more matching items than multiple choice or true–false items; and 80% of teacher-made tests are composed of items that test knowledge of terms, facts, and principles. Carter's (1984) research findings showed that teachers have difficulty identifying items that measure specific skills—especially higher order thinking skills. In addition, the technical quality of teacher-made items is not routinely evaluated (Stiggins & Bridgeford, 1985). The lack of attention paid to the technical quality of classroom assessments is further confounded by evidence that teacher-developed tests use too few items (Fleming & Chambers, 1983). Although there may be a tendency to associate classroom assessments with paper-and-pencil exams, teachers most frequently

---

[1]Research for the Classroom Assessment product profiles was supported by The Assessment Training Institute, Inc., 50 SW Second Avenue, Suite 300, Portland, OR 97204.

use informal observational assessments to gather information about students (Salmon-Cox, 1981). These findings, in conjunction with the increased emphasis on a variety of skills and objectives that may not lend themselves to traditional paper-and-pencil methods of assessment, suggest a need for modern information-processing technologies.

Although there are many newly available software products, this does not imply that assessment methodology is changing. It does mean that the kinds of tools available to implement various assessment methods are becoming much more diverse. What these new products offer is a way to make the job of gathering, recording, storing, and reporting evidence of student achievement much more efficient. For example, traditional multiple choice, true–false, and short answer assessments can be quickly generated and scored using software that has test banks and scanning capabilities. Speeches, artwork, and writing samples can easily be captured and stored using electronic portfolio software packages. Personal observations that teachers make can be written down and stored using pen-based computer technology instead of kept as "mental notes." Conventional gradebooks can be replaced with electronic gradebooks that can perform the traditional chores of averaging scores and weighting assessments. Moreover, these same gradebooks can link grades or scores to criterion-referenced descriptions of student achievement. These are a few examples of how technology can be used to enhance classroom assessment practices.

The majority of the products included here have been designed as tools for classroom teachers to incorporate into tasks already being performed. The teacher can use these products to facilitate the gathering, storing, and reporting of evidence of student learning. Technology can make these tasks more efficient and increase the amount of information available to teachers, students, and parents. For example, instead of giving a student a letter grade, this new technology can provide a variety of information that describes student learning and achievement. Parents would know that their children received a "B" in Math because they knew all the multiplication tables but were not as successful in using fractions. Products that link assessments to specific outcomes are able to flag differences in students' performances in more detail, without requiring additional teacher time and effort. Additionally, this added insight into where students are specifically succeeding and failing can be used to design instruction to reinforce students' strengths and improve relative weaknesses. Software that links assessment items with objectives often provides an item bank-type feature that allows for worksheets to be generated that emphasize a specific skill area. Improvement in a child's performance could be documented using an electronic portfolio of achievement that could be shown to the parents at the parent–teacher conference or sent home on a computer disk for parents to review. Changes in a student's attention to a topic or attitude toward a particular content area could be monitored using classroom observations recorded on a Newton Message Pad. Tests, portfolios, and observational assessments can all be carried out using specially designed software packages. Regardless of the software available, sound assessment practices are already a part of being an effective teacher and what technology offers is a way to make it a bit quicker and organizationally simpler for these educators.

The goal of increased student achievement through quality and efficient assessment must begin with a summary of available assessment tools. The products described here represent a wide range of classroom assessment tools. In order to make distinctions between the products, this original group was broken down into five categories: personal observation, written assessment, portfolio assessment, management of curriculum information, and electronic gradebooks. The classroom assessment-related software products and the electronic gradebook software packages are summarized in the sections that follow.

TOOLS FOR RECORDING PERSONAL OBSERVATIONS

The first category of classroom assessment products includes products designed to collect observational records. There are several key features to these products. First, observations are collected using a portable computer pad. Attached to the computer pad is a special pen that allows the user to write directly onto the screen of the computer pad. These notes are stored on a portable computer only temporarily because of the limited amount of memory in the portable pad. The pads are designed to link to a central computer workstation. The notes taken on the computer pad are uploaded onto the main computer, which has room for long-term storage of student information, observables, and assessments. Second, the handwritten notes are not "photocopied" into the computer but are actually read by the computer as if they had been typed in at a keyboard. The computer software packages are designed to "read" a teacher's handwriting. These notes can later be edited just like any word processing document. Third, the portable feature of these products encourages observations to be carried out anywhere or anytime—not necessarily when all students are on the same task. For example, if a teacher is interested in how a student carries out a science experiment, a list of observables or a checklist could be loaded onto the portable computer pad. Teachers would carry the computer and write on the screen as they observed students at work. The observables could be in a column format with adjacent columns representing different levels of achievement such as baseline, master, and proficient. The teacher would mark the appropriate column as the observations are made. Anecdotal information could be added to the observed outcome information, which may provide a more complete record of student achievement.

The personal observation category of products includes two different products: *Learner Profile* and the *Grady Profile Companion*. The software for these products was designed to organize the results of the information gathered by automatically timing and dating observations, producing graphs and reports, and pulling-up observables from which assessments can be quickly developed. The software defines what observables are included and what can be added. The software design also determines the options and formats that can be used to collect information. Different formats may be needed for different types of collected data. For example, attendance information may require different kinds of data to be recorded than behavioral or academic observations.

These products are not new but they are more sophisticated than previous products that used bar coding equipment. Original bar coding methods required the student's name to be scanned from a name tag that included a bar code. This was followed by scanning the appropriate level of achievement from a binder of bar codes. This bar code technology was the same technology that has been used in such places as libraries, supermarkets, and hardware stores. For example, checking out a library book requires the librarian to use a wand to scan the individual's library card and then the book. This method was awkward and limited when applied to the classroom, but it was the precursor to software that now allows teachers to make handwritten anecdotal notes on a portable computer pad.

The message pad software and hardware is designed to organize the results of observationally collected information, but additional training is needed in order to use this new technology as an assessment tool. A teacher has to learn how to use the computer screen pad in making daily observations of student work. Also, teachers need to learn how to share their observations with other teachers, because the notes made on the computer pad are all uploaded into a central computer station. And teachers must be trained in how to match observational data with relevant achievement goals. The training and expertise of the educator ultimately determines the quality and validity of the information collected, stored, and reported.

TOOLS FOR BUILDING OR SCORING WRITTEN ASSESSMENTS

The second category of classroom assessment products includes products with some type of generating or scoring capability for written assessments. A product falls into this category if it provides items for tests or worksheets. Also included are products that use scanning technology to increase the efficiency of scoring objective-item tests. These are the two dominant features of products in this category. Additional features of these types of products include space for resource information and outcomes because they are designed to link items to specific academic outcomes. The information stored and reported is a student's mastery of specified outcomes, which are specified by the teacher. This information is then used to track academic progress and is stored so that it can be passed to the student's next classroom teacher. These products are currently DOS or Windows-based systems; however, all software is currently being upgraded and many products are working toward becoming platform independent. Products that are platform independent allow for the software to be used on both Macintosh or Window-based computers.

Four products have been found to fit this category: *ABACUS Instructional Management System*, *CTB Classroom Manager*, *Objective Tracker*, and *The Assessor*. The first three products—ABACUS, Classroom Manager, and Objective Tracker—assume the responsibility for the quality of the items and their applicability to specific targets by providing items already linked to outcomes. All three of these products have the capability for teachers to add new items or edit existing ones. The items generated may mistakenly be assumed to be of a multiple choice format, however, generated items are not limited to selected response formats. Extended response questions are also available along with scoring rubrics, in order to make use of alternative assessment methods. ABACUS and Classroom Manager offer test banks of items that can be purchased for different content areas. Objective Tracker is unique in that it uses an algorithm to generate its test items. However, only math items are available with the Objective Tracker algorithm. These three products are especially useful in increasing the efficiency of building classroom assessments, especially for courses such as math and science, which tend to rely more heavily on paper-and-pencil assessments (Stiggins & Bridgeford, 1985). These products can reduce a teacher's time in both constructing a test and in scoring it. There are several issues relating to paper-and-pencil tests that are directly addressed by the item-bank technology. They include decreasing the amount of time used to write items, decreasing the time spent scoring exams, increasing the number of items available, increasing the variety of item formats, and increasing the range of cognitive abilities tested. The products reviewed here all address these issues to varying degrees. For those that provide items, they do so in objective and extended-response formats. The decision of which items to select is further simplified because all items are tied to specific outcomes.

The fourth product, *The Assessor*, relies on teacher-made tests for the items that make up an assessment. Therefore, no items or test banks accompany it. The Assessor relies on the teacher to write items that match specific outcomes. The Assessor, although not providing items, addresses the technical quality of teacher-made tests by supplying item characteristic information after the tests have been scored. This item characteristic information includes statistics for the entire test, as well as individual item analysis, which in turn is used to judge the quality and reliability of the classroom test.

The ease with which these products allow tests to be assembled, scored, and reported may lull teachers into an unwarranted sense of complacency. Are teachers testing what they think they are testing? The items provided in textbooks are not infallible, nor should these software products be expected to be so. The software is only a tool and it is the educator who has the responsibility of analyzing the match between outcome and test item, content and course coverage. Although these products offer a lot to the classroom teacher, the appropriateness, as well as the validity, of the test constructed relies on the teacher's assessment knowledge.

Tools for Creating Portfolio Assessments

The third category of products is designed to aid in the creation and storage of student portfolios using electronic portfolios. Instead of a single letter grade being used to describe a student's achievement, an electronic portfolio can describe a student's achievement through samples of student writing, audiotaped examples of student reading, and even video clips of a student giving a class presentation. This technology can encompass all three types of assessments (observational, written, and performance assessments) and store it all on an inexpensive portable computer diskette.

Three products described here are *Scholastic's Electronic Portfolio*, *Learning Quest's Electronic Portfolio*, and the *Grady Profile Portfolio Assessment*. Each product takes advantage of Macintosh technology to allow for the multimedia storage of student work. The different types of student work can be stored with attached annotations provided by the teacher. All three products capitalize on the storage capabilities of this technology. An obvious advantage of this technology is that evidence of student achievement can be stored on a computer disk and easily passed to subsequent classroom teachers. A teacher can much more easily store 25 student computer disks than a portfolio of student achievement that includes actual examples of tests, worksheets, and projects. Without this technology, reading examples would have to be stored on audiotapes and presentations would have to be stored on videotapes. If portfolios are already being used, electronic portfolios can be used to increase the storage efficiency as well as capturing all types of performances in the same medium—a single computer disk.

Although increasing the volume of information while at the same time shrinking the physical space required by the information is a key feature of portfolio products, their more subtle asset is in their potential to involve students in the assessment process. Students can be involved in choosing what pieces to include and what to leave out, which may have an effect on their participation and achievement by allowing them to have a more active role in the assessment of their work. Additionally, these products usually include space for students to write about why a specific piece was included or thoughts about their assignment. Engaging students in the assessment process can potentially lead to increased student motivation.

Scholastic's Electronic Portfolio has a broader target audience than just classroom portfolio creation for students. Scholastic is marketing its products for the classroom as well as promising the potential for a more comprehensive type of resume for job applicants or as an admissions requirement for students applying to college. This standardized use of portfolios raises many psychometric questions. However, for the classroom environment, the use of portfolios can be used to promote better communication about student achievement through actual examples of student work.

Learning Quest's Electronic Portfolio is unique in that it maintains documents in their original formats, allowing teachers to view and assess work as it was originally designed. Recent modifications to the software include a window menu that allows the user to tile or stack windows, as well as file loading that is now over 50 times faster than previous versions.

Grady Profile provides text area for comments, anecdotes, journal entries, and reflections. Teachers, students, and family members may enter their evaluations independently. An additional feature of the Grady Profile is its space for 990 pages of learner objectives that are used to link to specific samples of student work. This combination of multimedia storage of student learning examples tied to learner objectives is the foundation of the philosophy used to create the Grady Profile. Its design purpose was to maintain portfolios efficiently in the classroom and to use portfolios in the classroom setting to promote student learning. Extensive training for teachers is available on how to use this technology to promote student learning through the publishers of the Grady Profile.

Tools to Manage Curriculum Information

The purpose of the fourth category of products is primarily to manage curriculum information. *Teacher Instructional Mapping and Management System* (*TIMMS*), *Curriculum Designer,* and *IMSeries Instructional Solution* are three important examples of this type of product. None of these products promotes or generates classroom assessments directly. Rather, they speak to another component of the curriculum by providing information and resources to be used for classroom instruction. TIMMS is an electronic system designed to link and align curriculum, resources, and assessments. TIMMS provides the relational structure that curriculum specialists and teachers can use to develop their own databases. The Curriculum Designer is a tool that can efficiently and comprehensively create or modify a curriculum. The Curriculum Designer includes Comparison Consultant, which can compare the local curriculum to a chosen framework and list missing objectives and competencies. IMSeries Instructional Solution manages and integrates the core instructional processes—standards, curriculum, instruction, assessment, and validation. This system is designed to enable all constituents who are involved in a student's educational development, including administrators, teachers, parents, and students, to access the student's information online. All three of these products are similar in their ability to store vast amounts of information. They can also be

Electronic Gradebooks

The marketplace offers an abundant selection of software gradebook packages, many of which can be quickly downloaded from the Internet. Although there are many to choose from, most computerized gradebooks are designed around the idea of the traditional paper gradebook. The computer packages differ in their sophistication of screen displays, in the number of additional features they offer (including statistical computations and report graphing capabilities), and in the platforms on which they run. The electronic gradebooks can include a variety of data such as achievement, effort, attitude, or attendance. Differences exist between the programs on how data are weighted, scaled, and summarized. The majority of products report and store achievement data separately from attendance and behavior data. Many of the products provide maximum flexibility for teachers to design their own gradebook scoring scheme.

Conclusions

The products profiled in this summary represent a wide range of assessment-related tools. They hold great promise in increasing the quality and efficiency of classroom assessments. Unfortunately, they also have the potential to cause great harm because each product assumes an assessment literate user. Therefore, the promise of these new electronic assessment tools can only be realized in a school culture that is proficient in assessment. Educators are still the ones who choose what items to use in their classroom exams, what evidence to include in a student's portfolio, and what information to emphasize and store in the gradebook. Consequently, teachers have the final responsibility for the quality of classroom assessments and these electronic software applications can ease the recording, but not necessarily improve the quality or the value, of the data collected.

Appendix

Software Profiles Contents

I. *Software for Collecting Classroom Observation Records*
   Learner Profile
   Grady Profile Companion
II. *Software for Developing Classroom Assessments*

ABACUS Instructional Management System
CTB Classroom Manager
Objective Tracker
The Assessor
III. *Software for Creating Student Portfolios*
Scholastic's Electronic Portfolio
Grady Profile Portfolio Assessment
Learning Quest's Electronic Portfolio
IV. *Software for Managing Curriculum Information*
Teacher Instructional Mapping and Management System (TIMMS)
Curriculum Designer™
IMSeries
V. *Software for Using Gradebook Managers*
Bobbing Gradebook
Bobbing Gradebook PRO
ClassMaster 2.0+
Computerized Gradebook
Win School
Gradebook Manager for Windows
Gradebook Plus

PRODUCT: LEARNER PROFILE

Publisher: Sunburst Communications
Contact: Martin F. Boyle   Phone/Fax: 360-794-4690
Sound Solutions
P.O. Box 951
Monroe, WA 98272

Product Description. The Learner Profile is a synthesis of technology and assessment. The software is built around the hand-held Newton Computer from Apple. From a desktop computer, teachers are able to load the appropriate observables onto the Newton. They can easily carry the Newton to update student progress on specific observables and make handwritten notes throughout the day. Each notation is automatically timed and dated. Although the initial package of observables covers 18 different content areas, additional ones can be added.

Product Specifications. This software is available for Macintosh, Windows, or Network platforms. The recommended hardware requires 4 MB of RAM and 4 MB of hard disk space for both the Macintosh and Windows versions. Exact requirements should be checked based on a user's actual hardware. A scanner is not needed for this particular software, but the Starter Hardware Unit is required. Software requirements include a Macintosh Operating System of 7.0 or higher, the Newton software, and the Learner Profile software.

There are two different training options offered. Sunburst offers a Learner Profile Training Kit that includes overheads and duplicating masters, which are included in the district site license. The publishers also offer a 2-day workshop for $1,800 per day. Sound Solutions offers hands on training that includes technology, assessment, and instructional strategies for $750 per day for up to 15 participants. Two days of initial training with a 1-day follow-up is recommended.

Various passwords are used to allow different levels of security. Each teacher has an individual account and password. Students can also have their own passwords to access the software. Students are encouraged to be a part of the process by using the Learner Profile software in self-assessments.

The cost of the individual PC software is $299 and the Newton software is $109. Site licenses of 5, 10, or more are also available at reduced prices, including network versions. Learner Profile should be viewed as a core piece with the ability to integrate new pieces as they are developed.

PRODUCT: THE GRADY PROFILE COMPANION

Publisher: Aurbach & Associates
Contact: Liz Aurbach Phone: 800-774-7239
Aurbach & Associates, Inc. Fax: 314-432-7072
9378 Olive Street Road, Suite 102
St. Louis, MO 63132-3222
Web site: www.aurbach.com E-mail: aurbach@aol.com

Product Description. The Grady Profile Companion for the Newton Message Pad is software designed as an extension to the Grady Profile that makes the Grady Profile portable. All the Grady Profile subjects, skill sets, descriptors, observations, and student names can be put on the Companion. In addition, teachers can make handwritten observations to support the assessment of student performance. All the information recorded on the Companion can be copied to the Grady Profile on the Macintosh.

The newer versions of the Grady Profile Companion software work well with the newer models of the Newton (MP2xxx) and on the eMate. Version 1.0.6 offers both the older model and the new model versions of the software. When it is installed, the software prompts you to identify your Newton or eMate model.

Note: See Grady Profile Assessment Description.

PRODUCT: NCS ABACUSxp INSTRUCTIONAL MANAGEMENT SOFTWARE

Publisher: NCS ABACUS, Inc.
Contact: Marketing Services Phone: 800-736-4357
NCS ABACUS, Inc. & select option 2
837 W. Grove Ave. Fax: 602-827-7408
Mesa, AZ 85210

Product Description of ABACUSxp Instructional Management Software. ABACUSxp Instructional Management software is a cross-platform application software product for instructional management that addresses three major curriculum development and instructional support needs: (a) curriculum alignment to focus teaching and learning on defined curricular areas, instructional programs, specified outcomes linked to appropriate teaching resource materials; (b) defined measurement criteria for each instructional objective with test item banking, test generation, and scanning for classroom assessment, remediation, diagnostics, and learning accounting; (c) report generation of all curricular and instructional programs, resource materials, test libraries, and student to class to school to district performance mastery reporting.

Product Description of NCS MCADxp Model Curriculum and Assessment Database. MCADxp, the Model Curriculum and Assessment Database, is a complete electronic system of curriculum, assessment items, and correlations to state and national standards. The

MCADxp curriculum consists of statements of student learning, or objectives, that cover kindergarten through grade 12 in the four major content areas: language arts, mathematics, science, and social studies. The MCADxp assessments consist of 36,000 test questions in multiple choice and performance-based formats.

Product Specifications. ABACUSxp Instructional management software is now a cross-platform product. The hardware requirements for a single-user system or a local area network include a 486 PC (Pentium recommended) and 12 MB of RAM (16 MB of RAM recommended). The hard drive needs to have 150 MB plus 100 KB for each student file (250 MB and 200 KB are recommended). MCAD requires an additional 750 MB of available hard disk space. Any HP laser jet compatible printer can be used. A scanner is also required and can be an NCS OpScan3 or OpScan 5 with two read heads. The network software uses Novell 3.11 or higher. The software for both single-user or network system requires an Windows 95 or NT Workstation for PCs or the latest Mac OS version (System 7.5 minimum).

PRODUCT: CTB CLASSROOM MANAGER

Publisher: CTB/McGraw-Hill
Contact: CTB Customer Services Phone: 800-538-9547
20 Ryan Ranch Road
Monterey, CA 93940-5703

Product Description. The CTB Classroom Manager focuses on criterion-referenced test development by providing test banks organized by outcomes. Teachers choose appropriate outcomes and then the system provides test items that have been linked to the outcomes. The outcomes-based test banks are available for a wide range of levels and subjects. The purpose of the Classroom Manager is to generate and score classroom tests as well as track and report the results.

The Classroom Manager provides an efficient method for teachers to deal with their assessment responsibilities. It is a modular system that allows the system to grow. The base system includes modules for test generation, scanning, scoring, and reporting. Other available modules include tracking, prescription, gradebook, and lesson planning software.

Product Specifications. The currently available platforms include a DOS-based Network version and a Windows95 version. There are separate hardware requirements for each platform. The DOS system requires 640K RAM and a 60 MB hard drive. The DOS version can be run on a 286, but for better performance, a 486 is recommended. The Windows95 version will work on a 486 computer, but the Pentium is recommended. Eight MB RAM are needed, but 16 MB of RAM are recommended. A demonstration disk of the Windows95 version is available.

The software requirements include Novell Netware Version 2.12 or higher, a DOS operating system of 3.3 or higher (6.2 recommended), and Microsoft Windows version 3.1 or higher. Microsoft Windows is needed for the On-line Testing module. Scanners, a HP-compatible laser printer, and a mouse are all hardware pieces that are strongly recommended.

For administrator information, another software package called TestMate is available to complement the Classroom Manager product. This software provides item statistics as well as the aggregation of information by classroom or other specified groupings.

The average package cost, depending on components selected, ranges from $3,000 to $5,000. CTB provides field consultants in classroom assessment, and will work with school staff to determine their specific needs.

PRODUCT: OBJECTIVE TRACKER

Publisher:	IPS Publishing, Inc., a subsidiary of Advantage Learning Systems, Inc.		
Contact:	Chris Langlois, Systems Coordinator		
	12606 N.E. 95th St., C-110	Phone:	800-933-8378
	Vancouver, WA 98682	Fax:	360-944-9156
E-mail:	mathcheck@ipspub.com		

Product Description. Objective Tracker is a complete classroom management system designed to track student progress toward mastery of teacher-assigned math objectives on an individual student basis. Its algorithm-based technology generates fresh, objective-specific items every time a teacher prints a test or worksheet. This classroom tool assists the teacher with assessment and record-keeping needs.

Objective Tracker generates thousands of test questions because it uses algorithms rather than a test bank of static questions. Teachers choose the objective goals appropriate for a specific student or group of students. The program automatically creates and prints out tests or practice worksheets. Then, using a scanner, the teacher quickly inputs test scores into the program, which adjusts the content of the next tests or worksheets it prints to meet the needs of individual students. Objective Tracker is sold with one or more libraries of algorithms, from Grade 3 to Precalculus. A library customization program is available whereby content can be tagged to district, state, or publisher requirements. An upgrade to an Advantage Learning Systems product called Accelerated Math has also been released. Accelerated Math includes a number of innovations—it is networkable, offers such student interactive features as on-screen test taking, and is available for both Windows and Macintosh platforms.

Product Specifications. The hardware needed to run Objective Tracker includes a Pentium processor, 32 MB RAM, and at least 10 MB of free hard drive space. The demo requires a CD-ROM drive. Objective Tracker requires a Windows-compatible printer and an available serial port for an optional scanner. To date, the two compatible scanners are the Chatsworth Data 1100 and the Scanmark 2000. As with any Windows 3.11 or Windows 95 product, performance improves with a faster processor and more memory.

Special pricing is available for district purchases and other multiple-site sales.

PRODUCT: THE ASSESSOR

Publisher:	Software America, Inc.		
Contact:	Matthew S. Meldon	Phone:	800-860-8843
	Vice President & General Manager		630-554-6060
	Software America, Inc.	Fax:	630-554-6375
	P.O. Box 5125	E-mail:	sai@xnet.com
	Naperville, IL 60567		

Product Description. The Assessor-Curriculum Data Management & Test Scoring System is a bit different from the other test-generating packages that have been discussed thus far. It has been designed to automate the time-consuming process of scoring exams and performance assessments. In addition, it can provide a full description of item characteristics and standards-based item and mastery analysis information.

The Assessor's Assessment Management Module was written by system designers working together with a former superintendent of schools and a curriculum director to deal with the heart of Illinois schools' assessment and reporting needs and is now being marketed outside the state of Illinois. The system was designed to incorporate the flexibility of using teacher-made tests. The teacher ties the test items to the appropriate academic standards. After the test is designed, a scannable form is requested that includes each student's name with their ID.

The Assessor can automatically scan, score, and report on any form of student assessment, instantly. Scanners are used to input alternative assessments, forced choice items, or rubrics. The scoring is done by the system. The Assessor can then provide multiple informational reports, including ranked student results, student/teacher responses, assessment item analysis, and so on. The teacher requests the type of reports to be generated.

Product Specifications. The available platform is Windows95. The hardware requirements include a 486 IBM compatible PC, 4 MB of RAM, and 200 MB of hard drive space. A modem, for support purposes, is optional. A laser printer is recommended. The Assessor-supported scanners are from Scantron® or Scanning Systems®.

Additional Features. Results can be exported to an ASCII file. This allows assessment results to be exported for use in spreadsheets, graphing software, or word processing software. Also, student state testing results can be imported in order to make progress comparisons between local and state performances.

The cost for The Assessor can be obtained by contacting the publisher directly. A demonstration disk is available.

PRODUCT: SCHOLASTIC ELECTRONIC PORTFOLIO

Publisher: Scholastic, Inc.
Contact: Customer Service   Phone: 800-724-6527
Scholastic, Inc.
2931 East McCarty Street
Jefferson City, MO 65101

Product Description. This product's title represents what it truly is—a way to save a student's compilation of work on a computer. It is available for Macintosh computers and is intended for classroom use. The pieces of work that will be included have been produced outside of this program and then "pasted" in. It can accept import files from other Macintosh programs, including text, graphics, illustrations, and movies. Electronic Portfolio also allows the importation and playback of Hyperstudio products.

Product Specifications. The hardware requirements include 4 MB of RAM (8 MB is recommended), 30 MB of hard drive space, a CD-ROM drive, and a 256-color Macintosh with a 13" monitor (or larger). A printer is recommended as well as a color scanner. To include audio pieces, it is assumed that the microphone is already a component of the Macintosh computer.

The software required is an operating system of 7.0.1 or higher. (However, it is not compatible with operating system 7.5.3). A simple write program called Teachtext is included in the Electronic Portfolio software. However, if you have Microsoft Word available, this would be a preferable way to develop an essay before importing it into the Electronic Portfolio.

The security includes one master password and multiple student passwords, allowing students to work on their portfolios independently.

The Teacher's Edition current cost is $79.95, which includes a CD-ROM showing 16 real portfolios from a pre-Kindergartner through a junior in high school. Teachers may make one copy of this program for home use at no extra charge. There is a Lab Pack (5) available for $239.95. A site license is $799.95.

There is a training seminar available for an additional fee. The CD-ROM of portfolio examples also provides some self-training. Regional Scholastic representatives are available and can be contacted through the customer service number. There is a demonstration disk available free of charge.

PRODUCT: GRADY PROFILE PORTFOLIO ASSESSMENT

Publisher:	Aurbach & Associates		
Contact:	Liz Aurbach	Phone:	800-774-7239
	Aurbach & Associates, Inc.	Fax:	314-432-7072
	9378 Olive Street Road, Suite 102		
	St. Louis, MO 63132-3222		
Web site:	www.aurbach.com	E-mail:	aurbach@aol.com

Product Description. The main purposes of the Grady Profile are to maintain portfolios efficiently in the classroom setting and to promote student learning. The Grady Profile integrates the user-friendliness of the Macintosh computers and the sophistication of hypercard technology to provide a framework that can be furnished differently by each user. The software comes with 10 evaluation cards that the teacher can designate as specific areas of assessment, such as reading, math, thinking skills, or collaborative projects. Under each card are skill sets. The skill sets hold lists of observables that are used for student evaluations. The program provides examples of cards and skill sets. The program is organized by student folder and the first few screens of a student's folder include a place for demographic information and a (color) photo.

Product Specifications. This is a Macintosh-based system that allows examples of student writings, reading, pictures, and video clips to be stored. Also available is the Grady Profile Companion that uses the Newton Message Pad and eMate to make the Grady Profile portable.

The hardware required includes 4 MB of RAM (8 MB for a Power Macintosh) and 80 MB of hard drive space. A printer and graphical scanner are also recommended components. Assuming a Macintosh operating system of 7.0 or later, no additional software is needed.

There are different levels of access that allow the teacher global access and the students access to only their personal portfolios. Students are allowed to view their records without the capability of changing the teacher's evaluations. It is possible for the teacher to restrict access to anecdotal notes about students. The philosophy behind this is to make the student's work easily accessible to the student and the teacher. The portfolio itself is seen as a way to promote student teacher communication and encourage self-evaluation on the student's part.

The Grady Profile Portfolio Assessment is available on an individual basis or as a level site license package for $195 or $1,500, respectively. A demonstration disk is available. Two-day training sessions are also available and dates can be located on their web site.

PRODUCT: LEARNING QUEST'S ELECTRONIC PORTFOLIO

Publisher:	Learning Quest, Inc.	Phone:	541-753-6474
Contact:	Dr. Chris Moersch	Fax:	541-753-6461
	P.O. Box 61		
	Corvallis, OR 97339		
Web site:	www.learning-quest.com	E-mail:	dianna@learning-quest.com

Product Description. Learning Quest in conjunction with the National Business Education Alliance (NBEA) have developed the Electronic Portfolio software. Learning

Quest's Electronic Portfolio provides the technology for teachers to organize, store, and assess students' multimedia portfolios.

Electronic Portfolio is the support structure of the portfolio process that is based on an extensive survey of portfolio literature. The rubrics used to assess student works are designed by the teachers. Sample rubrics are included. Electronic Portfolio allows teachers to design their own reports of student achievement. The Electronic Portfolio maintains documents in their original formats, allowing teachers to view and assess the work as it was originally designed.

The system is designed to be user friendly by providing the following features:

> Window menu allows the user to tile or stack windows.
>
> Students and teachers have differing levels of password accessibility.
>
> Report system allows on screen display of reports without printing.
>
> File loading is now over 50 times faster.

Product Specifications. The software is Macintosh-based, however a WIN95 version is scheduled to be released soon. Training is available through workshops. The workshops include instruction on developing portfolio-based assessments electronically, multimedia authoring tools, capturing student work examples, and classroom management of student portfolios. The security provided allows for multiple users and different levels of access.

The workstation needed to run the software is a Macintosh LC computer or better. An LC should include a 14" color monitor. Color Quickdraw is needed, but it is already on all LCII Macs or later. A scanner is recommended. The Paperport VX by Visioneer is recommended because it is easy to use and inexpensive (around $200).

Other hardware recommended includes a cartridge drive (zip drive) for offline storage and a digital camera. For mobility purposes, a bar code reader or a Newton can be incorporated. The operating system needs to be MacOS System 7.0 or later. Three MB of RAM are also needed.

An individual station license and site licenses costs can be obtained by contacting Learning Quest directly. Demonstration software can be downloaded off of the Internet free of charge.

PRODUCT: TEACHER INSTRUCTIONAL MAPPING AND MANAGEMENT SYSTEM (TIMMS)

Publisher:	SYNECTICS, Ltd.		
Contact:	Lee Zobrist, Director or	Phone:	206-283-9420
	Jim Miller, President	Fax:	206-283-4538
	Educational Marketing & Services		
	SYNECTICS, Ltd.		
	2 Nickerson Street, Suite 100		
	Seattle, WA 98109-1652		
Web site:	synecticsltd.com	E-mail:	jimmsl@aol.com

Product Description. Teachers Instructional Mapping and Management System (TIMMS) has been developed by SYNECTICS, Ltd. to meet the needs of schools faced with tracking and accountability related to performance-based education. It is based on Microsoft NT/SQL Client/Server technology to maximize the utilization of existing classroom computers, minimizing hardware upgrade costs. Mac clients use thin client interfaces for exact compatibility for all PC and Mac users. More information about SYNECTICS and its services is available on its web site.

The focus of TIMMS is to support teachers to create high quality lessons aligned to the Essential Learnings (EL) using a variety of instructional and assessment resources, including Internet links; assign these lessons, track progress, and assess student accomplishments on their work using the equivalent of an electronic gradebook and task manager; analyze cumulative student progress toward meeting the essential learning benchmarks and report this progress to each student and parent using the performance report (PREP) as a report card with robust, editable comments; provide highly useful reports on school and district results on student progress; archive and transmit cumulative records of enrollment, withdrawals, and year after year records of student progress; provide a single, networked tool for all of the aforementioned at teachers' computers; and provide reports on curriculum framework, aligned resources, and assessable tasks.

Specifications. TIMMS is available as a PC-Network version with a Macintosh version being developed. The hardware requirements include a 486 PC or Pentium with 8 MB of RAM and 25 MB of hard drive space (100 MB of hard drive space recommended). The file server requires Windows NT and an SQL Server Database system. A Hewlett Packard 4 SI printer is recommended and any TWAIN compliant scanner. The client (teacher's) PC requires MS-Windows 3.X or higher.

Specific passwords allow different levels of access to the system. Administrators are able to aggregate student information by class or other designated groupings. Teachers can access curriculum information without concern about changing or deleting essential curriculum information.

The cost is approximately $150 to $200 per network user, depending on the modules selected, plus initial installation, customization, and training and support. Initial training is included and provides a half day of training for the technical staff and a 1-day in-service training for 20 to 25 teachers or key trainers. Additional training can be purchased. A Power Point slide show is available demonstrating the TIMMS software.

PRODUCT: CURRICULUM DESIGNER™

Publisher:	Tudor Publishing Company		
Contact:	Meredith Manning	Phone:	619-552-2244
	Vice President	Fax:	619-552-2248
	6815 Flanders Drive		
	San Diego, CA 92121-3914		
Web site:	www.tudorpub.com	E-mail:	mmanning@tudorpub.com

Product Description. Tudor Publishing Company (TPC) develops and markets educational software to improve student success. The focus of this endeavor is to provide products that pertain to the "what" and "did we," rather than the "how," of teaching. Curriculum Designer™ addresses the "what" by providing a desktop tool for creating curriculum for mathematics, language arts, and science. Curriculum Designer™ contains over 30,000 learning objectives that can be selected by a school district for inclusion in its curriculum. TPC's latest product, Skills Connection™, concentrates on the "did we." Skills Connection™ is an assessment product designed to bridge the gap between the classroom and home. Teachers can quickly assess students on vital skills and then send detailed tutorials home to parents.

Curriculum Designer has many features, a few of which are included here:

Comparison Consultant: This feature allows the user to compare curricula to note differences between alignments. It can be used to compare local frameworks with that of other states or assessment tools.

Bloom's Taxonomy Levels and Instructional Hours: Each objective in the Tudor Publishing database is classified according to a Bloom's Taxonomy level. This predetermined designation is easily modified by the user.

Edit and Print Curriculum: Users are able to add, delete, and modify learner outcomes from Tudor Publishing's database as they build and design their curriculum. A variety of report formats are available to publish a curriculum with attached resources for administrators, school board, teachers, parents, and students.

For further information about the Curriculum Designer™ or Skills Connection™, contact Tudor Publishing directly.

PRODUCT: IMSERIES™

Publisher:	Learning Technology Systems, Inc.		
Contact:	George S. Polos	Phone:	423-560-0261
	Learning Technology Systems	Fax:	423-769-5604
	2030 Falling Water Rd., #160		
	Knoxville, TN 37922		
Web site:	www.IMSeries.com	E-mail:	GPolos@IMSeries.com

Product Description. The IMSeries is designed to help educators align and manage what are often isolated and disjointed parts of an ideally cohesive instructional process. The core instructional processes—standards, curriculum, instruction, assessment, and validation—are both managed and integrated by IMSeries. The system is designed to enable all constituents who are involved in a student's educational development, including administrators, teachers, parents, and students, to access the online information, including access via a *web browser interface.* Persons who access the online information can make contributions as well as obtain information about the different instructional processes (e.g., survey outcomes, identify occurring instruction, review given assessments, and learn about student performance). Teachers can create lesson plans and assessments. Students can log on to check due dates and descriptions of pending homework assignments as well as do homework and take tests online. Parents can also access the system to check what has been taught, what is pending, what assignments have yet to be completed, and to evaluate their student's progress. Moreover, performance profiles can be generated for any knowledge and skill (even across courses and grade levels) in addition to the more traditional way of reporting achievement by using course grades. IMSeries is currently used in more than 200 K through 12 schools and several 2- and 4-year colleges, universities, and vocational institutions.

Product Specifications. This software is available for Macintosh or Windows operating systems. It can operate in true mixed-platform environments where a mixture of Macintosh and Windows workstations can be communicating with either a Macintosh or Windows server at the same time. The recommended hardware for workstations includes 32 MB of RAM and 100 MB of available hard disk space, and for servers includes 96 MB of RAM and 500 MB of available hard disk space. IMSeries is available for Windows NT as well as for Windows 95/98 and for Macintosh System 7.x or higher. The web browser interface operates with Netscape and Internet Explorer versions 3.x and above.

IMSeries can be licensed for sites (e.g., school buildings) or entire school districts, and its price is based on the number of students being served. In addition to software, licensing support services are provided to achieve successful full implementations of the IMSeries. Support services include implementation planning, training, consulting, and technical support for data conversion and custom development. The cost for full implementation varies based on the student population of the site or district.

PRODUCT: BOBBING GRADEBOOK AND BOBBING GRADEBOOK PRO

Publisher:	Bobbing Software		
Contact:	Bobbing Software		
	67 Country Oaks Drive	Phone:	800-688-6812
	Buda, TX 78610-9338	Fax:	512-479-9365
Web site:	www.moontower.com/bobbing/		
E-mail:	bobbing@moontower.com		

Product Description of Bobbing Gradebook. Bobbing GradeBook was rated number one in features, performance, look and feel, value, and satisfaction by *MacGuide* magazine. A slide show demonstration of this product can be downloaded to your computer if you have HyperCard 2.0, or later. However, Bobbing GradeBook is not a HyperCard program. Testimonials from users of the program are also available at the aforementioned Internet address. The versatility of this program is evident by the numerous and various categories that can be specified such as tests, quizzes, daily assignments, and extra credit, as well as student ID number, parent, and so on. And this versatility extends into ways to customize the look of your document such as adding spiral binding, grid lines, bold titles, and page dog-ears.

Information Storage and Reporting. The Bobbing Gradebook is able to handle a variety of grading schemes, including dropping the lowest or highest grades in a category. The categories can be summarized as a total or as an average value. All calculations are updated as you type. Annotations can be attached to any cell entry, with optional flags and there is a "Full Undo" that allows for trial-and-error recovery. The reporting capabilities include trend lines, histograms, statistics, and scatter plots.

Hardware and Software Requirements. The hardware required to run the Bobbing GradeBook is any Macintosh computer with over 350K of RAM, a 200K disk drive, and an 800K floppy disk drive. The operating system must be a Mac OS System 6 or 7. Only the original Mac 128K and the Mac 512K (Fat Mac) are incompatible. Site licenses are available.

Additional Features. This program has several more helpful capabilities, including: split scrolling that keeps names and titles on screen; unlimited students, assignments, and categories; and unlimited *Levels* of categories.

Product Description of Bobbing Gradebook Pro. The Bobbing GradeBook PRO is a much enhanced version of the original Bobbing GradeBook.

Information Storage and Reporting. Grades can be input as letters and output as letters or fractions. Assignment weights can be varied. Reports can have custom headers and footers. Cell notes can be put on reports. Multiple categories can be shown side by side instead of one at a time. And multiple trend lines and multiple scatter plots can be requested with one print command. Multiple reports can be printed on a single sheet of paper.

Hardware and Software Requirements. The required hardware includes any Mac with over 1 MB of RAM with an 800K disk drive. An 800K floppy disk drive is also required. Incompatible hardware includes the Mac 128K, Mac 512K, Mac 512KE, and the Mac Plus 1 MB. Site licenses are available.

Additional Features. This program has several other helpful features, including a 60-day money-back guarantee; a huge selection of fonts, sizes, styles, grids, and colors; and unique features that only GradeBook PRO has (see: http://www.jump.net/bob-bing/BGP_Features_Works.html).

PRODUCT: THE CLASSMASTER 2.0+

Publisher:	William K. Bradford Publishing Company, Inc.		
Contact:	P.O. Box 1355	Phone:	800-421-2009
	Concord, MA 01742		978-263-6996
		Fax:	978-263-9375
Web site:	www.wkbradford.com/titles/clms/clms.htm		
E-mail:	wkb@wkbradford.com		

Product Description. The ClassMaster 2.0+ is an electronic gradebook that has been designed to calculate, record, report, and forecast student and class performance. There are Windows and Macintosh versions. Transfer of class files between platforms is seamless, a simple key press lets you open your Windows files on a Mac. It has received several honors, including the 1991 Technology in Learning Software Award for Excellence, Finalist in the 1991–1992 Excellence in Software sponsored by the Software Publishers Association, and selected by *Media & Methods Magazine* for its 1992 Portfolio issue. The ClassMaster has been designed for use by K-12 teachers, college instructors, and professional trainers.

Information Storage and Reporting. The grading system will accept numbers, letters, checks, or any other system, in any combination. The grading scales can be set up using fractional percentages, varying weights, and specified maximum scores. The results can be rounded or based on a curve. Assignments can be recorded for extra credit, blank scores can be ignored, and even other scores can be recorded but not included for grading purposes. Reports include histograms of grade distributions for particular assignments or quizzes as well as histograms of individual student performance with overall class performance. Class rosters, attendance reports, and student grade reports can also be produced. Blank student roster grids can be printed. Individual progress reports can contain comments.

Hardware and Software Requirements. The requirements for the Macintosh version include 2MB of free RAM, System 6.7 or later, and a color monitor. The Windows version requires an IBM PC or compatible with 2 MB of RAM, Windows 3.1 or later, and a VGA monitor. Transfer of class files between platforms is seamless, a simple key press lets you open your Windows files on a Mac. Site licenses are available.

Additional Features. This software has other advantages. The flexible import/export feature lets you easily place information into other applications, such as WordPerfect and databases. And, you can save class lists and activity information as templates for reuse.

PRODUCT: COMPUTERIZED GRADEBOOK

Publisher:	Electronic Courseware Systems, Inc. (ECS Software)		
Contact:	1210 Lancaster Dr.	Phone:	800-832-4965
	Champaign, IL 61821		217-359-7099
		Fax:	217-359-6578

Product Description. This product is essentially the computerized version of the traditional gradebook. It provides a convenient and accurate method for keeping students' scores and assigning grades.

Information Storage and Reporting. Raw scores are entered and translated into standard scores that can be individually weighted. Final scores and their letter grade equivalents are computed. The program and data are stored on a diskette with password security. Student records and class rosters may be displayed and printed.

Hardware and Software Requirements. For the DOS version, an IBM PC with 128 K memory and 1 disk drive are required. Site licenses are available.

PRODUCT: WIN SCHOOL

Publisher:	Chancery Software, Ltd.		
Contact (US):	405-103 E. Holly St.	Phone:	800-999-9931
	Bellingham, WA 98225	Fax:	360-752-2201
(CN):	275-3001 Wayburne Drive	Phone:	800-999-9931
	Burnaby, BC, Canada V5G 4W1		604-294-1233
Web site:	www.chancery.com/chancery.html	Fax:	604-294-2225
E-mail:	chancery@chancery.com		

Product Description. This product is much more than an electronic gradebook. It is an entire administration system designed for public and private schools. It includes the following information: student demographics, discipline, attendance, health and immunization, scheduling, teacher gradebook (eClass Grades), report cards and transcripts, a report manager, query, ASCII import/export capabilities, and scanning capabilities. The gradebook is just one module in this integrated system.

Information Storage and Reporting. The information that can be stored includes percentages, letter grades, work habits, citizenship, and comments. Up to 15 grading scales that specify the relation between percentage, letter grade, grade points, earned credits, and pass/fail status can be specified. The report manager module combines report card information with attendance, discipline, and demographic information. The Honor Roll can be calculated on the requirements set by the school that may include a 3.0 grade point average, no failing marks, and no more than two unexcused absences.

Hardware and Software Requirements. Win School is a network system using Novell NetWare 4.x or Windows NT 4.0. Individual workstations must have Microsoft Windows 3.10 or later, 30 MB of hard disk space, and 8 MB of RAM (16 MB for Windows NT). Site licensing is available.

Additional Features. This program has the ability to design reports such as: report cards, eligibility lists, grade verification reports, academic probation letters, transcripts, progress reports, and so on.

PRODUCT: GRADEBOOK MANAGER FOR WINDOWS

Publisher:	CompuTech Computer Services
Contact:	6991 Lindsley Road
	Livonia, NY 14487
Web site:	members.aol.com/psavard/grademgr.html
E-mail:	psavard@frontiernet.net

Product Description. This product was written by teachers for teachers. This program is continually updated to reflect the features that teachers request and use most. This newest version works well with Windows 95. As a registered user, all future versions come at no additional cost.

Information Storage and Reporting. Scores can be stored numerically or as letter grades. Averages can be calculated for either kind of input. If scores are numeric, then averages are calculated using total points. If letter grades are used, then averages are calculated using the number of grades. Scores can be treated individually or grouped into categories. The reports are varied and include an attendance calendar and seating charts.

Hardware and Software Requirements. This program can be downloaded from the Internet. Version 4.3.9 is now available and requires approximately 740KB.

PRODUCT: GRADEBOOK PLUS

Publisher:	Projected Learning Programs	Phone:	800-248-0757
Contact:	P.O. 13060		405-416-3333
	Oklahoma City, OK 73113	Fax:	405-416-3336
		E-mail:	plp@pinsight.com

Product Description. Gradebook Plus was given the Award of Excellence from *Classroom Computer Learning.* There are separate versions for the Macintosh and IBM platforms.

Information Storage and Reporting. Teachers define their own grading scales for each class. Letter grades or raw scores can be entered and specific assignments may be exempted from the overall grade. Each score may be weighted. Gradebook Plus automatically calculates the mean, median, and standard deviation. Reports include individual or class reports, histograms, and progress reports. There is a built-in mini word processor that can be used to customize reports for parents. The scores can be easily imported and exported to programs such as Excel, AppleWorksGS, or Lotus 1-2-3.

Hardware and Software Requirements. The Macintosh version requires LC or better, 1 MB RAM, an operating System 6.0.7 or later, and a hard drive. The Windows version requires a 386/26 MHZ processor or better, 4 MB of RAM, a Windows 3.1 operating system or later, a hard drive, and a mouse. Building versions are available.

Additional Features. This software also has the ability to use more than one class in statistical analysis, and to generate a list of missing assignments for any student.

REFERENCES

ABACUSxp Instructional Management System for Macintosh or Windows (1998) [Computer Software]. Mesa, AZ: NCS Abacus.

Assessor, The [Computer Software]. (1997). Naperville, IL: Software America.

Aurbach, R. (1991). *Grady Profile Companion* (Version 1.0.5) [Computer Software]. St. Louis, MO: Aurbach & Associates.

Aurbach, R. (1998). *Grady Profile Portfolio Assessment* (Version 2.3) [Computer Software]. St. Louis, MO: Aurbach & Associates.

Bobbing GradeBook [Computer Software]. (1988). Buda TX: Bobbing Software.

Bobbing GradeBook PRO [Computer Software]. (1995). Buda TX: Bobbing Software.

Carter, K. (1984). Do teachers understand the principles for writing tests? *Journal of Teacher Education, 35*(6), 57–60.

ClassMaster 2.0+ [Computer Software]. (1997). Concord, MA: William K. Bradford.

Computerized Gradebook [Computer Software]. (1984). Champaign, IL: Electronic Courseware Systems.

CSL Win School Version 3.6 [Computer Software] (1998). Bellingham, WA: Chancery Software.

CTB Classroom Manager—DOS Version [Computer Software]. (1994). Monterey, CA: CTB/McGraw-Hill.

CTB Classroom Manager—Windows95 Version [Computer Software]. (1997). Monterey, CA: CTB/McGraw-Hill.

CTB Classroom Manager—Macintosh Version [Computer Software]. (1997). Monterey, CA: CTB/McGraw-Hill.

Curriculum Designer [Computer Software]. (1998). San Diego, CA: Tudor.

Dorr-Bremme, D. W. (1983). Assessing students: Teachers' routine practices and reasoning. *Evaluation Comment, 6*(4), 1–12.

Electronic Portfolio (Version 2.0) [Computer Software]. (1997). Corvallis, OR: Learning Quest.

Electronic Portfolio [Computer Software]. (1993). Jefferson City, MO: Scholastic.

Fleming, M., & Chambers, B. (1983). Teacher-made tests: Windows on the classroom. In W. F. Hathaway (Ed.), *Testing in the schools: New directions for testing and measurement, No. 19* (pp. 29–38). San Francisco: Jossey-Bass.

Gradebook Manager for Windows [Computer Software]. (1995). Livonia, NY: CompuTech Computer Services.

Gradebook Plus [Computer Software]. (1996). Oklahoma, OK: Projected Learning Programs.

IMSeries [Computer Software]. (1997–1999). Knoxville, TN: Learning Technology Systems.

Joyce, B. (1979a). *Teachers' thoughts while teaching* (Research Series No. 58). East Lansing: Michigan State University, Institute for Research on Teaching. (ERIC Document Reproduction Service No. ED 057 016)

Joyce, B. (1979b). *Teaching styles at South Bay School* (Research Series No. 57). East Lansing: Michigan State University, Institute for Research on Teaching. (ERIC Document Reproduction Service No. ED 187 666)

Learner Profile (Version 1.1.7) [Computer Software]. (1994). Pleasantville, NY: Sunburst Communications.

Morine-Dershimer, G. (1979). *Teacher conceptions of children* (Research Series No. 59). East Lansing: Michigan State University, Institute for Research on Teaching. (ERIC Document Reproduction Service No. ED 180 988)

Objective Tracker (Version 1.22) [Computer Software]. (1998). Vancouver, WA: IPS Publishing.

Salmon-Cox, L. (1981). Teachers and standardized achievement tests: What's really happening? *Phi Delta Kappan, 26*(9), 631–634.

Shulman, L. S. (1980). Test design: A view from practice. In E. L. Baker & E. S. Quellmalz (Eds.), *Educational testing and evaluation* (pp. 63–73). Los Angeles, CA: Sage.

Stiggins, R. J., & Bridgeford, N. J. (1985). The ecology of classroom assessment. Journal of *Educational Measurement, 22*(4), 271–286.

Stiggins, R. J., & Conklin, N. F. (1992). *In teachers' hands: Investigating the practices of classroom assessment.* Albany: State University of New York Press.

Teacher Instructional Mapping and Management System (1998). [Computer Software]. Seattle, WA: SYNECTICS.

Yeh, J. (1978). *Test use in the schools.* Los Angeles: University of California at Los Angeles, Center for the Study of Evaluation.

CHAPTER 11

HIGH STAKES, LOW STAKES TESTING: DO STAKES REALLY MATTER?

Lucy L. Payne
The University of St. Thomas, Minneapolis

A Policy of Pressure. As an accountability revolution sweeps through the nation's public schools, more students will be tested, and more schools will be compared. In Minnesota, testing will hit a new high, and the Legislature will consider a plan for state takeovers of failing schools.
—Minneapolis Star Tribune *(January 18, 1998; front page)*

Newspaper headlines are written to grab people's attention. Nothing captures newspaper headline attention like school test scores. As the state of Minnesota (only one of many possible examples) has moved toward using test scores as a minimum competency exam to graduate from high school, the attention-getting headlines are seen more often. Tests that have rewards (graduating from high school) or penalties (not graduating from high school) tied to the test results are considered to be "high stakes" tests. However, not all schools in the United States can be considered high stakes testing environments. Schools that do not have sanctions or rewards tied to the results of an exam cannot be viewed as high stakes testing environments. Instead, they are considered to be "low stakes" environments. A low stakes environment can still have a standardized achievement or criterion-referenced test, but the results will not be used automatically to make decisions about students, schools, or teachers.

As testing continues to increase across the nation's schools, in high stakes and low stakes environments, what effect do these tests have on the curriculum and instruction? In order to understand high stakes and low stakes testing, the growth in testing in this country must be examined.

THE GROWTH IN TESTING

In the early 1960s, policymakers began to gather information about the condition of American education and the effectiveness of mandated programs by examining standardized results (Madaus, 1985). State school boards and legislatures began to use test results as mechanisms of power. They began to administer rewards and sanctions based on students' performance on mandated tests, making them high stakes tests. Rewards and sanctions were seen as a way to motivate students, teachers, and schools. Test results in effect became a "triggering device" to make good and bad things happen automatically to individuals and schools (Madaus, 1988). As a result, an educational environment was created where test scores were the sole barometer of school district success (Corbett & Wilson, 1991). Policymakers also began to use standardized test data as indicators of the effectiveness of compensatory programs and curriculum development efforts tried during the 1950s and 1960s (Madaus, 1988).

Pressure to improve test scores increased in the 1970s (Frederiksen, 1984). As funding for education increased and the national average SAT score began to decline, school accountability became an important issue (Madaus, quoted in Brandt, 1989). The back to basics movement was a reaction to the decline in test scores. Along with the back to basics movement came a demand for accountability, or the use of test results to ensure quality (Rothman, 1995). During this time, policymakers quickly discovered the power test results had over reform and change (Madaus, 1985, 1988). Policymakers began to use this power over the curriculum more deliberately as minimum competency tests were adopted in 36 states (Rothman, 1995).

Testing continued to increase into the 1980s. The reform movement of this time worked to change instruction by imposing tests. It was the specific intention of reformers to modify instruction by mandating tests (Shepard & Dougherty, 1991). In the early 1980s, state departments of education began to collect test data in a systematic fashion to describe the status of education and to show equality of educational opportunity (Madaus, 1988). *A Nation At Risk* (National Commission on Excellence in Education, 1983) recommended "more rigorous and measurable standards and higher expectations for student performance" (p. 27) and proposed tests to measure these standards and expectations. Standardized tests were recommended to be administered at major transition points in education. The purposes of these tests were to certify or credential student competence to identify the need for remedial interventions, and to identify the opportunity for advance work. The testing was recommended as part of a national system of state and local standardized tests (Madaus, 1988, Rothman, 1995).

Today, classroom standardized test results are routinely used as information sources about the status of education and as a way to certify individual performance in the system (Airasian, 1987; Madaus, 1985). Standardized test data are often high stakes as they are used as the main indicator in monitoring the successes or failures of the schools (Airasian, 1987). Newspapers often rank school districts by test scores as a public service. Parents are expected to reward schools that have high test scores and put pressure to improve test scores on schools that perform at a lower level (Rothman, 1995). Test scores are even used by some school district personnel to determine merit pay and to make other personnel decisions. Some real estate agents have used school test scores to rate the quality of neighborhoods (Darling-Hammond & Wise, 1985; Haladyna, Nolen, & Haas, 1991; Paris, Lawton, Turner, & Roth, 1991; Rothman, 1995; Shepard, 1989; Smith, 1991a; Smith & Rottenberg, 1991).

Standardized achievement tests scores are increasingly being used for many different purposes, appropriate and inappropriate, by many different groups. Haladyna, Nolen, and Haas (1991) surveyed testing practices related to standardized testing and found 29 uses of standardized test information at all levels of schooling. Typical policy-oriented uses include assessing educational equity, providing evidence of effectiveness of schools and programs, allocating compensatory funds, evaluating teacher effectiveness, accrediting school districts, placing students in remediated settings, and certifying successful completion of high school or a given grade of elementary school (Airasian & Madaus, 1983). As of 1990, 46 states carried out mandated testing programs (U.S. Congress, OTA, 1992), 17 states link grade promotion or high school graduation (or both) directly to a test (Rothman, 1995), and at least 7 states have implemented programs to reward schools that demonstrate high levels of student performance (Rothman, 1995). Test results have also been used to argue for and against certain school aid or school reforms (Madaus, 1985). Some states have used the threat of taking over districts that perform poorly on tests as a way to motivate schools to improve test scores (Rothman, 1995).

TESTING PRACTICES

The development and use of a national assessment is still being discussed as a national voluntary eighth-grade test looms on the horizon. In the *Goals 2000* document, published by the U.S. Department of Education, one of the major stipulated goals for education is as follows:

> By the year 2000, all students will leave grades 4, 8, and 12 having demonstrated competency over challenging subject matter including English, mathematics, science, foreign languages, civics and government, economics, arts, history, and geography, and every school in America will ensure that all students learn to use their minds well, so they may be prepared for responsible citizenship, further learning, and productive employment in our Nation's modern economy. (U.S. Department of Education, 1995, p. 42)

To measure progress toward this goal, the creators of *Goals 2000* anticipated using the National Assessment of Education Progress (NAEP) exam. They also hoped to expand the NAEP exam in order to use results to rank states, districts, and perhaps even schools (Darling-Hammond, 1990), thereby making the NAEP exam a high stakes test.

In 1989, the National Commission on Testing and Public Policy estimated that 41 million students take 127 million tests a year. This is more than three tests a year for each student (Rothman, 1995). Others estimated the schools administered from 30 million to over 127 million tests each year (U.S. GAO, 1993). Of tests given to students in 1990–1991, 81% were achievement tests. These tests mainly assessed school achievement in math, reading, grammar, science, and history or social science (U.S. GAO, 1993). Also, 71% of the tests were norm referenced, and 71% of the tests were multiple choice format (U.S. GAO, 1993).

The National Commission on Testing and Public Policy estimated that the equivalent of 20 million school days are spent each year by children just taking tests and speculated from 10 to 20 times that many days are spent in preparation for the tests (Neill & Medina, 1989). In 1990–1991 the General Accounting Office (U.S. GAO, 1993) of the U.S. government studied the extent of school time dedicated to testing. Survey data indicated that, on the average, students spend less than 4 hours each year taking systemwide tests. However, one district did not give a systemwide test and six districts in the sample administered 10 or more systemwide tests. At the high end of testing, U.S. GAO (1993) found several districts that administered over 27 hours of systemwide tests in 1990–1991. It was also found that the national average of test preparation time was less than 7 hours a year (U.S. GAO, 1993). However, several districts claimed over 100 hours to prepare students for systemwide tests. Districts that devoted more time to testing and test preparation were those that were experienced in testing, that had a relatively high level of poverty, that administered high stakes tests, and that were located in the northeastern or southern states (U.S. GAO, 1993).

International comparisons of the number of systemwide tests encountered by students in their elementary and secondary career place the United States below the international average. U.S. students take significantly fewer systemwide tests, with a significantly lower number of tests being mandated or considered high stakes (Phelps, 1996; U.S. GAO, 1993). Internationally, students in some countries are taking up to 170 systemwide tests in their elementary and secondary education career, all of which are mandated and considered to be high stakes. U.S. students take an average of 40.8 systemwide tests, 25.2 of which are mandated and 10.8 of which can be considered high stakes (Phelps, 1996; U.S. GAO, 1993).

HIGH STAKES TESTING

In theory, educational tests are an unobtrusive method of estimating students' knowledge. Depending on the circumstances related to the test and test results, this can be true. In some situations, students take standardized exams and the scores are used appropriately. However, many educators, thinking of their own experiences in classrooms as students or as teachers, assert that tests influence students and teachers when they perceive that important consequences are connected to test results (U.S. Congress, OTA, 1992).

In an attempt to hold schools, teachers, and administrators accountable for student performance, some states (Minnesota) and school districts (Chicago) have implemented testing programs. These testing programs usually have consequences, real or perceived, assigned to the results (Rothman, 1995). External tests used in this fashion and other situations are considered to be high stakes tests. High stakes tests are "those whose results are seen rightly or wrongly—by students, teachers, administrators, parents or the public as being used to make important decisions that immediately and directly affect them" (Madaus, 1988, p. 87). Tests can become high stakes when policymakers mandate that the results of the tests be used automatically to make decisions on student graduation or promotion, the evaluation of teachers, schools or administrators, or the allocation of resources (Madaus, 1988). It is believed that high stakes tests will give students and schools an incentive to keep their "eyes on the prize" and work to improve student performance (Rothman, 1995). Teachers have reported extensive use of test results for external purposes such as comparing districts, ranking schools in the newspaper, and comparing schools (Shepard & Dougherty, 1991).

Not all high stakes tests are externally mandated. High stakes tests can be internally mandated. Any test can be viewed as high stakes if students, teachers, or administrators believe the results of an examination are important. High stakes effects are likely present based largely on what individuals perceive to be the case. The ACT and SAT college entrance tests are high stakes for college bound students, but for others they may have little or no impact. When people believe something to be true, their actions are guided by the importance perceived to be associated with it (Madaus, 1988; Meisels, 1989).

The concept of high stakes tests is a relative one. The stakes can vary depending on the context in which testing takes place. A high school graduation test is considered a high stakes test. Most students want to graduate from high school and most teachers will do what they can to help students achieve at the necessary level to get a diploma. However, if the content on the test is at a low level, and if the standard for passing the test is very low, the impact of the test on instruction will not be great for most students. Stakes, standards, and content work together to influence or not influence the curriculum and instruction presented to students (Airasian, 1988). The higher the perceived stakes on a test, the more attention in the curriculum it receives (Shepard, 1991).

Many tests have evolved to high stakes due to the considerable attention to test results in the press or elsewhere (L. B. Resnick & D. P. Resnick, 1989). The publicizing of test results is the most common method by which districts have placed high stakes on test results (Rothman, 1995; Shepard, 1990). Forty states have schools or districts ranked by achievement in the media (Shepard, 1990). Teachers have reported that the publication of test scores often produced feelings of shame, embarrassment, guilt, and anger and created the conditions for teachers to do what was necessary to avoid such feelings in the future (Smith, 1991a, 1991b, Smith & Rottenberg, 1991). Any educational assessment that receives publicity will stimulate educators to assure that their students perform well on that assessment (L. B. Resnick & D. P. Resnick, 1989).

TEACHING TO THE TEST

The focus on material that the high stakes test covers has resulted in a narrowing of the curriculum and a reduction of teachers' ability to adapt, create, or diverge from that curriculum. In other words, high stakes testing environments lead teachers to teach to the test. Teaching to the test can narrow the curriculum to only things measured by the test (Madaus, 1988). Tests do not cover the full range of important instructional objectives, but they can control what is taught (Worthen & Spandel, 1991). They can influence education in terms of curriculum materials and classroom instruction affecting what is taught, how it is taught, the rate and sequence of teaching, the degree and depth of teaching, and attitudes about teaching (Alderson & Wall, 1993). Teaching to the test is not good or bad in the abstract. Few would disagree that the content of the instruction and the content of the test should be related to the educational objectives (Mehrens & Kaminski, 1989). However, if the content of the test changes the content of instruction in a negative way, teaching the test can be viewed as educationally unsound. Some researchers view teaching to the test as cheating (Cohen & Hyman, 1991; Mehrens & Kaminski, 1989). If students practice the tasks on a test, then the test scores become meaningless.

Standardized tests were developed to obtain valid and reliable information about the whole domain of knowledge, not just the sample of tasks that appear on the test (U.S. Congress, OTA, 1992). Standardized achievement tests, which are high stakes tests in many situations, attempt to sample what is most typically taught to students taking the test (Worthen & Spandel, 1991). Often the content of standardized achievement tests is mismatched with the content emphasized in a school's curriculum and classrooms. When there are stakes associated with the test, many schools have aligned their curriculum to the high stakes test. This alignment occurs "so students do not spend hours studying materials on which they will never be tested—regardless of the value of those materials or the benefits that students might derive from studying them" (Neill & Medina, 1989, p. 694).

In a survey of teachers, superintendents, testing coordinators, and principals, a considerable majority reported that their district curriculum had changed to match the skills measured by the test. Over 70% reported that some curriculum changes went as far as to match curricula to particular test questions. Over three fourths of the respondents perceived that teachers taught some information only because it is included on the standardized test (Hall & Kleine, 1992). Testing directors in high stakes states nearly unanimously agree that teachers spend more time teaching specific objectives on the tests than they would if the tests were not required (Shepard, 1990).

High stakes tests tend to encourage disproportionate attention to material that is covered in the tests, thereby excluding many other worthwhile educational objectives and experiences (Madaus, 1988, 1991; Suarez & Gottovi, 1992). High stakes tests tend to inhibit the development of the curricular variety that may be necessary to serve local and individual needs (Madaus, 1991). Basic skills in math and reading are viewed as more important than the teaching of nontested subjects (social studies, science, fine arts), reading of books, discussions of ideas, problem solving, writing, creative activities, and projects requiring research and critical thinking (Darling-Hammond, 1990). Teachers claim to put most emphasis on the basic skills (Herman & Golan, 1990, 1993) and tended to slight topics within math and reading that the test does not cover (Smith 1991a, 1991b; Smith & Rottenberg, 1991). Reading instruction, for instance, sometimes entails reading short passages and recognizing one correct answer rather than students inventing their own questions and possible answers. In writing, students practice finding mistakes rather than creating their own writing (Darling-Hammond, 1990; Shepard, 1991). Mathematics instruction would entail simple one step problems that focus on basic facts rather than on problems that involve mathematical thinking and reasoning.

Most high stakes tests are a multiple choice format (U.S. GAO, 1993), a factor that might in itself affect instruction by the limiting thinking and skills that they can assess. "Instruction is becoming more and more a matter of getting kids ready for multiple choice tests" (Madaus, as quoted in Brandt, 1989). Teachers devote substantial amounts of class time to the types of thinking and learning assessed by the tests (Airasian, 1988; Madaus, 1988). Among the problems, the multiple choice format does not measure a student's ability to organize relevant information and present a coherent argument (Shepard, 1989). Teachers have reported less concern for higher order thinking skills (Herman & Golan, 1990, 1993). Therefore, instruction in higher level thinking and learning skills is sometimes lost or de-emphasized because most standardized tests assess lower level thinking skills (Cohen & Hyman, 1991; Suarez & Gottovi, 1992). Teachers often overemphasize rote memorization and drill and practice teaching methods that lead to cramming by students (Madaus, 1991; Shepard, 1989). Classroom instruction becomes dominated by tasks that resemble the test, often resulting in less than enlightened pedagogy (Shepard, 1991). For example, in one school where test scores fell just short of one year's growth in language, the principal created a daily review program that required pupils to answer multiple choice questions on grammar, usage, punctuation, and capitalization. The teaching methods that teachers used were narrowed and the act of teaching was in some ways deskilled. Over time and with increased testing stakes, teaching became more testlike (Smith, 1991a, 1991b; Smith & Rottenberg, 1991).

By narrowing the instructional purview of curriculum to testable items, a clear constraint is placed on the creativity and flexibility of teachers, with the eventual effect of stunting the professional judgment of educators (Meisels, 1989). Teachers, in fact, often suffer conflicts between the mandate to teach to the test and the desire to be better attuned to children's learning needs (Shepard, 1991). When discussing high stakes standardized testing, teachers reported they were pressured to "teach the test" (Darling-Hammond & Wise, 1985) and raise test scores (Shepard & Dougherty, 1991). They gave specific examples, such as being asked to write curriculum materials similar to the test to give their students practice, and giving up on essay tests so that classroom experiences would more closely parallel standardized tests. Teachers view standardized tests as a means for ensuring that a testable body of knowledge was covered in the curriculum.

Teachers have reported that in planning for instruction they looked at prior tests to make sure the curriculum included all or most of the test content and test objectives. They reported that to some extent they adjusted their instructional plans based on test performance of the class taught the previous year and even more so on the most recent test performance of their current class. They also adjusted the sequence of their curriculum based on what was included in the test (Herman & Golan, 1990, 1993).

TEST PREPARATION

In addition to the effect of testing on the character of normal instruction, testing also distorts instruction because of the vast amount of time given to test preparation in place of normal instruction. In general, teachers reported spending from 1 to 4 weeks of class time on test preparation activities, which included having students complete worksheets that reviewed expected test content, having students practice item formats expected on the test, and instructing students in test-taking strategies (Herman & Golan, 1990, 1993). Teaching to the test has become important enough in this country for a commercial industry to develop for student preparation techniques for high stakes testing (Madaus, 1988). In one study, over 40% of teachers in a high stakes district claimed to use these materials (Nolen, Haladyna, & Haas, 1992). Many publishers offer test preparation programs to increase students' level of achievement by teaching them how to follow directions, how to use time wisely, and how to review skills that will be on the test (Mehrens & Kaminski, 1989). Textbooks have also realized the focus on test preparation and market their books based on standardized test alignment. In the front of most textbooks there are charts and tables summarizing the textbook as it relates to various standardized tests.

Some teachers emphasize subject matter that is included on the standardized test and some change their teaching methods to prepare students for the test (Edelman, 1981). Teachers report that testing programs reduced the time available for instruction. Three to 4 weeks of the school year were "lost" to test preparation, testing, and test recovery (Smith 1991a, 1991b; and Smith & Rottenberg, 1991). Half of the teachers in one study spent 4 or more weeks giving students worksheets to review content expected to be on the test and giving students practice with the kinds of item formats that were on the test (Shepard & Dougherty, 1991). Teaching the test has led to substantial amounts of class time devoted to test-taking skills (Suarez & Gottovi, 1992). The U.S. General Accounting Office (1993) found, on the average, high stakes testing environments spent 43% more time in test-related activities, mostly test preparation activities.

In a study by Fish (1988), it was found that teachers in one high stakes district devoted substantial time to preparing students for the high stakes test. Ninety-seven percent of the teachers in the study prepared their students all year, 86% aligned the content of the tests with the regular curriculum, and 94% practiced the content of the tests using the test format. Another study revealed that two thirds of teachers in a representative sample from a high stakes state report they always or usually teach or review topics covered on the test prior to test week (Nolen et al., 1992). The site administrators for these teachers claimed that 70% of the teachers at their site taught or reviewed topics covered on the test prior to test week (Nolen et al., 1992).

TEST RESULTS

High stakes test results are often viewed by parents and students as the main objectives of schooling (Madaus, 1988, 1991). Political pressures and media attention given to high stakes test results can lead to misuses of norms that can artificially inflate scores. The most publicized incident of this sort was presented by Cannell and labeled as the Lake Wobegon effect (Shepard, 1991). Cannell (1988) found that all 50 states claimed their elementary standardized test results were above the national average. In order to show themselves as above average, schools picked a set of norms that allowed this to be shown.

High stakes test results for individual students are often used to serve a variety of purposes for which they may not have been designed (Madaus, 1991). High stakes standardized test results have been used in the awarding of scholarships, the diagnosis and classification of students, and in teacher and school evaluation (Madaus, 1991). These misuses of test results have harmful side effects in schools. They can limit the programs that students can enter and dictate where students are placed with the effect of increasing the existing inequities in educational services, particularly for minority or low income students (Medina & Neill, 1990; Neill & Medina, 1989).

LOW STAKES TESTING

The research literature clearly shows the effects of high stakes testing in the curriculum. However, not all U.S. schools can be considered high stakes testing environments. Low stakes testing is not addressed as often as high stakes, but is used to denote environments that lack the pressures of high stakes environments. Madaus (1988) defined low stakes tests in contrast to high stakes tests: "Low stakes tests are those which are perceived as not having important rewards or sanctions tied directly to test performance" (p. 88). Testing can still take place, but the results are not used as the sole source of information to make decisions about students, teachers, or schools. Teachers have the option to disregard test results they feel are inaccurate (Madaus, 1988). Most districts surveyed by the U.S. General Accounting Office (1993) reported that they were low stakes testing environments.

NAEP

The current NAEP exam is considered to be a low stakes test. The NAEP is a congressionally mandated exam designed to study longitudinal achievement in the United States. The exam is given to a representative sample of students from the school population in the 4th, 8th, and 12th grades that are selected through a scientifically designed stratified random sampling procedure (Educational Testing Service [ETS], 1994). Each student in the sample only completes a sample of the test items. Scores are not reported by individual, school, district, or state achievement level. There are no sanctions or rewards currently attached to the NAEP exam.

In addition to gathering data about school achievement, NAEP also surveys teachers and students about the school experience. The 1992 NAEP data from teacher surveys reported that 90% of fourth-grade teachers put heavy emphasis on numbers and operations in mathematics. Students and teachers reported that since 1990 there has been an increase in daily problem solving from textbooks (ETS, 1994). However, textbook problem solving usually does not resemble the types of problems described in the National Council of Teachers of Mathematics (NCTM, 1989) *Curriculum and Evaluation Standards for School Mathematics* as problem solving (Romberg, Wilson, Khaketta, & Chavarria, 1989). Students and teachers reported very little change in the frequency with which students were asked to engage in extended problem-solving activities that involved mathematical reasoning and communication (ETS, 1994).

The NAEP results in mathematics reflect student achievement in the nation. Based on the recommendations in the *Standards* and other reform recommendations by mathematics groups, the NAEP recently implemented changes in its mathematics test given to 4th-, 8th-, and 12th-graders. In part, NAEP added two new sections to the mathematics section of the exam. The new NAEP exam now includes questions and tasks that ask students to construct their own responses. These student constructed response tasks are of two types. The first type, regular constructed response questions, require only a short constructed answer. The second type, extended constructed response tasks, requires students to demonstrate, in writing, their mathematical reasoning and problem solving abilities by solving problems requiring a greater depth of understanding, and then explaining, at some length, specific features of their solutions (ETS, 1994).

In 1992, the NAEP mathematics assessment was at a lower level of performance on both regular and extended constructed response questions among all three age groups than on the multiple choice items. On the other hand, average student performance on the traditional multiple choice format increased for all age groups, across gender and racial lines. Because this was the first use of the constructed response questions, there were no previous data against which comparisons could be made. The Office of Educational Research and Improvement (OERI) summarized the following from the new NAEP data gathered:

> Approximately one-third to two-thirds of the students provided incorrect responses to these extended [response] questions, indicating little evidence of understanding the mathematics concepts involved or even the questions being asked.... Substantial percentages of students, sometimes as many as one-fifth, simply left their papers blank.... Most students who did seem to understand the problems had difficulty explaining their work. (ETS, 1994, p. 9)

The NAEP results show a gain in basic math skills but discouraging results in higher order thinking skills. The negative results have been partly attributed to the influence of standardized testing on teaching and learning (Shepard & Dougherty, 1991). The current achievement level in multiple choice items versus extended response items raises concern about mathematics teaching in the nation's schools. Studies of the mathematics classroom have revealed a considerable homogeneity in mathematics instruction (Stodolsky, 1988). Mathematics instruction can be characterized as focusing on algorithmic learning. Mathematics programs emphasize number operations through individual seatwork and recitation. There is typically little attention to group work, discussion, or problem solving (Stodolsky, 1988).

The NAEP results and studies of mathematics classrooms are of concern to mathematics educators as they are disturbing to the vision of mathematics instruction outline in the *Standards*. The data seem to reflect the characteristics of high stakes environments even when data were collected from both high and low stakes environments. If mathematics teaching has been found to be homogeneous, then high and low stakes environments are possibly presenting similar mathematics instruction. With the reform of mathematics teaching presented in the *Standards,* why would low stakes environments have similar instruction as high stakes environments when they lack high stakes pressures? Could this mean there are influences at work in low stakes environments that influence instruction to be similar to high stakes environments? Low stakes, in fact, might be a misconception because of the unintended influences on mathematics instruction that might be at work in low stakes environments.

A Closer Look at Low Stakes Mathematics Instruction

A concentrated look at fourth-grade mathematics curriculum and instruction in three low stakes elementary schools revealed a mathematics curriculum and teacher instruction that was very similar to what would be expected in a high stakes environment. Low stakes mathematics instruction was dominated by instructional formats that centered around teacher talk and independent student work. Although such interactions could be based on high quality instructional principles that encourage the application of skills, inquiry learning, hypothesis testing, and the general articulation of ideas, the character of the classroom discussion was dominated by instructional techniques based on a continuous stream of lower cognitive level, recalling knowledge or simple ideas, one correct answer questions. Most often questions asked in the classroom were procedural in nature. Teachers would show students the steps to follow to find the correct answer to a computational problem and would then work through similar problems with the students. The low stakes environments support this, because no school spent large amounts of time on instructional formats that encouraged the type of thinking and learning (project work, use of technology, cooperative learning) emphasized in the *Standards* (NCTM, 1989).

Influences on the low stakes environment lead the curriculum and instruction to be similar to teaching to the test found in the high stakes environments (Payne, 1997). The instructional behaviors displayed by the teachers in the low stakes testing environments did not differ much from the instructional behaviors that might be expected in high stakes testing environments described earlier. Mathematics instruction consisted of a relatively monolithic method of recitation and seatwork.

The predominate instructional formats found in the low stakes testing environments studied were seatwork, guided seatwork, and recitation. Again, such engagement did not include large amounts of group work, discussion, problem solving, or connections between ideas and content, but were devoted to instruction that focused on lower level question–answer sessions between the students and the teacher. The teacher was seen as the sole authority in mathematics, the person who knew all the answers and posed the problems. The students job was to work many similar problems and find correct answers to these problems.

The mathematics curriculum in all schools was based on skill-drill and generally failed to promote educational experiences underscored by the NCTM *Standards*. Students, for instance, were rarely asked to explain their thinking, justify their answer, or give a lengthy response. Students seldom, if ever, were asked to formulate a problem for themselves. Generally speaking, the learning was fragmented, narrow, and dedicated to the mastery of isolated skills. Connections between mathematical ideas and concepts were not emphasized. Students spent very little time in activities that engaged higher levels of thinking, mathematical reasoning, or problem solving. Teachers devoted a substantial amount of class time to the type of thinking and learning that might traditionally be labeled as simple knowledge recall, skill acquisition, and basic facts.

The mathematics curriculum was dominated by basic computational skills. The basic mathematics content taught at the three schools was very similar. Although the teachers, district curriculum guides, and textbooks were different, the sequence of topics taught was very similar. All three schools began the year with place value or addition and subtraction of whole numbers and continued with a curriculum primarily focused on multiplication and division.

The curriculum materials presented to students were dominated by rote memorization and repetitive practice seatwork assignments. Typical seatwork assignments were mathematics worksheets from the supporting textbook materials or a series of problems from the textbook. The textbook encouraged the mathematical skills to be taught in an isolated manner. The chapters and objectives within the textbooks focused on one or two mathematical ideas or skills. There were few, if any, connections made between mathematical ideas. The textbook did offer suggestions for making connections to real-life situations, but these were largely ignored by the teachers. Teachers never asked students to explain, orally or in writing, their thinking or mathematical reasoning. The only open question used by the teachers was, "Do you have any questions about this?" Little creativity was observed in mathematics instruction or curriculum materials used. Teachers followed the same basic lesson plan through most mathematics instruction. Teachers described their mathematics teaching style by describing their typical lesson in mathematics. There was little variation in the actual instructional device or model used to guide instruction. The teachers, in fact, were unsure of how else to present lessons besides what the textbook had suggested they do or what they had done in the past.

Test preparation, beyond the teaching of test taking skills, for the low stakes test occurred at only one school site. The school site with the highest number of lower income students. The teachers at the other schools did not use specific materials or spend instructional time in standardized test preparation activities beyond an explanation of the purposes of the tests and teaching test taking skills. However, the mathematics textbook publishers advertised their materials as being aligned with the most popular standardized tests, including the low stakes test to be administered. Of course, the textbook should cover material that will be tested, but in this case, there was an exclusive reliance on only selected parts of the textbook for instruction.

The classroom assessment materials were taken from the textbook support materials or were developed based on those materials. These tests were sometimes given to students in a multiple choice format, but more importantly the tests were designed by the textbook publisher to be specifically aligned with standardized tests. In some cases, the textbook claimed there were item-by-item associations between the textbook assessment materials and standardized tests.

Finally, the low stakes testing environments examined were similar to high stakes environments described in the literature in the way that parents viewed test scores. Teachers at the three schools discussed the use of results in communicating with parents. Parents, according to the teachers, were eager to receive the results and focused on the percentile rank of their child. In high stakes situations, test results are often viewed as the main objective of schooling. In a low stakes environment, the test results deemphasize career or curriculum consequences, and stress the diagnostic power of the tests. To the parents, however, the tests always seem to have "high stakes" consequences, and if parents are moved by the scores, teachers and principals will not be able to ignore the influence. Parents in this study, according to the teachers, put a lot of emphasis on the standardized test scores. They were seen as an important indicator of how their child was achieving in school. Teachers were aware of parents' focus on the test results. Parents and teachers often relied on these scores as a single measure of what students knew or as a verification of report card grades.

INFLUENCES ON LOW STAKES INSTRUCTION

Teachers in the low stakes testing environments were influenced by many factors. In reflecting on their teaching, they referred to their own teachers, university professors, authors of curriculum materials, past experiences, traditions in the school, and the mathematics textbook. Classroom observations confirmed the mathematics textbook as the largest influence on mathematics instruction across the three schools in this study. The 1992 and 1994 NAEP data support this as they revealed that the mathematics classroom instruction still relies on lecture and textbooks (Lindquist, 1997).

Another influence on low stakes mathematics instruction was the tradition of how mathematics had been taught in years past at each of the schools. Two teachers in this study had completed their student teaching in the schools in which they were now employed. They had been trained and had mathematics teaching modeled for them by teachers who had been at the school site for many years. Some teachers, especially the less experienced ones, also discussed the need to keep in line with the form of practice used by the other teachers.

A first-year teacher in the study felt very compelled to teach as the teachers around her did. She selected her mathematics content by working with and following the other fourth-grade teachers. In an effort to help the new teacher through her first year of teaching, the other teachers shared their materials, ideas, and past experiences. The new teacher spoke of feeling trapped in her mathematics teaching. She did not feel she was able to "go against what the other teachers were doing in mathematics." A teacher at another school site completed her student teaching with the other fourth-grade teacher at the school many years ago. The newer teacher felt her mathematics teaching was greatly influenced by the time she spent in her colleague's classroom student teaching. As a result, she felt their mathematics classrooms were very similar.

TEXTBOOK DRIVEN CURRICULUM

The teachers in this low stakes environment used their mathematics textbook for teaching suggestions, lesson materials, assignments, and assessment materials. The teachers used the textbook almost exclusively in their mathematics teaching. In the lesson plans reviewed, the textbook and publisher's support materials were included in 84% of the planned mathematics lessons. The classroom observations showed the textbook as the primary source for the mathematics curriculum. The textbook was used in 90% of the lessons observed. Other influences on instruction were modest in comparison to the role of the textbook. NAEP data shows that more than three fourths of the students in fourth grade use textbooks daily (Lindquist, 1997).

As early as 1913, Cubberly noted the important role that textbooks played in instruction. Studies of teaching have continued to show the dominance of the textbook in the classroom (see Bagely, 1931; Barton & Wilder, 1966; Cahen, Filby, McCutcheon, & Kyle, 1983; Educational Products Information Exchange, 1977; Gross, 1952; Lindquist, 1997; Turner, 1988; Woodward & Elliott, 1990a, 1990b, 1990c). Goodlad (1984) found

> mathematics teachers, somewhat more than other teachers (except foreign language teachers), generally reported that the textbooks recommended by states and districts were of relatively high influence. Our data on instructional materials strongly support the generalization that the mathematics curriculum was dominated by textbooks in the classrooms we studied. (p. 208)

Kuhs and Freeman (1979) argued that the textbook content potentially establishes the content of instruction. Similarly, Dreeben (1985) argued that mathematics instruction was based on the curricular materials teachers used. Researchers have concluded that textbooks dictate the content addressed in the classroom (Barr, 1988; Barr & Dreeben, 1983; Stake & Easley, 1978; Westbury, 1990; Woodward & Elliott, 1990a). In a qualitative study of mathematics instruction, Barr (1988) found that seven of nine fourth-grade teachers used their textbooks by moving lesson by lesson through the book. Other studies (Sosniak & Stodolsky, 1993) have shown differing levels of textbook use between teachers.

The teachers in this study used the textbook to determine the majority of the mathematics content they would teach. When describing the mathematical ideas to be taught, all the teachers in this study referred to textbook chapters they would or would not include. The majority of the curricular materials in the low stakes testing environment came from the textbook or its supporting materials. Teachers in all the schools regularly skipped pages in their textbooks that asked students to explain what they had learned, to work in teams or cooperative groups, to collect and analyze their own data, and to use problem-solving strategies. This raises an interesting question, because even where more principled teaching might be encouraged in the textbook, it tended to be ignored. The textbooks then, seem to suit an established style or tradition of teaching. When the textbook departs from this style or tradition, the pages are generally skipped or ignored. Interestingly, the pages and teaching suggestions skipped by the teachers in this study were often highlighted as being compatible with the *Standards*.

The Textbook, The *Standards*, and Standardized Tests

Textbook publishers often claim to review recent research to be aware of the teaching needs facing their "customers" throughout the nation (Squire & Morgan, 1990). This information is used in the development of materials in an effort to please all schools and sell more books in a national market (Woodward & Elliott, 1990a). Some research evidence, however, indicates that textbooks are widely used, yet most are poorly written and poorly conceived and most are concerned about lower order facts and skills rather than higher cognitive activities (Woodward & Elliott, 1990a).

All the schools examined administered the 1992 edition of the Iowa Test of Basic Skills (ITBS). The mathematics test has three sections: Math Concepts and Estimation, Math Problem Solving and Data Interpretation, and Math Computation. The Math Computation section is optional, but is used in the three schools in this study. The NCTM *Curriculum and Evaluation Standards for School Mathematics* were published in 1989 and were influential in the revisions made to the 1992 edition of the ITBS. Changes in the ITBS include the use of calculators, the inclusion of a subtest of estimation, a larger focus on problem solving or applying problem-solving strategies, the focus on data interpretation, and allowing the Math Computation section to be optional (Riverside Publishing, 1993).

In studies of earlier mathematics textbook editions and earlier editions of standardized tests (Callahan & Alford, 1986; Freeman, et al., 1983; Mehrens & Phillips, 1986), several researchers found that "textbooks emphasized computation far more than did any test" (Callahan & Alford, 1986, p. 25). This may be the case even more so today, especially because the Math Computation test has become optional. Mathematics textbooks in the aforementioned studies were found to be aligned with the standardized tests between 20% and 97% of the time. The degree of alignment between mathematics textbooks and standardized tests was affected by how many problems were viewed as giving students a reasonable opportunity to learn, by how broadly topics were defined, and by whether the content of textbooks from earlier grades was included (Callahan & Alford, 1986). Curriculum alignment is a term often heard and used, but seldom defined. As the previous studies indicate, the definition of curriculum alignment affects the degree to which tests and textbooks are considered to be aligned.

The mathematics textbooks used in this study claimed to be aligned with the most popular standardized tests (including the test given in all the schools studied). However, the publication dates on the textbooks were 1991, 1993, and 1994. The ITBS given in the schools studied was published in 1992. The 1991 textbook and most likely the 1993 textbook were aligned, according to the publisher, with a previous edition of the ITBS. The publisher did not define what was meant by alignment, but the meaning is pretty clear. The textbook has been expressly designed to cover the ideas, facts, skills (and perhaps items) on the ITBS and other tests. Some degree of curriculum alignment arguably would exist between the various components of the curriculum (objectives, materials, instructional experiences, and tests). At some level, the curriculum needs to be coordinated in order to secure a coherent and unified school experience. The question is what fundamentally becomes the source of alignment? Does it start with the objective and purposes, as it arguably should, or does it start with the standardized test?

The 1994 textbook included chapter objectives with standardized test correlations. This edition of the textbook included what is on the ITBS, but other objectives as well. An informal comparison of the 1994 textbook and the 1992 ITBS revealed that the ITBS had similar questions as the textbook on the "correlated" objectives. However, the textbook also emphasized computation far more than the standardized test and covered more objectives than the ITBS, as the book worked to be correlated with five different standardized tests and to be all things to all people in a national textbook market. Thus, the publishers' claim to alignment is not precisely accurate. The text is not aligned to the ITBS as much as it simply covers testable material used on the ITBS. This being the case, the test may not turn out to be the driving force behind textbook driven instruction after all.

The textbooks used by the teachers in this study also claimed to support the *Standards*. Mathematics textbooks adopted by the districts in this study offered teaching suggestions and activities that were in support of the *Standards*. The margins of the teacher's editions had suggestions for using manipulatives, communication, critical thinking, math reasoning, problem solving, math connections, subject integration, group work, and more. However, these were largely ignored by the classroom teachers. Teachers focused on answering the computational and story problems in the textbook.

The mathematics textbooks used by the teachers in this study were more recently published than the mathematics textbooks used in past studies of textbook and test alignment. Changes that occur in textbooks have historically been more evolutionary than revolutionary, as they respond over time to a wide range of emerging influences (Elliott, 1990). This was apparent when examining the two editions of *Addison-Wesley Mathematics* (1991, 1993). An examination of textbook chapters indicates that the only changes made between the 1991 and 1993 editions were in photographs and graphics. All the student problems, notes to teachers, and support materials were identical. If textbooks change slowly while major changes are occurring to standardized tests (such as the ITBS), then the textbooks are possibly more aligned to the previous standardized tests than the tests currently used. The important issues are the content selected from these textbooks to be taught in the mathematics curriculum and the way in which they are taught.

Teachers in this study selected mathematics curriculum materials and instructional techniques that reflected teaching to the test as defined in the high stakes literature. The bulk of the literature on the high stakes testing environment and teaching to the test was created prior to the publication of the *Standards* and the revised edition of the ITBS.

INSTRUCTIONAL TRADITIONS IN THE CURRICULUM

Although the mathematics textbook drives the mathematics curriculum, it might not be the only reason teachers in low stakes environments tend to show little instructional variance. Mathematics instruction in the schools in this study was also influenced by what might be called tradition, that is, by the actual content and instructional techniques that had traditionally been taught in mathematics at the school site. The traditional mathematics curriculum of skill-drill computation influenced teachers to select what they would teach from the mathematics textbook. Stake and Easley (1978) found the mathematics curriculum to deviate little from the traditional curriculum. Traditional mathematics teaching is not aligned with the *Standards*. This is reflected in the teachers choice to ignore or skip over sections of the mathematics textbook based on the *Standards*.

Teachers at each school were encouraged to teach in similar manners. Teachers expressed the importance of offering similar experiences for all students at the same grade level. Students would be regrouped in the next grade and needed, according to their teacher, to have similar experiences and a common knowledge base. Teachers at each site would meet and discuss what mathematics content would be taught and how it would be taught. The more experienced teachers at the school site seem to lead the mathematics teaching traditions. The less experienced teachers referred to the more experienced teachers as being an influence on their instruction. Informal interactions between the two teachers revealed the more experienced teacher as the curriculum and instructional leader of the two, offering teaching suggestions, materials, and ideas. By teaching in a similar fashion, teachers were able to share the work of preparing lessons. Teachers would have classroom assistants or volunteers duplicate copies of worksheets for all the students in the fourth grade.

Teachers' beliefs about mathematics and mathematics teaching may be limiting instructional variance because, as previous studies have shown, teachers have inappropriate beliefs about these areas (Frank, 1988, 1990; Garofalo, 1989; Schoenfeld, 1985, 1992; Spangler, 1992; Zollman, 1992). If teachers believe mathematics to be computation and only computation, then instructional variance is not going to exist. Beliefs have been found to develop slowly over long periods of time. Prior to becoming teachers, teachers had spent more than 13 years in classrooms as students. These experiences influenced their beliefs about what mathematics is (Thompson, 1985). Teachers come into classrooms remembering what their own mathematics instruction entailed, and tend to teach as they were taught (Pajares, 1993). This causes traditions in mathematics instruction to continue.

The fact of the matter is that the 1989 publication of National Council of Teachers of Mathematics' *Curriculum and Evaluation Standards* has had little effect on mathematics instruction in these low stakes testing environments, although teacher awareness and familiarity with the *Standards* varied among the schools studied. When asked, teachers said they were familiar with the *Standards*, but they could not explain or give examples of any of the goals or standards. Of the teachers in the TIMSS, 42% reported being very aware of the current ideas about the teaching and learning of mathematics and 53% reported being somewhat aware. However, only 33% mentioned the NCTM *Standards* by name (Stigler, 1995). This is better than in 1993, when only 18% of teachers in grades 1–4 were "well aware" of the NCTM Standards documents (Weiss, 1994).

Teachers prepare students for what they believe to be important. If something is important it will be assessed (Grouws & Meier, 1992), but there is evidence to also show that if something is assessed it will be important. Although there was no palpable pressure to teach to the test, teachers and administrators nevertheless wanted their students to do their best on the standardized tests. These tests were seen as important because of the information they produced about a student's achievement. Teachers stressed to students the importance of doing their best in order to find out what they know. They stressed that the information would be used to help them as teachers, to decide what to teach for the remainder of the year.

CONCLUSIONS

Schools and school researchers need to closely examine the effects of low stakes and high stakes testing in order to fully appreciate the contrast. The low stakes mathematics classrooms examined, while considered to be low stakes, embraced instructional methods that differed little from what might be expected in a traditionally high stakes testing environment. Influences on the low stakes mathematics curriculum, including the role the textbook plays and the pervasiveness of a skill-driven tradition in mathematics instruction, cause mathematics instruction to take on instructional characteristics similar to those found in the traditional high stakes testing environments. The reasons or influences for the kind of instruction that prevails in low stakes and traditionally high stakes testing environments might be different, but the instruction is nonetheless similar.

Theoretically speaking, in low stakes environments teachers should expect to exercise their intelligence and creativity. The curriculum is more likely to be based on problem solving, mathematical reasoning, communication, connections within mathematics, and vital interdisciplinary connections, the very ideas highlighted in the *Standards* in a low stakes testing environment. The materials and instructional methodologies available to the teachers in this study, however, very much affected these possibilities.

Clearly, this issue transcends the debate between low stakes and high stakes environments. Other important factors are at work. Generally, these factors revolve around a complex curriculum condition that harbors a subtle design for teachers to teach to the test, as described in the literature. The textbook, standing as an authoritative curriculum source for the teacher, and the strength of instructional traditions exerts a pull on the teacher that influences instruction to be similar to what is described in the high stakes literature as teaching to the test. Teachers seem to be teaching to what they believe the test is. The test has undergone some changes, but teachers' instruction does not seem to change. They continue to teach in the same traditional way.

The relation between the textbook and the test is directionally misplaced, as text publishers tout a linkage with the standardized test, they acknowledge the real authority in the curriculum. This helps to create an instructional climate that does not encourage much variance or innovation. But the text does not act alone. Teachers tend to be inclined to use the text in ways that are most suitable for raising scores. With high stakes pressures absent, teachers nevertheless gravitate to instructional approaches that lack any real principled direction and that certainly show little responsiveness to the *Standards*.

SUMMARY

The changed use of test results has established high stakes environments in some public schools. The research clearly shows the effects of high stakes environments on curriculum and instruction. The curriculum has become more narrow due to teaching to the test, instructional formats that resembled the high stakes test, and test preparation. There is limited research on the low stakes environment. Research on mathematics instruction has shown the homogeneity of the mathematics curriculum. The mathematics curriculum has been found to be narrow in content and presentation.

An in-depth look at the low stakes testing environments is lacking. Without looking at the opposing side of high stakes testing, how do educators know that they are different? The possibility exists that instruction in high and low stakes environments is very similar.

Moreover, the selection of the research that is based on classrooms fails to examine specific subject areas. A teacher's philosophy could be very different in different academic areas due to prior experiences, beliefs about the content, as well as other factors. Reading could be taught using a child-centered philosophy, whereas mathematics in the same classroom could be taught using a highly subject-centered philosophy. Each subject area must be examined.

A FINAL THOUGHT

High stakes, low stakes, do stakes really matter? As testing continues to receive media attention, educational leaders need to look beyond the tests and examine what is occurring in the classrooms and why it is happening. Concerns and attention should stay focused on students and what and how they are learning.

REFERENCES

Airasian, P. W. (1987). State mandated testing and educational reform: Context and consequences. *American Journal of Education, 95*(3), 393–412.

Airasian, P. W. (1988). Measurement driven instruction: A closer look. *Educational Measurement: Issues and Practice, 7*(4), 6–11.

Airasian, P. W., & Madaus, G. (1983). Linking testing and instruction: Policy issues. *Journal of Educational Measurement, 20*(2), 103–118.

Alderson, J. C., & Wall, D. (1993). Does washback exist? *Applied Linguistics, 14*(2), 115–129.

Bagely, W. C. (1931). The textbook and methods of instruction. In G. M. Whipple (Ed.), *The textbook in American education, Thirtieth yearbook of the national society for the study of education* (pp. 7–26). Bloomington, IL: Public School Publishing Company.

Barr, R. (1988). Conditions influencing content taught in nine fourth-grade mathematics classrooms. *Elementary School Journal, 88*(4), 387–411.

Barr, R., & Dreeben, R. (1983). *Education policy and the working of schools.* (ERIC Document Reproduction Service No. ED 231908)

Barton, A. H., & Wilder, D. E. (1966). Research and practice in the teaching of reading: A progress report. In M. B. Miles (Ed.), *Innovation in education* (pp. 361–398). New York: Teacher's College Press.

Brandt, R. (1989). On misuse of testing: A conversation with George Madaus. *Educational Leadership, 46*(7), 26–29.

Cahen, L. S., Filby, N., McCutcheon, G., & Kyle, D. W. (1983). *Class size and instruction.* New York: Longman.

Callahan, L. G., & Alford, L. E. (1986). Alignment of textbook and test content. *Arithmetic Teacher, 34*(3), 25.

Cannell, J. J. (1988). National normed elementary achievement testing in America's public schools: How all 50 states are above the national average. *Educational Measurement: Issues and Practice, 7*(2), 5–9.

Cohen, S. A., & Hyman, J. S. (1991). Can fantasies become facts? *Educational Measurement: Issues and Practice, 10*(1), 20–23.

Corbett, H. D., & Wilson, B. L. (1991). *Testing, reform, and rebellion.* Norwood, NJ: Ablex.

Cubberly, E. P. (1913). Textbooks. In P. Monroe (Ed.), *Cyclopedia of education* (Vol. 5, pp. 576–578). New York: Macmillan.

Darling-Hammond, L. (1990). Achieving our goals: Superficial or structural reforms? *Phi Delta Kappan, 72*(4), 286–295.

Darling-Hammond, L., & Wise, A. E. (1985). Beyond standardization: State standards and school improvement. *Elementary School Journal, 85*(3), 315–336.

Dreeben, R. (1985, April). *The social organization of mathematics and reading instruction.* Paper presented at the annual meeting of the American Educational Research Association, Chicago. (ERIC Document Reproduction Service No. ED262877)

Edelman, J. (1981). The impact of the mandated testing program on classroom practices: Teacher perspectives. *Education, 102*(1), 56–59.

Educational Products Information Exchange (1977). *Report on a national study of the nature and quality of instructional materials most used by teachers and learners.* New York: EPIE Institute.

Educational Testing Service (1994). *America's mathematics problem: Raising student achievement. A synthesis of finding from NAEP'S 1992 mathematics assessment* (Report No. 23-FR-03). Washington, DC: U.S. Government Printing Office.

Elliott, D. L. (1990). Textbooks and the curriculum in the postwar era 1950–1980. In D. L. Elliott & A. Woodward (Eds.), *Textbooks and schooling in the United States: Eighty-ninth yearbook of the national society for the study of education* (pp. 42–55). Chicago: University of Chicago Press.

Fish, J. (1988). *Responses to mandated standardized testing.* Unpublished doctoral dissertation, University of California, Los Angeles.

Frank, M. L. (1988). Problem solving and mathematical beliefs. *Arithmetic Teacher, 35*(5), 32–34.

Frank, M. L. (1990). What myths about mathematics are held and conveyed by teachers? *Arithmetic Teacher, 37*(5), 10–12.

Frederiksen, N. (1984). The real test bias. *American Psychologist, 39*(3), 193–202.

Freeman, D. J., Kuhs, T. M., Porter, A. C., Floden, R. E., Schmidt, W. H., & Schwille, J. R. (1983). Do textbooks and tests define a national curriculum in elementary school mathematics? *Elementary School Journal, 83*(5), 501–513.

Garofalo, J. (1989). Beliefs and their influence on mathematical performance. *Mathematics Teacher, 82*(7), 502–505.

Goodlad, J. (1984). *A place called school: Prospects for the future.* New York: McGraw-Hill.

Gross, R. E. (1952). American history teachers look at the book. *Phi Delta Kappan, 33*(5), 290–291.

Grouws, D. A., & Meier, S. L. (1992). Teaching and assessment relationships in mathematics instruction. In G. C. Leder (Ed.), *Assessment and learning of mathematics* (pp. 83–106). Hawthorne, Victoria: Australian Council for Educational Research.

Haladyna, T. M., Nolen, S. B., & Haas, N. S. (1991). Raising standardized achievement test scores and the origins of test score pollution. *Educational Researcher, 20*(5), 2–7.

Hall, J. L., & Kleine, P. F. (1992). Educators' perceptions of NRT misuse. *Educational Measurement: Issues and Practice, 11*(2), 18–22.

Herman, J. L., & Golan, S. (1990). *Effects of standardized testing on teachers and learning - another look.* Los Angeles, CA: National Center for Research on Evaluation, Standards and Student Testing (CRESST), UCLA Graduate School of Education. (ERIC Document Reproduction Service No. ED341738)

Herman, J. L., & Golan, S. (1993). The effects of standardized testing on teaching and schools. *Educational Measurement: Issues and Practice, 12*(4), 20–25, 41–42.

Kuhs, T. M., & Freeman, D. J. (1979). *The potential influence of textbooks on teachers' selection of content for elementary mathematics.* Paper presented at the annual meeting of the American Education Research Association, San Francisco. (ERIC Reproduction Document Service No. ED175856)

Lindquist, M. M. (1997). NAEP findings regarding the preparation of classroom practices of mathematics teachers. In P. A. Kenney & E. A. Silver (Eds.), *Results from the sixth mathematics assessment of the NAEP* (pp. 61–86). Reston, VA: NCTM

Madaus, G. F. (1985). Public policy and testing profession—You've never had it so good? *Educational Measurement: Issues and Practice, 4*(4), 5–11.

Madaus, G. F. (1988). Influence of testing on the curriculum. In L. N. Tanner (Ed.), *Critical issues in curriculum: Eighty-seventh yearbook of the national society for the study of education* (pp. 83–121). Chicago: University of Chicago Press.

Madaus, G. F. (1991). The effects of important tests on students: Implications for a national examination system. *Phi Delta Kappan, 73*(3), 226–231.

Medina, N. J., & Neill, D. M. (1990). *Fallout from the exams undermine equity and excellence in America's public schools* (3rd ed., rev.). Cambridge, MA: National Center for Fair and Open Testing (FairTest).

Mehrens, W. A., & Kaminski, J. (1989). Methods for improving standardized test scores: Fruitful, fruitless, or fraudulent? *Educational Measurement: Issues and Practice, 8*(1), 14–22.

Mehrens, W. A., & Phillips, S. E. (1986) *Sensitivity of item statistics to curricular validity.* Research series no. 2. East Lansing: Michigan State University Department of Counseling, Educational Psychology and Special Education.

Meisels, S. J. (1989). High stakes testing in kindergarten. *Educational Leadership, 46*(7), 16–22.

National Commission on Excellence in Education. (1983). *A nation at risk: The imperative of educational reform.* Washington, DC: U.S. Government Printing Office.

National Council of Teachers of Mathematics (1989). *Curriculum and evaluation standards for school mathematics.* Reston, VA: NCTM.

Neill, M., & Medina N. J. (1989). Standardized testing: Harmful to educational health. *Phi Delta Kappan, 70*(9), 688–696.

Nolen, S. B., Haladyna, T. M., & Haas, N. S. (1992). Uses and abuses of achievement test scores. *Educational Measurement: Issues and Practice, 11*(2), 9–15.

Pajares, F. (1993). Preservice teachers' beliefs: A focus for teacher education. *Action in Teacher Education, 15*(2), 45–53.

Paris, S. C., Lawton, T. A., Turner, J. C., & Roth, J. L. (1991). A developmental perspective on standardized achievement testing. *Educational Researcher, 20*(5), 12–19.

Payne, L. L. (1997) *Fourth grade mathematics instruction in classically low stakes testing environments.* Unpublished doctoral dissertation, University of Iowa, Iowa City.

Phelps, R. (1996). Are U.S. students the most heavily tested on earth? *Educational Measurement: Issues and Practice, 15*(3), 19–26.

A policy of pressure. (1998, January 18). *Minneapolis Star Tribune*, p. A1.

Resnick, L. B., & Resnick, D. P. (1989). Tests as standards of achievement in schools. *The uses of standardized tests in American education. Proceedings of the 1989 ETS invitational conference* (pp. 63–80. Princeton, NJ: ETS.

Riverside Publishing (1993). *Iowa Tests of Basic Skills: Interpretive guide for teachers and counselors.* Chicago: Houghton Mifflin.

Romberg, T. A., Wilson, L., Khaketla, M., & Chavarria, S. (1992). Curriculum and test alignment. In T. Romberg (Ed.), *Mathematics assessment and evaluation* (pp. 61–74). Albany: State University of New York Press.

Rothman, R. (1995). *Measuring up: Standards, assessments, and school reform.* San Francisco, CA: Jossey-Bass.

Schoenfeld, A. H. (1985). Metacognitive and epistemological issues in mathematical understanding. In E. A. Silver (Ed.), *Teaching and learning mathematical problem solving: Multiple research perspectives* (pp. 361–379). Hillsdale, NJ: Lawrence Erlbaum Associates.

Schoenfeld, A. H. (1992). Learning to think mathematically: Problem solving, metacognition, and sense making in mathematics. In D. A. Grouws (Ed.), *Handbook of research on mathematics teaching and learning* (pp. 334–370). New York: Macmillan.

Shepard, L. A. (1989). Why we need better assessments. *Educational Leadership, 46*(7), 4–9.

Shepard, L. A. (1990). Inflated test scores gains: Is the problem old norms or teaching to the test? *Educational Measurement: Issues and Practice, 9*(3), 15–22.

Shepard, L. A. (1991). Will national tests improve student learning? *Phi Delta Kappan, 73*(3), 232–238.

Shepard, L. A., & Dougherty, K. C. (1991). *Effects of high stakes testing on instruction.* Paper presented at the annual meeting of the American Educational Research Association and the National Council on Measurement in Education, Chicago. (ERIC Document Reproduction Service No. ED337468)

Smith, M. L. (1991a). Meaning of test preparation. *American Educational Research Journal, 28*(3), 521–542.

Smith, M. L. (1991b). Put to the test: The effects of external testing on teachers. *Educational Researcher, 20*(5), 8–11.

Smith, M. L., & Rottenberg, C. (1991). Unintended consequences of external testing in elementary schools. *Educational Measurement: Issues and Practice, 10*(1), 7–11.

Sosniak, L. A., & Stodolsky, S. S. (1993). Teachers and textbooks: Materials use in four fourth grade classrooms. *Elementary School Journal, 93*(3), 248–275.

Spangler, D. A. (1992) Assessing students' beliefs about mathematics. *Arithmetic Teacher, 40*(3), 148–152.

Squire, J. R., & Morgan, R. T. (1990). The elementary and high school textbook market today. In D. L. Elliott & A. Woodward (Eds.), *Textbooks and schooling in the United States: Eighty-ninth yearbook of the national society for the study of education* (pp. 107–126). Chicago: University of Chicago Press.

Stake, R. E., & Easley, J. A. (1978). *Case studies in science education: Vol. 2. Design, overview and general findings.* Urbana: Illinois University, Center for Instructional Research and Curriculum Evaluation. (ERIC Document Reproduction Service No. ED166059)

Stigler, J. W. (1995). *The TIMSS Technical Report.* Unpublished draft, Department of Psychology, University of California, Los Angeles.

Stodolsky, S. S. (1988). *The subject matters: Classroom activity in math and social studies.* Chicago: University of Chicago Press.

Suarez, T. M., & Gottovi, N. C. (1992). The impact of high stakes assessments on our schools. *NASSP Bulletin, 76*(545), 82–88.

Thompson, A. G. (1985). Teachers' conceptions of mathematics and the teaching of problem solving. In E. A. Silver (Ed.), *Teaching and learning mathematical problem solving: Multiple research perspectives* (pp. 281–294). Hillsdale, NJ: Lawrence Erlbaum Associates.

Turner, R. R. (1988). How the basals stack up. *Learning, 17*(8), 62–64.

U.S. Congress. Office of Technology Assessment (OTA). (1992, February). *Summary: Testing in American schools: Asking the right questions.* Washington, DC: Author. (OTA-SET-520)

U.S. Department of Education. (1995). *An invitation to your community building community partnerships for learning goals 2000 a world-class education for every child.* Washington, DC: Author.

U.S. General Accounting Office. (1993, January). *Student testing: Current extent and expenditures, with cost estimates for a national examination.* Washington, DC: Author. (GAO/PEMD-93-8)

Weiss, I. (1994). *A profile of science and mathematics education in the United States.* Chapel Hill, NC: Horizon Research, Inc. (ERIC Document Reproduction Service No. ED382461)

Westbury, I. (1990). Textbooks, textbook publishers, and the quality of schooling. In D. L. Elliott & A. Woodward (Eds.), *Textbooks and schooling in the United States: Eighty-ninth yearbook of the national society for the study of education* (pp. 1–22). Chicago: University of Chicago Press.

Woodward, A., & Elliott, D. L. (1990a). Textbook use and teacher professionalism. In D. L. Elliott & A. Woodward (Eds.), *Textbooks and schooling in the United States: Eighty-ninth yearbook of the national society for the study of education* (pp. 178–193). Chicago: University of Chicago Press.

Woodward, A., & Elliott, D. L. (1990b). Textbooks: Consensus and controversy. In D. L. Elliott & A. Woodward (Eds.), *Textbooks and schooling in the United States: Eighty-ninth yearbook of the national society for the study of education* (pp. 146–161). Chicago: University of Chicago Press.

Woodward, A., & Elliott, D. L. (1990c). Textbooks, curriculum and school improvement. In D. L. Elliott & A. Woodward (Eds.), *Textbooks and schooling in the United States: Eighty-ninth yearbook of the national society for the study of education* (pp. 222–232). Chicago University of Chicago Press.

Worthen, B. R., & Spandel, V. (1991). Putting the standardized test debate in perspective. *Educational Leadership, 48*(5), 65–69.

Zollman, A., & Mason, E. (1992). The standards' beliefs instrument (SBI): Teachers' beliefs about the NCTM Standards. *School Science and Mathematics, 92*(7), 359–364.

Part V

Scheduling

SCHEDULING, AS ANY SCHOOL leader knows, can have a profound impact on educational programs. Although the annual task of creating an effective schedule demands considerable time and effort of school leaders, scheduling rarely receives its due in research and even in professional literature. The recent renewed interest in block scheduling warrants a reexamination of that practice and of other scheduling options for elementary, middle, and secondary schools. This part examines scheduling options and reviews related literature about the impacts of block scheduling. Henry Traverso briefly summarizes past attention devoted to scheduling, particularly during the 1930s and 1960s, as well as recent efforts to implement what he calls "intensive," or block, scheduling. He presents an overview of scheduling options as well. Robert Lynn Canady and Michael D. Rettig provide a comprehensive treatment of the origins, rationale, practices, and emerging research on block scheduling in K–12 settings. Canady and Rettig are optimistic about the potential of block scheduling, but they caution that the evidence for its effectiveness, although promising, remains preliminary.

CHAPTER 12

SECONDARY SCHOOL SCHEDULING

Henry Traverso
*Connecticut Association for Supervision
and Curriculum Development*

SECONDARY SCHOOL SCHEDULING HAS TAKEN A PROMINENT position in the list of educational concerns being addressed in this decade. Along with performance-based assessment, interdisciplinary education, inclusion, multiple intelligences in the classroom, bilingual education, multicultural education, and standards-based education—to cite a few of the issues facing school administrators—school scheduling has resurfaced in its unique 30-year cycle of intensive scrutiny. However, unlike the efforts for restructuring of school scheduling models in the 1930s and 1960s, the implementation of "intensive scheduling" designs during the 1990s is more widespread and more thoroughly documented and promoted than in preceding national movements for scheduling reform (Traverso, 1996).

Earlier Movements

References to secondary school scheduling appear in the literature as far back as the 1890s. However, the earliest period of intense interest in high school scheduling practices occurred in the 1930s. Douglas (1932), Langftt (1938), and Puckett (1931) conducted surveys of contemporary scheduling practices and published their findings in periodicals and scholarly texts. Avoiding the promotion of one design over another, these authors served as resources to school administrators on common practices of their contemporaries. No one model was promulgated as most advantageous or purported to improve the instructional process. Research on the effectiveness of various models was absent in the literature of the period.

This purely academic approach of the 1930s contrasts with innovative movements of the 1960s. Advocates during that decade became heralds for alternative forms of scheduling the American high school (Bush & Allen, 1964). At regional conferences throughout the country, developers of new scheduling models vigorously promoted their adoption by school administrators.

A stimulus for significant changes in school scheduling was the availability of new computer technology for high schools. More complex designs of secondary school schedules could now be developed because of the capacity of main frame computers to schedule a myriad of new departmental approaches to implementing the curriculum. Instruction could be provided in less rigid, more distinct and creative patterns. The most noteworthy product of this period was the flexible-modular schedule (Petrequin, 1968). Although more of historical note than practical utility to high school principals today, the "flex-mod" design enabled each high school department to organize classes into large group, small group, and independent study units. Classes in each subject did not meet daily in uniform period lengths but at various times during the scheduling cycle of from 20 to 120 minutes.

Concurrent with implementation of the flex-mod schedule were controversial social changes on high school campuses. The introduction of the "open campus" and unsupervised free time for students, coupled with occasional campus unrest during the 1960s, produced a negative reaction to such changes in the traditional high school setting. School communities that implemented the new scheduling format were quick to return to the conventional schedule. By the early 1970s, the flex-mod schedule remained in use in only a small number of schools.

What is "intensive scheduling" and what does an educational leader need to know about scheduling the secondary school program? Intensive scheduling refers to a redesigned secondary school schedule that lengthens the amount of time students and teachers remain together within an instructional period. Whereas in more traditional schedules a class length runs from 45 to 55 minutes, instructional periods in schools that have adopted any of the various forms of intensive scheduling are found to run from 80 to 90 minutes in one widely adopted model, to as many as 230 minutes in models that adopt a more extended use of time. For present and aspiring school administrators, knowledge of the current movement in secondary school scheduling and its relation to previous innovative efforts is essential (Gilman & Knoll, 1984). Effective scheduling of the secondary school is viewed by most educators to be one of the greatest challenges to an administrator's management skill (Shaten, 1982). It is the principal's responsibility to ensure that all the students and teachers, the curriculum, the instructional materials, and physical space are systematically united into a compatible arrangement that provides an ideal learning environment (Cawelti, 1994).

Although the major portion of this chapter is devoted to the scheduling options prominent both in the nation's schools as well as in today's literature on secondary school scheduling, it would be incomplete without a reference to the widely recurring consideration of year round education (Sommerfield, 1995). Expanding school populations, overcrowded school buildings, and revolts of taxpayers have forced many school districts to reconsider the school calendar and jettison the 180-day "agrarian" calendar so widespread throughout the country. For the school administrator, change from a traditional to a year-round calendar will necessitate the construction of more than one master schedule at the high school level. Up to five distinct master schedules may have to be designed by the school scheduler, depending on the size of the student body and the number of "tracks" needed to accommodate the enrollment. Schools with 12-month calendars exist in over half the states at the present time, thus suggesting that administrators may well be required to become knowledgeable about this topic (Brekke, 1992). A host of references is available for examination in college libraries and in the general press.

SCHEDULE OPTIONS IN PERSPECTIVE

Most writers on secondary school scheduling share agreement on two issues: Administrators need not rely on the literature or the practices of their contemporaries to identify or to create a schedule model that best fits the needs of an particular school, and the continuous search since early in this century for the "perfect" schedule attests to the fact that there is no such entity (Canady & Rettig, 1995). Thus, the scheduling models presented here are examples of past and contemporary practices of school administrators.

TRADITIONAL SCHEDULES

Although a large number of high schools have adopted some form of intensive scheduling, most institutions still retain the traditional schedule with its roots in the "recitation" model of colonial America (Boyer, 1983). Considered by many to be a time-tested model, with opportunities for variations to meet the particular needs of a department (i.e., science labs), the goals of certain students (i.e., early release for work experience programs), or the outcomes of special programs (i.e., built-in activity periods), the traditional schedule possesses the following characteristics:

> All periods are equal in length, thus standardizing instruction into equal time blocks.
>
> Full-credit courses meet at the same time daily throughout the week.
>
> The weekly cycle repeats itself throughout the semester or year.
>
> Shared faculty (or part-time teachers) are easily accommodated.
>
> Work experience programs and alternating sessions with vocational-technical schools can be readily scheduled. (See Fig 12.1.)

Period	Monday	Tuesday	Wednesday	Thursday	Friday
1	A	A	A	A	A
2	B	B	B	B	B
3	C	C	C	C	C
4	D	D	D	D	D
5	E	E	E	E	E
6	F	F	F	F	F
7	G	G	G	G	G

FIG. 12.1. Traditional schedule.

VARIATIONS ON CONVENTIONAL SCHEDULES

Resourceful and creative secondary school administrators have also learned to reshape the traditional schedule so that it meets a greater diversity of curricular goals, provides more variety within the school day, and yet maintains all necessary connections with collaborating secondary schools (vo-tech) and special staffing circumstances.

One such variation is the rotating period schedule. (See Fig. 12.2.) Within a conventional seven-period schedule, periods have been rotated so that all of a student's courses meet at different times throughout the week. Administrators, teachers, and students recommend this rotation in order to achieve greater variety in the school day and to take advantage of "optimal" learning times in each course. It is argued that some students learn better in the morning, whereas others prefer afternoon periods for instruction. Thus, a student's mathematics class might meet during the first period on Monday, the last period on Tuesday, the sixth period on Wednesday, and so on. A parallel model is used in schools where students are released either for morning or afternoon attendance at a vocational-technical school or early release for a work experience assignment. (See Fig. 12.3.) While still providing a degree of rotation, this model works well when part-time or shared staff are members of the faculty (Traverso, 1996).

Period	Monday	Tuesday	Wednesday	Thursday	Friday
1	A	B	C	D	E
2	B	C	D	E	F
3	C	D	E	F	G
4	D	E	F	G	A
5	E	F	G	A	B
6	F	G	A	B	C
7	G	A	B	C	D

FIG. 12.2. Rotating period schedule.

Period	Monday	Tuesday	Wednesday	Thursday	Friday
1	A	B	C	D	A
2	B	C	D	A	B
3	C	D	A	B	C
4	D	A	B	C	D
5	E	F	G	E	F
6	F	G	E	F	G
7	G	E	F	G	E

FIG. 12.3. A parallel model schedule.

Another format found across the country is the flexible period schedule. (See Fig. 12.4.)

Providing varying time units for each course throughout the week, this model permits both regular instruction and elongated periods for audiovisual presentations, student group discussions, or laboratory-oriented activities in each subject area.

	Monday	Tuesday	Wednesday	Thursday	Friday
1	A	A	A	A	A
2	B	B	B	B	B
3	C	C	C	C	C
4	L	U	N	C	H
5	D	D	D	D	D
6	E	E	E	E	E
7	F	F	F	F	F

FIG. 12.4. Flexible period schedule.

A more widely used model, especially in schools experimenting with the concept of the intensive period, is the single-double rotation schedule. (See Fig. 12.5.) Each course meets for five periods but only during 4 days because each subject meets for two consecutive periods on one of the days. Although it is clear that this model functions if there are an even number of total periods daily, some schools have introduced a seven-period schedule by "freezing" one period across the five days of the week for a single period each day. Although this model has been used in many schools for decades, it has been widely adopted by schools as a stepping-stone, or trial, prior to implementing the intensive schedules reviewed later in this chapter (Traverso, 1991). All departments and faculty members are provided with a brief but concrete experience with instructing in a time block of up to 90 minutes. Some schools have subsequently decided to adopt more comprehensive forms of intensive scheduling and others have either retained the single-double rotation model and continued to provide staff development in order to better utilize the longer instructional periods or have returned to their previous schedules and continued their study of alternatives.

Period	Monday	Tuesday	Wednesday	Thursday	Friday
1	A	A	A	A	B
2	A	B	B	B	B
3	C	C	C	D	C
4	D	C	D	D	D
5	E	E	E	E	F
6	F	F	E	F	F

FIG. 12.5. Single-double rotation schedule.

INTENSIVE SCHEDULING

The use of intensive scheduling varies at the two levels of secondary education: the middle school and the high school. Although the term *block scheduling* is used to describe the arrangement of time within the daily schedule at both levels, the model found in many middle schools seeks to provide a large block of flexible time for teams of teachers to offer instruction to a fixed group of students for both their academic core subjects as well as their elective and exploratory courses (see Fig. 12.6). Within this model, a group of from 80 to 120 students is scheduled with a four or five teacher team for core courses such as language arts, science, social studies, and mathematics (and often a foreign language), and then individually or collectively with teachers of electives or exploratory courses. This large block of time arrangement allows the team of teachers to vary the length of instructional time on any day to accommodate field trips, laboratories, film viewing, group library visitations, and other activities best offered in longer time blocks (Braddock, 1980).

Periods	
1	⎫ Five-period block
2	⎪ Of core subjects:
3	⎬ Language arts, science,
4	⎪ Mathematics, social
5	⎭ Studies, and foreign language
6	Elective / Exploratory
7	Elective / Exploratory
8	Elective / Exploratory
9	Elective / Exploratory

FIG 12.6. Schedule for approximately 120 students with a five-teacher team.

At the high school level, the intensive schedule is experienced in a variety of models. Most prevalent in American and in Canadian schools is the "4 x 4" block schedule (see Fig. 12.7).

Period	Semester 1	Semester 2
1	Course A	Course E
2	Course B	Course F
3	Course C	Course G
4	Course D	Course H

FIG. 12.7. 4 x 4 block schedule

Although widely used in Canadian secondary schools for over 20 years, and reported in use in some American schools for as long, the 4 x 4 block schedule has only been implemented in this country during the past 7 years. Viewed as a key to improving secondary education by many practitioners, the 4 x 4 block is highly controversial to many members of the school community. However, it is rapidly being introduced in schools from one coast to another (Canady & Rettig, 1993).

Adoption of the block schedule alters the basic configuration of the school curriculum into a semester model (Edwards, 1993). What were traditionally full-year courses offered daily for 180 or so days, are now scheduled for 90 days in either semester by roughly doubling the length of the instructional period. In addition, a host of special considerations must be addressed with the incorporation of this new scheduling option. These are the need to determine if the school day must be lengthened, the need to examine the existing teachers' contract and renegotiate any provisions, to make special provisions for year-long music programs that cannot be accommodated in a semester model, to incorporate advanced placement courses into a semestered approach, and to schedule sequential courses in foreign language and mathematics so as to reduce the time gap between successive levels (i.e., Spanish I offered in the fall of one year and Spanish II not offered until the spring of the next year, a time span of 12 months). Interestingly, the issues and problems that the block schedule brings to the surface have not deterred many hundreds of high school administrators from examining and adopting such a schedule (Alam & Seick, 1994).

Adoption of a block (or intensive) schedule results in the following changes to the traditional operation of the high school:

> Students are enrolled in four periods per day, instead of six or seven (Dismuke, 1994).
>
> Teachers teach three periods daily, with one preparation period.
>
> There are no study halls for students because they are fully scheduled.
>
> Students take eight courses yearly, for a possible total of 32 by graduation.
>
> Additional faculty members may be needed for proper implementation.

As with any change introduced in an organization, the use of the block scheduling concept produces a number of predictable problems common to most high schools. In addition, special concerns may arise due to the unique nature of many of American high schools. These must be researched and identified in advance of any implementation. However, educators who have adopted the block schedule have documented the following advantages of this administrative option:

> Opportunities for personalized attention and instruction for students is expanded; teachers have fewer students each semester, allowing time for individualization.

Faculty members have no more than three class preparations daily; the fourth period is assigned as a planning period.

The student load for teachers is reduced from up to 125 daily to 60 to 80, as teachers are only responsible for three classes a day.

Upper level courses can be expanded because students are eligible to enroll in up to 32 courses over 4 years.

Students also have fewer preparations and homework assignments daily and are more able to attend to these subjects, as students only have four classes daily instead of six or seven.

Expanded use of team teaching and interdisciplinary organization are possible.

Students failing a course in one semester can repeat it in the next, avoiding summer school make ups and remaining on track for graduation (i.e., an algebra I course failed in the fall semester can be retaken in the spring semester).

Fewer subjects need to be made up when absent students return to school following illness or other reasons.

The textbook budget for new books can be cut in half because two sets of students can use the books in the same year.

More lab-oriented activities can take place in all courses because of the longer time block (e.g., hands-on activities, inductive reasoning, use of the computer lab and media center, etc; Traverso, 1996).

Some schools have adopted an alternative form of block scheduling called "the alternate day" block or Day 1/Day 2 block (or A/B block). This is illustrated in Fig. 12.8 (Traverso, 1991).

Period	Day 1	Day 2	Day 3	Day 4
1	Course A	Course E	Course A	Course E
2	Course B	Course F	Course B	Course F
3	Course C	Course G	Course C	Course G
4	Course D	Course H	Course D	Course H

FIG. 12.8. Alternate day block schedule.

Schools have chosen the alternate day block schedule for a variety of reasons. Among these are a desire to meet with students throughout the year in a particular course; to address the special problems unique to the music department and for upper level courses, particularly advanced placement courses that are tested in

May; to eliminate the lengthy time gaps that can occur between sequential courses; to avoid conflicts with existing teacher contracts; and to gain many of the benefits inherent in the longer instructional period.

However, a number of the advantages of the 4 x 4 block schedule are sacrificed with the alternate day schedule, such as: students failing a course cannot make it up during the next semester and must attend summer school; students are still scheduled for six or more courses daily throughout the year; few opportunities exist for accelerating a student's program, especially for those gifted in one or more areas; teachers must continue to maintain grades and records for over 100 students; teachers must prepare for five or six classes each day and attempt to provide the instructional needs for well over 100 students daily; and students have six or more subjects to make up following an absence.

A less frequently used intensive schedule adopts the concept of the macroschedule (Carroll, 1989). Paralleling the trimester model found on many college campuses, this "Copernican" schedule was developed by Joseph M. Carroll (see Fig. 12.9). A former teacher and school administrator, Carroll retired as superintendent of the Masconomet Regional School District in northeastern Massachusetts, where the Copernican plan was implemented and evaluated by a team of Harvard researchers (Carroll, 1994).

Period Length*	Option A (60-Day Period)	Period Length*	Option B (30-Day Period)
8:00 - 10:00 a.m.	Class I	8:00 a.m. - 12 noon	Class I
10:00 a.m. -12 noon	Class II	12 noon - 12:30 p.m.	Lunch
12 noon - 12:45 p.m.	Interdisciplinary Seminar or Elective or P.E./Health	12:30 - 1:15 p.m.	Interdisciplinary Seminar or P.E./Health or Elective
12:45 - 1:15 p.m.	Lunch	1:15 - 2:15 p.m.	Elective or P.E./Health or Study or Tutorial
1:15 - 2:15 p.m.	Elective or P.E./Health or Study or Tutorial	2:15 - 5:00 p.m.	Activities/Sports
2:15 - 5:00 p.m.	Activities/Sports		

*Schools determine passing time allotments based on building characteristics and local needs.

FIG. 12.9. Macroschedule.

The Copernican plan consists of two distinct patterns for offering instruction: An up-to-4-hour class daily for a term of 30 days or two 2-hour classes each day for a total of 60 days. These intensive approaches to the core curriculum are offered in conjunction with periods for interdisciplinary seminars, electives, physical education, study periods, and tutorial assistance from teachers. According to the author of the program, it allows a high school to lower the average class size by up to 20%, lower the average teacher's student load from 60% to 80% and increase the number of sections offered in the master schedule by 20%.

Another example of a form of trimester scheduling is found in a western Canadian province (see Fig. 12.10).

PERIOD	PERIOD LENGTH
A	130 minutes
Break	20 minutes
B	130 minutes
Break	20 minutes
C	130 minutes

(During each of the periods there is a midperiod break of 10 minutes)

FIG. 12.10. Trimester schedule.

During these 60-day cycles, a student is able to take as many as nine courses or a total of 36 courses over a 4-year period.

Another variation of trimester scheduling is illustrated in Fig. 12.11 (Traverso, 1996). Following a 10-month calendar, this model divides the year into three 60-day sessions, from mid-August to early November, followed by the second session through mid-February, with the final session ending just before June. Proponents argue that students have more time to concentrate on particular classes as well as instructional objectives within each class; that students are able to enroll in more classes yearly, yet have extended time for extracurricular activities; that students can repeat any courses failed in lieu of summer school; that students have more room for electives that meet specific needs; and that teachers enjoy the extended time for adopting new teaching strategies, such as increased use of technology.

Period	Time	Lunch Schedule
1	8:00 - 9:15 a.m.	
2	9:15 - 11:00 a.m.	
3	11:00 a.m. - 1:15 p.m.	First Lunch 11:00 - 11:30 a.m. Class A 11:40 a.m. - 12:15 p.m Class B 11:10 - 11:48 a.m. Second Lunch 11:57 a.m. - 12:18 p.m. Class B 12:37 - 1:15 p.m. Class C 11:10 a.m. - 12:25 p.m. Third Lunch 12:25 - 1:15 p.m.
4	1:25 - 2:40 p.m.	
5	2:50 - 4:05 p.m.	

FIG. 12.11. Sample trimester schedule (school maintains three lunch waves).

TRADITIONAL SEMESTER COURSES

It is important to note that an intensive schedule has the effect of compressing a traditional block of time into a much shorter period. In the same way that a 4 x 4 block schedule reduces full-year courses into semester courses (by increasing the daily meeting time), so are former semester or half-credit courses reduced to quarter courses, those meeting only one conventional marking period. The following model (see Fig. 12.12) illustrates the compression graphically.

\multicolumn{9}{c}{Sample high school schedule: Semester 1}
Period 1		Period 2		Period 3				Period 4
History	P A S S I N G	1st Quarter Sociology	Lunch	Algebra II		P A S S I N G		1st Quarter Ceramics
		2nd Quarter Theater						2nd Quarter Psychology
\multicolumn{9}{c}{Sample high school schedule: Semester 2}
Period 1		Period 2		Period 3				Period 4
3rd Quarter P.E.	P A S S I N G	English III	Lunch	French III		P A S S I N G		Chemistry
4th Quarter Health								

FIG. 12.12. Sample high school schedule: Semester 1 & 2.

Critical to the success of extended time schedules is their adaptability to unique circumstances of particular secondary schools. Within Fig. 12.12, for example, advanced placement courses meet for the first three terms so that the conclusion of the course better coincides with the nationally determined dates of the exams. At that point, the student is able to take a traditional semester course, which is now scheduled for the remaining quarter in the same period in which the AP course met.

School schedulers are also able to ensure that at least 25% of the faculty has a common planning period, thus allowing for an increase in the number of interdisciplinary courses.

OTHER CONSIDERATIONS

An earlier reference in this chapter to year-round education indicated that burgeoning enrollments required schools to adopt this alternative, especially when taxpayers vetoed any attempt to increase building capacity through additional construction. There are two other popular alternatives that administrators have used to address the issue of large school populations or declining budgets. These are the "4-day week" and the "house plan."

The introduction of the 4-day week was prompted by economic constraints, and affects over 100 schools in 10 states (Barton, Johnson, & Brulle, 1986). Achieved by lengthening the school day by up to 120 minutes and reducing the number of days in session from five to four, this alternative produces savings in heating and electrical costs, in bus gasoline expenses, and in the general wear and tear of the faculty. Reported benefits center on cost savings in particular parts of the budget; the ability to schedule field trips on the "fifth" day; the increased teacher and student attendance; make ups for inclement weather days; and the use of the "fifth" day for professional staff development and personal matters of teachers, parents, and students, such as medical appointments.

The problems inherent in the 4-day week model include difficulty in establishing cooperative arrangements with vocational programs and university collaboration, and in scheduling performing group schedules and athletic contests. Conflicts with the existing teacher contract can sometimes also pose a problem.

The implementation of the concept of a "house plan" has its roots in the early part of the century when urban high schools had upward of from 5,000 to 8,000 students. Often referred to as schools-within-schools, house plans assigned smaller groups of students to a generally self-contained unit of from 700 to 1,200 students, each with its own administrator ("housemaster"), faculty, and assigned set of classrooms. Secondary educators have long believed that school climate is improved when students identify with a smaller unit within a large high school. The type of house plan is a function of the size of the student body vis-à-vis the number and size of the specialized facilities found in most high schools, such as gymnasiums, laboratories, cafeterias, and computer facilities (Cawelti, 1993).

The literature on secondary school scheduling attests to the search for the ideal secondary school schedule (Adler, 1982). In the next decade, administrators will be challenged by recommendations from national organizations, from the actions of their colleagues in neighboring schools, and even from their own faculties wishing to examine conscientiously and professionally the type of schedule in use in the school, to determine its suitability to meet the educational needs of all students. In their review, administrators will have a wide range of options to consider. The decision to remain pat may well be in the best interests of the school community presently being served. It is more likely that a decision will be made to modify the schedule or to adopt an entirely different one that seeks to benefit from the concept of extended time.

School administrators today have the benefit of a wealth of literature on the topic of secondary school scheduling, more than was available during the 1930s and 1960s combined (when national attention was sharply focused on scheduling innovations). In addition, schools in every state have implemented various forms of intensive scheduling, especially the two forms of block scheduling (Schoenstein, 1994). Thus, administrators and their faculties have the opportunity to visit sites of innovative practices and to communicate with their peers. No principal can argue against the consideration of adopting a new schedule because of insufficient information. It is a function of the willingness to examine the status quo and determine if a need for change is warranted.

REFERENCES

Adler, M. J. (1982). *The Paideia proposal: An educational manifesto.* New York: Macmillan.

Alam, D., & Seick, Jr., R. E. (1994, May). A block schedule with a twist. *Phi Delta Kappan,* pp. 732–733.

Barton, L. E., Johnson, H. A., & Brulle, A. R. (1986). An evaluation of the effectiveness of an extended year program. *Journal of the Association for Persons with Severe Handicaps, 2,* 136–138.

Boyer, E. L. (1983). *High school: Report of secondary education in America.* New York: Harper.

Braddock, J. H. II. (1980, May). Tracking the middle grades: National patterns of grouping for instruction. *NASSP Bulletin,* pp. 93–96.

Brekke, N. R. (1992, May). Year-round schools. *School Business Affairs,* pp. 62–65.

Bush, R. N., & Allen, D. W. (1964). *A new design for high education—Assuming a flexible schedule.* New York: McGraw-Hill.

Canady, R. L., & Rettig, M. D. (1993, December). Unlocking the Lockstep High School schedule. *Phi Delta Kappan,* pp. 310–314.

Canady, R. L., & Rettig, M. D. (1995). *Block scheduling: A catalyst for change in high schools.* Princeton, NJ: Eye on Education.

Carroll, J. M. (1989). *The Copernican plan: Restructuring the American high school.* Andover, MA: The Regional Laboratory for Educational Improvement of the Northeast and Islands.

Carroll, J. M. (1994). *The Copernican plan evaluated: The evolution of a revolution.* Topsfield, MA: Copernican Associates.

Cawelti, G. (1993). Restructuring large high schools to personalize learning for all. *ERS Spectrum*, Summer, pp. 111–114.

Cawelti, G. (1994). *High school restructuring: A national study.* Arlington, VA.: Educational Research Service.

Dismuke, D. (1994). Students go for four. *NEA Today*, p. 19.

Douglas, H. R. (1932). *Organization and administration of secondary schools.* New York: Ginn & Company.

Edwards, C. M., Jr. (1993, September). Restructuring to improve student performance. *NASSP Bulletin*, pp. 77–88.

Gilman, D.A., & Knoll. S. (1984). Increasing instructional time: What are the priorities and how do they affect the alternatives? *NASSP Bulletin, 68*, 41–44.

Langfitt, R. E. (1938). *The daily schedule and high school organization.* New York: Macmillan.

Petrequin, G. (1968). *Individualizing learning through modular-flexible programming.* New York: McGraw-Hill.

Puckett, R. (1931). *Making a high school schedule of recitations.* New York: Longman, Green.

Schoenstein, R. (1994, December). Block schedules. *Virginia Journal of Education.*

Shaten, N. (1982, April). Building the schedule. *NASSP Bulletin, 48*, 56–59.

Sommerfield, M. (1995, May 11). Longer year, day proposed for schooling. *Education Week*, pp. 1,12.

Traverso, H. (1991, October). Scheduling: From micro to macro. *The Practitioner, 18*(1).

Traverso, H. (1996). *New directions in scheduling the secondary school.* Reston, VA: NASSP.

CHAPTER 13

BLOCK SCHEDULING: WHAT WE HAVE LEARNED

Robert Lynn Canady
University of Virginia

Michael D. Rettig
James Madison University, Harrisonburg, Virginia

One outcome of the ongoing debate about public schools during the late 1980s and early 1990s was that educators in elementary, middle, and high schools began to investigate ways to use time more productively. This chapter reviews the issues that made alternative scheduling models an attractive option, examines the manner in which block scheduling has been implemented in schools, and describes the results of research related to current scheduling models.

First, the Issues

For high schools and middle schools, the search for alternative scheduling was influenced by several factors. First, in many states the number of course credits required for graduation with an academic diploma rose to as many as 24 Carnegie units. In schools with a traditional six- or seven-period day, this left little room for elective courses like music and fine arts or vocational education courses.

In response to increased graduation requirements, many high schools added one or two periods to the schedule; however, some students became overwhelmed adjusting to eight or more teachers a day and juggling multiple notebooks, homework assignments, and tests for an entire school year. Further, adding periods without lengthening the school day reduced class periods to as few as 38 minutes in some schools, which raised serious questions as to how teachers and students could work productively in such short, fragmented time periods. The rise in the use of technology also exacerbated the problem of the short period. For example, teachers found it difficult to settle into the computer lab, log on, and have time to investigate a problem on the Internet in 40 minutes.

Proponents of block scheduling also argued that an impersonal environment was created by the "assembly-line, single-period daily schedule" and that disciplinary problems were exacerbated by schedules that release thousands of students into hallways 6 to 10 times a day for 3 to 5 minutes of noise and stress (Canady & Rettig, 1995). In 1994, a report from the National Education Commission on Time and Learning indicated that traditional ways of organizing schools contributed to these problems; the report even referred to students as "prisoners of time."

Elementary schools confronted similar issues. Various state and federal programs, added over the last two decades, gradually led to the fragmentation of the elementary school day. Teachers complained they sometimes felt like mere traffic cops, with students being "pulled out" of class to participate in Title I classes, special education programs, or talented and gifted instruction. Some educators even began to question the value of such programs.

To address this fragmentation, as well as the isolation and stigmatization of students attending support and enrichment programs, educators began to seek ways to blend support programs with regular programs. The push to blend programs gained momentum as some federal programs, such as Title I, became less restrictive, and as inclusion became more acceptable as a way to serve selected special education populations.

Elementary schools also had other concerns. Earlier reports of positive relationships between reduced class size and pupil achievement (Glass, Cahen, Smith, & Filby, 1979) were reinforced by new studies (Achilles, 1997; Achilles, Finn, & Bain, 1997–1998). As some stressed the need to give additional attention to teaching young children "phonemic awareness" (Yopp, 1995), teachers contended that such teaching had to occur in groups of from 5 to 10, with instruction repeated throughout the day. Some state governors even developed political platforms related to reducing class sizes in the early grades, and popular magazines carried feature stories on the emphasis on lowering class size in California (Toch & Streisand, 1997).

In many schools, grouping issues became a political concern. Some parents insisted that their children be grouped homogeneously, at least in reading and mathematics; other forces, along with research results, suggested that elementary teachers and administrators should group heterogeneously. In some communities, this debate seemed to present school personnel with a no-win situation.

Another issue facing elementary schools was the form of classroom instruction. Arguments were raised in favor of increasing the amount of teacher-directed instruction (Brophy, 1982; Rosenshine, 1983) and engaging students in more active learning; typical seatwork and independent activities lost favor. Teachers faced the challenge of providing instruction to an increasingly diverse student population, preferably in small groups, while reducing their dependence on seatwork for the rest of the class.

Finally, calls for school accountability grew louder. In some states, students were required to pass end-of-grade tests or other barrier examinations before advancing to the next grade, and schools faced a need to raise test scores.

In response to these issues and the forces underlying them, many elementary schools began to reexamine the manner in which their classrooms and days were structured and to apply alternative scheduling models.

MODELS OF ELEMENTARY SCHOOL ORGANIZATION

Although the dominant model for organizing elementary schools during the past 30 years has been to assign one teacher to a self-contained classroom with from 20 to 35 students, various other models have been tried. In team teaching, for example, two to five teachers work with perhaps 50 to 150 students. In blended classrooms, a regular classroom teacher and a full-time resource teacher typically share a larger class that includes from 10 to 15 Title I and special education resource students; in multi-age classrooms, the students have an age span of 3 to 5 years, crossing two or more grade levels. In a scheduling model called the Joplin plan, flexible, focused, homogeneous groups are formed across grade levels for special instructional periods in reading and mathematics.

The Success for All reading program, developed at Johns Hopkins University by Robert E. Slavin, is primarily a curriculum-based reading program; however, it does offer a way to reduce groups for instruction by employing principles of the Joplin plan. In each of the Success for All schools, the day begins "with a highly structured, 90-minute reading period during which children gather in groups according to reading ability, rather than age. Every certified teacher—from the gym coach to the librarian—is assigned a reading class, to keep class sizes small" (Olson, 1998, p. 44).

Parallel block scheduling (PBS) is another organizational plan for elementary schools developed in the 1960s that has regained national attention during the 1990s because of its potential to address student achievement, class size, support services, and grouping issues. The following sections take a closer look at this model and the data available from selected schools.

PARALLEL BLOCK SCHEDULING (PBS) IN THE ELEMENTARY SCHOOL

Parallel block scheduling calls for two parallel blocks of instruction, during which some students attend classes or activities in average-sized groups, and teachers work with smaller groups for extended periods of time, usually in reading or mathematics. PBS is a flexible model that can be adapted easily to meet the needs of elementary schools with unique student populations and resources. Each variation, however, is built on the following premises:

> The regular or base teacher's instructional program takes precedence over scheduling considerations for special programs and support services.
>
> Every day, large blocks of instructional time are reserved for reading, language arts, and mathematics. Interruptions during these periods are limited to real emergencies.
>
> Classroom instruction in language arts and mathematics is provided in reduced-size groups. Ideally, homeroom or base teachers work with one group of students, while the other students receive support services, enrichment, or attend large group instruction and practice sessions, either in computer labs or in what PBS schools call an "extension center."

Support services, such as special education resource programs and Title I programs that still use a "pull-out" model, are scheduled during extension time.

Schedules for language arts, reading, mathematics, social studies, science, special programs, and support services are coordinated by an administrator or designee. This may be an individual or a committee of teachers and staff within the school. (Hopkins & Canady, 1997, 13.109–13.131)

Several studies have been conducted of schools using parallel block scheduling. To begin the review, results are reported from one school that has been operating a parallel block schedule for 5 years. Following this in-depth look at Whittier Elementary School, other relevant studies are summarized.

Parallel Block Scheduling: One School's Story

Five years after PBS was implemented at Whittier Elementary School in Mesa, Arizona, Whittier principal Roger Vanderdye described the resulting changes (Garber, 1997; Vanderdye, personal communication, February 1998). Some of the effects were planned; others were serendipitous. Whereas implementing a new schedule may not have caused these effects, Vanderdye would argue that PBS certainly facilitated at least nine positive changes.

Class Size Was Significantly Reduced for Selected Periods of the School Day. Whittier teachers spend from 400 to 900 minutes each week working on mathematics and/or reading with half their homeroom classes, in what are called direct instructional groups (DIGs) Note that some schools call these directed reading groups (DRGs) and directed math groups (DMGs). Two years after the program was implemented, Vanderdye reported that the district-created criterion referenced test (CRT) scores began to rise dramatically across all grade levels.

Direct Teacher Instructional Time Increased Significantly. With fewer children in the classroom being taught specific skills at one time, children's time on task and the sheer number of student–teacher interactions increased exponentially. Vanderdye observed that the average teacher, while teaching the entire class, had a bit less than two student–teacher interactions per pupil during each 50-minute period. During DIG time, with half the class, student–teacher actions increased to over five interactions per pupil in the 50-minute period.

Classroom Pull-Outs Were Eliminated That Also Reduced Fragmentation of the School Day. Typical "pull-out" activities and classes–such as band, orchestra, choral music, English as a second language/English as a foreign language, LD resource, computers, foreign language, gifted/talented, speech, Title/Chapter I, Reading Recovery, DARE–were scheduled during the extension period.

Grouping Concerns Became a Moot Issue. Teachers had complete flexibility to group by performance or not to group at all. Students could be moved freely in and out of groups. No children were stigmatized as different, because all students were either in extension classes or in the classroom receiving instruction at their level.

Classroom Management Improved. With a considerably lower student–teacher ratio, behavior problems diminished. Children were less distracted; teachers had more time to individualize instruction; the level of instruction was more appropriate. Because children were successful academically, behavior became more positive schoolwide.

Instructional Alignment Improved. Because PBS encourages teachers to maximize their teaching time with students during the DIG phase, Whittier teachers focused on content of instruction and delineated clear curricular expectations. Both horizontal and vertical curricular alignment followed within a very short time.

All Children Participated in Gifted Activities. Extension centers piqued the open-ended curiosity of all children. Centers, cooperative groups, pedagogical discussion groups, and process folios for all children became standard in extension groups. Activities were designed to stimulate the "seven smarts" (word, number, picture, music, body, people, and self) described by Gardner's (1983) theory of multiple intelligences.

Teachers Gained Flexibility to Marshal Resources Where Needed. Hard and soft money, technology, grants, and staff could be applied creatively. PBS facilitated the use of part-time teachers and aides, as well as the commingling of funds from various monetary sources.

Inclusion of Students With Special Needs Was Enhanced. Probably the most notable and easily identifiable benefit of PBS, aside from the greater number of student–teacher interactions, was the tremendous increase in learning opportunities for children with special needs. Whittier reduced the number of special education (SPED) students, mostly LD referrals, by half in the very first year of PBS. Because pull-outs for SPED occurred during extension, children leaving the classroom experienced less stigmatization. SPED students could "double-dip"—for example, receiving special reading help in the resource room, but also joining a reading group with their peers and their classroom teacher. SPED students with significant difficulties, such as behavioral or emotional problems (at Whittier, there were five classes of children labeled as such), could still phase into extension classes and DIGs with peers. After 4 years of PBS at Whittier, the total number of referrals dropped to approximately 2%, and the mainstreaming of all special education children was complete. In 1997, Whittier Elementary School won a National Title I Distinguished School Award.

At Whittier Elementary School there was a dramatic increase in test scores from August 1992 to May 1996. Garber (1997) explored the underlying causes, with particular attention to the school's nontraditional scheduling and the innovative allocation of categorical resources. Garber interviewed teachers, school principals, and district administrators to evaluate their perceptions of the changes at Whittier. Except for one teacher, all participants were favorable toward the scheduling changes (primarily the implementation of PBS). The researcher found these positive responses to be particularly remarkable because the interviews took place during the next-to-the-last week of school, traditionally a low point for staff morale and energy. To increase the credibility of her study, Garber triangulated data from 32 interviews, 28 observations, and over 500 pages of documentation. The critical findings related to instructional outcomes were as follows:

> The principal was an agent for change.
>
> Parallel block scheduling allowed for smaller classes in reading and mathematics.
>
> The extension program provided a way to address varying student needs and to extend learning time for selected students.
>
> Most interviewees perceived that the small class sizes in reading and/or mathematics influenced the improved test scores.
>
> Fragmentation of the school day was perceived both to have decreased and to have increased.
>
> Stigmatization decreased because all students left the room systematically; as a growing "ripple effect" of PBS, the integration of services and funds (when permitted) provided opportunities to use federal and state categorical funding more effectively while meeting the intent of the law.

Garber noted two additional positive outcomes of parallel block scheduling: first, a significant reduction in the number of students identified with specific learning disabilities, and second, enhanced inclusion, with integration of general and most special needs students (including gifted and talented students) into common learning experiences through the extension center program.

Although many teachers and other educators at Whittier and in the district attributed the school's gains in student test scores to the small class sizes in reading and mathematics provided through PBS, other schools with small classes have not demonstrated the same level of success. Garber concluded that other components of the Whittier experience contributed to students' performance: "One single innovation cannot account for the success at Whittier. All of these factors working together seem to have produced these improved outcomes, and the researcher's opinion is that it is the unique synergy produced by these variables [brought together by PBS] that partially explains the noted increases in student test scores" (Garber, 1997, p. 159).

PBS AND STUDENT ACHIEVEMENT

The primary goal of parallel block scheduling is to improve student achievement through uninterrupted classroom instruction with smaller classes for language arts and mathematics. Data from numerous individual schools indicate that implementing PBS leads to improved student achievement, as measured on norm-referenced and criterion-referenced tests. Table 13.1 summarizes the results for several schools using parallel block scheduling.

As with most organizational changes, of course, it is difficult to demonstrate with "hard data" that simply adopting the PBS model will raise student achievement. Many other factors influence student achievement, such as the home environment, the teacher, and the match between curriculum and testing; however, there is evidence that once PBS is in place, more research-based instructional practices are likely to occur. Such practices include the following: increasing student–teacher interactions, reducing instructional group size, protecting teaching time, reducing the stigmatization of students in special programs, and so on.

TABLE 13.1
Pre- and Post-parallel Block Scheduling Standardized Test Results

Name of School	Reading Comprehension Pre PBS	Reading Comprehension Post PBS	Mathematics Composite Pre PBS	Mathematics Composite Post PBS	Name of Test
Sleepy Hollow Elementary School (VA)	(1988) 66	(1991) 79	(1988) 72	(1991) 90	Iowa Test of Basic Skills
Whittier Elementary (AZ)	(1991) lowest in district	(1995) highest of all Title I schools	(1991) lowest in district	(1995) highest of all Title I schools	Mesa, Arizona criterion-referenced tests
Wilkes County (GA)	(1995) 36	(1997) 53	(1995) 48	(1997) 71	Iowa Test of Basic Skills

Note: Sleepy Hollow results from a personal communication from Harriet Hopkins, Coordinator Elementary Education, Area III, Fairfax County Public Schools, VA. Whittier Elementary results from Garber (1997). Wilkes County data from Delany, Tobuson, Hooten, and Dozier (1997–1998).

OTHER RESULTS OF PARALLEL BLOCK SCHEDULING

Data also are available from other elementary schools that have adopted parallel block scheduling. In an Indiana study (Wilson, 1993) of data from Indiana Statewide Testing for Educational Progress (ISTEP), statistically significant differences were found in mathematics achievement in favor of PBS classes, although no statistically significant differences were found in reading achievement. Wilson also reported statistically significant differences in students' beliefs about how well they were learning, attitudes toward themselves as learners, and beliefs about how others saw them as learners—all in favor of PBS classes. Responses from interviews of teachers using parallel block scheduling indicated that the teachers believed PBS had benefited students in terms of achievement and attitudes toward school and learning and had enhanced their own effectiveness as teachers.

An outside evaluation of Monroe Elementary School, an ethnically diverse school in Utah, has shown increases in students' performance on state criterion-referenced tests in reading and mathematics.

In other studies, schools using parallel block scheduling have reported the following:

The stigma attached to students receiving support services—special education, remedial classes, even gifted and talented classes—is reduced (Garber, 1997; Hopkins, 1990). Children not in such programs also move to the extension center for supplemental and enrichment activities to support the classroom program. This reduces the perception that certain students are treated differently.

Grouping issues are addressed. In numerous studies of grouping, Oakes (1985) found that ability grouping, or "tracking," students appeared to foster mediocre classroom experiences for most students and erected special barriers to the educational success of poor, Black, and Hispanic youngsters. In certain instances, however, temporary groupings of students for remediation, practice, or enrichment may be advantageous (Slavin, 1987). PBS allows teachers to create flexible skills groups within the controlled, heterogeneously grouped homeroom.

Principals in PBS schools report significantly fewer discipline problems. During language arts and mathematics, students in PBS schools were on task and attentive for approximately 86% of the time, as compared to 57% for students in traditionally scheduled schools (Fogliani, 1990). Children who are on task are out of trouble. This factor also may contribute to the increased achievement reported in PBS schools.

Special education enrollment is reduced. It can be argued that because children are receiving more individualized assistance without missing critical classroom time, many of their educational needs are identified sooner and remedial efforts begin earlier (Delany, Tobusen, Hooten, & Dozier, 1997–1998; Garber, 1997). The reduced need for special education support services allows school districts to allocate more money to other programs.

These reports indicate that parallel block scheduling has produced positive results in many different situations. The model has been adapted to meet the needs of individual schools and different populations of students. It also has been adapted to support current educational initiatives, such as the integration of curriculum and the inclusion of special education students (Snell, Lowman, & Canady, 1996).

Block Scheduling in Middle Schools and High Schools

Although there are several hybrids and modifications of block scheduling in place today, almost all represent some variation of two basic forms. The first form, called the alternate-day block schedule, is also referred to as *A/B*, or *Day 1/Day 2*, or sometimes the eight-block schedule. Essentially, whether there are six, seven, or eight periods in the schedule, students and teachers meet every other day for extended blocks of time, usually from 80 to 110 minutes.

The second basic form is the 4/4 schedule. Students complete four year-long courses each semester. Each course meets for 90 minutes every day, over a 90-day semester. Students earn eight credits per year; thus, they can complete a total of 32 credits during their 4 years in high school. Because students can earn 24 credits in 3 years and can possibly graduate early, this version also is called the "accelerated" schedule.

A comparison of these two scheduling models finds that each has positive aspects and each presents issues that need to be addressed:

Positive Aspects of the Alternate-Day Block Schedule

The scheduling of transfer students is easier than in the 4/4 schedule.

Few curriculum changes are needed before implementation; for example, pacing guides are not as critical as in the 4/4 schedule.

Most principals say singletons pose fewer scheduling conflicts.

Sequencing of courses, or gaps, for example, between a language I and a language II class, is not a major issue.

Full-year programs, such as band, chorus, yearbook, newspaper, or ROTC, are accommodated more readily.

Semester courses, such as research courses and various types of writing classes, seem to be accommodated better in the alternate-day block schedule.

Both teachers and students experience a greater variety of classes by meeting different classes each day over a 2-day period.

Teachers report that when discipline problems arise, both teacher and student have time to "cool off" because one or more days elapse between classes.

Both politically and administratively, the alternate-day block schedule is easier to implement than the 4/4 schedule.

Major Concerns With the Alternate-Day Block Schedule

Students are responsible for the same number of courses as in the single-period schedule.

There is no reduction in the number of classes for teachers; record-keeping requirements do not change.

The number of teacher preparations during any one term remains the same.

More review may be necessary on some days, for example, when a class meets Thursday and then not until Monday.

Longer gaps ensue over long weekends, snow days, or other days off.

There are no savings in textbook expenditures.

Students have limited opportunities for acceleration or for extended learning time in courses with a high failure rate, such as algebra I.

In most schools, the number of course choices remains the same.

Students failing a course must continue to attend, and they have no opportunity to retake the class until summer or the following fall. (This may not be an issue in schools with a low failure rate.)

Positive Aspects of the 4/4 Semester Schedule

Teachers are responsible for fewer classes during each term.

Students have fewer classes, preparations, and tests each term.

Teachers' record-keeping responsibilities during any one term are lower.

Fewer textbooks are needed; estimated savings amount to about 40%.

It is easier to offer extended learning time and allow class repeats for struggling students (see Rettig & Canady, 1998).

It is easier to provide special programs for students in grade 9.

Both teachers and students report that the school day is less stressful.

It is easier to accelerate higher achieving students; for example, students may complete 4 years of two different foreign languages and up to 8 years of mathematics.

Major Concerns with the 4/4 Block Schedule

Scheduling electives (singletons) and some year-long classes, such as music, can be a problem.

Many people see the 4/4 plan as more difficult for transfer students.

Because instructional time is compressed, it may be harder to manage subjects such as foreign language, mathematics, and subjects requiring large amounts of reading.

Many teachers argue that compressing semester courses to 9 weeks reduces their status and effectiveness.

Student absences are viewed as being a greater problem in the 4/4 plan.

Some vocational students are asked to spend one semester at the regular school and one semester at a vocational center; this disconnects them from their regular program and from the "spirit" of the school.

Balancing student schedules is critical; some schools do not recognize the importance of this factor during the first year of implementation.

Because of the issue of retention of learned material, special consideration must be given to the scheduling of classes that lead to AP and state-mandated tests.

Report cards and other progress reports are a scheduling concern, because course time is compressed.

Some teachers report problems with instructional pacing, especially in mathematics.

Some language and math teachers say they cannot "stack" two lessons in one day; as a result, covering the material becomes an issue.

RESULTS OF BLOCK SCHEDULING IN HIGH SCHOOLS

Inquiry into the effects of high school block scheduling is still in its infancy, although some Canadian studies were reported in the mid-1970s. This research can be divided into three strands: effects on school climate, effects on academics, and factors affecting the change to a block schedule.

Effects on School Climate. Overall, in spite of some challenges that the use of block scheduling presents to teachers, the majority report that, after 2 or more years, block scheduling is favorable. Students and parents also are positive. (Angola High School, 1997; Cawelti, 1997; Conner, 1997; Cunningham, 1997; DiRocco, 1998–1999; Eineder, 1996; Freeman, 1996; Guskey & Kifer, 1994; Hundley, 1996; Jones, 1997; Irvine, 1995; King, Clements, Enns, Lockerbie, & Warren, 1975; Mistretta & Polansky, 1997; North Carolina Department of Public Instruction, 1997a; Phelps, 1996; Pulaski County High School, 1994; Sessoms, 1995; Shortt & Thayer, 1998–1999; Snyder, 1997; Staunton, 1997a, 1997b). There is evidence that teachers who have practiced in the block longer and teachers who have more years of experience develop even a stronger preference for the block (Staunton, 1997b). There also is evidence that school principals are the most supportive of block scheduling (compared with teachers, students, and parents); principals are nearly unanimous in their preference for this organizational model over the single period schedule (North Carolina Department of Public Instruction, 1997a). Initially, there is greater stress for teachers until they learn how to plan and teach in a larger block of time, but school eventually becomes less stressful for both teachers and students (Angola High School, 1997; Fleck, 1996; Freeman, 1996; Kramer, 1997a; North Carolina Department of Public Instruction, 1997a; O'Neil, 1995; Salvaterra & Adams, 1995; Schoenstein, 1995; Sessoms, 1995; Snyder, 1997; Staunton, 1997a).

One of the reasons that principals may be so supportive of block scheduling is the positive effect it has on school discipline. There is evidence that the number of discipline referrals to the office is reduced by 25% to 35% (Carroll, 1994; Collins, 1998; Eineder, 1996; Freeman, 1996; Guskey & Kifer, 1994; Hackmann, 1995; Meadows, 1995; Phelps, 1996; Pisapia & Westfall, 1996; Pulaski County High School, 1994; Vawter, 1998). In one school in Florida, the number of referrals was reduced by 50% (Sessoms, 1995). Evidence exists that in-school suspensions also decline (Angola High School, 1997; Eineder, 1996; Snyder, 1997). In one middle school, aggressive student behavior was reduced substantially (86%) after 3 years on a block schedule (Link-Jobe, 1996).

There is evidence that both student and teacher attendance will likely improve, although gains are small (Angola High School, 1997; Chesapeake Public Schools, 1997; Eineder, 1996; Kramer, 1997a; Pisapia & Westfall, 1996; Schoenstein, 1995; Snyder, 1997; Vawter, 1998). It is unlikely that "school-haters" will be persuaded to attend more often by a different schedule. For obvious reasons, the number of class tardies also is reduced (Angola High School, 1996; Eineder, 1996; Guskey & Kifer, 1994; Hoeland, 1997; Snyder, 1997).

Unless special plans are in operation, students may experience difficulty in recovering from absences. In Fairfax County, Virginia, teachers felt students had an easier time recovering from absences in 47-minute periods, although students reported that it was easier to catch up in the block (Irvine, 1995; Jones, 1997). However, there are some indications that because of this factor, the "more motivated" students have fewer absences (Jones, 1997; Kramer, 1996, 1997b; Mistretta & Polansky, 1997).

EFFECTS ON STUDENT PERFORMANCE AND ACHIEVEMENT

Effects on academics have been explored, including the following: grade point average and honor roll achievement, numbers of failures and dropout rates, and students' performance on standardized tests. It should be noted that there have been very few large-scale studies of block scheduling; much of the research reported is based on individual school evaluation reports.

There is consistent evidence that students' grades, as reported by grade point averages, increase and the number of students on the A, B Honor Roll increases. (Angola High School, 1997; Collins, 1998; Edwards, 1995; Eineder, 1996; Governor Thomas Johnson High School, 1995; Guskey & Kifer, 1994; Hottenstein & Malatesta, 1993; Jones, 1997; King, 1996; O'Neil, 1995; Pelham High School, 1996; Pisapia & Westfall, 1996; Pulaski County High School, 1994; Reid, 1994; Reid, Hierck, & Vergin, 1995; Snyder, 1997; Stumpf, 1995; Vawter, 1998). There also is evidence that grade improvement may be greater in 4/4 schools than in A/B schools (Jones, 1997; Pisapia & Westfall, 1996).

There is evidence that failure rates in 4/4 schools decline (Governor Thomas Johnson High School, 1995; Hackmann, 1995; Hottenstein & Malatesta, 1993; Reid, 1995; Reid, Hierck, & Vergin, 1995; Schoenstein, 1995; Vawter, 1998). Some students often labeled at-risk are more likely to stay in school; this is especially true in the 4/4 schedule, probably because students may repeat several classes and still graduate with their class (Reid, 1995; Sharman, 1990). There is evidence that students complete more courses in the 4/4 plan than in the A/B or single-period schedules (Canady & Rettig, 1995; Edwards, 1995; Irvine, 1995; O'Neil, 1995). Graduation rates at least hold in block scheduled schools, and there is evidence that graduation rates improve (Carroll, 1994; Eineder, 1996; Hottenstein & Malatesta, 1993; Pulaski County High School, 1995; Reid, 1995; Reid et al., 1995; Sessoms, 1995). Some data suggest that graduation rates are likely to increase more with the 4/4 plan than with the A/B plan (Hottenstein & Malatesta, 1993; Sessoms, 1995).

Although the aforementioned data are important when considering the effects of block scheduling, considerable controversy has arisen regarding studies reporting "hard data" on student performance, specifically student performance on standardized measurements. Most studies have been focused on the effect of the 4/4 plan on student achievement; little evidence exists regarding student performance in A/B schedules.

Data regarding the improvement of standardized test scores under block scheduling vary. Several studies have been reported based on data from Canadian schools, where the 4/4 plan has been used for more than 20 years and continues to be used (Bateson, 1990; Gore, 1996; Marshall, Taylor, Bateson, & Bridgen, 1995; Raphael, Wahlstrom, & McLean, 1986). More recently, studies from the United States have become available (Angola High School, 1997; Averett, 1994; Chesapeake Public Schools, 1997; Hamdy, 1996; Hoeland, 1997; Jones, 1997; Kramer, 1996, 1997a, 1997b; Lockwood, 1995; North Carolina Department of Public Instruction, 1997b; Pisapia & Westfall, 1996; Schroth & Dixon, 1995; Shortt & Thayer, 1998–1999; Snyder, 1997; Vawter, 1998; Wronkovich, Hess, & Robinson, 1997; York, 1997). Readers should analyze all studies carefully. Key questions include the following: What evidence is provided that measurements are valid and reliable? What attempts were made to control for other variables (socioeconomic status, SES; prior achievement level; consistency of testing conditions; and the like) that might influence test scores?

The largest U.S. study to date has been completed by the Department of Instruction in North Carolina (1997b). Over the past few years the number of schools operating on the 4/4 schedule in North Carolina has increased to more than 65%. It has been possible to compare the performance of block and nonblocked schools systematically through the use of statewide end-of-course (EOC) examinations in algebra I, English I, biology, U.S. history, and economics, legal, and political systems. Data have been presented for 3 years of EOC testing. Tests were administered at the completion of each course; thus first semester 4/4 students took their examinations at the end of the first semester; second semester 4/4 students and nonblocked students took their examinations at the end of the school year. Researchers used two controls to equalize the populations taking the EOC tests because they discovered that lower performing schools and schools with students having lower socioeconomic status (SES) had moved to the 4/4 schedule more rapidly than higher performing schools. Schools adopting the 4/4 had a lower "starting point"; their test scores in nearly every area were lower prior to block scheduling than in nonblocked schools. In addition, the "parents' education level," a proxy for SES, was lower for blocked schools. Thus it would have been methodologically improper to compare blocked and unblocked schools without statistically controlling for the difference in populations. The study reported that "overall, students in block and non-block scheduled schools have equivalent End-of-Course test scores" (North Carolina Department of Public Instruction, 1998, p. 5) With adjustment for parents' educational level and "starting point," blocked schools scored significantly higher in English I, biology, and U.S. history in 1994, blocked schools scored significantly higher in all five EOC tests in 1995; and blocked schools scored significantly higher in U.S. history in 1996. It should be noted that the population of blocked and nonblocked schools changed each year as more schools adopted the 4/4 schedule. In addition, no relation was found between the length of time in a block schedule and students' EOC scores.

In a study frequently cited by critics of block scheduling, Bateson (1990) reported significantly lower achievement in science for students in schools operating the 4/4 schedule. Nonblocked students scored statistically higher than blocked students in each of the six domains of science knowledge that were part of the Third Provincial Assessment of Science. Test items were validated, and the statistical analysis of results was sound. The assessment of science achievement, however, was not designed to compare blocked and nonblocked performance. The educational significance of this study and similar studies (Gore, 1996; Marshall, Taylor, Bateson, & Bridgen, 1995; Raphael, Wahlstrom, & McLean, 1986) has been questioned by Kramer (1997b) and others for the following reasons.

In the Bateson study, the testing timetable favored students in year-long classes. The examination was given to all students in May 1986, regardless of when they took science that year. For students who had completed the class during the fall semester, the exam was taken nearly a full semester after completion of the course. Spring semester students missed 2 days of instruction for every 1 day missed by full-year students. The testing time frame itself could have had an effect on the results.

As mentioned previously in the North Carolina study (1997b), higher achieving schools satisfied with their students' progress have not adopted the 4/4 schedule as quickly as lower achieving schools, who are searching for ways to improve. Prior to implementation of the block schedule, 4/4 schools are lower achieving and serve a lower SES population. The Bateson study did collect a variety of background variables, including three that could somewhat logically serve as proxies for SES: future course plans in science, whether they have and use a computer at home, and future educational plans. Because no differences were found among the differently scheduled groups on these background items, it was assumed that the comparison groups were equivalent. Critics of the Bateson study argue that owning a personal computer was not commonplace in 1986; in fact, so few people owned a computer as to make this variable an inappropriate proxy for SES. Also, the use of future educational plans as a proxy for SES is questioned. The differences in populations caused by this "volunteer effect" could account partially for the differences in achievement that have been reported.

In addition, there are several important differences in the manner in which the 4/4 semester block schedule has been implemented in Canada and the United States. For example, it has been reported in Canada that blocks range from 60 to 80 minutes in length (Raphael et al., 1986); we are aware of only one 4/4 school in the United States with less than 80 minutes per block; most have classes from 85 to 90 minutes in length. It also has been reported that in Canada little staff development was provided in how to adapt instruction and course pacing (Kramer, 1996); in most U.S. implementations, staff development and pacing have been addressed at least to some extent. Teachers in Canada often were provided planning time only one semester (Kramer, 1997b); teachers in the United States generally have been allocated one of four blocks for lesson planning each semester.

Each student tested was given a 40-item multiple choice test from the 120 test item bank. Based on the data reported, the mean raw score for full-year science students was 22.1/40, the mean raw score for fall semester science students was 20.6/40 (93% of full-year students), and the mean raw score for spring semester science students was 21.1/40 (95% of full-year students). Statistically significant differences favoring year-long science participation were reported. It can be argued, however, that these differences can be explained by the volunteer effect and/or the testing timetable. Additional research in the appropriate context, which employs adequate controls, is still needed.

The long-term effect of the 4/4 schedule on student retention of learned material is still a matter of debate (Angola High School, 1997; Carroll, 1994; Kramer, 1996, 1997b; Smythe, Stennett, & Rachar, 1974; Stennett & Rachar, 1973). Tentatively, "it seems safest to conclude that a gap in instruction may reduce recall of recently learned material but that it will probably have no long-term negative effects on student learning" (Kramer, 1996, p. 763).

The effect of the 4/4 schedule on student performance on AP examinations is unclear. Many schools report greater numbers of students taking AP courses and stable or increasing pass rates. Data analysis conducted by the College Board has suggested that students who take AP courses for only one semester score lower on some AP examinations than students who are enrolled in courses for the entire academic year (College Board, 1996a, 1996b). This may be more a testing issue than a learning issue; students who have completed an AP course in the fall must wait until May for the exam, whereas students enrolled in the spring semester are tested long before the course is completed (unless the school year begins in early August). Also, the comparison released by the College Board did not control for economic differences among the schools or for the previous test scores at those schools. Furthermore, students in block-scheduled schools where AP courses extended over two semesters were classified with the year-long comparison group.

The fixed May testing date has forced many schools on the 4/4 plan to make special adaptations. In some schools, AP classes are one semester; for lab classes, they are often scheduled over two semesters; and some AP classes are scheduled for 27 weeks. Further investigation of the relation between the time provided for AP courses and AP test scores is needed. (Chesapeake Public Schools, 1997; Edwards, 1995; Governor Thomas Johnson High School, 1995; Guskey & Kifer, 1994; Jones, 1997; Keen, 1996; Pisapia & Westfall, 1996; Salvaterra & Adams, 1995; Vawter, 1998). In addition, there is some evidence that participation in AP courses increases (Chesapeake Public Schools, 1997; Jones, 1997).

There is evidence that the needs of students with disabilities may be better met in block schedules; additional evidence suggests that the 4/4 plan may be preferable to the A/B plan for special education students (Jones, 1997; Santos & Rettig, 1999).

EFFECTS ON SPECIFIC COURSES AND CURRICULUM

Debate continues about which courses are most appropriately taught within the 4/4 plan. In a survey by the North Carolina Department of Public Instruction (1997a), using a 3-point scale (1 = does not work well, 2 = makes no difference, 3 = works well), all courses were rated above 2 by teachers, students, and principals. The lowest ratings by teachers were for band and orchestra (2.13) and AP courses (2.16); the highest ratings were for PE and health (2.72) and science courses (2.67) other than biology (2.52). The lowest ratings by students were for foreign language (2.31), special education (2.35) and AP courses (2.37); the highest ratings by students were for PE and health (2.59) and honors courses (2.58). Principals rated all courses at or above 2.5 (band) and most courses above 2.8. In another study in California, teachers agreed that their subjects adapted well to a block schedule (on a Likert scale of 0–4, 2.911; Staunton, 1997b).

In some courses, such as mathematics, teachers may cover less material; however, many teachers say that the material covered is taught better and in greater depth. Again, this finding is reported more often under the 4/4 plan (Kramer, 1996). In 1996, the Third International Mathematics and Science Study included a comparison of mathematics curricula in the United States and other industrialized countries. It was reported that the U.S. curriculum was less focused and covered more topics superficially; the Japanese curriculum covered fewer topics in much greater depth. The United States ranked 28th; Japan ranked 3rd.

There is limited evidence that math performance under a block schedule initially may drop and then improve; this is probably a pacing issue that can be corrected (Kramer, 1996).

In both the A/B and 4/4 plans, foreign language teachers report difficulty covering the equivalent of two classes of material during a double-length period (Sessoms, 1995). There is evidence, however, that more "intense" instruction produces greater learning in foreign language (Blaz, 1998; Edwards, 1976; Larson & Smalley, 1972; Stern, 1976; Williamson, 1968). In the 4/4 plan, foreign language must be carefully sequenced; the first 2 years should be offered in consecutive semesters, preferably in the same academic year. Students who have completed a year of foreign language in middle school should be scheduled for level II in their first semester of high school to maintain continuity. This recommendation is based on the premise that the second year of a language is the most critical and has the highest failure rate of any of the 4 to 5 years of language instruction. One study of adults in community college compared compressed term (6 weeks, 10 hours per week) versus standard term (15 weeks, 4 hours per week) and found achievement at similar levels except for vocabulary and structure, where the compressed term instruction was found to be statistically better (at the .05 level; Schoenfeldt, 1997). Many foreign language teachers in the 4/4 schedule state that students receive adequate exposure to subject material (Blaz, 1998; Staunton, 1997a).

Also, based on discussions with many high school principals from across the nation, it is not unusual for some social studies teachers to experience difficulty moving away from a great deal of factual teaching to more conceptual teaching. Social studies teachers often report that current state and national testing programs force them to rely heavily on factual teaching.

The scheduling of performing arts classes within the 4/4 plan also must be addressed. There is evidence that enrollments may decline if the schedule is not adapted. By implementing modifications, such as split blocks or an embedded A/B schedule, it is possible to maintain both quality and enrollment (Angola High School, 1997; Miles & Blocher, 1996; Milleman, 1996a, 1996b; Music Educators National Conference, 1995; Rettig & Canady, 1999; Snyder, 1997). One study indicated that enrollments in art increased with the implementation of a block schedule (Smith, 1997).

Curriculum adjustments need to be made with block schedules, especially with the 4/4 plan, to accommodate pacing issues and the more in-depth study that hopefully occurs. For example, some students may be expected to take additional foreign language and math courses (Canady & Rettig, 1995; Kramer, 1996; personal communication, Diane Frost, curriculum coordinator in the Asheboro City Schools, North Carolina; North Carolina Department of Public Instruction, 1997a).

The students in the 4/4 plan enrolling in additional math courses seem to be of two types: those who fail a course and repeat it, and those who take math courses, such as statistics, for enrichment (Kramer, 1996). These factors may explain why schools report needing additional math teachers after 3 or 4 years on the 4/4 plan. This effect may necessitate changes in the way teachers are assigned to schools. For example, when schools are assigned faculty slots by subject areas, difficulties may arise if and when a significant number of students enroll in additional math, music, or foreign language classes, either as retakes or for enrichment (Averett, 1994; Canady & Rettig, 1995).

In all types of block schedules, because teachers spend more time with whole-class groups in the media center, additional staff and materials are needed in the media center. Circulation may increase as well. (Note: In the 4/4 plan, fewer textbooks are required; this may free some funds for the media center budget.) Additional computer labs also are needed; math teachers tend to make greater use of computer labs and English teachers of writing labs (Angola High School, 1997; Sessoms, 1995; Snyder, 1997). Finally, the number of interdisciplinary teams and studies is likely to increase with block scheduling (Pisapia & Westfall, 1996; Sessoms, 1995).

Data about the amount of homework completed in block-scheduled schools vary. Some teachers report more homework completed; others report less (Blaz, 1998; Kramer, 1996, 1997b; North Carolina Department of Public Instruction, 1997a; Pulaski County High School, 1994; Ross, 1977).

One concern has been that too many teachers allow too much time in class for homework. In a statewide study in North Carolina, 89.7% of teachers reported allowing less than 90 minutes per week (less than 18 minutes per day) of in-class homework; 63.9% allowed 30 minutes or less per week. Also, 93.5% of students reported doing less than 2½ hours of homework during class time per week (less than 40 minutes per week per course; North Carolina Department of Public Instruction, 1997a).

FACTORS INFLUENCING THE SUCCESS OF BLOCK SCHEDULING

One factor critical to the success of block scheduling in middle and high schools is whether the massive educational bureaucracy that has developed around the "given" of daily single-period schedules will accommodate block scheduling. Examples of the existing practices that are issues to be addressed include having state requirements for a specific number of hours of seat time per Carnegie unit of credit and providing only one AP testing date each year. Moreover, if high stakes state tests are administered several weeks before the end of the semester, schools in the 4/4 schedule are disadvantaged. Allowing only one set of requirements for participation in sports also can limit scheduling flexibility (Furman & McKenna, 1995; Sessoms, 1995; Tanner, 1996).

There is evidence that teachers' level of satisfaction with block scheduling is affected by how and when they are involved in the process of changing the schedule. Teachers who were involved at the beginning and throughout the planning and implementation phases were significantly more satisfied with the change than teachers who were less involved. In addition, teachers with greater involvement reported a higher degree of instructional change (Brandenburg, 1995; North Carolina Department of Public Instruction, 1997a; Vawter, 1998).

Finally, the key to successful implementation of block scheduling is sustained staff development. Most teachers in block-scheduled schools plan lessons that include at least three different activities. The two most difficult aspects of a lesson plan for teachers seem to be developing and implementing the application phase of a lesson and managing the transitions within the block. Interestingly, whereas elementary school teachers are taught or otherwise develop skills in classroom transitions, this is relatively new to many high school teachers. Lesson pacing is also a problem for some high school teachers in a block schedule. It appears that just providing teachers with staff development in various teaching strategies is not sufficient; many teachers also need assistance in building those strategies into appropriate lesson plans (Sessoms, 1995; Tanner, 1996; Vawter, 1998).

However, the results of a Minnesota study (Center for Applied Research and Educational Improvement, 1995) indicate that students in longer block-scheduled classes had a higher engagement rate than did students in the shorter, traditional schedule. This appeared to be true for all subject areas, including mathematics. It is strongly suspected that this occurs only after teachers have received assistance in developing lessons to engage learners (Center for Applied Research and Educational Improvement, 1995; O'Neil, 1995).

An overwhelming majority of teachers in a block schedule lecture less and gradually engage students in more active learning structures; as a result, students become less passive in their learning and eventually take more ownership of the learning process (Brandenburg, 1995; Bryant, 1995; Jones, 1997; King, 1996; Kramer, 1996, 1997a; Mayes, 1997; O'Neil, 1995; Phelps, 1996; Pisapia & Westfall, 1996; Quinn, 1997; Sessoms, 1995; Staunton, 1997b; Vawter, 1998).

In reviewing the research about block scheduling at all levels of schooling, there is overwhelming evidence that the school environment is affected by the manner in which the school is scheduled. Block scheduling alone is not a panacea for the many problems of American schools. A school schedule can, however, have an enormous impact on a school's instructional climate. The schedule is not merely a means of moving teachers and students to various spaces during selected periods of time:

> A schedule can be viewed as a resource; it is the schedule that permits the effective utilization of people, space, time, and resources in an organization.
>
> A schedule can help solve problems related to the delivery of instruction or a schedule can be a major source of problems.
>
> A schedule can facilitate the institutionalization of desired programs and instructional practices.

A strong belief, and a review of the relevant research, supports the notion that scheduling is an untapped resource that can serve as a catalyst for school improvement.

REFERENCES

Achilles, C. M. (1997, October). Small classes, big possibilities. *The School Administrator,* pp. 6–15.

Achilles, C. M., Finn, J. D., & Bain, H. P. (1997–1998). Using class size to reduce the equity gap. *Educational Leadership, 55*(4), 40–44.

Angola High School. (1996). *The 4x4 block schedule survey.* Angola, IN: Author.

Angola High School. (1997). *Statistical report.* Angola, IN: Author.

Averett, C. P. (1994). *Block scheduling in North Carolina high schools.* Raleigh, NC: Department of Public Instruction.

Bateson, D. J. (1990). Science achievement in semester and all-year courses. *Journal of Research in Science Education, 27*(3), 233–240.

Blaz, D. (1998). *Teaching foreign languages in the block.* Larchmont, NY: Eye on Education.

Brandenburg, A. C. (1995). *An analysis of block scheduling models and their impact on a positive school climate.* Unpublished doctoral dissertation, Pepperdine University, Malibu, CA.

Brophy, J. (1982). Successful teaching strategies. *Phi Delta Kappan, 63,* 527–532.

Bryant, R. H. (1995). *A comparative study of teaching strategies used in block and traditionally scheduled high schools in the state of Wyoming.* Unpublished doctoral dissertation, University of Wyoming, Laramie.

Canady, R. L., & Rettig, M. D. (1995). *Block scheduling: A catalyst for change in high schools.* Larchmont, NY: Eye on Education.

Carroll, J. M. (1994). *The Copernican plan evaluated: The evolution of a revolution.* Topsfield, MA: Copernican Associates.

Cawelti, G. (1997). *Effects of high school restructuring: Ten schools at work.* Arlington, VA: Educational Research Service.

Center for Applied Research and Educational Improvement. (1995). *Report study of the four period schedule for Anoka-Henepin district no. 11.* Minneapolis, MN: Author. (http://carei.coled.umn.edu/blockscheduling/Research/REPORTs.HTM)

Chesapeake Public Schools. (1997). *4X4 block schedule evaluation follow-up achievement data, Western Branch High School 1996–97.* Chesapeake, VA: Author.

College Board. (1996a, September 19; revised March 10, 1997). *AP and January examinations* [Press release]. Princeton, NJ: The College Board.

College Board. (1996b, December 12). *Performance of AP students who are block scheduled* [Press release]. Princeton, NJ: The College Board.

Collins, R. D. (1998). *An analysis of a rural high school's first year in a 4 X 4 block schedule.* Unpublished doctoral dissertation, George Washington University, Washington, DC.

Conner, S. R. (1997). *The influences of block scheduling in secondary agriculture science programs in East Texas.* Unpublished doctoral dissertation, Stephen F. Austin University, Stevensville, TX.

Cunningham, D. J. (1997). *Implementation of an alternate day block schedule: A case study.* Unpublished doctoral dissertation, Virginia Polytechnic Institute and State University, Blacksburg.

Delany, M., Tobusen, L. Hooton, B., & Dozier, A. (1997–1998). Parallel block scheduling spells success. *Educational Leadership, 55*(4), 61–63.

DiRocco, M. D. (1998–1999). How an alternating-day schedule empowers teachers. *Educational Leadership, 56*(4), 82–84.

Edwards, C. M., Jr. (1995). The 4x4 plan. *Educational Leadership, 53*(3), 16–19.

Edwards, H. P. (1976). Evaluation of the French immersion program offered by the Ottawa Roman Catholic Separate School Board. *Canada Modern Language Review, 33,* 137–142.

Eineder, D. (1996). *The effects of block scheduling in a high school.* Unpublished doctoral dissertation, Appalachian State University, Boone, NC.

Fleck, L. M. (1996). *Block scheduling: A descriptive study of its effect on student distress.* Unpublished doctoral dissertation, Memphis State University.

Fogliani, A. E. (1990). *A case study of parallel block scheduling: An instructional management strategy.* Unpublished doctoral dissertation, University of Virginia.

Freeman, C. J. (1996). *Block scheduling: A vehicle for school change.* Unpublished doctoral dissertation, University of Minnesota, Minneapolis.

Furman, J., & McKenna, J. B. (1995). Dover renew 2000: Implementation of a block schedule. *ERS Spectrum, 13*(2), 29–36.

Garber, M. G. (1997). *Parallel block scheduling: A study of integrated services and funding resulting in improved student achievement.* Unpublished doctoral dissertation, University of Virginia.

Gardner, H. (1983). *Frames of mind: The theory of multiple intelligences.* New York: Basic Books.

Glass, G. V., Cahen, L. S., Smith, M. L., & Filby, N. N. (1979). Class size and learning—New interpretation of the research literature. *Today's Education, 68,* 42–44.

Gore, G. R. (1996). Provincial exam results and timetables. *Catalyst, 39*(3).

Governor Thomas Johnson High School. (1995). *Three year summary report 1992–95.* Frederick, MD: Author.

Guskey, T., & Kifer, E. (1994). *Program evaluation: Block scheduling at Governor Thomas Johnson High School* (second year report). Unpublished manuscript, College of Education, University of Kentucky.

Hackmann, D. G. (1995). Ten guidelines for implementing block scheduling. *Educational Leadership, 53*(3), 24–27.

Hamdy, M. (1996). *Block scheduling: Its impact on academic achievement, and the perceptions of students, teachers, and administrators.* Unpublished doctoral dissertation, Florida Atlantic University, Boca Raton.

Hoeland, J. M. (1997). *The effect of block classes on student achievement of high school freshmen.* Unpublished doctoral dissertation, University of Denver, Denver, CO.

Hopkins, H. J. (1990). *A comparison of the effectiveness of pull out programs in a parallel block scheduled school and in a traditionally scheduled school.* Unpublished doctoral dissertation, University of Virginia, Charlottesville.

Hopkins, H. J., & Canady, R. L. (1997). Parallel block scheduling for elementary schools. In *ASCD curriculum handbook* (pp. 13.109–13.131). Alexandria, VA: ASCD.

Hottenstein, D., & Malatesta, C. (1993). Putting a school in gear with intensive scheduling. *High School Magazine, 1*(2), 28–29.

Hundley, W. W. (1996). *A comparative study of classroom environments in traditional and block scheduled classes.* Unpublished doctoral dissertation, Seattle Pacific University, Seattle.

Irvine, T. H. (1995). *An evaluation of flexible scheduling in an urban high school.* Unpublished doctoral dissertation, Northern Arizona University, Flagstaff.

Jones, B. (1997). *A status report of block scheduling in nine high schools.* Office of High School Instruction and K–12 Curriculum Service, Fairfax County Public Schools, 7423 Camp Alger Avenue, Falls Church, VA 22077.

Keen, C. M. (1996). *An investigation of the achievement of 4 x 4 block-scheduled advanced placement calculus A/B students.* Unpublished doctoral dissertation, College of William and Mary, Williamsburg, VA.

King, A. J. C., Clements, J. L., Enns, J. G., Lockerbie, J. W., & Warren, W. K. (1975). *Semestering the secondary school.* Toronto: Ontario Institute for Studies in Education.

King, B. B. (1996). *The effects of block scheduling on learning environment, instructional strategies, and academic achievement.* Unpublished doctoral dissertation, University of Central Florida, Orlando.

Kramer, S. L. (1996). Block scheduling and high school mathematics instruction. *The Mathematics Teacher, 89*(9), 758–767.

Kramer, S. L. (1997a, February). What we know about block scheduling and its effects on math instruction: Part I. *NASSP Bulletin*, pp. 18–24.

Kramer, S. L. (1997b, March). What we know about block scheduling and its effects on math instruction: Part II. *NASSP Bulletin*, pp. 68–82.

Larson, C. N., & Smalley, W. A.. (1972). *Becoming bilingual: A guide to language learning.* South Pasadena, CA: William Carey Library.

Link-Jobe, J. L. (1996). *Reducing aggressive student behaviors through block scheduling.* Unpublished doctoral dissertation, Oregon State University, Corvallis.

Lockwood, S. L. (1995). Semesterizing the high school schedule: The impact on student achievement in algebra and geometry. *NASSP Bulletin, 79*(595), 102–110.

Marshall, M., Taylor, A., Bateson, D., & Bridgen, S. (1995). *The British Columbia assessment of mathematics and science: Preliminary report (DRAFT).* Victoria: British Columbia Ministry of Education.

Mayes, L. M. (1997). *Relationship of instructional changes in high schools with intensive scheduling models.* Unpublished doctoral dissertation, Widener University, Chester, PA.

Meadows, M. E. (1995). *A preliminary program review of the four-period day as implemented in four high schools.* Unpublished doctoral dissertation, University of Maryland, College Park.

Miles, R. B., & Blocher L. R. (1969). *Block scheduling: Implications for music education.* Springfield, IL: Focus on Excellence.

Milleman, J. (1996a). The 4x4 block schedule and Angola High School band. *Indiana Musicator, 41*(4), 8–10.

Milleman, J. (1996b). The 4x4 block schedule and Angola High School band. *BD Guide, 10*(5), 28–30.

Mistretta, G. M., & Polansky, H. B. (1997, December). Prisoners of time: Implementing a block schedule in the high school. *NASSP Bulletin*, pp. 23–31.

Music Educators National Conference. (1995). *Scheduling time for music.* Reston, VA: Music Educators National Conference.

North Carolina Department of Public Instruction, Division of Accountability Services. (1997a). *1997 Block scheduling survey—Executive summary: Critical issues.* Raleigh, NC: Department of Public Instruction. (Available at http://www.dpi.state.nc.us/block_scheduling/)

North Carolina Department of Public Instruction, Division of Accountability Services. (1997b). *1997 Blocked scheduling end-of-course test scores evaluation brief.* Raleigh: NC: Department of Public Instruction. (Available at http://www.dpi.state.nc.us/block_scheduling/)

Oakes, J. (1985). *Keeping track: How schools structure inequality.* New Haven, CT: Yale University Press.

Olson, D. (1998, February 4). Will success spoil Success for All? *Education Week*, pp. 42–45.

O'Neil, J. (1995). Finding time. *Educational Leadership, 53*(3), 11–15.

Pelham High School. (1996). *Report card for Pelham High School.* Pelham, NH: Author.

Phelps, C. R. (1996). *An examination of 8-block scheduling: A case study of three selected Illinois schools.* Unpublished doctoral dissertation, Southern Illinois University, Carbondale.

Pisapia, J., & Westfall, A. L. (1996). *Alternative high school scheduling: Student achievement and behavior.* Richmond, VA: Metropolitan Educational Research Consortium.

Pulaski County High School. (1994). *Survey report: Four-four block schedule.* Dublin, VA: Author.

Quinn, K. M. (1997). *The effects of intensified scheduling on instructional methodologies.* Unpublished doctoral dissertation, Immaculata College, PA.

Raphael, D., Wahlstrom, M. W., & McLean, L. D.. (1986). Debunking the semestering myth. *Canadian Journal of Education, 11*(1), 36–52.

Reid, W. M. (1994). The Copernican timetable and mathematics: Grade 12 exam results at L. V. Rogers Secondary School. *Vector,* Spring, 50–51.

Reid, W. M. (1995). *Restructuring secondary schools with extended time blocks and semesterized courses.* Unpublished doctoral dissertation, Gonzaga University, British Columbia.

Reid, W. M., Hierck, T., & Vergin, L. (1995). Measurable gains of block scheduling. *The School Administrator, 51*(3), 32–33.

Rettig, M. D., & Canady, R. L. (1998). High failure rates in required mathematics courses: Can a modified block schedule be part of the cure? *NASSP Bulletin, 596,* 56–65.

Rettig, M. D., & Canady, R. L. (1999, March). The effects of block scheduling. *School Administrator,* pp. 14–19.

Rosenshine, B. (1983). Teaching functions. *Elementary School Journal, 83,* 335–351.

Ross, J. A. (1977). An evaluation of timetable innovation in Ontario. *Canadian Journal of Education, 3,* 23–35.

Salvaterra, M., & Adams, D. (1995). Departing from tradition: Two schools' stories. *Educational Leadership, 53*(3), 32–36.

Santos, K. E., & Rettig, M. D. (1999, January/February). Going on the block: Meeting the needs of students with disabilities in high schools with block scheduling. *Teaching Exceptional Children,* pp. 54–59.

Schoenfeldt, A. Y. (1997). *Achievement and satisfaction in adult Spanish language courses with compressed and standard formats.* Unpublished doctoral dissertation, Florida Atlantic University, Boca Raton.

Schoenstein, R. (1995). The new school on the block schedule. *The Executive Educator, 17*(8), 18–21.

Schroth, G., & Dixon, J. (1996). The effects of block scheduling on student performance. *International Journal of Educational Reform, 5*(4), 472–476.

Sessoms, J. C. (1995). *Teachers' perceptions of three models of high school block scheduling.* Unpublished doctoral dissertation, University of Virginia, Charlottesville.

Sharman, R. G. (1990). Student dropouts and scheduling patterns in secondary schools: An exploratory study. *Alberta Journal of Educational Research, 4,* 325–336.

Shortt, T. L., & Thayer, Y. V. (1998–1999). Block scheduling can enhance school climate. *Educational Leadership, 56*(4), 76–81.

Slavin, R. E. (1987). Ability grouping and student achievement in elementary schools: A best-evidence synthesis. *Review of Educational Research, 57,* 293–336.

Smith, A. D. (1997). *The role of art in restructured schools: A case study of two restructured high schools.* Unpublished doctoral dissertation, Indiana University, Bloomington.

Smythe, O. G., Stennett, R. G., & Rachar, B. (1974). *Longterm retention of numeric and algebraic skills in semesterized and non-semesterized programmes.* London, Ontario: London Board of Education. (Micromedia Limited Use Microlog order number ON00774)

Snell, M. E., Lowman, D. K., & Canady, R. L. (1996). Parallel block scheduling: Accommodating students' diverse needs in elementary schools. *Journal of Early Intervention, 20*, 265–278.

Snyder, D. (1997, October). *4-Block scheduling: A case study of data analysis of one high school after two years.* Paper presented the annual meeting of the Midwest Educational Research Association, Chicago.

Staunton, J. T. (1997a). *A study of teacher beliefs on the efficacy of block scheduling.* Unpublished doctoral dissertation, University of Southern California.

Staunton, J. T. (1997b, December). A study of teacher beliefs on the efficacy of block scheduling. *NASSP Bulletin*, pp. 73–80.

Stennett, R. G., & Rachar, B. (1973). *Gains in mathematics knowledge in grade 10 semesterized and non-semesterized programmes.* London, Ontario: London Board of Education. (Micromedia Limited Use Microlog order number ON00775)

Stern, H. H. (1976). The Ottawa-Carleton French project: Issues, conclusions, and policy implications. *Canadian Modern Language Review, 33*, 216–233.

Stumpf, T. (1995). A Colorado school's un-rocky road to trimesters. *Educational Leadership, 53*(3), 20–33.

Tanner, B. M. (1996). *Perceived staff needs of teachers in high schools with block schedules.* Unpublished doctoral dissertation, University of Virginia, Charlottesville.

Third International Mathematics and Science Study. (1996). *Mathematics achievement in the middle school years.* TIMSS International Study Center: Boston College.

Toch, T., & Streisand, B. (1997, October 13). Does class size matter? *U.S. News & World Report*, pp. 22–20.

Vawter, D. H. (1998). *Changes associated with the implementation of block scheduling in American secondary schools.* Unpublished doctoral dissertation, University of Virginia, Charlottesville.

Williamson, V. G. (1968). A pilot program in teaching Spanish: An intensive approach. *Modern Language Journal, 52*, 73–78.

Wilson, L. J. (1993). *The effects of parallel block scheduling versus surface scheduling on reading and mathematics achievement on students' attitudes toward school and learning.* Unpublished doctoral dissertation, Ball State University, Muncie, IN.

Wronkovich, M., Hess, C. A., & Robinson, J. E. (1997, December). An objective look at math outcomes based on new research into block scheduling. *NASSP Bulletin*, pp. 32–41.

Yopp, H. K. (1995). Teaching reading. *The Reading Teacher, 48*(6), 538–542.

York, T. (1997). *A comparative analysis of student achievement in block and traditionally scheduled high schools.* Unpublished doctoral dissertation, University of Houston.

AUTHOR INDEX

A

ABACUSxp Instructional Management System for Macintosh or Windows, *298*
Achilles, C. M., 349, *367*
Adams, D., *372*
Adelson, J., 67, *90*
Adler, M. J., 343, *344*
Adler, S. A., *132*
Airasian, P. W., 303, 304, 306, 308, *322*
Alam, D., 338, *344*
Alba, R. D., 115, 116, *129*
Alderson, J. C., 307, *322*
Alford, L. E., *322*
Alleman-Brooks, J. E., 88, *94*
Alliance for Service-Learning in Education Reform, 82, *90*
Almond, G. A., 51, *53*
Alnot, S. D., *259*
Alter, G., 43, 44, *53*
American Association of College for Teacher Education, 145, *165*
American Association of School Administrators, 236
American Education Research Association, 239, *259*
American Federation of Teachers, 236
Ammon, R., 44, *60*
Anderson, C., 43, *53*, 68, *90*
Anderson, F. J., 73, *90*
Anderson, L., 3, 7, 9, 11, 13, 22, *29*, 43, *53*
Andre, T., 50, 51, *56*
Angell, A., 52, *56*
Angola High School, 359, 360, 361, 363, 365, *367*
Appiah, K. A., 113, *129*
Araboulou, A., 69, *91*
Archbald, D. A., 156, *165*
Armento, B. J., 40, *59*
Aronson, E., 44, *53*
Ashburn, E., 145, *177*
Assessment Training Institute, 236
Assessor, The, 282, *298*
Astin, A., 16, 23, *29*
Atwood, V. A., 80, *91*

Au, K. H., 151, *166*
Aurbach, R., *298*, *299*
Averett, C. P., 361, 365, *367*

B

Bagely, W. C., 316, *322*
Bain, H. P., *367*
Baker, K. A., 158, *166*
Balch, S. A., 141, *166*
Banaszak, R. A., 65, *91*
Banks, C., 42, *53*, 109, *129*
Banks, J. A., 42, *53*, *54*, 66, 71, *91*, 106, 107, 108, 109, 110, 111, 112, 125, *129*, 138, 139, 140, 144, 146, 148, 163, *166*
Barber, B. R., 6, 7, 45, *54*
Barker, R. G., 51, *54*
Barr, R., *54*, 316, *322*
Barth, J., *54*
Barton, A. H., 316, *322*
Barton, L. E., 343, *344*
Bateson, D. J., 361, *368*, *370*
Battistoni, R. M., 35, 39, 47, 48, *54*
Beal, G., 44
Beane, J. A., 83, *95*
Beaulieu, L. J., 160, *166*
Beck, I., 12, 13, *31*
Becker, D. F., 250, 253, 255, *259*
Beckerman, M., 48, *57*
Benbow, C. P., 184, 185, *193*, *196*
Beneson, W., 86, *91*
Bennally, A., 148, *166*
Bennett, C. E., 68, *91*
Bennett, C. L., 106, 107, 109, 113, 119, 121, *129*
Bennett, S., 23, *29*
Bennett, W. J., 39, *54*, 78, *91*
Berelson, B., 113, *130*
Berlin, J., 272, *274*
Berliner, C. C., *96*
Berliner, D., 84, *91*
Berry, B. W., 44, *56*, 149

375

Berry, G. L., *166*
Berson, M. J., 85, 86, *91*
Bertocci, T. A., 82, *96*
Beyer, B., 49, *54,* 78, 79, *91*
Biemiller, A. J., 185, *194*
Birkey, C. J., 41, *59*
Blaz, D., 364, 365, *368*
Blocher, L. R., *371*
Bloom, B. S., 84, *91*
Bobbing GradeBook, *299*
Bobbing GradeBook Pro, *299*
Boocock, S. S., 48, *54,* 81, *91*
Boone, R., 86, *94*
Borland, J. H., 192, *194*
Bossung, J., 145, *175*
Bouljon, G., 273, *274*
Bowers, C. A., 85, *91*
Bowman, B., 146, *166*
Boyer, E. L., 83, *91,* 334, *344*
Braddock, J. H. II, 337, *344*
Bradley Commission of History in Schools, 39, 54
Brameld, T., 139, *166*
Brandenburg, A. C., 366, 367, 368
Brandhorst, A., 67, *91*
Brandt, R. S., 72, *95, 96, 322*
Branson, M., 16, 17, *29*
Braun, J. A., 86, *91*
Braxton, J., 25, *30*
Brekke, N. R., 333, *344*
Bridgeford, N. J., 300
Bridgen, S., *370*
Broadnax, W. D., *54*
Brody, R., 19, *29*
Brophy, J., 84, *91,* 349, *368*
Broudy, H S., 140, *166*
Browder, C. S., *195*
Brown, A. L., 84, *97*
Brown, W., *98*
Bruner, J. S., 192, *194*
Bryant, R. H., 367, *368*
Burch, H. R., 69, *92*
Burstyn, J. N., 87, *92*
Bush, R. N., 332, *344*
Butterfield, E. C., *194*
Buttery, T., 145, *166*
Butts, R., 37, *54,* 105, *130*

C

Cahen, L. S., 316, *322, 369*
Calderon, M., 151, *167*
Callahan, C. M., 184, 192, *194*
Callahan, L. G., 317, *322*
Campbell, P., *174*
Canady, R. L., 334, 338, *344,* 348, 360, 365, *368, 370, 372, 373*
Cannell, J. J., 310, *322*

Carnegie Council on Adolescent Development, 156, *167*
Carpenter, T., *259*
Carroll, J. D., 41, *54*
Carroll, J. M., *340, 344,* 359, 360, 363, *368*
Carter, G. R., 83, *92*
Carter, K., 278, *299*
Cawelti, G., 333, 343, *345,* 359, *368*
Cazden, C. B., 157, 158, *167*
Center for Applied Research and Educational Improvement, 366, 367, *368*
Center for Civic Education, 6, 19, 20, 21, 40, *54,* 64, 85, *92,* 105, 107, 123, 124, *130*
Chambers, B., *299*
Chandler, K., 26, *31*
Chaney, B., 26, *31*
Chapman, C., 26, *31*
Chavarria, L., *325*
Cherryholmes, C. H., 48, *54,* 81, *92*
Chesapeake Public Schools, 359, 361, 363, *368*
Cheville, J., *275*
Chilcoat, G., 50, *54*
Chilcott, J. H., 66, *92*
Chinn, P., 146, *169*
Classmaster 2.0+, *299*
Clegg, A. A., Jr., 66, 71, 81, 84, *91, 92, 99*
Clements, J. L., *370*
Cochran-Smith, M., 151, *167*
Cohen, M. N., 113, *130*
Cohen, S. A., 307, 308, *322*
Colby, A., 77, *92*
Cole, M., *175*
College Board, *167,* 363, *368*
Collins, J., *173*
Collins, M., 152, *167*
Collins, R. D., 359, 360, *368*
Colomb, R., 50, *54*
Computerized Gradebook, *299*
Condon, W., *274*
Conklin, N. F., *236,* 300
Connell, R., 67, *92*
Conner, S. R., 359, *368*
Conrad, B. D., 73, *92*
Conrad, D., 70, 83, *92*
Contreras, G., *54*
Cook-Gumperz, J., 157, *167*
Cooper, E., 156, *167*
Cooper, L., 155, *167*
Corbett, H. D., 302, *322*
Cornbleth, C., 22, *29,* 49, *50, 54,* 147, *167*
Cortes, C. E., 149, *167*
Costa, A., 84, *92*
Costell, P. J. M., 49, *54*
Covington, M., 205, *236*
Cramer, R. H., 186, 187, *194*
Crawford, J., 158, *167*
Cremin, L. A., 128, *130*
Crisman, F., 75, *92*
Csikszentmihalyi, M., 189, *194*

AUTHOR INDEX

CSL Win School Version 3.6, *299*
CTB Classroom Manager—Macintosh Version, *299*
CTB Classroom Manager—Windows 95 Version, *299*
Cuban, L., 41, *55*
Cubberly, E. P., 316, *322*
Cummins, J., 140, 151, *167*
Cunningham, D. J., 359, *368*
Curriculum Designer, *299*
Curtis, C., 44, 45, *55*
Czarra, F., 68, *92*

D

Dalton, R. J., 23, *29*, 38, *55*
Damon, W., 77, *92*
D'Andrade, R., 113, *130*
Dantonio, M., 84, *92*
Darling-Hammond, L., 146, 147, 155, 156, 157, *168*, 303, 304, 307, 308, *322*, *323*
Davidman, L., 109, 112, *130*
Davidman, P. T., 109, 112, *130*
Davis, D. G., 146, 156, *168*
Davis, J. E., 37, *55*
Davis, O. L., 41, *59*
DeKanter, A. A., *166*
Delany, M., 354, 356, *368*
Delpit, L. D., 151, *168*
Despain, L., 272, *274*
Dewey, J., 49, *55*, 70, 71, 79, 84, *93*, *274*
Diaz, E., *167*
Diaz, S., 151, *168*
Dickinson, G., 38, *55*
Dillon, J. T., 79, *93*
DiRocco, M. D., 359, *368*
Dismuke, D., 338, *345*
Dixon, J., *372*
Donato, R., *172*
Dorr-Bremme, D. W., 278, *299*
Dorricott, D., 85, *97*
Dougherty, K. C., *325*
Douglas, H. R., 332, *345*
Dozier, A., *368*
Dreeben, R., 316, *322*, *323*
Dunbar, S. B., *259*
Dunn, W. W., 62, 69, *93*
Duran, R., 151, *168*
Dynneson, T. L., 63, *93*

E

Easley, J. A., *326*
Edelman, J., 309, *323*
Edens, K. M., 44, *56*
Education for Democracy Project, *55*
Educational Products Information Exchange, 316, *323*
Educational Testing Service, 311, 312, *323*
Edwards, C. M., Jr., 338, *345*, 360, 363, 364, *369*

Edwards, H. P., *369*
Ehman, L. H., 20, *29*, 42, 47, 51, *55*, 71, 74, 85, 86, *93*
Eineder, D., 359, 360, *369*
Eisner, E. W., 47, *55*
Elbow, P., 264, 266, 267, *274*
Electronic Portfolio, *299*
Electronic Portfolio Version 2.0, *299*
Elkind, D., 39, *55*
Elliott, D. L., 318, *323*, *327*
Elshtain, J. B., 114, *130*
Engle, S. H., 7, 8, 9, 14, 21, *30*, 48, *55*, 78, 81, *93*
Enns, J. G., *370*
Epstein, J., 160, *168*
Erickson, F. D., 157, *168*
Essed, P., 142, *168*
Estes, G., 146, *168*
Evans, R. W., 69, *93*
Eyler, J., 25, *30*

F

Fagan, B. M., 118, *130*
Fancett, V., 41, *55*
Farlow, L., 50, *55*
Farnen, R. F., 18, *31*, 51, *60*
Feinberg, W., 105, *130*
Feldt, L. S., 250, *259*
Fennema, E., 255, *259*
Ferguson, P., 23, 24, 25, *30*, 49, *55*
Fernandez, R. R., *176*
Fernlund, P. M., 37, *55*
Fetterman, D. M., *194*
Filby, N., *322*, *369*
Finley, M. K., 146, *168*
Finn, C., 22, 24, *31*, 41, *58*, *367*
Fish, J., 309, *323*
Fleck, L. M., 359, *369*
Fleming, M., 278, *299*
Floden, R. E., *323*
Fogliani, A. E., 355, *369*
Foner, E. F., 120, *130*
Ford, D. Y., 189, *194*
Forsyth, R. A., *259*
Foster, M., 151, 152, 159, *168*, *169*
Fraisse, P., 39, *55*
Frank, M. L., 319, *323*
Franke, M. L., *259*
Franklin, J. H., 119, *130*
Franzosa, S. D., 36, 37, *55*
Frech, W., 66, *93*
Frederiksen, N., 302, *323*
Freeland, K., 35, 38, 39, *55*
Freeman, C. J., 359, *369*
Freeman, D. J., 317, *323*, *324*
Frisbie, D. A., *259*
Frueh, T., *58*
Fu, D., 262, *274*
Fueyo, J., 265, 272, *274*
Furman, J., 366, *369*

G

Gagnon, P., 63, *93*
Gall, M. D., 79, 80, *93*
Gallagher, J. J., 185, 187, 191, 193, *194*
Garber, M. G., 351, 353, 354, 355, 356, *369*
Garcia, E. E., 151, 152, 162, *169*
Garcia, J., 44, *56, 57, 58*
Gardner, H., 352, *369*
Garman, B., 25, *30*
Garofalo, J., 319, *323*
Garraty, J. A., 120, *130*
Garrod, A., 71, *96*
Gartner, A., 45, *57*
Gay, G., 106, 113, *130,* 139, 148, 163, *169*
Gee, J. P., 157, *169*
Geography Education Standards Project, 65, *93*
Giles, D., 25, *30*
Gilligan, C., 77, *93*
Gilliom, M. E., 49, *56,* 71, *94*
Gilman, D. A., 333, *345*
Gilmore, A., 41, 57
Giroux, H. A., 141, *169*
Gitlin, T., 111, 112, *130*
Glaser, R., 155, 157, *169*
Glass, G. V., 349, *369*
Glazer, N., 111, 115, 116, 117, *130,* 140, *169*
Glenn, A. D., 48, *56,* 85, 86, *93*
Goel, M. L., 51, *58*
Golan, S., *324*
Goldman, S., 151, *169*
Gollnick, D., 146, *169*
Gonzalez, A., 44, *53*
Good, T., 84, *91*
Goodlad, J. I., 22, *30,* 41, *56,* 86, *94,* 316, *323*
Goodman, J., 71, *94*
Goodman, Y., 151, *169*
Gore, G. R., 361, 362, *369*
Gottovi, N. C., *326*
Governor Thomas Johnson High School, 360, 363, *369*
Gradebook Manager for Windows, *299*
Gradebook Plus, *299*
Granger, B., 44, *56*
Granger, L., 44, *56*
Grant, C. A., 137, 138, 139, 140, 142, 145, 147, 150, 155, 163, 164, *169, 170, 175*
Grant, S. G., 52, *60*
Graue, M. E., 160
Graves, D., *172,* 262, 264, *274*
Greenberg, K., 272, *274*
Griffin, A. F., 78, *94*
Gross, M. U. M., 186, *194*
Gross, R. E., 63, *93,* 316, *323*
Grosshans, R. R., 65, *99*
Grouws, D. A., 320, *323*
Guiton, G., 184, 190, *194*
Gump, P.V., 51, *54*
Gumperz, J. J., *167*

Guskey, T., 359, 360, 363, *369*
Gutmann, A., 122, 127, *131*

H

Haas, N. S., *323, 325*
Haberman, M., 145, 146, *166, 170*
Hackmann, D. G., 359, 360, *369*
Hackney, S., 113, *131*
Hadaway, N. L., 44, *56*
Hahn, C. L., 51, 52, *56*
Hakuta, K., 153, *173*
Haladyna, T. M., 38, *59,* 303, *323, 325*
Hale-Benson, J. E., 151, *170*
Hall, J. L., 307, *324*
Hall, N., 151, *170*
Hallam, R. N., 39, *56*
Hamdy, M., 361, *369*
Hamp-Lyons, L., 272, *274*
Han, L., 251, 253, 254, *259*
Hanks, M., 51, *56*
Hansen, J., 262, *274*
Hanvey, R. G., 43, *56,* 68, *94*
Harbeck, K. M., 164, *170*
Hardin, J., 13, 14, *30*
Harmin, M., 76, *97*
Harrington, C., 42, *56*
Harris, M., 113, *131*
Hartshorne, H., 78, *94*
Harvill, L. M., 248, *259*
Harwood, A., 18, 19, *30*
Hawke, S., 41, 55
Hawkins, M. L., 41, *57*
Heath, J. A., 51, *56*
Heath, S. B., 151, 157, 158, 160, *170*
Helburn, N., 64, *94*
Helburn, S. W., 41, *59*
Heller, K. A., *195*
Henning-Stout, M., 257, *259*
Henze, R., *172*
Herbert, E. A., 262, *274*
Herman, A., 113, *131*
Herman, J. L., *308, 309,* 324
Hertzberg, H. W., 121, *131*
Hess, C. A., *374*
Hess, R. D., 38, *56*
Hidalgo, N. M., 160, *170*
Hierck, T., *372*
Hieronymus, D. A., *259*
Higgins, K., 86, *94*
Higham, J., 110, 113, 115, 116, *131*
Hilgers, T. L., *274*
Hilliard, A. G., 151, *171*
Hirsch, E. D., Jr., 140, *171*
Hoeland, J. M., 359, 361, *369*
Hoffman, C. M., 144, 145, *175*
Hoge, J. D., 7, 8, 9, 11, 13, 14, 15, 16, 17, 20, 21, 22, *31,* 34, 35, 42, 47, *58*
Holland, A., 50, 51, *56*

Hollinger, D. A., 109, 110, 111, 112, 116, 117, *131*
Holm, W., *174*
Holmes, C. T., 156, *171*
Hooton, B., *368*
Hoover, H. D., 240, 241, 243, 247, *259, 260*
Hopkins, H. J., 351, 355, *369, 370*
Hottenstein, D., 360, *370*
Houston, R., 145, *166*
Howard, G., 113, *131*
Howe, L., *97*
Howley, A., *195*
Hughes, C. S., *95*
Humphreys, L. G., 185, *194*
Hundley, W. W., 359, *370*
Hunt, M. P., 78, *94*
Huot, B., 272, *275*
Hurd, P. D., 67, *94*
Hursh, D., 69, *94*
Hyde, J. S., 255, *260*
Hyman, J. S., *322*

I

Imseries, *299*
Irvine, J. J., 151, 154, *171*
Irvine, T. H., 359, 360, *370*
Ishler, R. E., 44, *56*
Ivie, S. D., 140, *171*

J

Jackson, N. E., 185, 188, 189, 191, *194, 195*
Jacobs, V. R., *259*
Jaffe, S., *260*
Janos, P. M., *195*
Jarilomek, J., 8, 14, *31*, 34, 42, 47, *58*
Jenkins, L., *29*
Jhally, S., *172*
Johnson, D. W., 44, *57*, 72, *94*, 155, *167, 171*
Johnson, R. T., 72, *94, 171*
Johnson, V., 86, *93*
Jones, B., 359, 360, 361, 363, 367, *370*
Jones, B. F., *95*
Jones, V. L., 66, 67, *98*
Joyce, B., 278, *299, 300*
Joyce, W. W., 88, *94*
Junn, J., 11, 12, 13, 21, 22, *30, 31*

K

Kallen, H., 110, 112, *131*
Kaminski, J., *324*
Karst, K. L., 121, *131*
Kassen, L., *196*
Katz, P. A., 44, *56*
Kean, M. H., 256, *260*
Keating, T., 48, *56*
Keen, C. M., 363, *370*
Kennedy, K. J., 63, 87, *94*
Kenny, R. A., Jr., 71, *96*

Khaketla, M., *325*
Kielsmeier, J., 25, *30*
Kifer, E., *369*
Kim, B. U., 65, *99*
Kim, C., 44, *57*
Kim, S., 48, *57*
King, A. J. C., 359, *370*
King, B. B., 360, 367, *370*
King, J. E., 149, *171*
Kirschenbaum, H., 76, *94, 97*
Klass, P. H., 86, *91*
Klein, E. J., *195*
Klein, S. S., 44, *57*, 144, *171*
Kleine, P. F., *324*
Kline, S., *172*
Knipping, N. Y., 51, 52, *57*
Kohl, H., 152, *171*
Kohlberg, L., 76, 77, *94, 95*
Kohn, A., 205, 236
Koretz, D., 262, *275*
Korn, W., 16, *29*
Kotovsky, K., *196*
Kourilsky, M. L., 41, *57*
Kraft, R., 25, *30*
Kramer, S. L., 359, 360, 361, 362, 363, 364, 365, 367, *370*
Kuhs, T. M., 316, *323, 324*
Kulik, C. C., 192, 193, *195*
Kulik, J. A., 192, 193, *195*
Kunc, N., 44, *57*
Kunjufu, J., 151, *171*
Kyle, D. W., *322*

L

Ladson-Billings, G., 106, 109, *131*, 151, 152, *171*
Landry, B., 108, *131*
Landsness, R. M., 82, *96*
Lane, R. E., 64, *95*
Langfitt, R. E., 332, *345*
Laosa, L. M., 158, *171*
Lareau, A., 160, *171*
Larkins, A. G., 41, *57*
Larson, C. N., 364, *370*
Lawton, T. A., *325*
Learner Profile, *300*
Lee, C. D., 158, 161, 162, *171*
Lee, S. J., 143, 145, *172*
Lehwald, G., *195*
Leifer, A. D., 149, *172*
Leiss, W., 149, *172*
Lello, J., 39, *57*
Leming, J. S., 29, 42, 47, 51, *57*, 76, 77, 78, *95*
Lerner, R., 108, 119, *131*
Lesko, N., *176*
Levi, L. W., 121, *259*
Levstik, L., 39, *57*
Levy, L. W., *131*
Levy, S., 85, *95*
Lewis, B., 126, *131*

Lickona, T., 78, 95
Lieberson, S., 115, 116, *132*
Lindblom, K. J., 74, *95*
Lindquist, E. F., *259*
Lindquist, M. M., 315, 316, *324*
Link-Jobe, J. L., 359, *370*
Lintz, A., *172*
Lipka, R. P., 83, *95*
Lipset, S. M., 128, *132*
Lipsky, D. K., 45, *57*
Lissitz, R. W., 236
Litcher, J. H., 44, *57*
Livingston, S. A., 81, *95*
Lockerbie, J. W., *370*
Lockwood, S. L., 361, *370*
Loewen, J. W., 108, 109, *132*
Lomawaima, K. T., 148, *172*
Long, C., *168*
Longstreet, W. C., 154, *172*
Lowman, D. K., *373*
Lucas, T., 159, *172*
Lynch, R., *166*

M

MacDonald, W., *29*
Mackey, J. A., 67, 75, 92, *95*
Madaus, G., 198, *199*, 302, 303, 304, 305, 306, 307, 308, 309, 310, 311, *322, 324*
Magee, B., 128, *132*
Mahoney, D. J., 121, *131*
Maier, P., 126, *132*
Malatesta, C., *370*
Mann, T. E., *54*, 156
Manzo, K. K., 128, 129, *132*
Margalef-Bogda, S., 44, *58*
Margolin, L., 188, *195*
Margolis, H., 72, *95*
Marshall, M., 361, 362, *370*
Martin, A., 52, *57*, 145, *175*
Martin, D. J., 250, 253, *260*
Martorella, P. H., 66, 67, 70, 71, 74, 80, *95*
Marzano, R. M., 84, *95*
Mason, E., *327*
Massachusetts Advocacy Center and the Center for Early Adolescence, 156, *172*
Massaro, T. M., 124, 125, *132*
Mathews, D., *57*
Mattai, P. R., 141, *172*
Matthews, K. M., 35, *171*
May, M., 78, *94*
Mayes, L. M., 367, *370*
McBrien, J. L., 72, *96*
McCabe, P. O., 72, *95*
McCarthy, C., 141, 149, 150, *172*
McCarty, T., *166*
McCormick, T. E., 42, *57*, 145, *172*
McCutcheon, G., *322*
McGhee, P. E., 44, *58*

McKenna, J. B., *369*
McKeown, M., 12, 13, *31*
McLean, L. D., *372*
Meadows, M. E., 359, *371*
Medina, N. J., 310, *324, 325*
Mehan, H., 157, 158, 159, *168, 172*
Mehlinger, H., 71, *93*
Mehrens, W. A., 307, 309, 317, *324*
Meier, S. L., *323*
Meisels, S. J., 306, 308, *324*
Merriam, C., 63, *96*
Merryfield, M. M., 68, *96*
Metcalf, L. E., 78, *94*
Mesa-Bains, A., 143, 145, *172*
Messick, S., 242, *260*
Meyer, K., 264, 265, 273, 274, *275*
Michaels, S., 157, *167, 173*
Milbrath, L. W., 51, *58*
Miles, R. B., 365, *371*
Milleman, J., 365, *371*
Miller, J., 24, *30*
Miller, J. J., 112, 116, *132*
Miller, S. L., 40, *58*, 65, *96*
Mills, S., 79, *96*
Minami, M., 157, *173*
Mistretta, G. M., 359, 360, *371*
Mock, K., 146, *173*
Mohatt, G., *168*
Moll, L. C., *168*
Monks, F. J., *195*
Moran, C. E., 153, *173*
Morgan, R. T., *326*
Morine-Dershimer, G., 278, *300*
Morris, J. W., Jr., 86, *99*
Mosher, R., 71, *96*
Moss, A. A., Jr., 119, *130*
Mullis, I., *29*
Murphy, J., 84, *98*
Murphy, S., 262, 267, *275*
Murrell, P., 151, *173*
Music Educators National Conference, 365, *371*

N

NAEP Civics Consensus Project, 105, 107, *132*
Nagai, A. K., 108, 119, *131*
National Assessment of Educational Progress, 8
National Assessment of Educational Progress Civics Consensus Project, 6, 7, 9, 14, 20, 21
National Center for Education Statistics, 2, 136, *173*
National Center for History in the Schools, 63, *96*
National Coalition for Women and Girls in Education, 144, *173*
National Commission on Excellence in Education, 303, *324*
National Council on Economic Education, 65, *96*
National Council for the Social Studies, 7, 8, 14, 43, 52, *58*, 67, 79, 82

National Council for the Social Studies (NCSS) Task Force, 96
National Council for the Social Studies (NCSS) Task Force on Ethnic Studies Curriculum Guidelines, 69, 96
National Council of Teachers of Mathematics, 311, 313, 324
National Education Association, 144, 173
Neill, D. M., 324
Neill, M., 256, 257, 260, 305, 307, 310, 325
New Standards Project, 264, 265, 275
Newmann, F. M., 49, 58, 82, 96, 165
Nicholls, J. G., 185, 195
Niemi, R., 11, 12, 13, 21, 22, 30, 31
Nieto, S., 151, 173
Nitko, A. J., 245, 260
Noddings, N., 255, 260
Nolen, S. B., 309, 310, 323, 325
Nolin, M. J., 26, 31
North Carolina Department of Public Instruction, Division of Accountability Services, 359, 361, 362, 364, 365, 366, 371
Norton, D. E., 44, 58

O

Oakes, J., 146, 155, 156, 173, 174, 194, 355, 371
Objective Tracker, 300
Ochoa, A. S., 7, 8, 9, 14, 21, 30, 78, 81, 93
O'Connell, B. E., 83, 95
Oden, M. H., 196
Ogbu, J. U., 141, 174
Ogle, D., 84, 96
Oickle, E., 175
Okamoto, D., 172
Oldenquist, A., 87, 96
Olneck, M., 141, 174
Olson, D., 350, 371
Omi, M., 142, 174
O'Neil, J., 359, 360, 367, 371
Oppenheim, A. N., 18, 31, 51, 60
Orfield, G., 142, 143, 174
Orimoloye, P. S., 88, 94
Ormseth, R., 174
Ornstein, N. J., 54
Ovando, C. J., 173
Owen, R. C., 66, 96

P

Pahl, R. H., 48, 58, 85, 96
Pai, Y., 109, 132
Pajares, F., 319, 325
Palincsar, A. S., 84, 97
Palmer, J., 73, 90
Pang, V. O., 148, 151, 174
Pangle, L. S., 105, 129, 132
Pangle, T. L., 105, 132
Pappas, C. C., 39, 57
Paris, S. C., 303, 325

Parker, W. C., 8, 14, 31, 34, 37, 38, 43, 47, 58, 78, 79, 97, 111, 113, 114, 132, 135, 174
Parks, S., 48, 57
Passow, A. H., 185, 192, 195
Passow, A. J., 184, 195
Patashnick, M., 195
Patrick, J. J., 7, 8, 9, 11, 13, 14, 15, 16, 17, 20, 21, 22, 31, 34, 35, 39, 42, 47, 50, 58, 71, 93, 108, 123, 124, 132
Patterson, S. H., 69, 92
Payne, L. L., 313, 325
Peck, K. L., 85, 97
Pelham High School, 360, 371
Pendarvis, E., 184, 189, 190, 191, 192, 193, 195
Perkins, D. N., 49, 58, 79, 98
Perleth, C., 191, 195
Peterson, J., 187, 190, 195
Petit, C. W., 119, 133
Petrequin, G., 332, 345
Phelps, C. R., 359, 367, 371
Phelps, R., 305, 325
Philips, S. U., 157, 158, 174
Phillips, S. E., 324
Piaget, J., 39, 58, 192, 195
Pisapia, J., 359, 360, 361, 363, 365, 367, 371
Polansky, H. B., 371
A policy of pressure, 325
Popkewitz, T. P., 141, 174
Popper, K. R., 128, 133
Porter, A. C., 323
Portes, P. R., 138, 174
Potts, J., 262, 264, 265, 266, 275
Pratte, R., 58
Presseisen, B. Z., 95
Price, R. D., 41, 58
Pritchard, I., 47, 58
Puckett, R., 332, 345
Pugh, S., 44, 58
Pulaski County High School, 359, 360, 365, 371
Purves, A., 264, 275

Q

Quinn, K. M., 367, 371

R

Raasch, C., 24, 31
Rachar, B., 373
Ramey, D. R., 174
Ramirez, J. D., 158, 174
Ramsett, D. E., 40, 58
Rankin, S C., 95
Raphael, D., 361, 362, 372
Raths, K. L., 76, 97
Ravitch, D., 22, 31, 41, 58, 141, 174
Reid, W. M., 360, 372
Reis, S. M., 195
Remy, R. C., 20, 31, 82, 97
Renzulli, J. S., 187, 189, 191, 195, 196

Resnick, D. P., *325*
Resnick, L. B., 306, *325*
Rettig, M. D., 357, 365, *368, 372*
Rex, J., 113, *133*
Reyes, D. J., 74, *97*
Rhody, T., 79, *93*
Rice, C. T., *96*
Richardson, S., 48, *59*
Rief, L., *275*
Riggs, E., 16, *29*
Riverside Publishing, 317, *325*
Robinson, J. E., *374*
Robinson, N. M., *195*
Roedding, G. R., 85, *97*
Rogers, K. B., 192, *196*
Romberg, T. A., 311, *325*
Rosenbaum, J., 146, *174*
Rosenshine, B., 349, *372*
Rosier, P., 158, *174*
Ross, E. W., 62, *97*
Ross, J. A., 365, *372*
Rossi, J. A., 69, *97*
Rotberg, I. C., 258, *260*
Roth, J. L. , *325*
Rothman, R., 303, 304, 305, 306, *325*
Rothman, S., *131*
Rottenberg, C., *326*
Rousseau, W. W., 79, *96*
Rowe, M. B., 80, *97*
Rudnitski, R. A., *195*
Rutter, R. A., *176*
Ryan, F. L., 44, *57*
Ryan, K., 78, *99*

S

Sacks, P., 238, *260*
Sadker, M. P., 144, *175*
Salmon-Cox, L., 279, *300*
Salvaterra, M., 359, 363, *372*
Salvio, P. M., 262, *275*
Santos, K. E., 363, *372*
Sapon-Shevin, M., 192, *196*
Saville-Troike, M., 159, *175*
Saxe, D., 45, 46, *60,* 83, *98*
Schafer, W. D., 202, 236
Schechter, S. L., 74, *97*
Schild, E. O., 81, *91*
Schine, J., 82, *97*
Schlesinger, A. M., Jr., 111, 112, 113, *133*
Schmidt, A. J., 111, *133*
Schmidt, W. H., *323*
Schoenfeld, A. H., 319, *325*
Schoenfeldt, A. Y., 364, *372*
Schoenstein, R., 344, *345,* 359, 360, *372*
Schoggen, M., 51, *59*
Schoggen, P., 51, *59*
Schroth, G., 361, *372*
Schug, M. C., 40, 41, *59*
Schultz, J. B., 78, *97*

Schwartz, E., 72, *95*
Schwille, J. R., *323*
Scribner, S., 151, *175*
Sears, J. T., 164, *175*
Secada, W. G., 145, *170*
Seefeldt, C., 39, *59*
Seldes, G., 63, *97*
Serma, I., *176*
Sessoms, J. C., 359, 360, 364, 365, 366, 367, *372*
Sharman, R. G., 360, *372*
Shaten, N., 333, *345*
Shaughnessy, J. M., 38, *59*
Shaver, J. P., 36, 38, 41, *59*
Shearmur, J., 128, *133*
Shepard, L. A., 303, 306, 307, 308, 309, 310, 312, *325*
Shephard, L., 156, *175*
Sherk, J., *167*
Shermis, S., *54*
Sherry, F. T., 48, *59*
Shortt, T. L., 359, 361, *372*
Shulman, L. S., 278, *300*
Sidelmick, D., 16, *31*
Siebert, M., *196*
Siegler, R., 188, *196*
Simon, S. B., 76, *97*
Sinatra, G., 12, 13, *31*
Sinclair, R. L, *176*
Sizemore, B. A., 161, 162, *175*
Slaughter-Defoe, D. T., *171*
Slavin, R. E., 44, 50, *59,* 72, 73, *98, 155, 175,* 355, *372*
Sleeter, C. E., 113, *133,* 137, 138, 139, 140, 141, 147, 150, 155, 164, *170, 175*
Smalley, W. A., *370*
Smith, A., 68, *92*
Smith, A. D., 365, *373*
Smith, F., 151, *175*
Smith, G. A., *176*
Smith, L. H., *196*
Smith, M. A., *275*
Smith, M. L., *175,* 303, 306, 308, 309, *326, 369*
Smith, R. B., 74, *97*
Smith, R. M., 40, *59*
Smythe, O. G., 363, *373*
Snell, M. E., 356, *373*
Snyder, D., 359, 360, 361, 365, *373*
Snyder, T. D., 144, 145, *175*
Social Science Education Consortium, 71, *98*
Sommerfield, M., 333, *345*
Sosniak, L. A., 316, *326*
Sowder, J. T., 255, *260*
Sowell, T., 116, *133*
Spandel, V., *327*
Spangler, D. A., 319, *326*
Spener, D., 157, *175*
Spring, J., 149, *175*
Squire, J. R., 317, *326*
Stahl, N., *54*
Stahl, R., 50, *59*

AUTHOR INDEX

Stake, R. E., 316, 319, *326*
Stallings, J. S., 145, *175*
Stanley, J. C., *193*
Stanley, W., 49, *60*
Stansbury, K., *168*
Staunton, J. T., 359, 364, 367, *373*
Steiner, G. A., 113, *130*
Stennett, R. G., 363, *373*
Stern, H. H., 364, *373*
Stern, J. D., 144, *176*
Sternberg, R. J., 188, *196*
Stevens, L., 86, *98*
Stiehm, J., *54*
Stiggins, R., 202, 222, 224, 236, 278, *300*
Stigler, J. W., 320, *326*
Stodolsky, S., 41, *60*, 312, *326*
Stoll, C. S., 81, *95*
Stotsky, S., 112, *133*, 141, *176*
Streisand, B., *373*
Strickland, D., 151, *176*
Stufflebeam, D., 198, *199*
Stumpf, T., 360, *373*
Suarez, T. M., 307, 308, 309, *326*
Subotnik, R., 189, *196*
Suhor, C., *95*
Sullivan, J., 44, *60*
Summers, E., *196*
Sunstein, B., 264, 273, *274*, *275*
Swartz, R. J., 79, *98*
Swiatek, M. A., 193, *196*

T

Taba, H., 84, *98*
Tabors, P., *167*
Takaki, R., 107, 117, *133*, 147, *176*
Talbert, J. E., 146, *176*
Tanner, B. M., 366, *373*
Tannenbaun, A., 187, *196*
Tarlov, S., 83, *99*
Tate, W. F., 145, *170*
Taylor, A., *370*
Taylor, C., 117, 118, *133*
Teacher Instructional Mapping and Management System, 292, *300*
Terman, L. M., 188, 189, *196*
Thayer, Y. V., *372*
Third International Mathematics and Science Study, *373*
Thomas, M. D., 140, *176*
Thompson, A. G., 319, *326*
Thompson, D. F., 64, *98*
Thompson, S., 210, 236
Thorkildsen, T. A., 185, *196*
Thorndike, R. M., 242, 247, 248, *260*
Tierney, R., 263, 275
Tikunoff, W. J., 154, *176*
Times Mirror Center for the People and the Press, 17
Timm, J. T., 120, *133*
Tobin, K. G., 80, *98*

Tobusen, L., *368*
Tocci, C., 52, *56*
Toch, T., 349, *373*
Tooker, E., 121, *133*
Torney, J. V., 18, *31*, 38, 51, *56*, *60*
Traverso, H., 332, 335, 336, 339, 341, *345*
Trevisan, M., 202, 236
Trimble, K., 156, *176*
Trueba, H., 169, 176
Turnell, M., 44, *60*
Turner, J. C., *325*
Turner, M., 29
Turner, R. R., 316, *326*
Tussman, J., 5, *31*
Tyack, D. B., 156, *176*

U

Ueda, R., 108, 109, 110, 115, 117, *133*
U. S. Commission on Immigration Reform, 106, *133*
U. S. Congress, Office of Technology Assessment, 304, 305, 307, *326*
U. S. Department of Education, 304, *326*
U. S. General Accounting Office, 304, 305, 308, 309, 311, *327*

V

VanSickel, R. L., 48, 50, *59*, *60*, 81, *98*
VanSledright, B. A., 52, *60*
Vars, G. F., 67, *98*
Vawter, D. H., 359, 360, 361, 363, 366, 367, *373*
Verba, S., 51, *53*, *64*, *98*
Vergin, L., *372*
Vik, P., 51, *56*
Vocke, D. E., 72, *98*
Vockell, E. L., 86, *98*
Vygotsky, L. S., 192, *196*

W

Wade, R. C., 25, *31*, 45, 46, *60*, 83, *98*
Wahlstrom, M. W., *372*
Wall, D., *322*
Wallace, S., *166*
Walstad, W. B., 40, 41, *59*, *60*
Warren, W. K., *370*
Waters, M. C., 115, 116, *132*, *133*
Waters, M. M., 151, *176*
Watts, M., 41, *60*
Waugh, D., 147, *167*
Webster, Y. O., 112, *133*
Wehlage, G. G., 156, *176*
Weil, J., *97*
Weil, M., 74, 84, *98*
Weiss, I., 320, *327*
Wells, A. S., 155, *176*
Wertheimer, M., 66, 67, *98*
Wertsch, J. V., 151, *176*
Wesser, A., *196*

West, T. G., 126, *133*
Westbury, I., 316, *327*
Westfall, A. L., *371*
Wexler, P., 65, *99*
Wheelock, A., *176*
Whelen, M., 37, *60*
White, C. S., 86, *93*, 108, *132*
White, E., 264, 272, 273, *275*
White, H., 40, *60*
Wiggins, G., 156, *176*, 256, *260*, 262, *275*
Wilder, D. E., *322*
Wilderson, F., *167*
Wilen, W. W., 78, 79, 80, 84, *91*, *99*
Wilkinson, J. H., 112, *133*
Williams, W. L., 164, *175*
Williamson, V. G., 364, *373*
Willig, A. C., 158, *177*
Wills, J. S., *172*
Wilson, B. L., *322*
Wilson, L., *325*
Wilson, L. J., 355, *373*
Winant, H., 142, *174*
Windrim, R. J., 72, *99*
Winner, E., 186, *196*
Winston, B. J., 40, *60*
Wise, A. E., *323*
Wolf, D. P., 263, *275*
Wolff, L., *275*

Woodson, J., 164, *177*
Woodward, A., 316, 317, *327*
Wooster, J., *29*
Worthen, B. R., 307, *327*
Woyach, R. B., 64, *99*
Wronkovich, M., 361, *374*
Wynne, E., 78, *99*

Y

Yeager E. A., 86, *99*
Yeager, T., 66, 67, *98*
Yeh, J., 278, *300*
Yopp, H. K., 349, *374*
York, D. E., *171*
York, T., 361, *374*
Yuen, S. D., *174*

Z

Zalk, S. R., 44, *56*
Zebroski, J. T., 262, *275*
Zeldin, S., 83, *99*
Zempher, N., 145, *177*
Zevin, J., 66, *96*
Zhang, Q. H., 65, *99*
Zollman, A., 319, *327*

Subject Index

A

Achievement, 10–14
Assessment, 202–236, 238–260, 262–273, 278–300, 302–327
    competencies for educational leaders, 208–211
    literacy, 222–226
    and policy, 226–228, 255–258, 302–304
    users of, 218–221
    see also Achievement; Authentic assessment; Testing
Assimilation, 115–117
Authentic assessment, 156–157, 262–273, 279–280, 283–284, 290–292

C

Character education, 75–78
Citizenship education, 6–31, 34–60, 62–99
    defined, 36–38
    and democracy, 6–7, 104–111, 128–129
    in elementary school, 37–60
    history of, 34–35
    and knowledge, 26–27, 38–42, 62–67, 70–71, 118–122
    outcomes of, 8–14, 104–106, 123
    and values, 12–14
Civic participation, 23–26, *see also* Political participation skills
Classroom climate, 19, 51–52
Concept learning, 74–75
Cooperative learning, 47–48, 50, 72–74, 154–155
Critical thinking, 49–50, 78–80, 127–127
Cultural determinism, 112–113
Cultural pluralism, 107
Cultural responsiveness, 150–151

D

Decision-making, 48–49, 78
Democracy, 6–7, 106–107, 110–111
    and citizenship education, 7–8, 128–129

see also Political attitudes

E

Extracurricular activities, 27, 50–51

G

Gifted and talented education, 180–196
    defined, 185–187
    effectiveness of, 190–192
    and equity, 184–185
    research on, 189–190
    selection criteria, 189–190
Global education, 42–44, 68–69
Gradebook, electronic, 295–298

H

Hidden curriculum, 47
Home influences, 160

I

Inclusion, 44–45
Interdisciplinary curriculum, 67–70
Issues-centered education, 51–52, 69–70, 124

L

Law-related education, 13
Leadership in education, 161–162, 203–205, 208–211, 231–236
Learning styles, 154

M

Media influences, 149–150
Multicultural education, 42–44, 68–69, 104–133, 136–177
    and citizenship education, 106–107

and civic mythmaking, 108–109
critique of, 111–122, 140–142
and curriculum, 122–128, 147–150
history of, 138–140
and identity, 107–110, 112–115
and instruction, 150–157
and language, 157–159
and students, 142–144
and teachers, 144–147
see also Assimilation; Cultural determinism; Cultural pluralism; Cultural responsiveness

O

Outcomes, 8–14, 104–106, 123, 212–218, 284, 287–289, 292–293

P

Participatory learning, 47–48
Political attitudes, 14–20, 27, 46, 128
Political participation skills, 20–26, 28, 46–50
 see also Civic participation
Portfolios, *see* Authentic assessment

Q

Questioning, 84

R

Role playing, 80–82

S

Scheduling, 332–345, 348–374
block, 336–341, 348–374
effects of, 358–366
in elementary school 349–356
history of, 332–333
house plan, 343
in middle school, 356–358
options, 334–342
in secondary school, 256–358
successful practices, 366–367
Service learning, 25, 45–46, 82–83
Simulations, 80–82
Standards, 317–319

T

Technology, 85–86, 278–300
Testing, 155–156, 221, 238–260, 278–279, 302–327
administration of, 249–250, 304–305
and high stakes, 302–327
interpretation of data, 229–230, 245–248
item development, 241–245
and low stakes, 310–311
preparation for, 309–310
proliferation of, 302–304
teaching to, 306–309
see also Assessment
Textbooks, 315–316
Thematic instruction, 42–47n